NINE STONES

CREATED, WRITTEN, AND DRAWN BY
SAMUEL SPANO

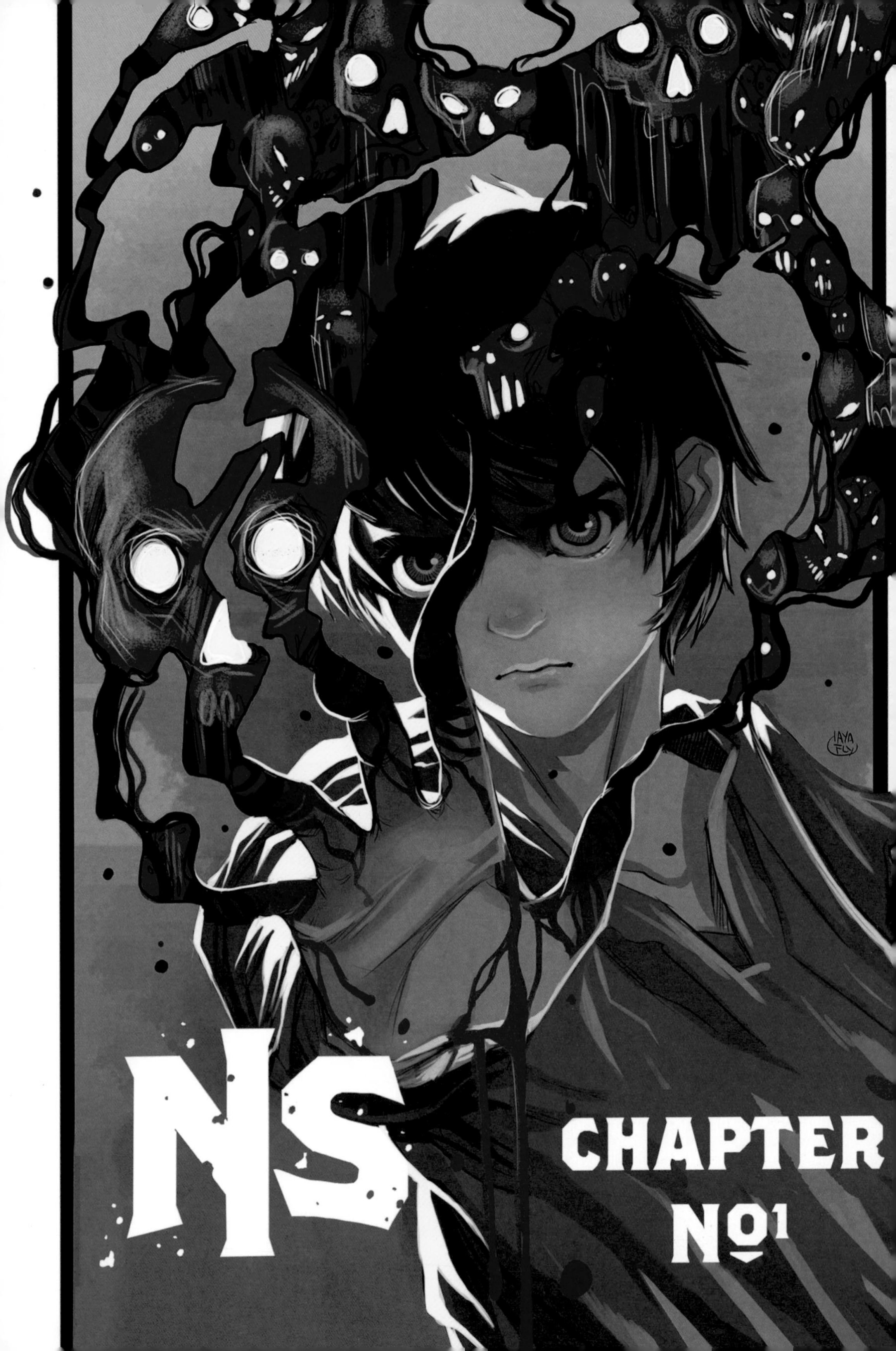
NS
CHAPTER
Nº1

SHADOW.

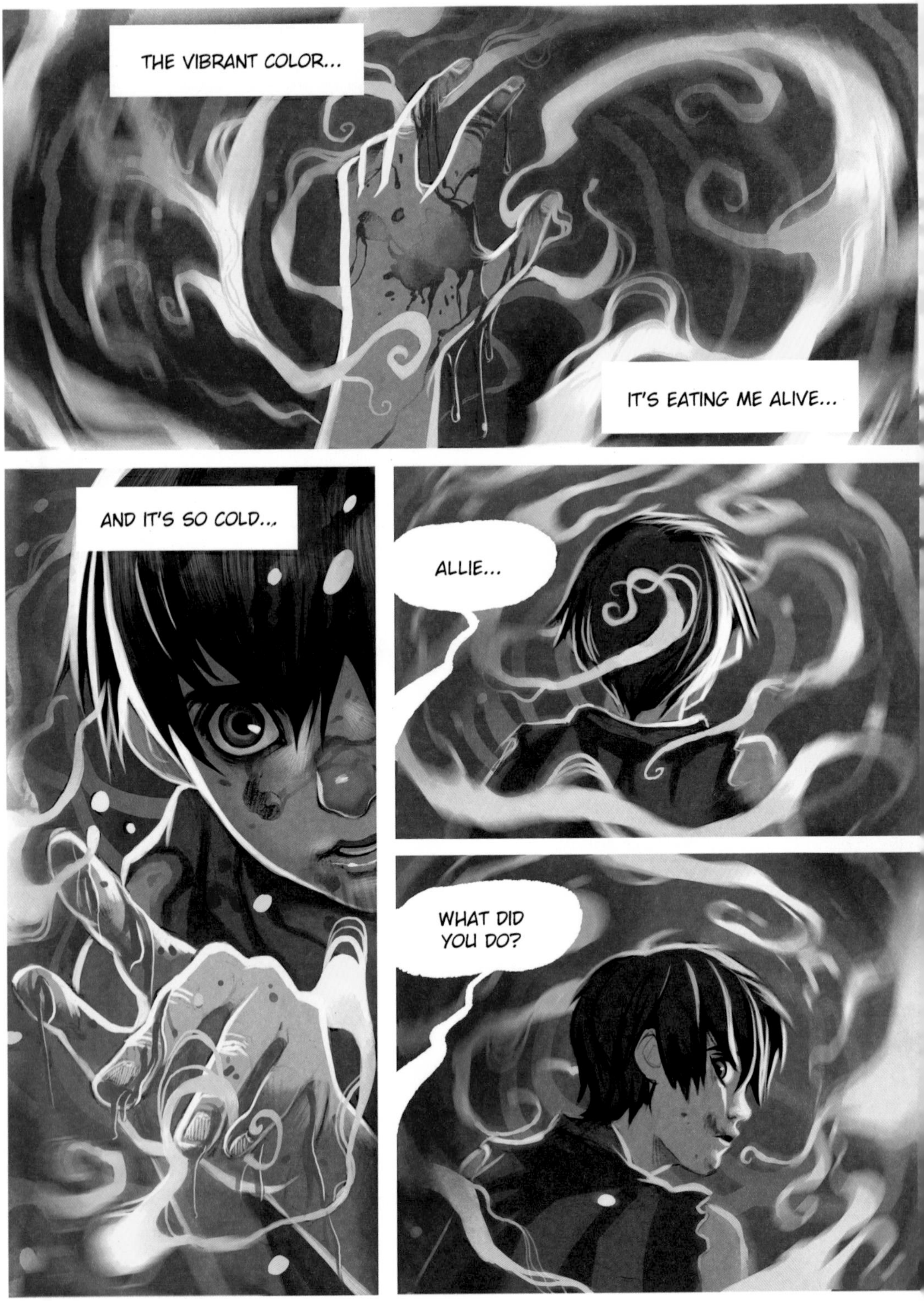
THE VIBRANT COLOR...
IT'S EATING ME ALIVE...
AND IT'S SO COLD...
ALLIE...
WHAT DID YOU DO?

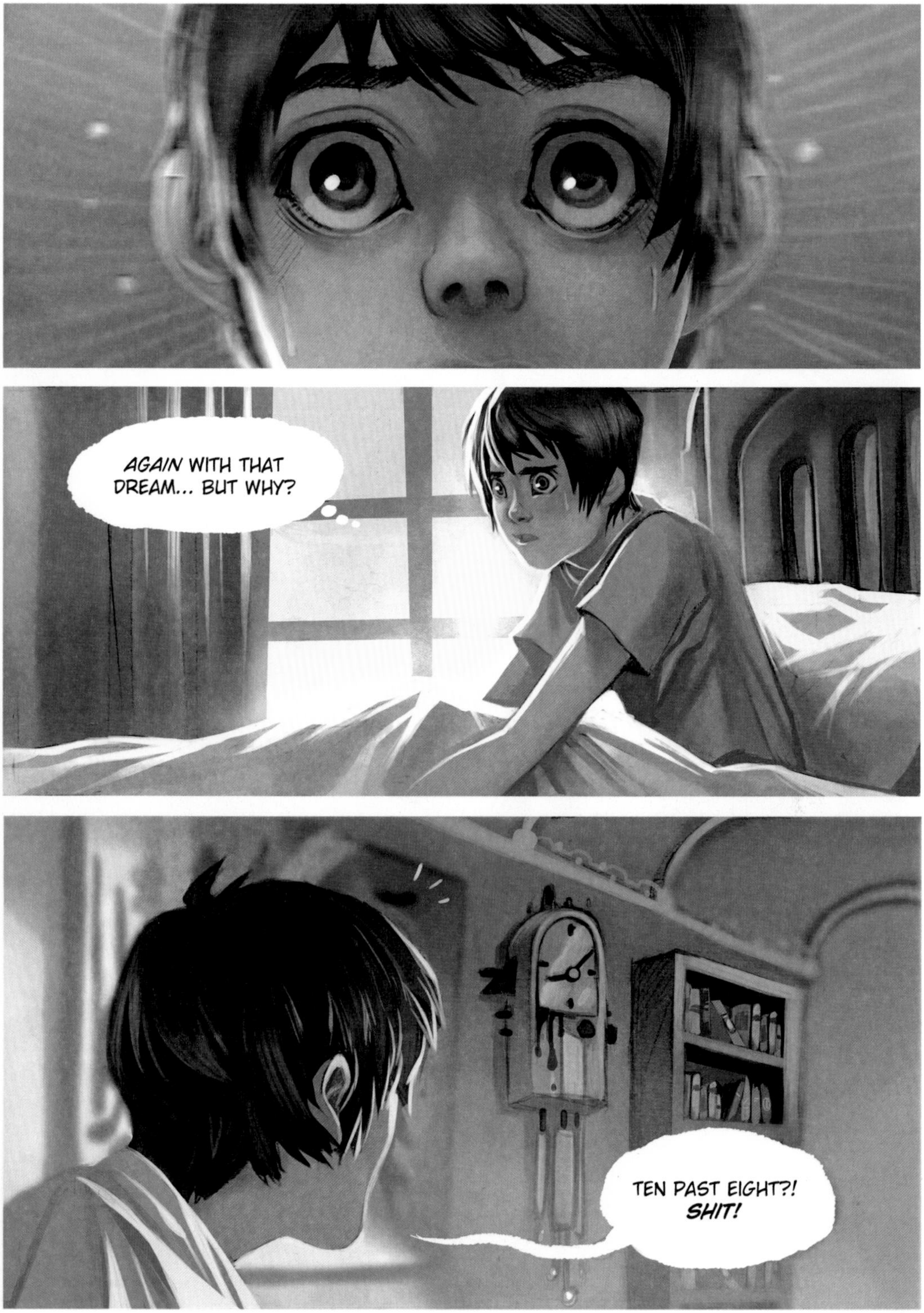
AGAIN WITH THAT DREAM... BUT WHY?
TEN PAST EIGHT?! SHIT!

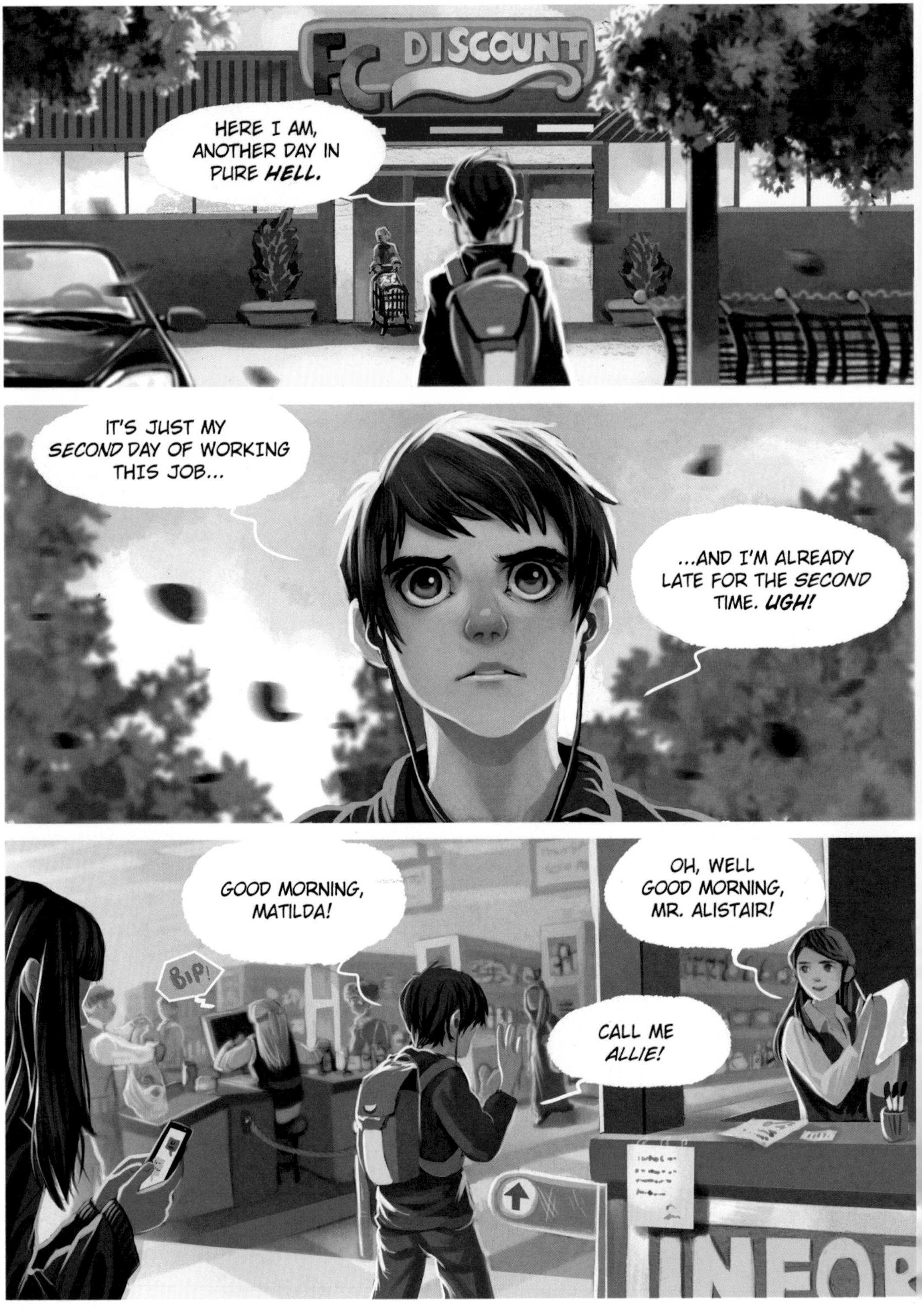
FC DISCOUNT
HERE I AM, ANOTHER DAY IN PURE *HELL.*
IT'S JUST MY *SECOND* DAY OF WORKING THIS JOB...
...AND I'M ALREADY LATE FOR THE *SECOND* TIME. *UGH!*
BIP!
GOOD MORNING, MATILDA!
OH, WELL GOOD MORNING, MR. ALISTAIR!
CALL ME *ALLIE!*
INFOR

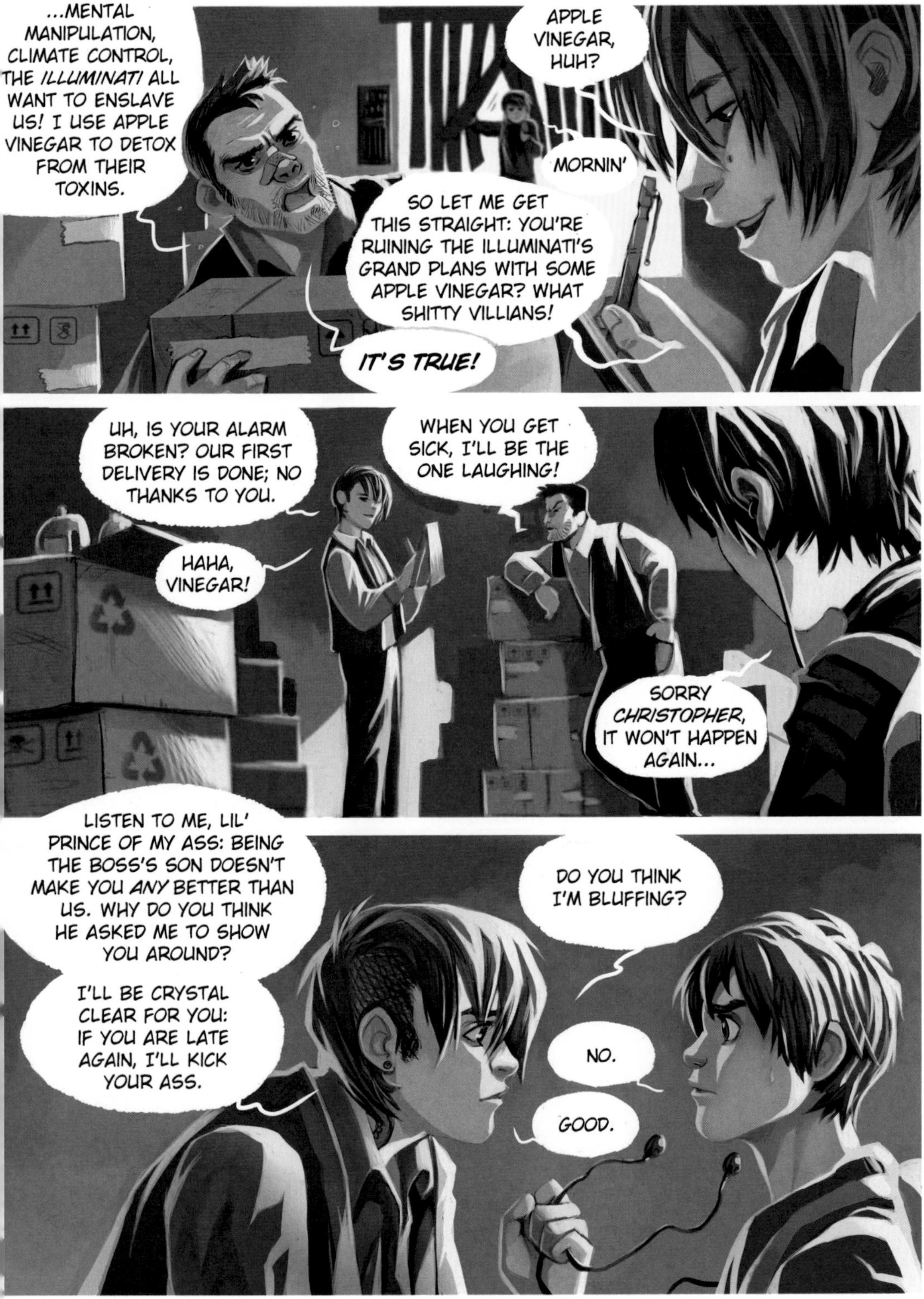
...MENTAL MANIPULATION, CLIMATE CONTROL, THE *ILLUMINATI* ALL WANT TO ENSLAVE US! I USE APPLE VINEGAR TO DETOX FROM THEIR TOXINS.
APPLE VINEGAR, HUH?
MORNIN'
SO LET ME GET THIS STRAIGHT: YOU'RE RUINING THE ILLUMINATI'S GRAND PLANS WITH SOME APPLE VINEGAR? WHAT SHITTY VILLIANS!
IT'S TRUE!
UH, IS YOUR ALARM BROKEN? OUR FIRST DELIVERY IS DONE; NO THANKS TO YOU.
WHEN YOU GET SICK, I'LL BE THE ONE LAUGHING!
HAHA, VINEGAR!
SORRY *CHRISTOPHER*, IT WON'T HAPPEN AGAIN...
LISTEN TO ME, LIL' PRINCE OF MY ASS: BEING THE BOSS'S SON DOESN'T MAKE YOU *ANY* BETTER THAN US. WHY DO YOU THINK HE ASKED ME TO SHOW YOU AROUND?
I'LL BE CRYSTAL CLEAR FOR YOU: IF YOU ARE LATE AGAIN, I'LL KICK YOUR ASS.
DO YOU THINK I'M BLUFFING?
NO.
GOOD.

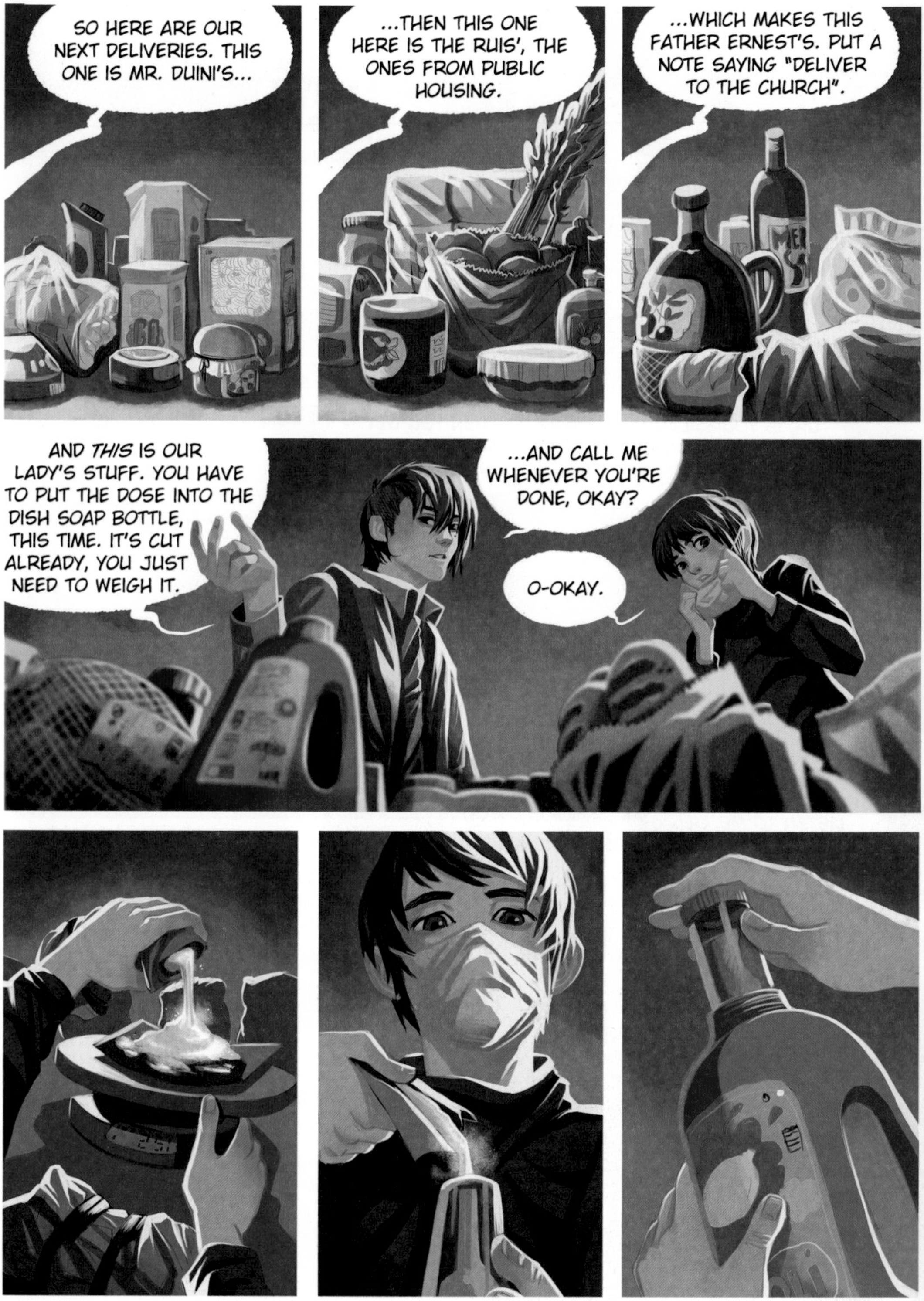
SO HERE ARE OUR NEXT DELIVERIES. THIS ONE IS MR. DUINI'S...
...THEN THIS ONE HERE IS THE RUIS', THE ONES FROM PUBLIC HOUSING.
...WHICH MAKES THIS FATHER ERNEST'S. PUT A NOTE SAYING "DELIVER TO THE CHURCH".
AND *THIS* IS OUR LADY'S STUFF. YOU HAVE TO PUT THE DOSE INTO THE DISH SOAP BOTTLE, THIS TIME. IT'S CUT ALREADY, YOU JUST NEED TO WEIGH IT.
...AND CALL ME WHENEVER YOU'RE DONE, OKAY?
O-OKAY.

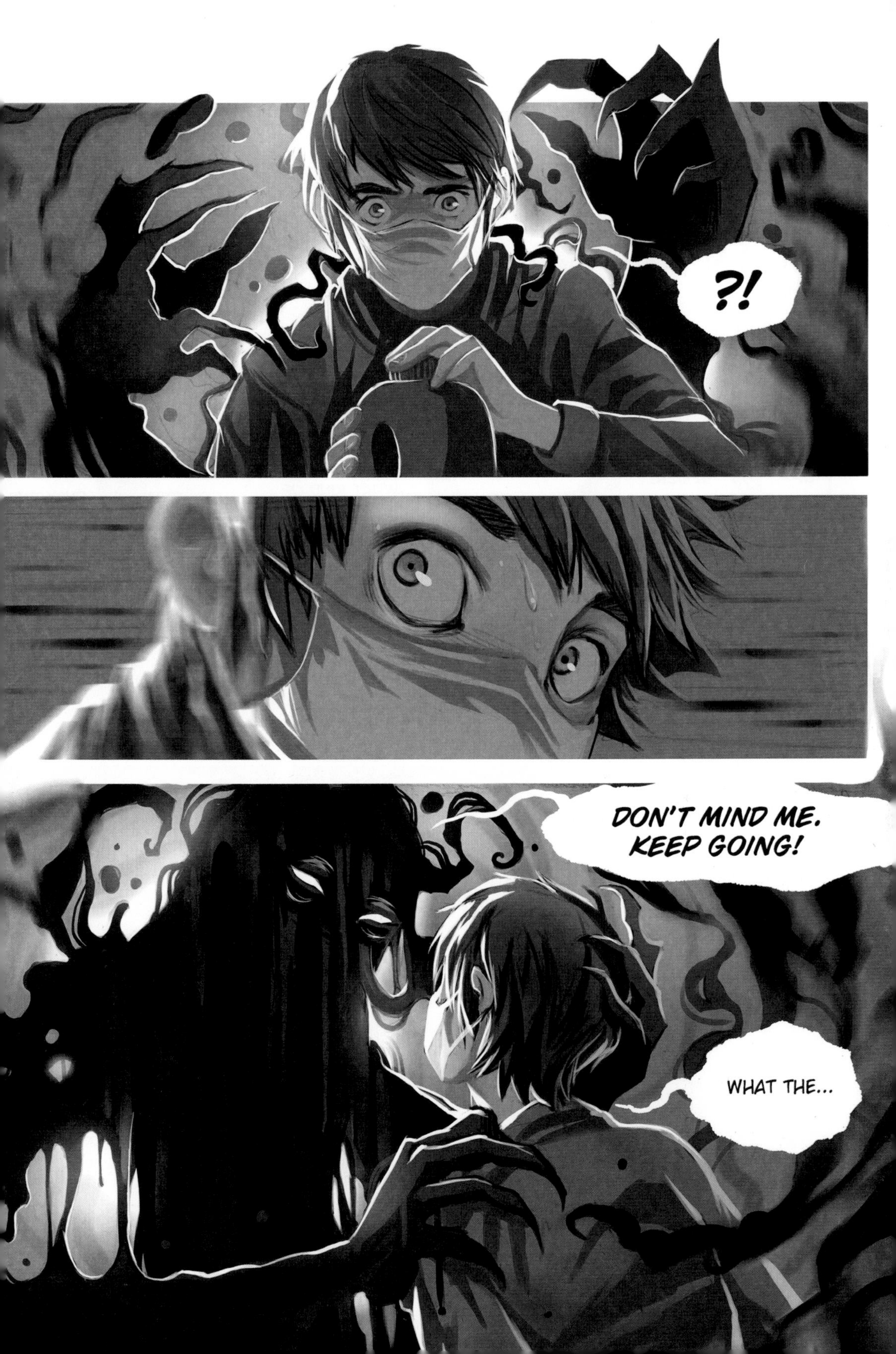
?!
DON'T MIND ME. KEEP GOING!
WHAT THE...

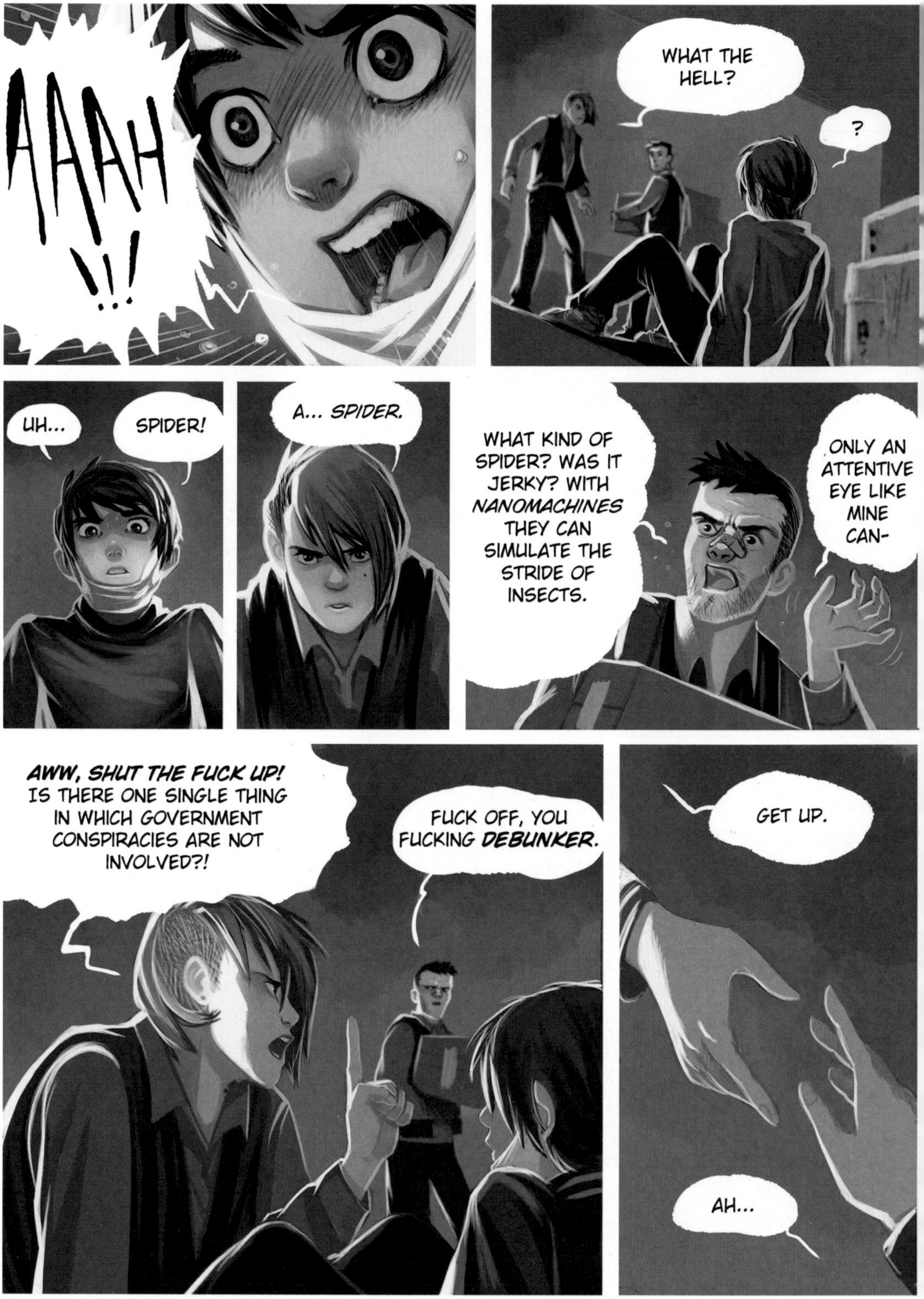
AAAH!!!
WHAT THE HELL?
?
UH...
SPIDER!
A... SPIDER.
WHAT KIND OF SPIDER? WAS IT JERKY? WITH NANOMACHINES THEY CAN SIMULATE THE STRIDE OF INSECTS.
ONLY AN ATTENTIVE EYE LIKE MINE CAN-
AWW, SHUT THE FUCK UP! IS THERE ONE SINGLE THING IN WHICH GOVERNMENT CONSPIRACIES ARE NOT INVOLVED?!
FUCK OFF, YOU FUCKING DEBUNKER.
GET UP.
AH...

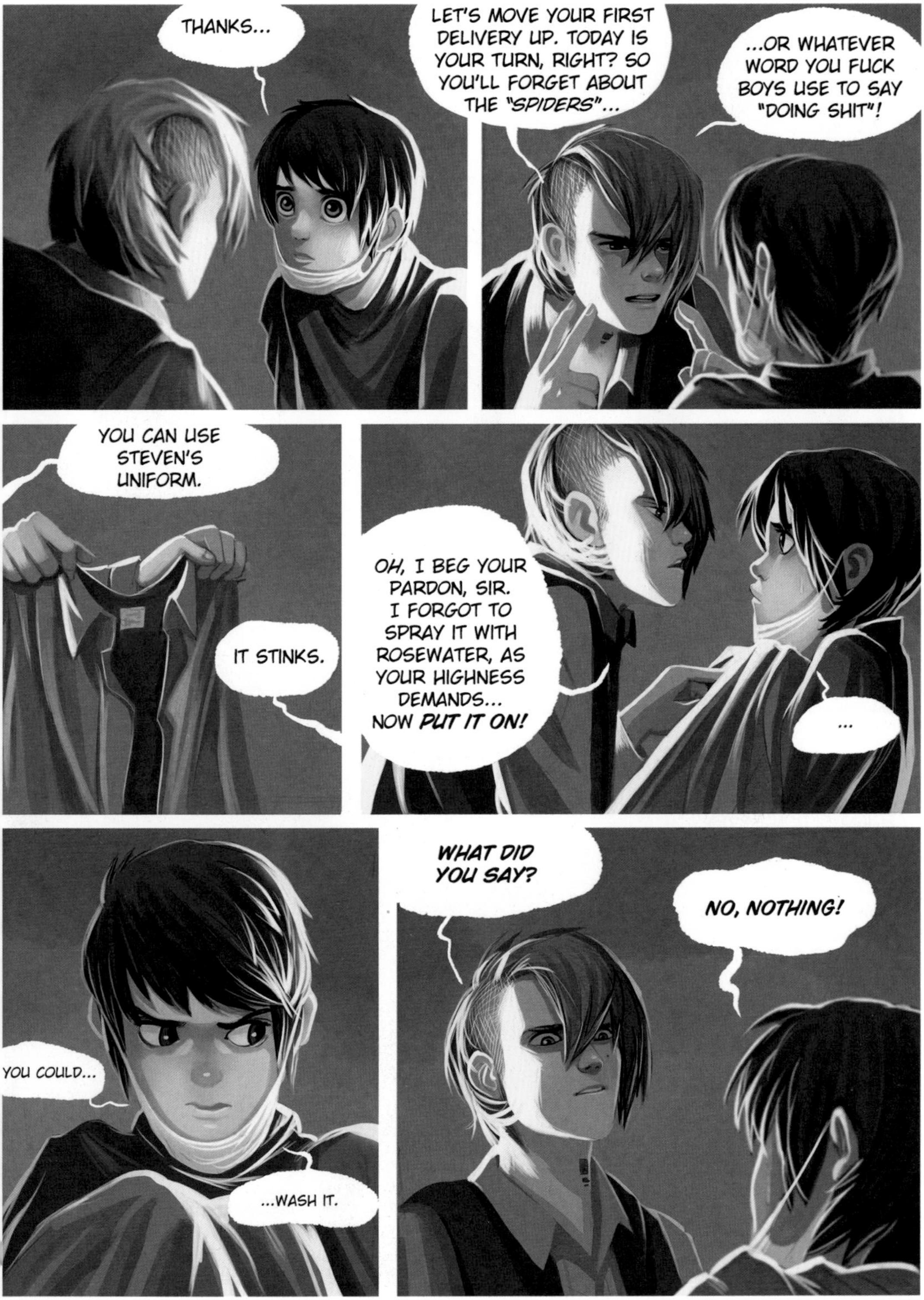
THANKS...
LET'S MOVE YOUR FIRST DELIVERY UP. TODAY IS YOUR TURN, RIGHT? SO YOU'LL FORGET ABOUT THE "SPIDERS"...
...OR WHATEVER WORD YOU FUCK BOYS USE TO SAY "DOING SHIT"!
YOU CAN USE STEVEN'S UNIFORM.
IT STINKS.
OH, I BEG YOUR PARDON, SIR. I FORGOT TO SPRAY IT WITH ROSEWATER, AS YOUR HIGHNESS DEMANDS... NOW PUT IT ON!
...
YOU COULD...
...WASH IT.
WHAT DID YOU SAY?
NO, NOTHING!

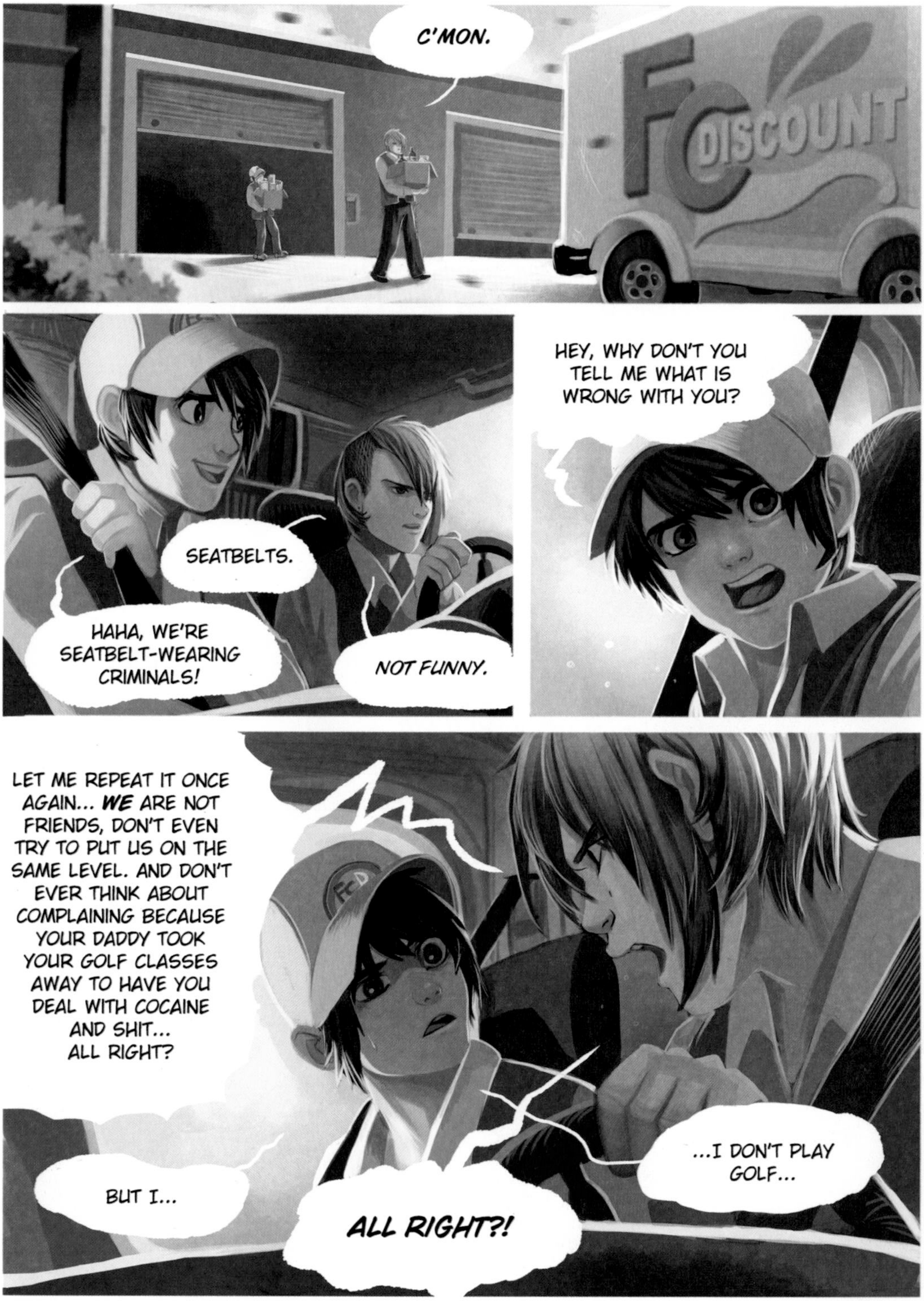
C'MON.
FC DISCOUNT
SEATBELTS.
HAHA, WE'RE SEATBELT-WEARING CRIMINALS!
NOT FUNNY.
HEY, WHY DON'T YOU TELL ME WHAT IS WRONG WITH YOU?
LET ME REPEAT IT ONCE AGAIN... WE ARE NOT FRIENDS, DON'T EVEN TRY TO PUT US ON THE SAME LEVEL. AND DON'T EVER THINK ABOUT COMPLAINING BECAUSE YOUR DADDY TOOK YOUR GOLF CLASSES AWAY TO HAVE YOU DEAL WITH COCAINE AND SHIT... ALL RIGHT?
BUT I...
...I DON'T PLAY GOLF...
ALL RIGHT?!

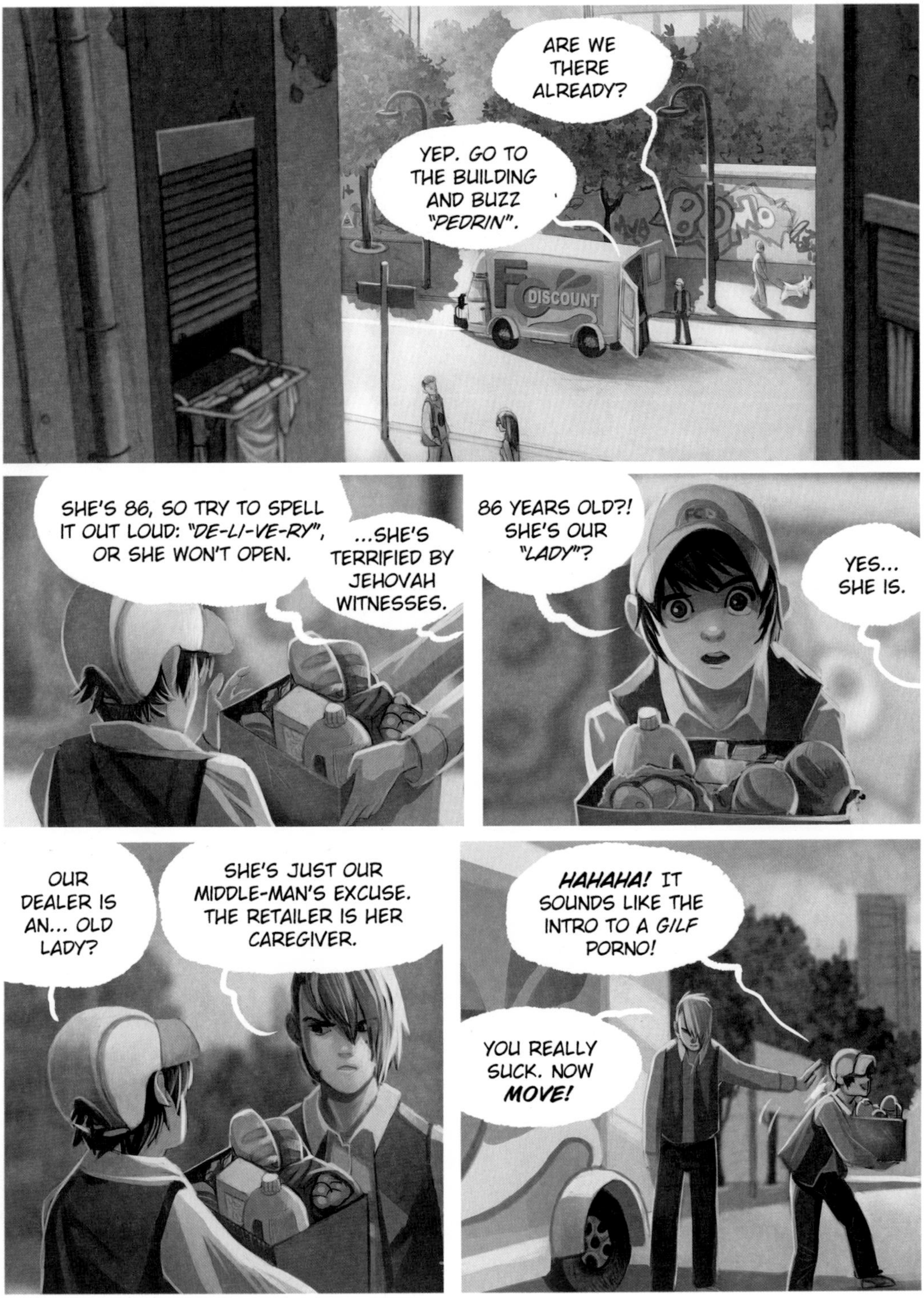

ARE WE THERE ALREADY?
YEP. GO TO THE BUILDING AND BUZZ *"PEDRIN"*.
FC DISCOUNT
SHE'S 86, SO TRY TO SPELL IT OUT LOUD: *"DE-LI-VE-RY"*, OR SHE WON'T OPEN.
...SHE'S TERRIFIED BY JEHOVAH WITNESSES.
86 YEARS OLD?! SHE'S OUR *"LADY"*?
YES... SHE IS.
OUR DEALER IS AN... OLD LADY?
SHE'S JUST OUR MIDDLE-MAN'S EXCUSE. THE RETAILER IS HER CAREGIVER.
HAHAHA! IT SOUNDS LIKE THE INTRO TO A *GILF* PORNO!
YOU REALLY SUCK. NOW ***MOVE!***

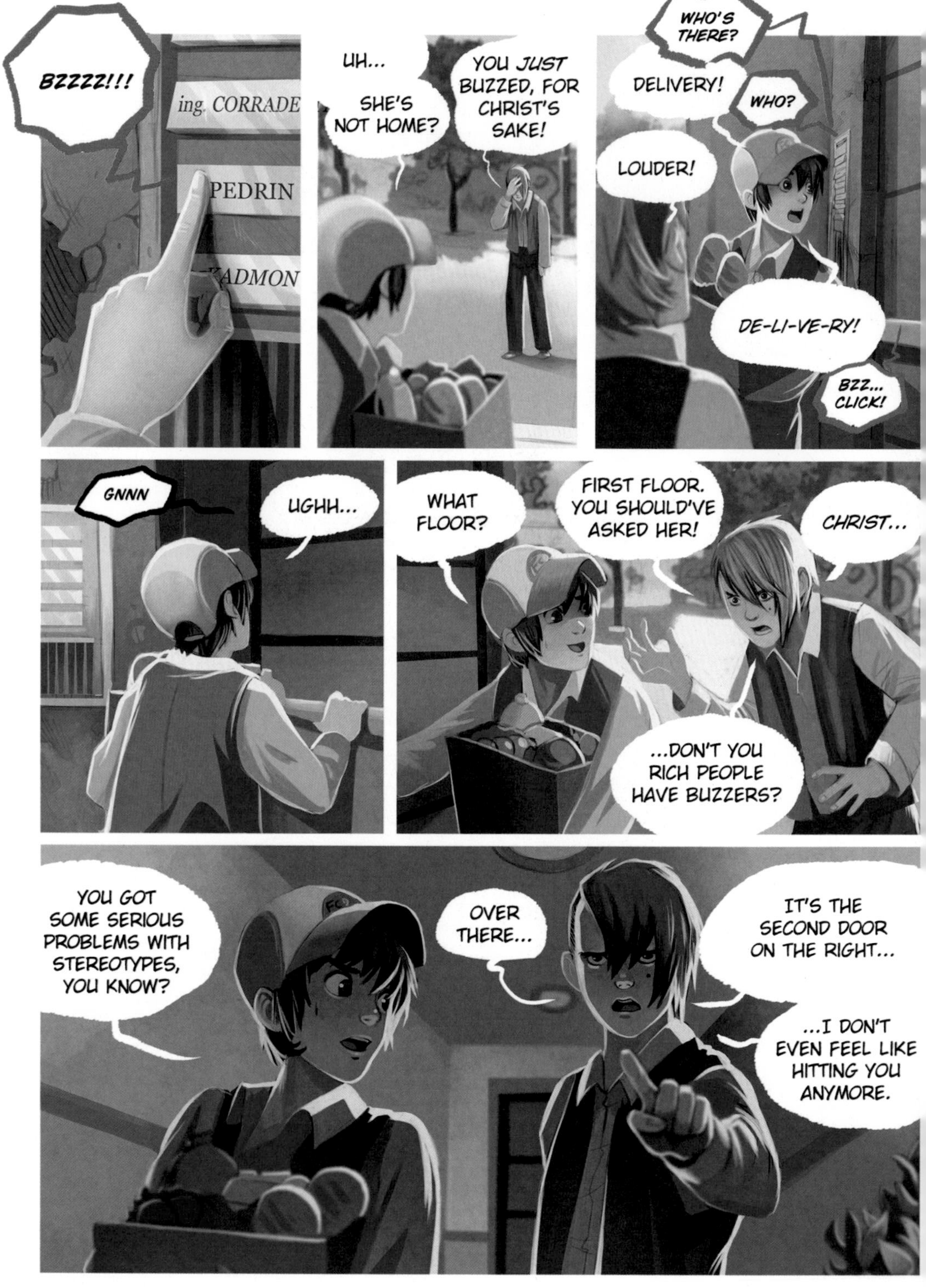
BZZZZ!!!
ing. CORRADE
PEDRIN
KADMON
UH...
SHE'S NOT HOME?
YOU JUST BUZZED, FOR CHRIST'S SAKE!
WHO'S THERE?
DELIVERY!
WHO?
LOUDER!
DE-LI-VE-RY!
BZZ... CLICK!
GNNN
UGHH...
WHAT FLOOR?
FIRST FLOOR. YOU SHOULD'VE ASKED HER!
CHRIST...
...DON'T YOU RICH PEOPLE HAVE BUZZERS?
YOU GOT SOME SERIOUS PROBLEMS WITH STEREOTYPES, YOU KNOW?
OVER THERE...
IT'S THE SECOND DOOR ON THE RIGHT...
...I DON'T EVEN FEEL LIKE HITTING YOU ANYMORE.

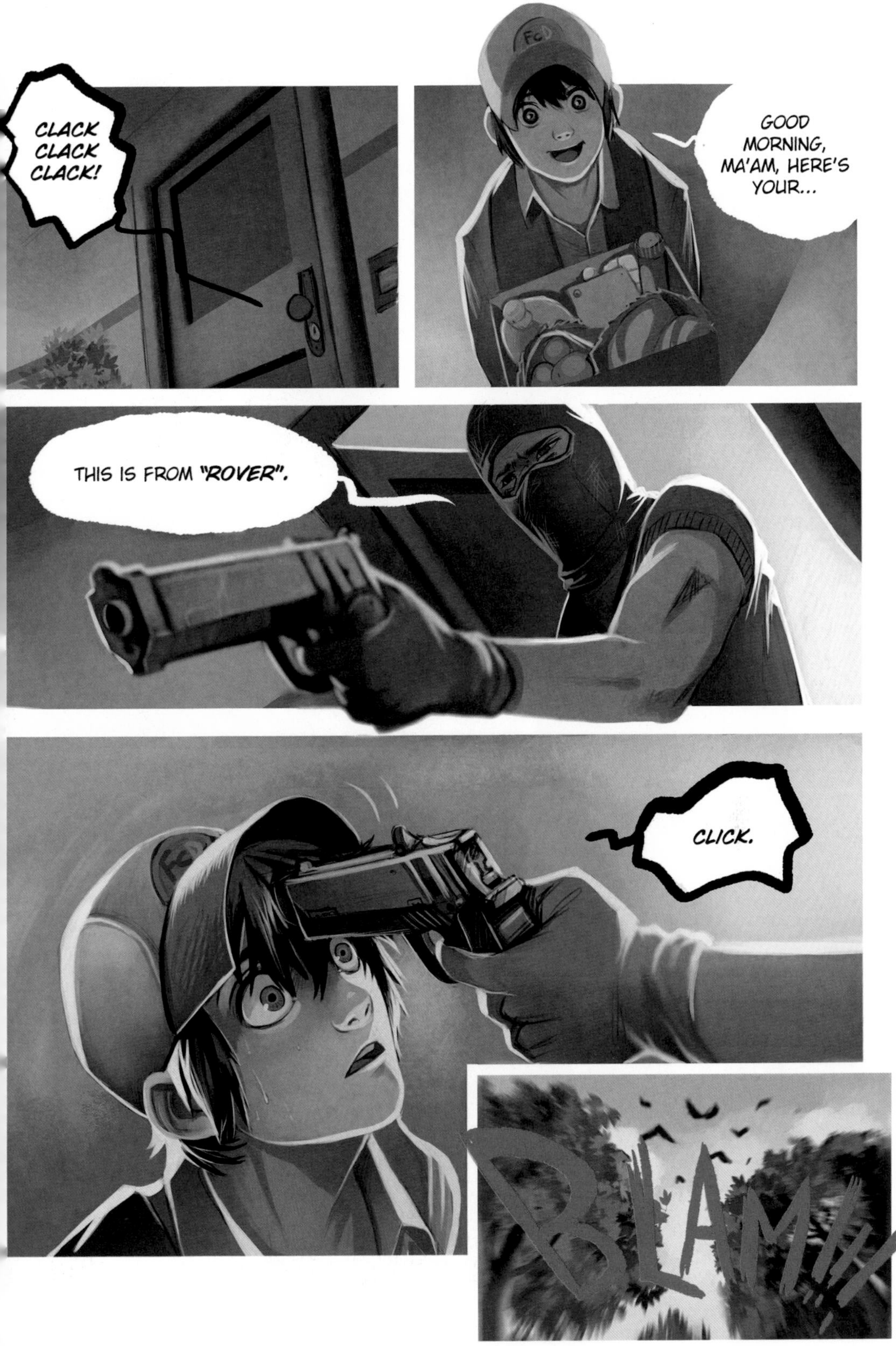
CLACK CLACK CLACK!
GOOD MORNING, MA'AM, HERE'S YOUR...
THIS IS FROM "ROVER".
CLICK.
BLAM!!!

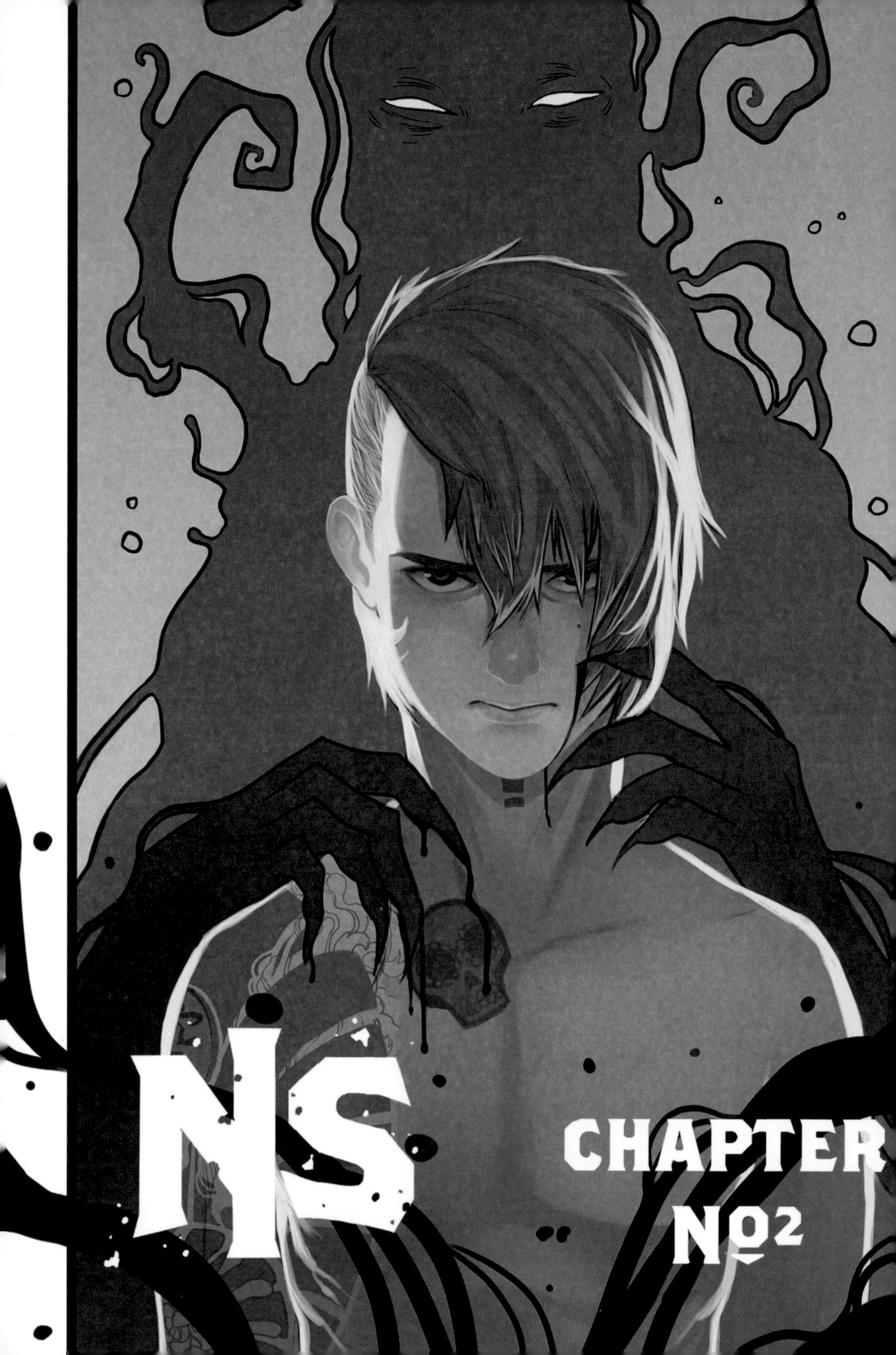

NS
CHAPTER
№2

ARE YOU HUNGRY?

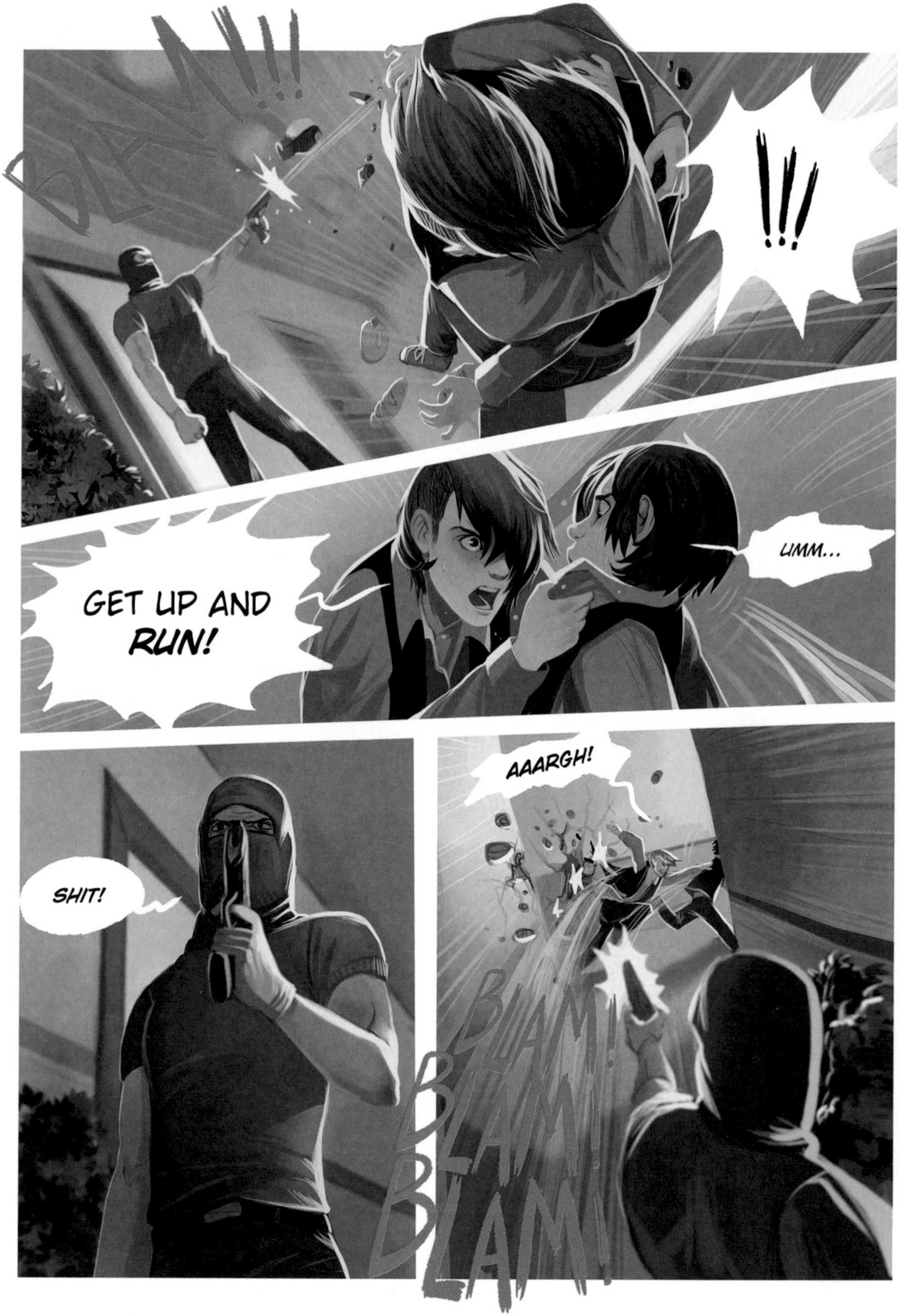
BLAM!!!
!!!
GET UP AND RUN!
UMM...
SHIT!
AAARGH!
BLAM! BLAM! BLAM! BLAM!

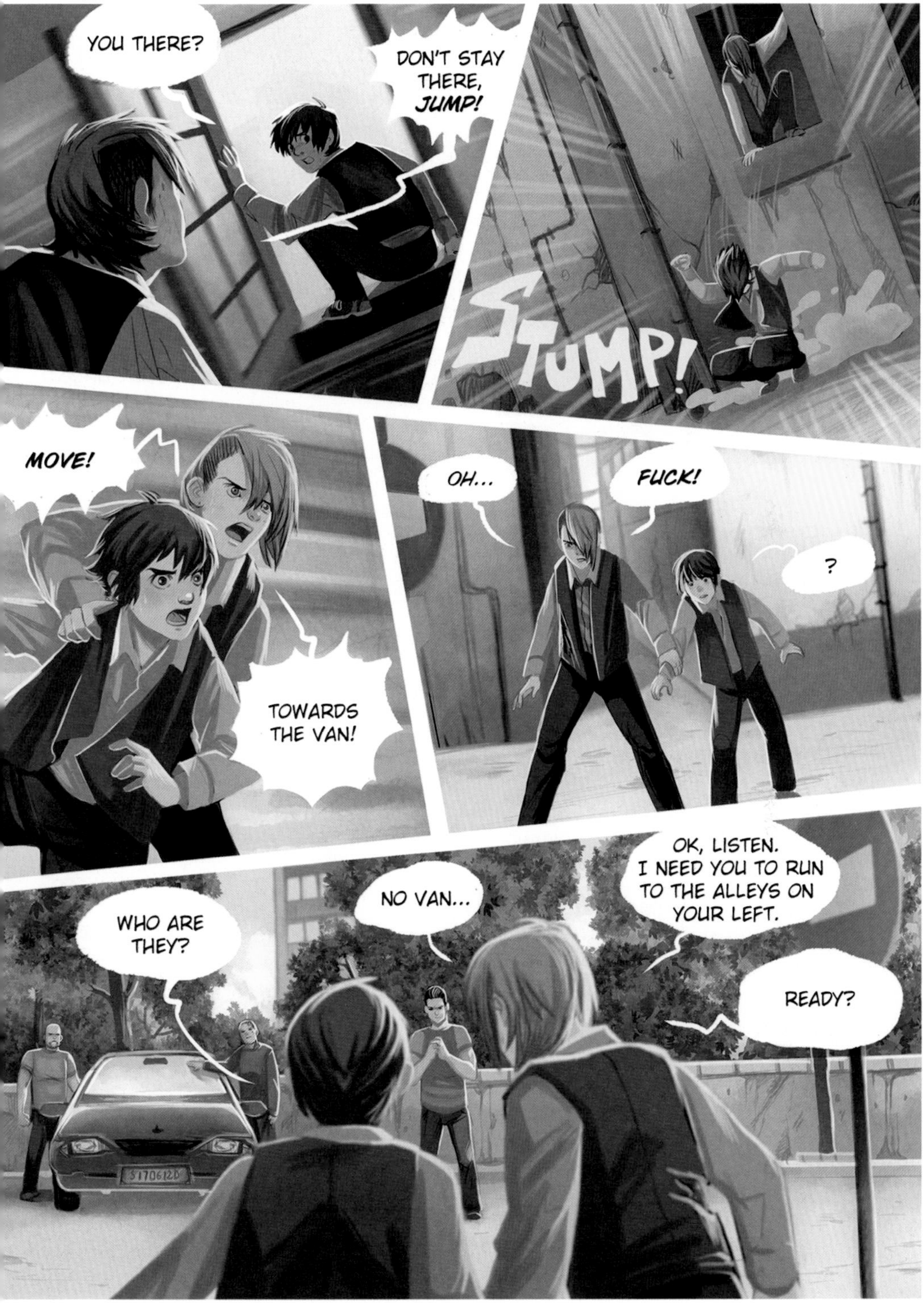
YOU THERE?
DON'T STAY THERE, JUMP!
STUMP!
MOVE!
TOWARDS THE VAN!
OH...
FUCK!
?
WHO ARE THEY?
NO VAN...
OK, LISTEN. I NEED YOU TO RUN TO THE ALLEYS ON YOUR LEFT.
READY?

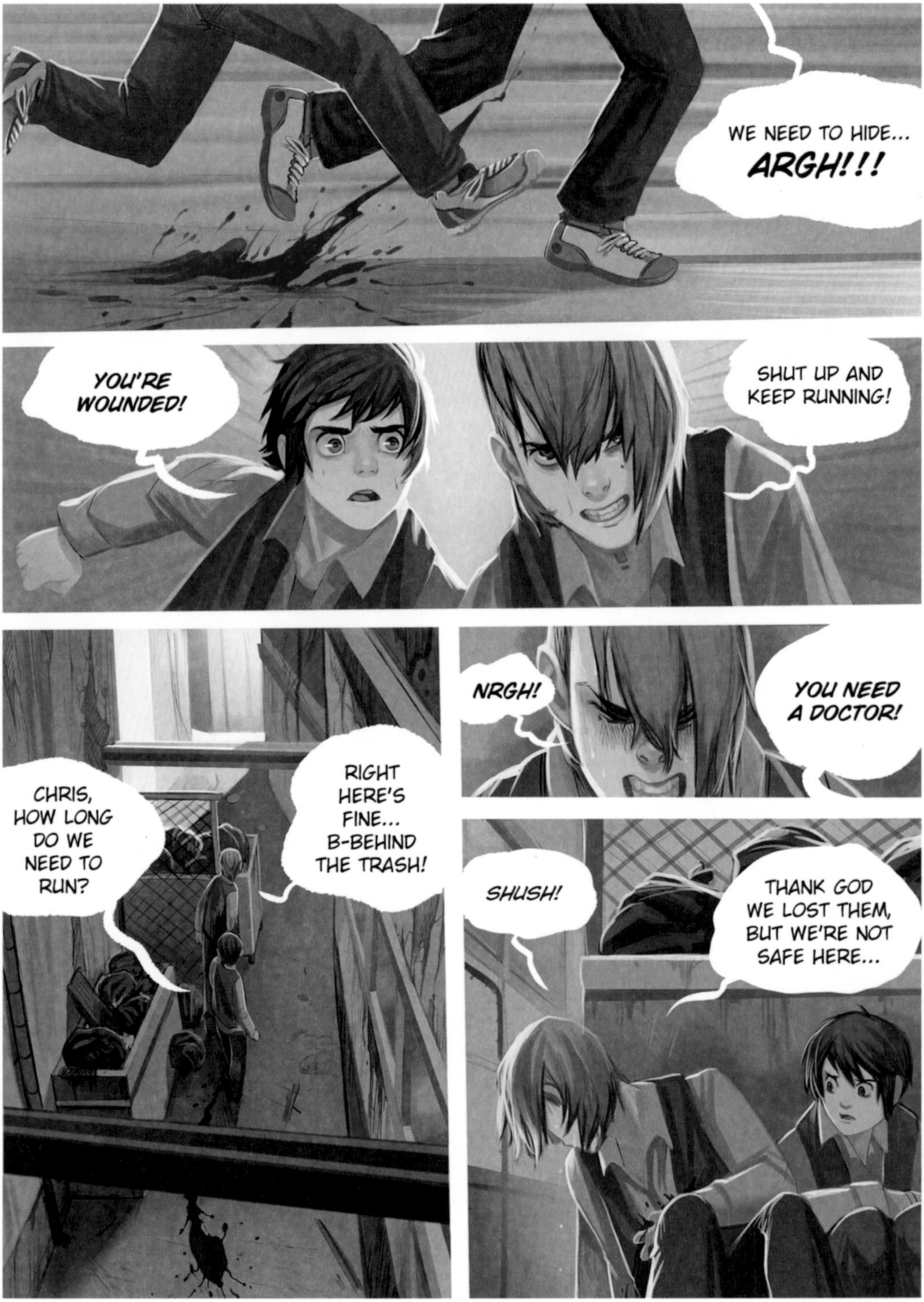
WE NEED TO HIDE... ARGH!!!
YOU'RE WOUNDED!
SHUT UP AND KEEP RUNNING!
CHRIS, HOW LONG DO WE NEED TO RUN?
RIGHT HERE'S FINE... B-BEHIND THE TRASH!
NRGH!
YOU NEED A DOCTOR!
SHUSH!
THANK GOD WE LOST THEM, BUT WE'RE NOT SAFE HERE...

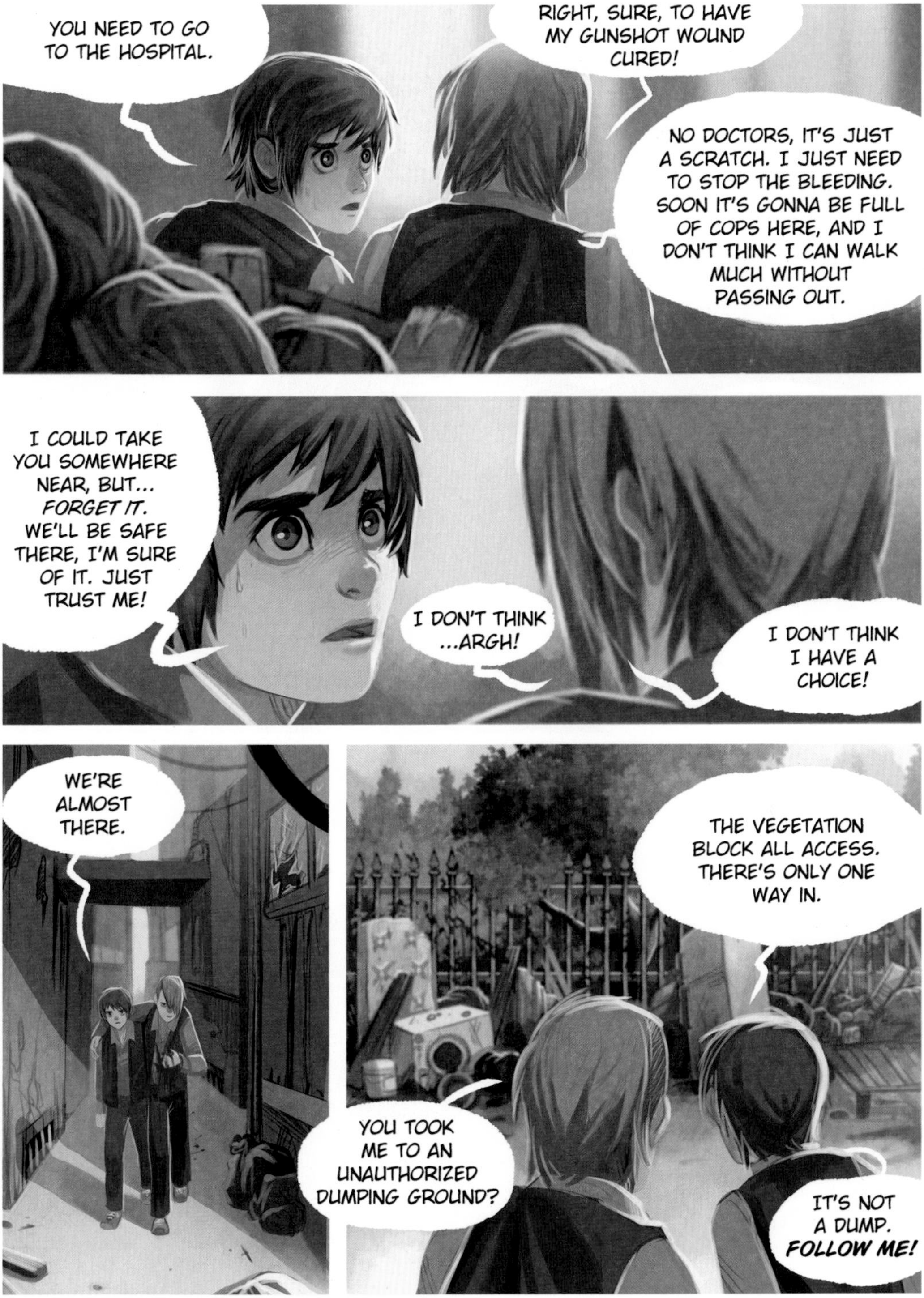
YOU NEED TO GO TO THE HOSPITAL.
RIGHT, SURE, TO HAVE MY GUNSHOT WOUND CURED!
NO DOCTORS, IT'S JUST A SCRATCH. I JUST NEED TO STOP THE BLEEDING. SOON IT'S GONNA BE FULL OF COPS HERE, AND I DON'T THINK I CAN WALK MUCH WITHOUT PASSING OUT.
I COULD TAKE YOU SOMEWHERE NEAR, BUT... *FORGET IT.* WE'LL BE SAFE THERE, I'M SURE OF IT. JUST TRUST ME!
I DON'T THINK ...ARGH!
I DON'T THINK I HAVE A CHOICE!
WE'RE ALMOST THERE.
THE VEGETATION BLOCK ALL ACCESS. THERE'S ONLY ONE WAY IN.
YOU TOOK ME TO AN UNAUTHORIZED DUMPING GROUND?
IT'S NOT A DUMP. ***FOLLOW ME!***

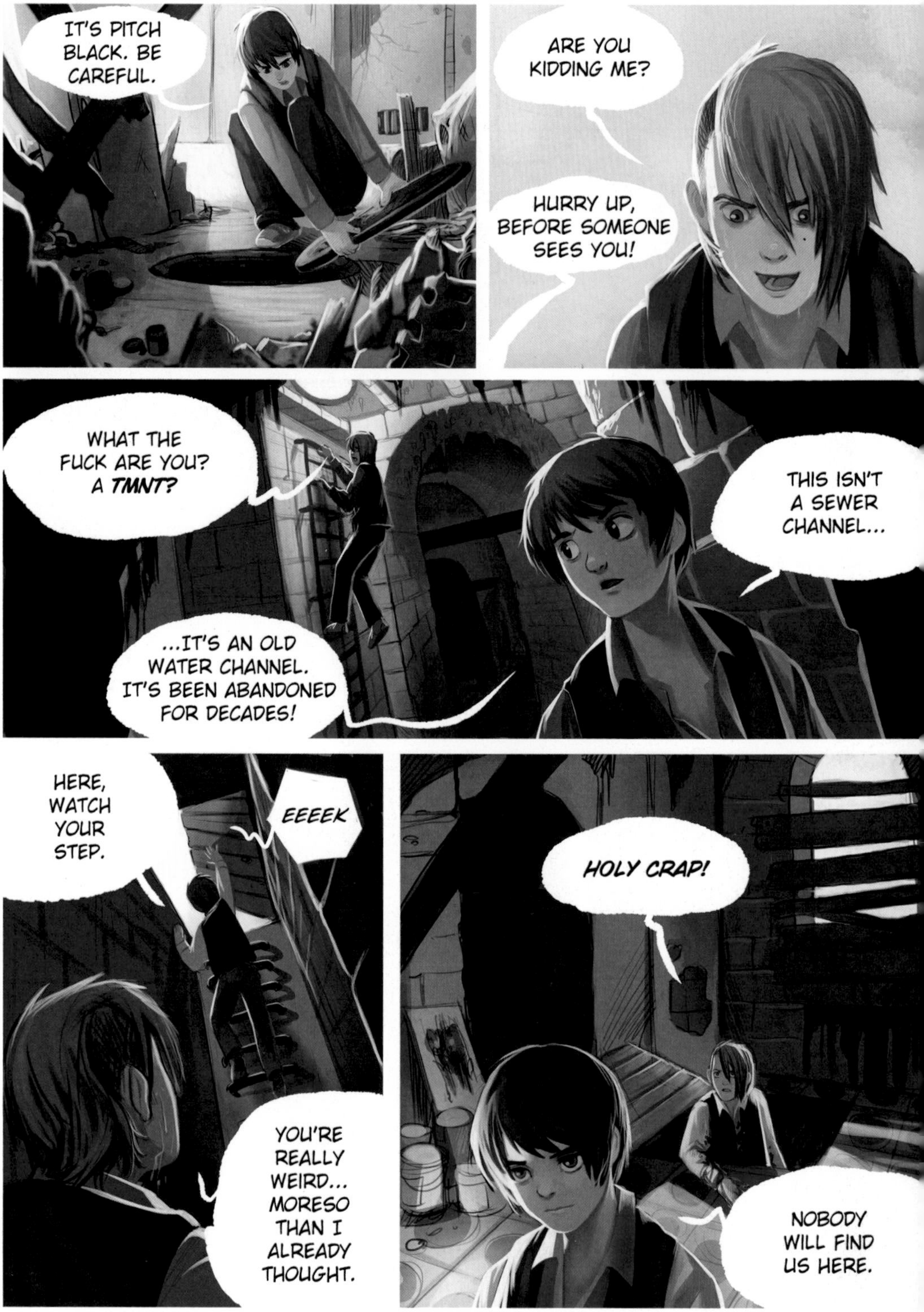
IT'S PITCH BLACK. BE CAREFUL.
ARE YOU KIDDING ME?
HURRY UP, BEFORE SOMEONE SEES YOU!
WHAT THE FUCK ARE YOU? A TMNT?
THIS ISN'T A SEWER CHANNEL...
...IT'S AN OLD WATER CHANNEL. IT'S BEEN ABANDONED FOR DECADES!
HERE, WATCH YOUR STEP.
EEEEK
YOU'RE REALLY WEIRD... MORESO THAN I ALREADY THOUGHT.
HOLY CRAP!
NOBODY WILL FIND US HERE.

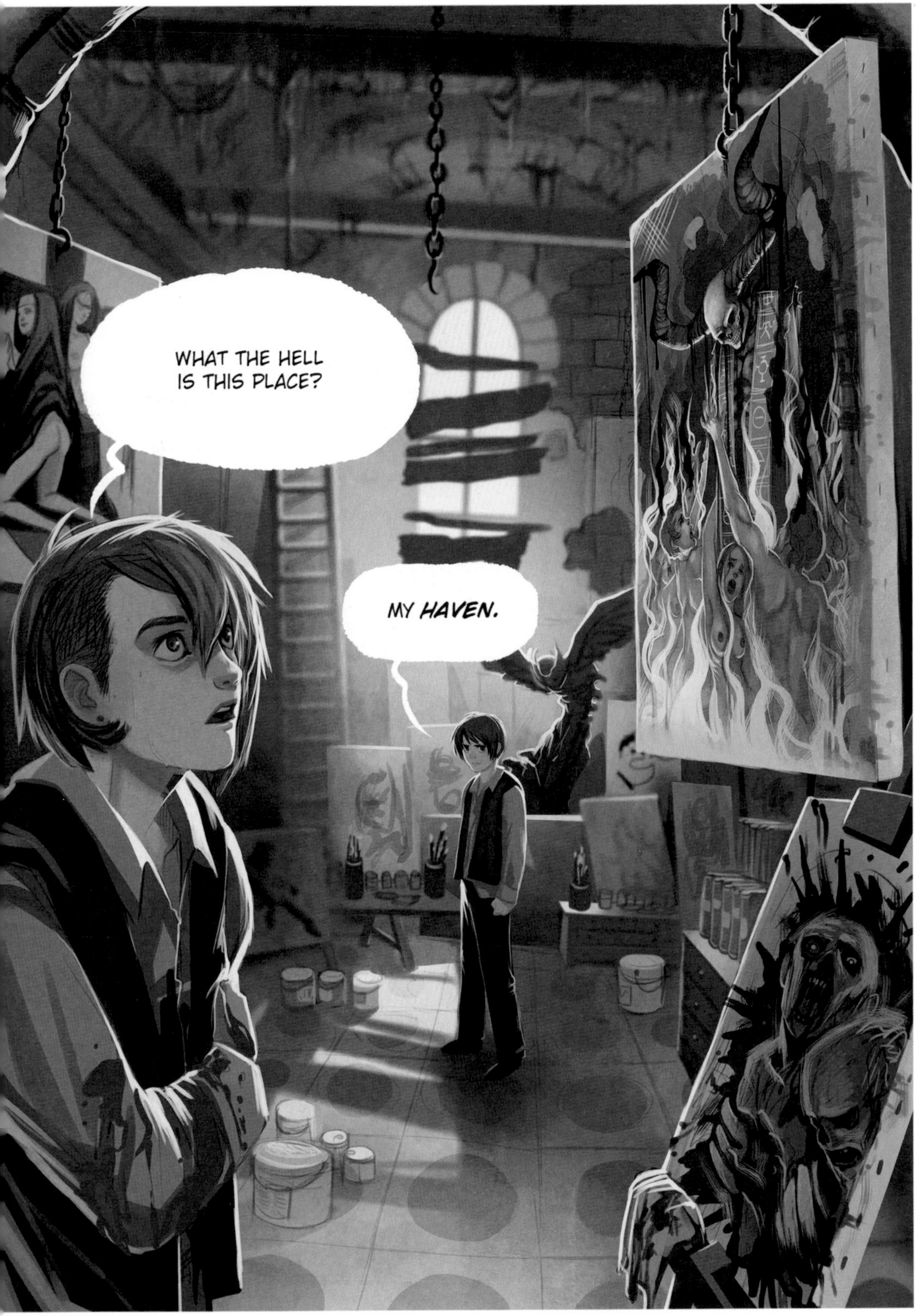
WHAT THE HELL IS THIS PLACE?
MY HAVEN.

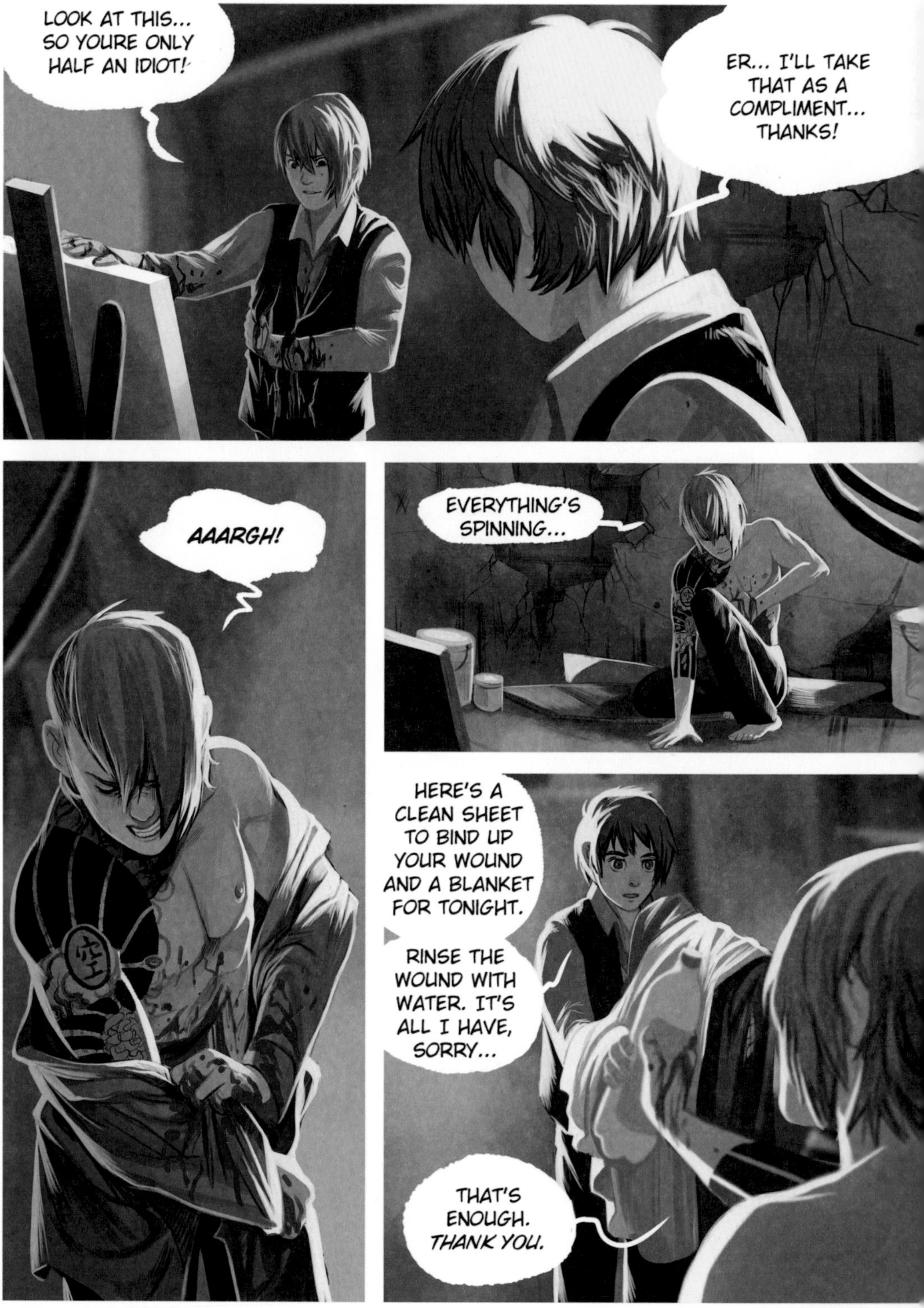
LOOK AT THIS... SO YOURE ONLY HALF AN IDIOT!
ER... I'LL TAKE THAT AS A COMPLIMENT... THANKS!
AAARGH!
EVERYTHING'S SPINNING...
HERE'S A CLEAN SHEET TO BIND UP YOUR WOUND AND A BLANKET FOR TONIGHT.
RINSE THE WOUND WITH WATER. IT'S ALL I HAVE, SORRY...
THAT'S ENOUGH. THANK YOU.

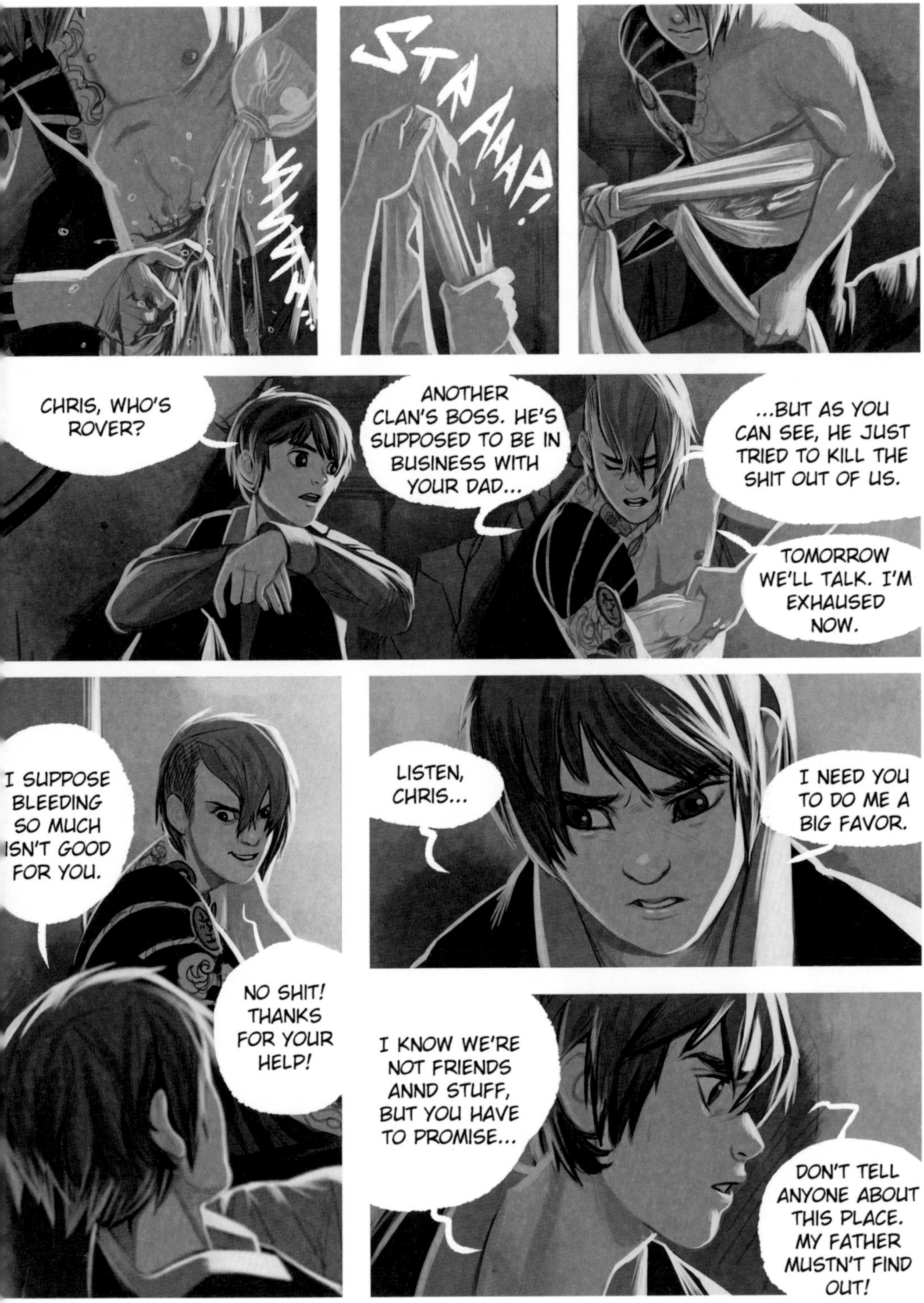
SSSSH!
STRAAAP!
CHRIS, WHO'S ROVER?
ANOTHER CLAN'S BOSS. HE'S SUPPOSED TO BE IN BUSINESS WITH YOUR DAD...
...BUT AS YOU CAN SEE, HE JUST TRIED TO KILL THE SHIT OUT OF US.
TOMORROW WE'LL TALK. I'M EXHAUSED NOW.
I SUPPOSE BLEEDING SO MUCH ISN'T GOOD FOR YOU.
NO SHIT! THANKS FOR YOUR HELP!
LISTEN, CHRIS...
I NEED YOU TO DO ME A BIG FAVOR.
I KNOW WE'RE NOT FRIENDS ANND STUFF, BUT YOU HAVE TO PROMISE...
DON'T TELL ANYONE ABOUT THIS PLACE. MY FATHER MUSTN'T FIND OUT!

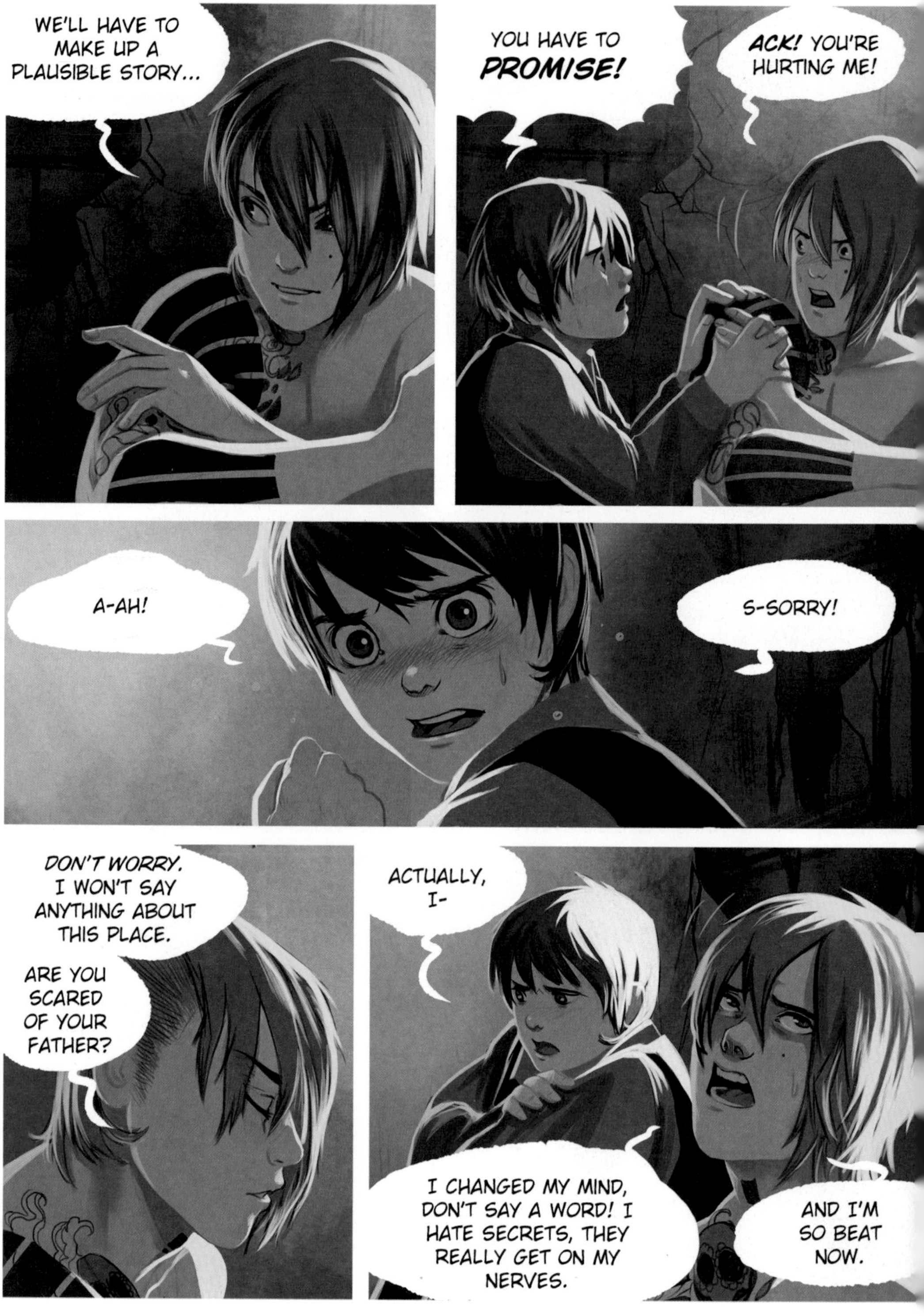
WE'LL HAVE TO MAKE UP A PLAUSIBLE STORY...
YOU HAVE TO PROMISE!
ACK! YOU'RE HURTING ME!
A-AH!
S-SORRY!
DON'T WORRY. I WON'T SAY ANYTHING ABOUT THIS PLACE.
ARE YOU SCARED OF YOUR FATHER?
ACTUALLY, I-
I CHANGED MY MIND, DON'T SAY A WORD! I HATE SECRETS, THEY REALLY GET ON MY NERVES.
AND I'M SO BEAT NOW.

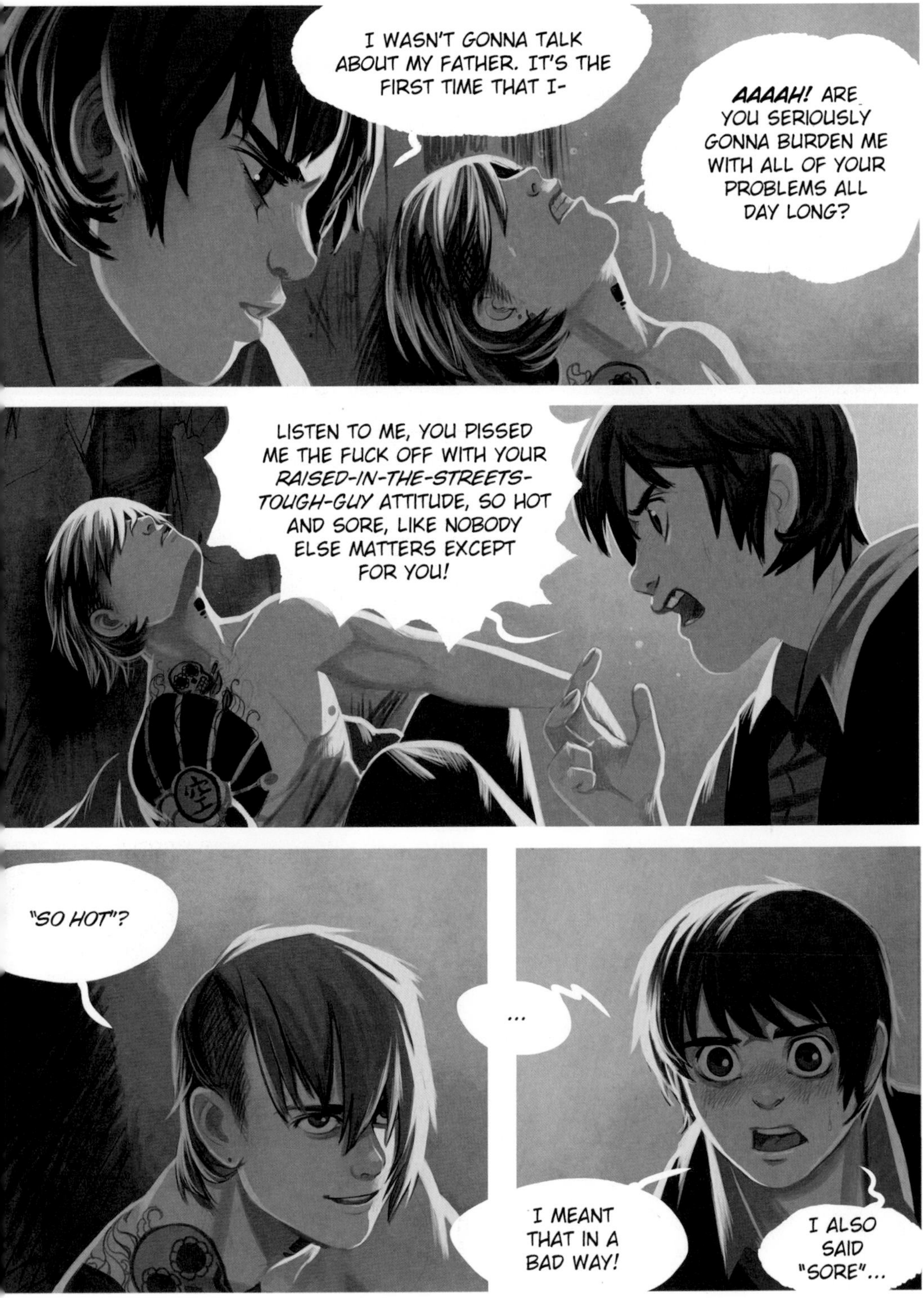
I WASN'T GONNA TALK ABOUT MY FATHER. IT'S THE FIRST TIME THAT I-
AAAAH! ARE YOU SERIOUSLY GONNA BURDEN ME WITH ALL OF YOUR PROBLEMS ALL DAY LONG?
LISTEN TO ME, YOU PISSED ME THE FUCK OFF WITH YOUR RAISED-IN-THE-STREETS-TOUGH-GUY ATTITUDE, SO HOT AND SORE, LIKE NOBODY ELSE MATTERS EXCEPT FOR YOU!
"SO HOT"?
...
I MEANT THAT IN A BAD WAY!
I ALSO SAID "SORE"...

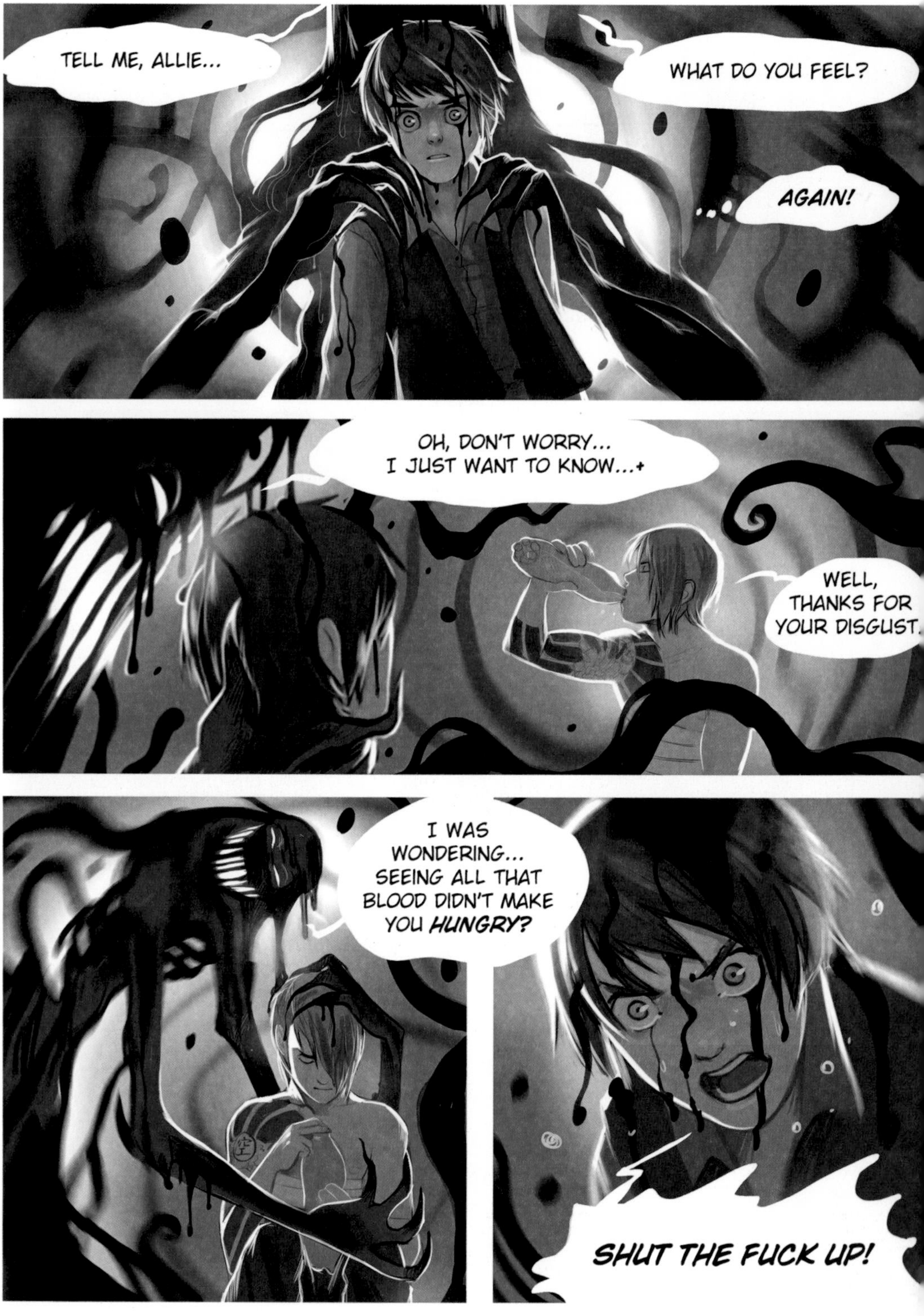
TELL ME, ALLIE...
WHAT DO YOU FEEL?
AGAIN!
OH, DON'T WORRY... I JUST WANT TO KNOW...+
WELL, THANKS FOR YOUR DISGUST.
I WAS WONDERING... SEEING ALL THAT BLOOD DIDN'T MAKE YOU HUNGRY?
SHUT THE FUCK UP!

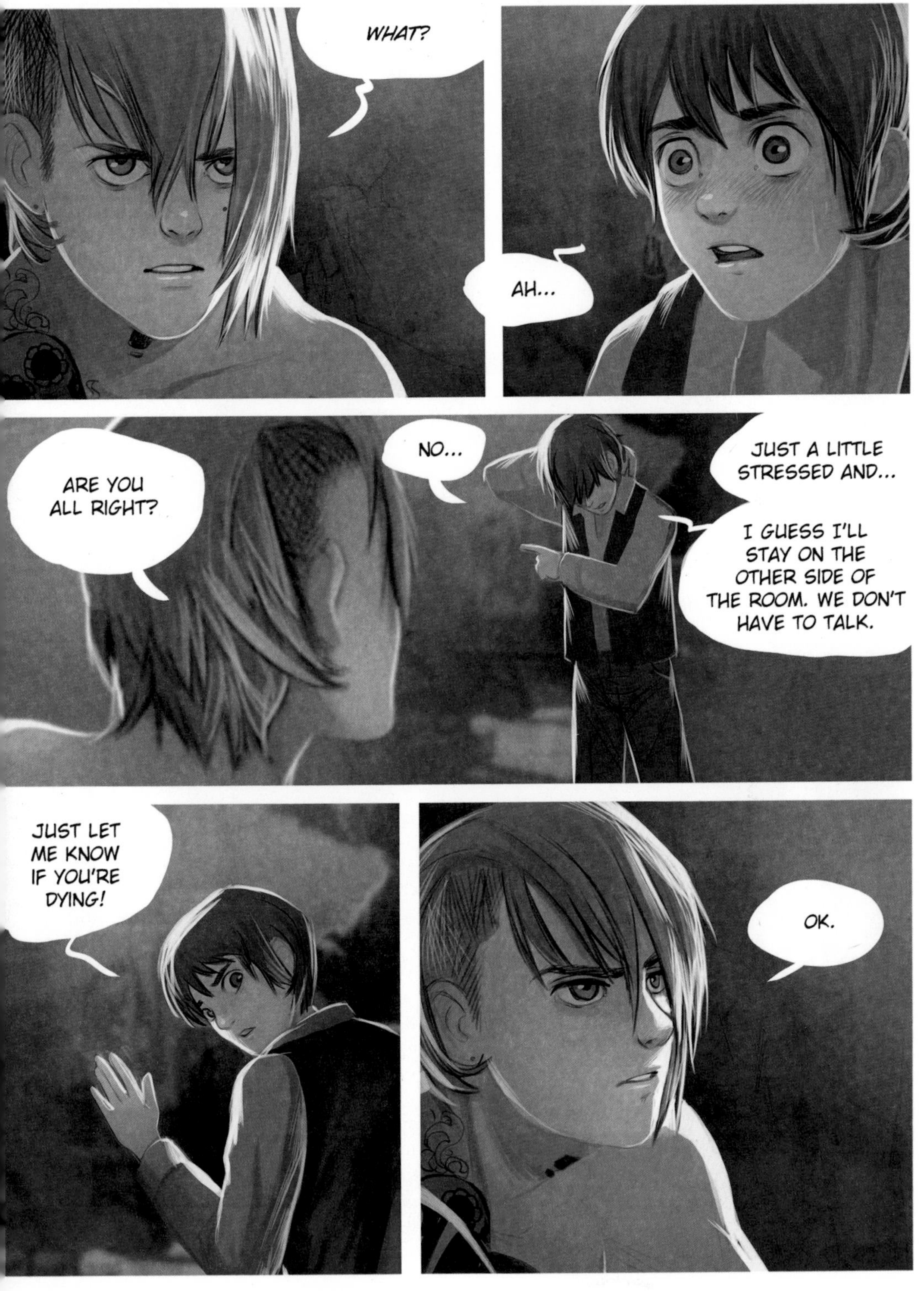
WHAT?
AH...
ARE YOU ALL RIGHT?
NO...
JUST A LITTLE STRESSED AND...
I GUESS I'LL STAY ON THE OTHER SIDE OF THE ROOM. WE DON'T HAVE TO TALK.
JUST LET ME KNOW IF YOU'RE DYING!
OK.

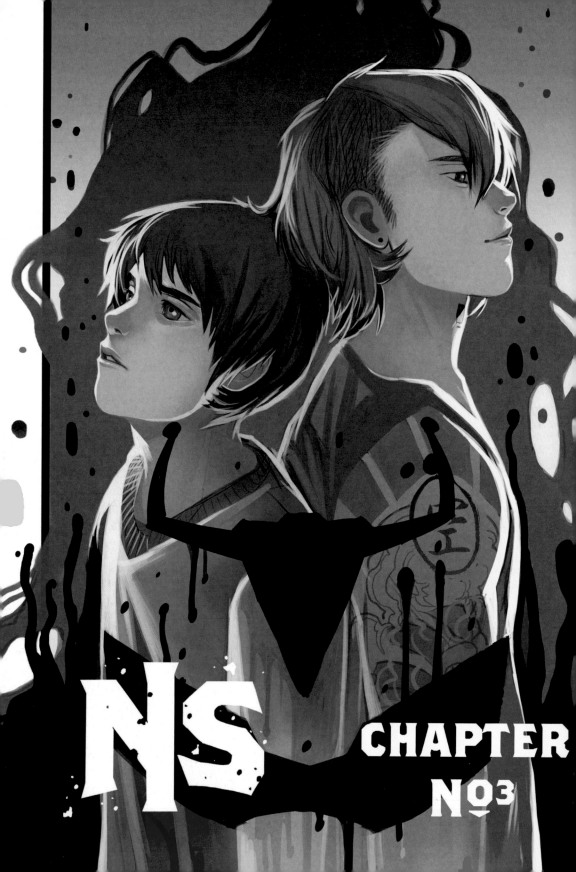

NS

CHAPTER Nᵒ3

THE PRESENT.

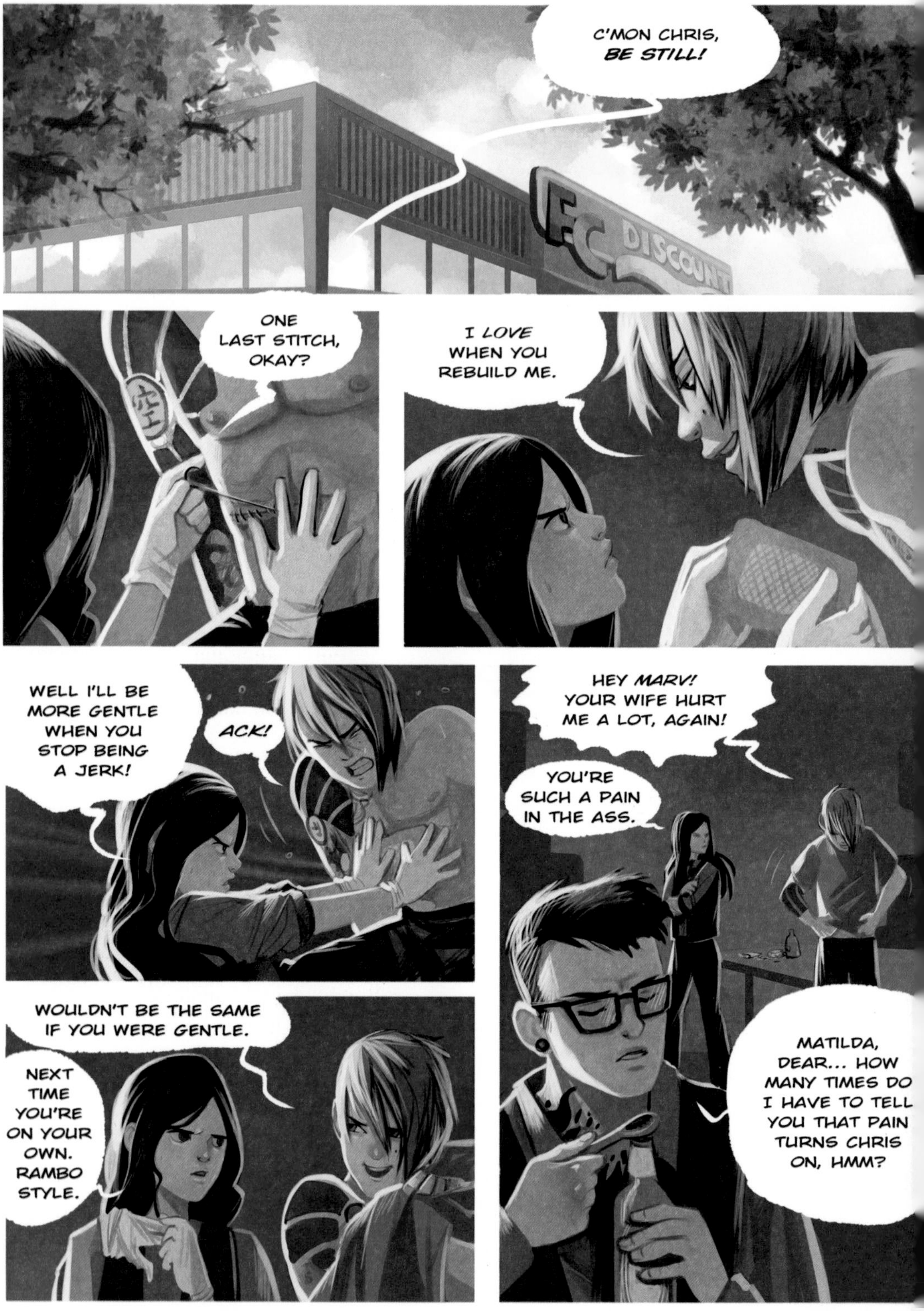
C'MON CHRIS, BE STILL!
FC DISCOUNT
ONE LAST STITCH, OKAY?
I LOVE WHEN YOU REBUILD ME.
WELL I'LL BE MORE GENTLE WHEN YOU STOP BEING A JERK!
ACK!
HEY MARV! YOUR WIFE HURT ME A LOT, AGAIN!
YOU'RE SUCH A PAIN IN THE ASS.
WOULDN'T BE THE SAME IF YOU WERE GENTLE.
NEXT TIME YOU'RE ON YOUR OWN. RAMBO STYLE.
MATILDA, DEAR... HOW MANY TIMES DO I HAVE TO TELL YOU THAT PAIN TURNS CHRIS ON, HMM?

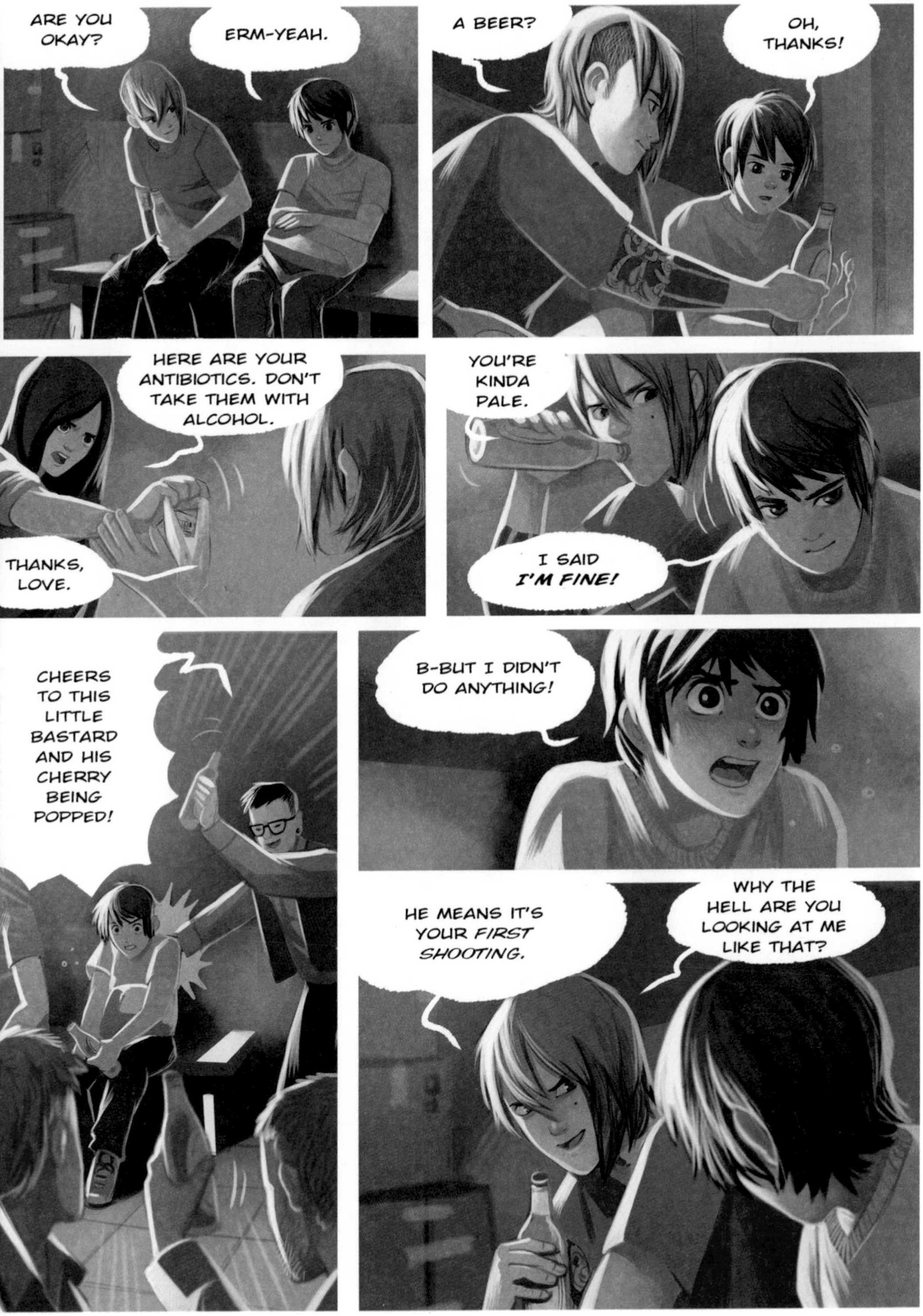
ARE YOU OKAY?
ERM-YEAH.
A BEER?
OH, THANKS!
HERE ARE YOUR ANTIBIOTICS. DON'T TAKE THEM WITH ALCOHOL.
THANKS, LOVE.
YOU'RE KINDA PALE.
I SAID *I'M FINE!*
CHEERS TO THIS LITTLE BASTARD AND HIS CHERRY BEING POPPED!
B-BUT I DIDN'T DO ANYTHING!
HE MEANS IT'S YOUR *FIRST* *SHOOTING.*
WHY THE HELL ARE YOU LOOKING AT ME LIKE THAT?

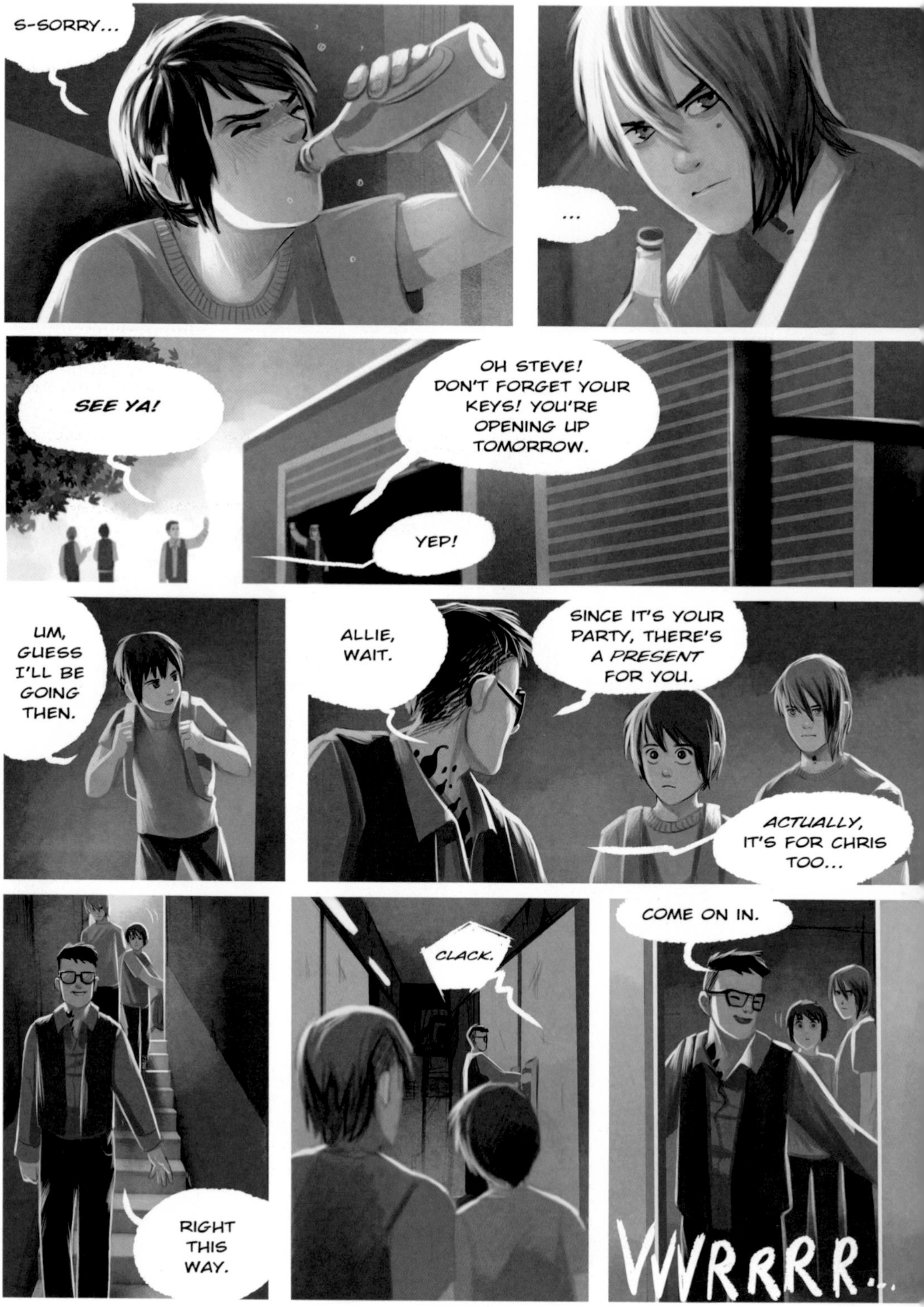
S-SORRY...
...
SEE YA!
OH STEVE! DON'T FORGET YOUR KEYS! YOU'RE OPENING UP TOMORROW.
YEP!
UM, GUESS I'LL BE GOING THEN.
ALLIE, WAIT.
SINCE IT'S YOUR PARTY, THERE'S A *PRESENT* FOR YOU.
ACTUALLY, IT'S FOR CHRIS TOO...
RIGHT THIS WAY.
CLACK.
COME ON IN.
VVVRRRR...

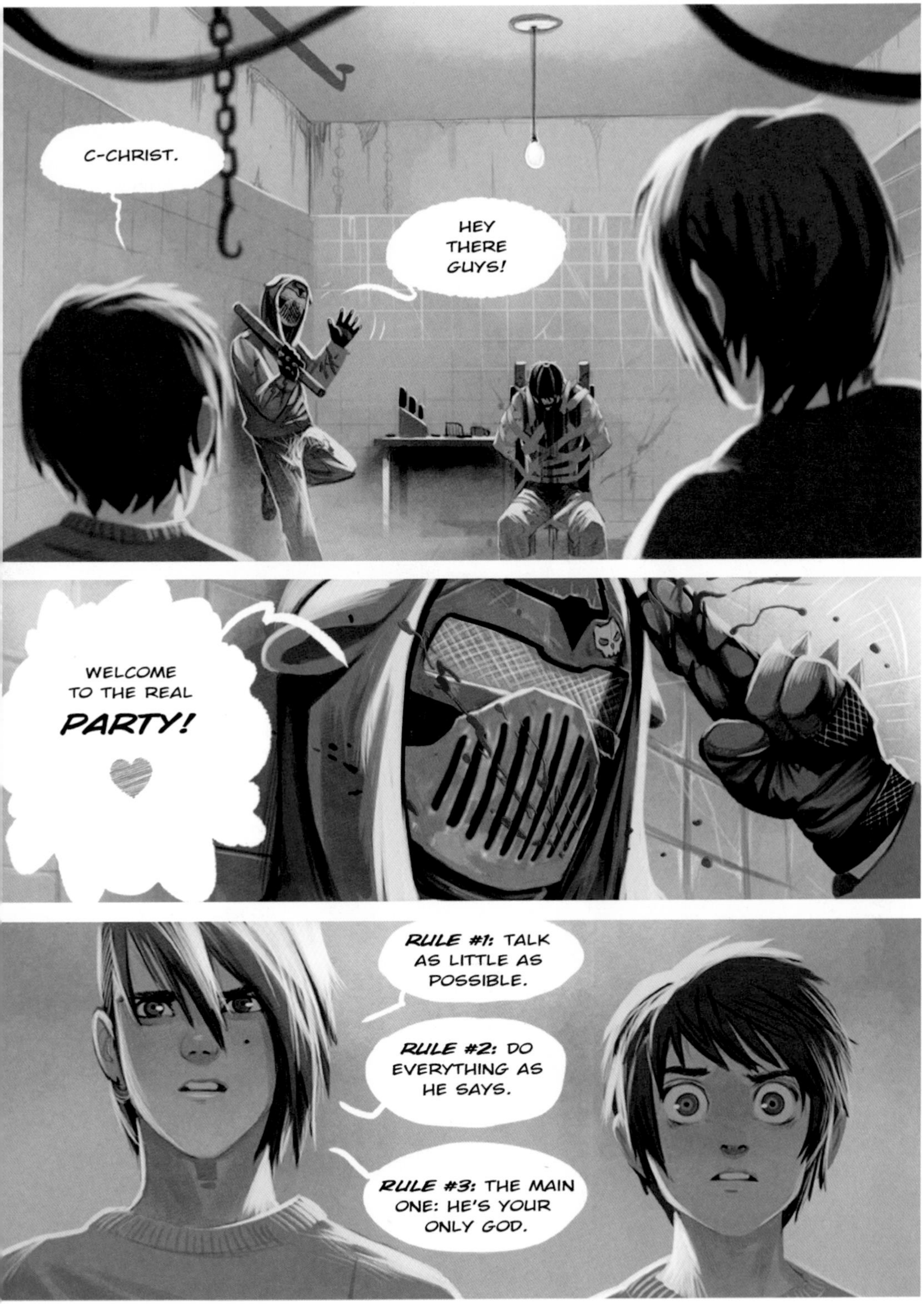
C-CHRIST.
HEY THERE GUYS!
WELCOME TO THE REAL ***PARTY!***
RULE #1: TALK AS LITTLE AS POSSIBLE.
RULE #2: DO EVERYTHING AS HE SAYS.
RULE #3: THE MAIN ONE: HE'S YOUR ONLY GOD.

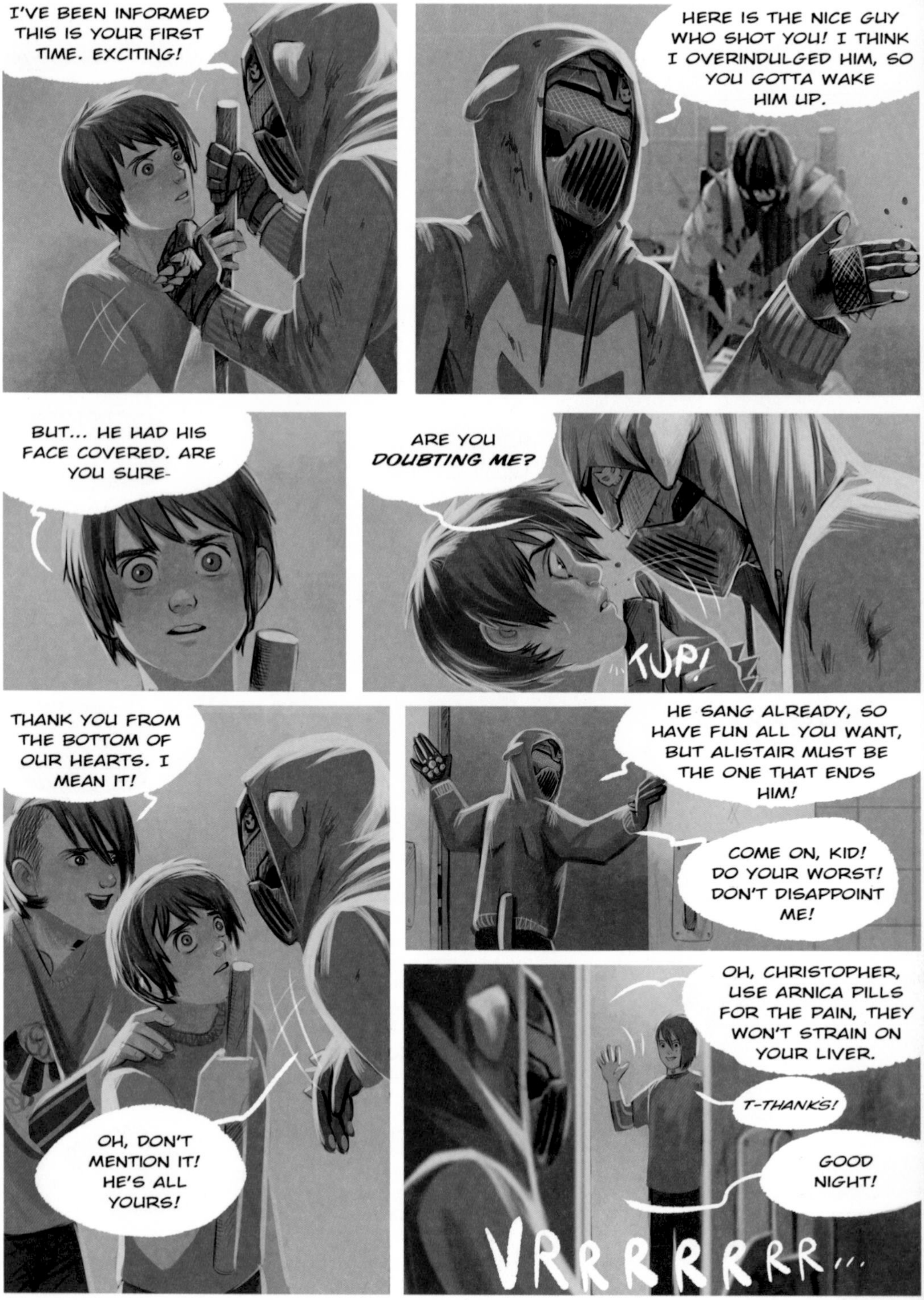
I'VE BEEN INFORMED THIS IS YOUR FIRST TIME. EXCITING!
HERE IS THE NICE GUY WHO SHOT YOU! I THINK I OVERINDULGED HIM, SO YOU GOTTA WAKE HIM UP.
BUT... HE HAD HIS FACE COVERED. ARE YOU SURE-
ARE YOU *DOUBTING ME?*
TUP!
THANK YOU FROM THE BOTTOM OF OUR HEARTS. I MEAN IT!
OH, DON'T MENTION IT! HE'S ALL YOURS!
HE SANG ALREADY, SO HAVE FUN ALL YOU WANT, BUT ALISTAIR MUST BE THE ONE THAT ENDS HIM!
COME ON, KID! DO YOUR WORST! DON'T DISAPPOINT ME!
OH, CHRISTOPHER, USE ARNICA PILLS FOR THE PAIN, THEY WON'T STRAIN ON YOUR LIVER.
T-THANKS!
GOOD NIGHT!
VRRRRRRR...

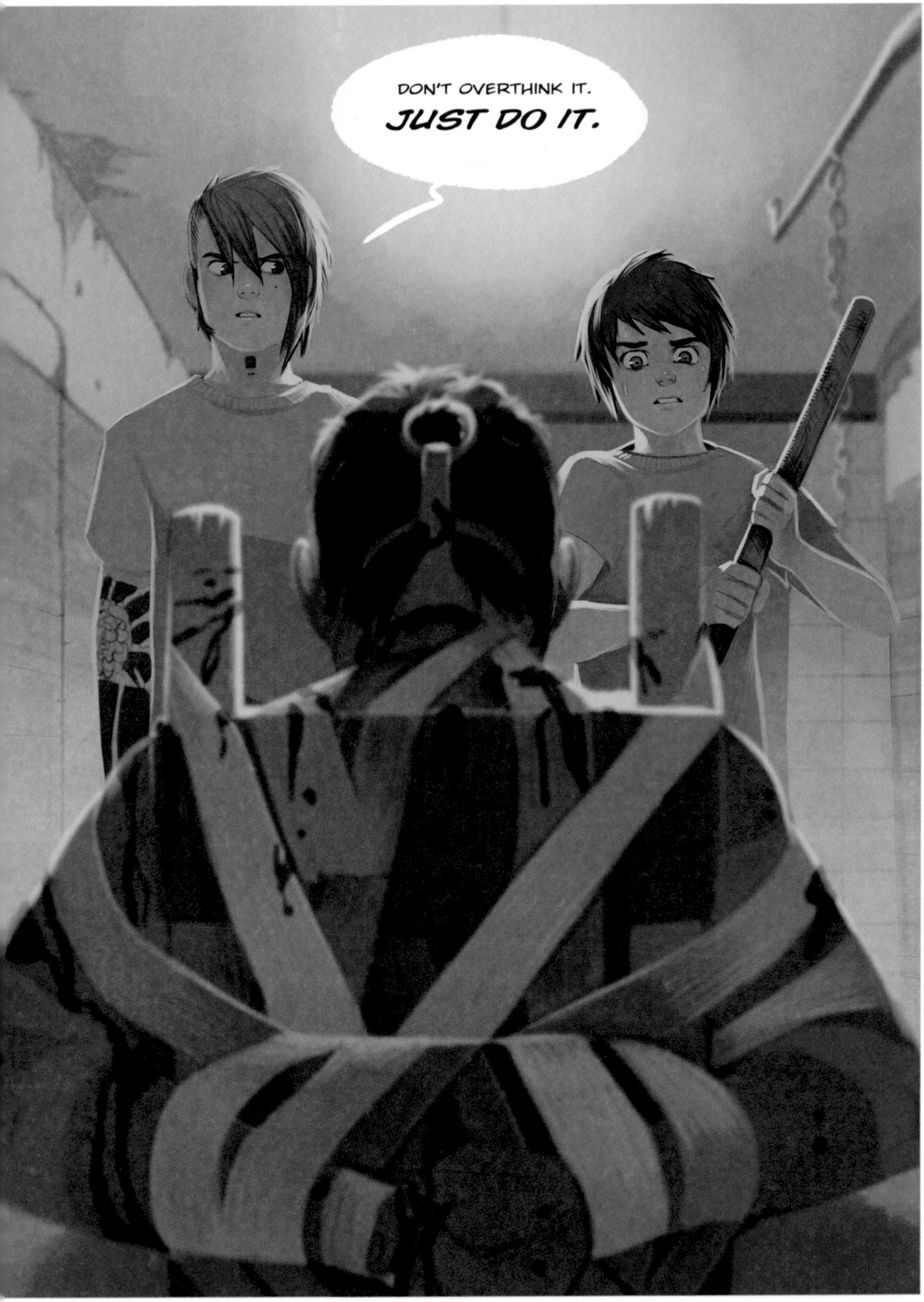
DON'T OVERTHINK IT.
JUST DO IT.

CRIII... CRIII... CRIII... CRIII...

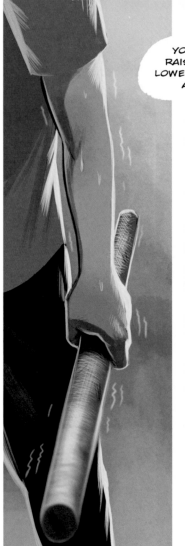

YOU KEEP RAISING AND LOWERING YOUR ARM...

...IF YOU DON'T MOVE, HE'LL WAKE UP AND IT'S JUST BETTER IF YOU DO THIS WHILE HE'S UNCONSCIOUS.

I GOT IT, NO NEED TO REPEAT IT. JUST GIVE ME A SECOND...

LISTEN, HE'S ALREADY DOOMED. IF YOU DON'T KILL HIM, FELIX WILL. BUT THAT'D MEAN YOU DISOBEYED, AND I SUGGEST THAT YOU NEVER DO THAT.

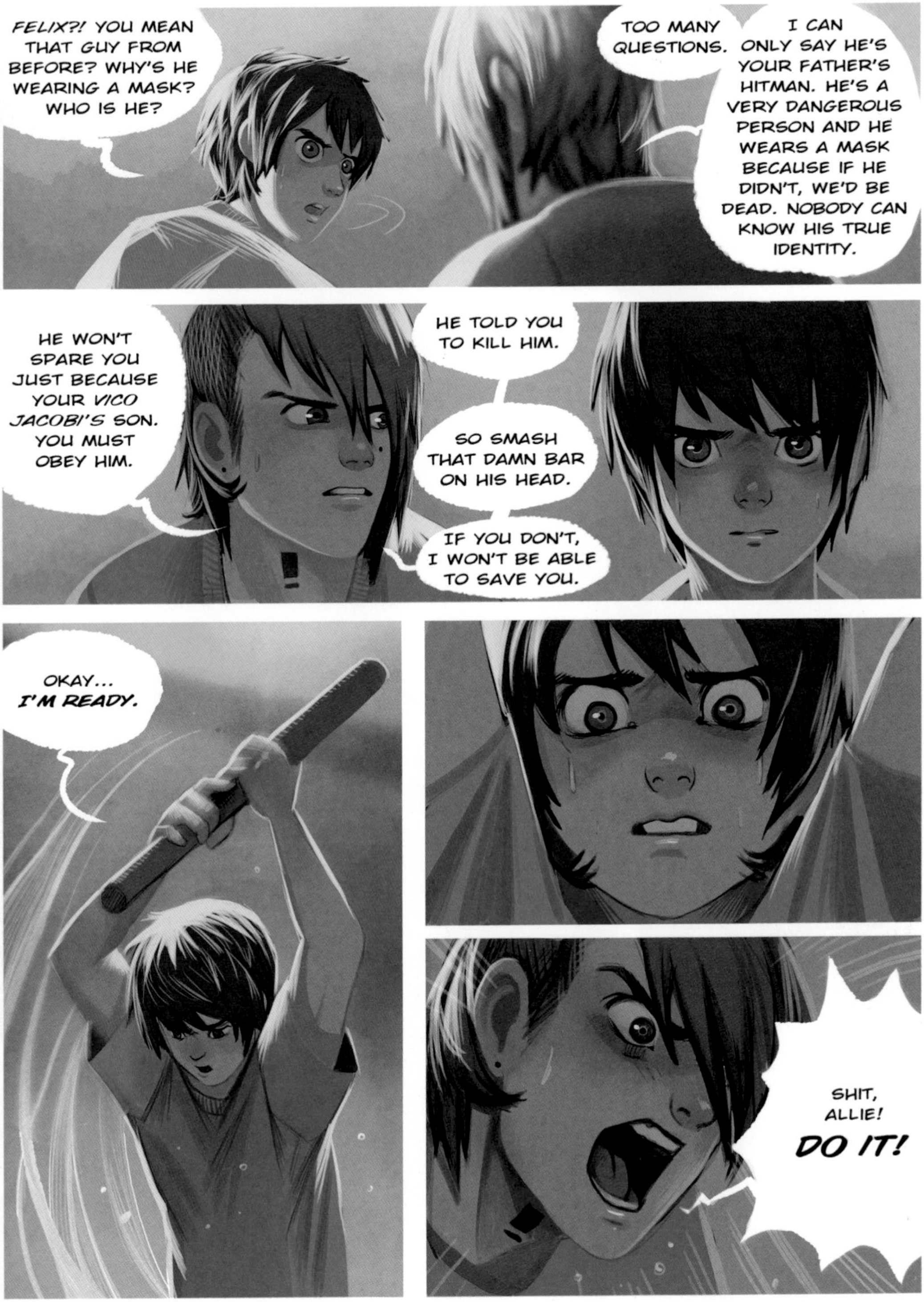
FELIX?! YOU MEAN THAT GUY FROM BEFORE? WHY'S HE WEARING A MASK? WHO IS HE?
TOO MANY QUESTIONS.
I CAN ONLY SAY HE'S YOUR FATHER'S HITMAN. HE'S A VERY DANGEROUS PERSON AND HE WEARS A MASK BECAUSE IF HE DIDN'T, WE'D BE DEAD. NOBODY CAN KNOW HIS TRUE IDENTITY.
HE WON'T SPARE YOU JUST BECAUSE YOUR *VICO JACOBI'S* SON. YOU MUST OBEY HIM.
HE TOLD YOU TO KILL HIM.
SO SMASH THAT DAMN BAR ON HIS HEAD.
IF YOU DON'T, I WON'T BE ABLE TO SAVE YOU.
OKAY... ***I'M READY.***
SHIT, ALLIE!
DO IT!

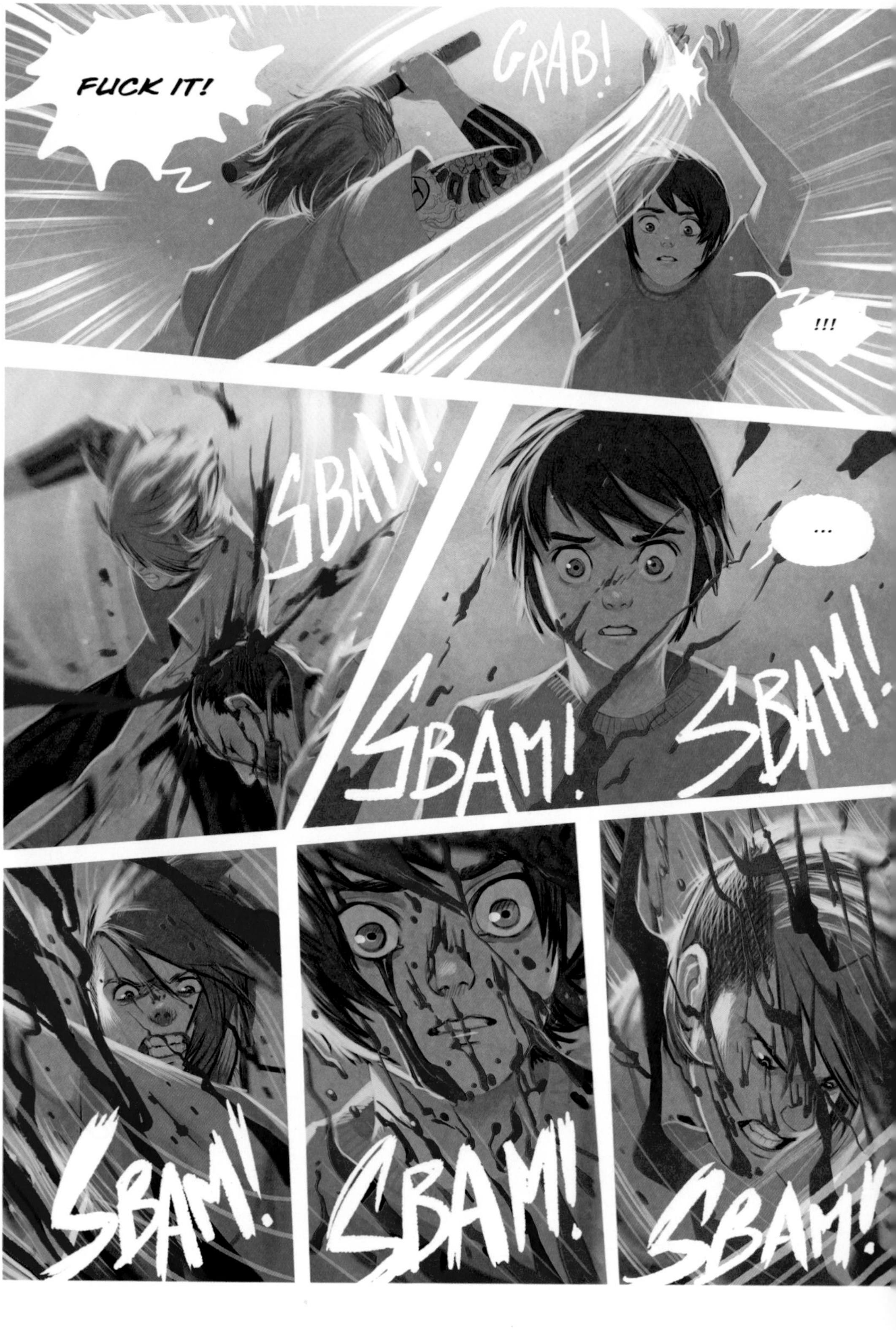
FUCK IT!
GRAB!
!!!
SBAM!
...
SBAM!
SBAM!
SBAM!
SBAM!
SBAM!

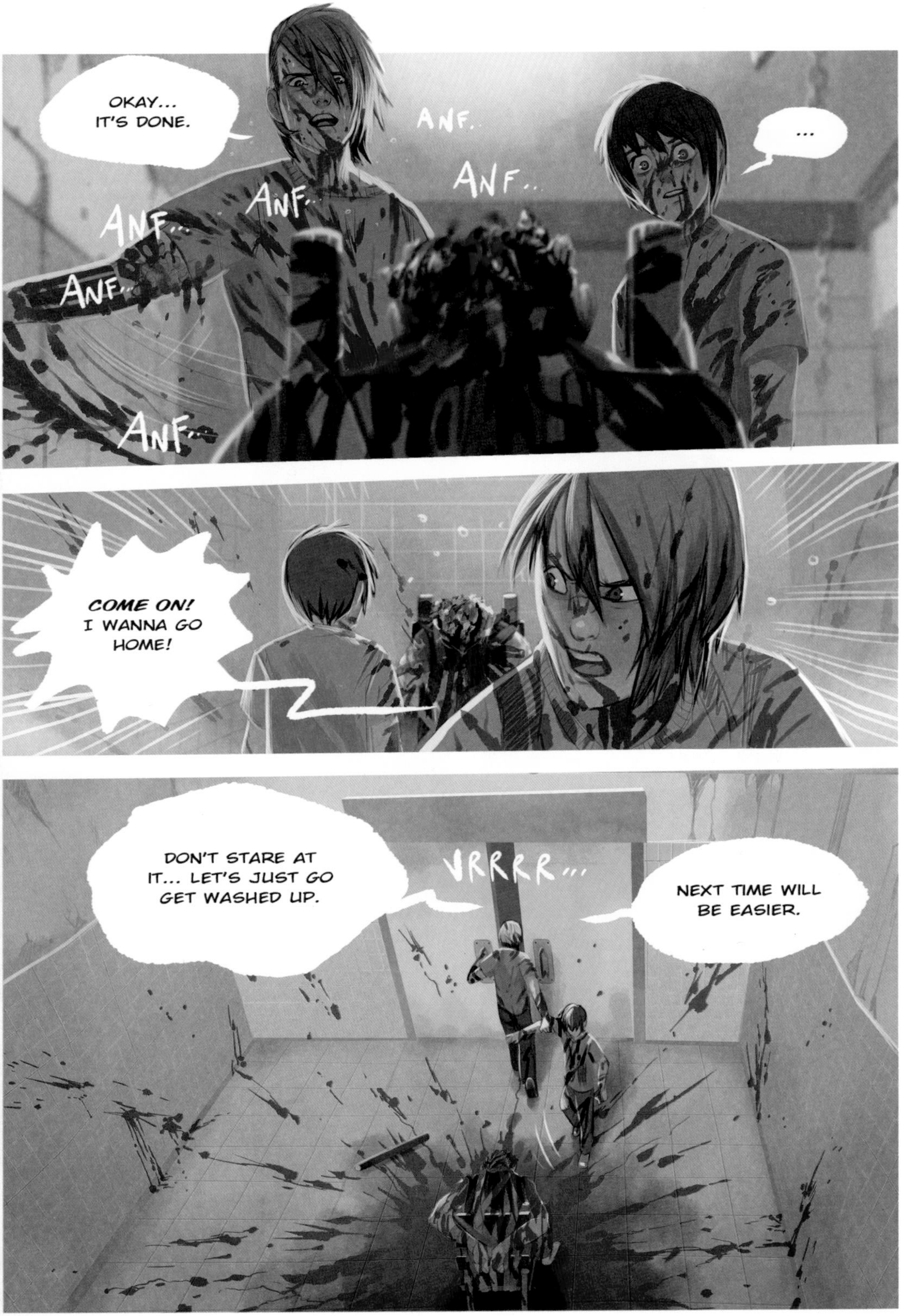
OKAY... IT'S DONE.
ANF.
ANF...
ANF...
ANF...
ANF...
ANF...
...
COME ON! I WANNA GO HOME!
DON'T STARE AT IT... LET'S JUST GO GET WASHED UP.
VRRRR...
NEXT TIME WILL BE EASIER.

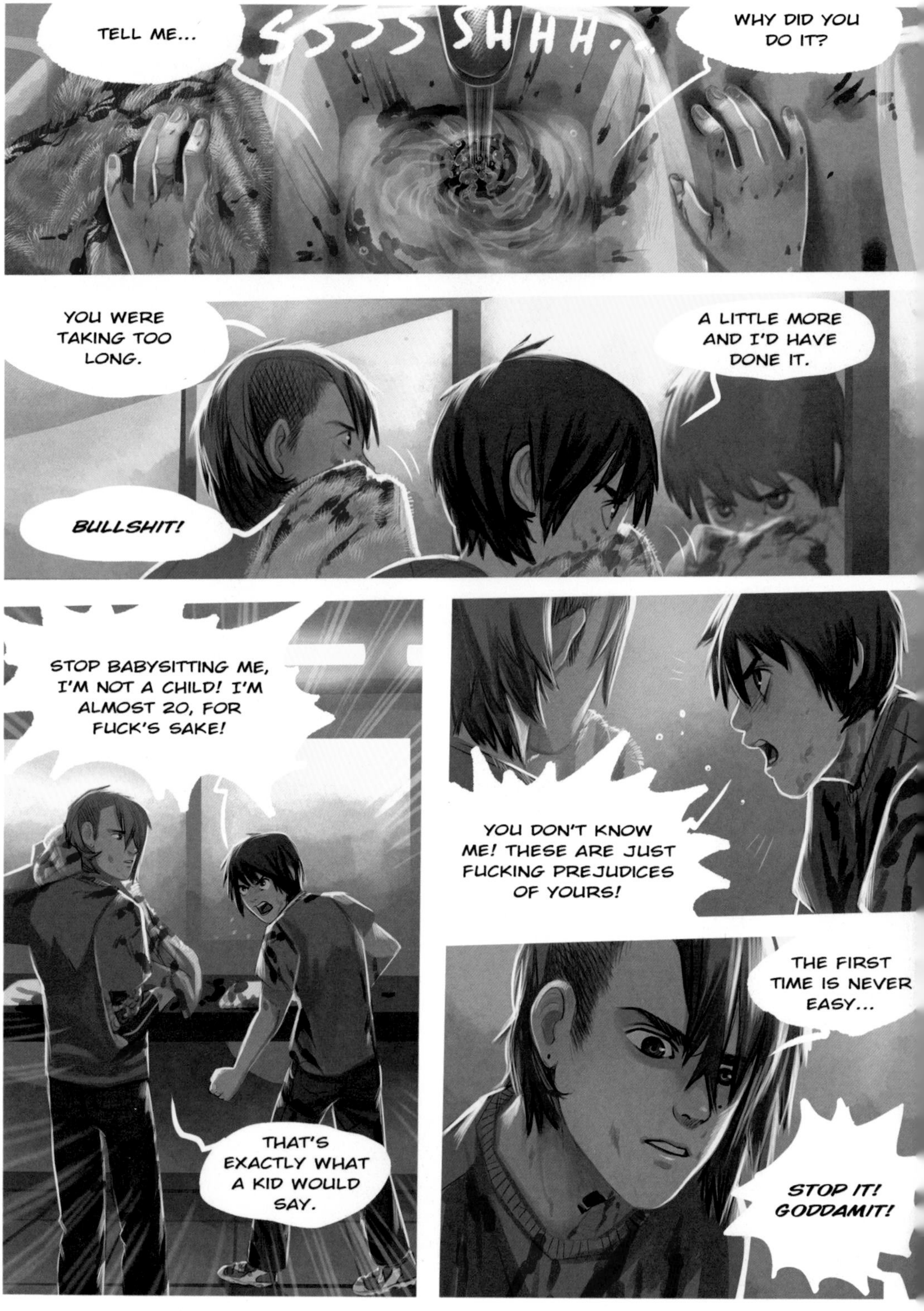
TELL ME...
SSSSSHHH.
WHY DID YOU DO IT?
YOU WERE TAKING TOO LONG.
A LITTLE MORE AND I'D HAVE DONE IT.
BULLSHIT!
STOP BABYSITTING ME, I'M NOT A CHILD! I'M ALMOST 20, FOR FUCK'S SAKE!
THAT'S EXACTLY WHAT A KID WOULD SAY.
YOU DON'T KNOW ME! THESE ARE JUST FUCKING PREJUDICES OF YOURS!
THE FIRST TIME IS NEVER EASY...
STOP IT! GODDAMIT!

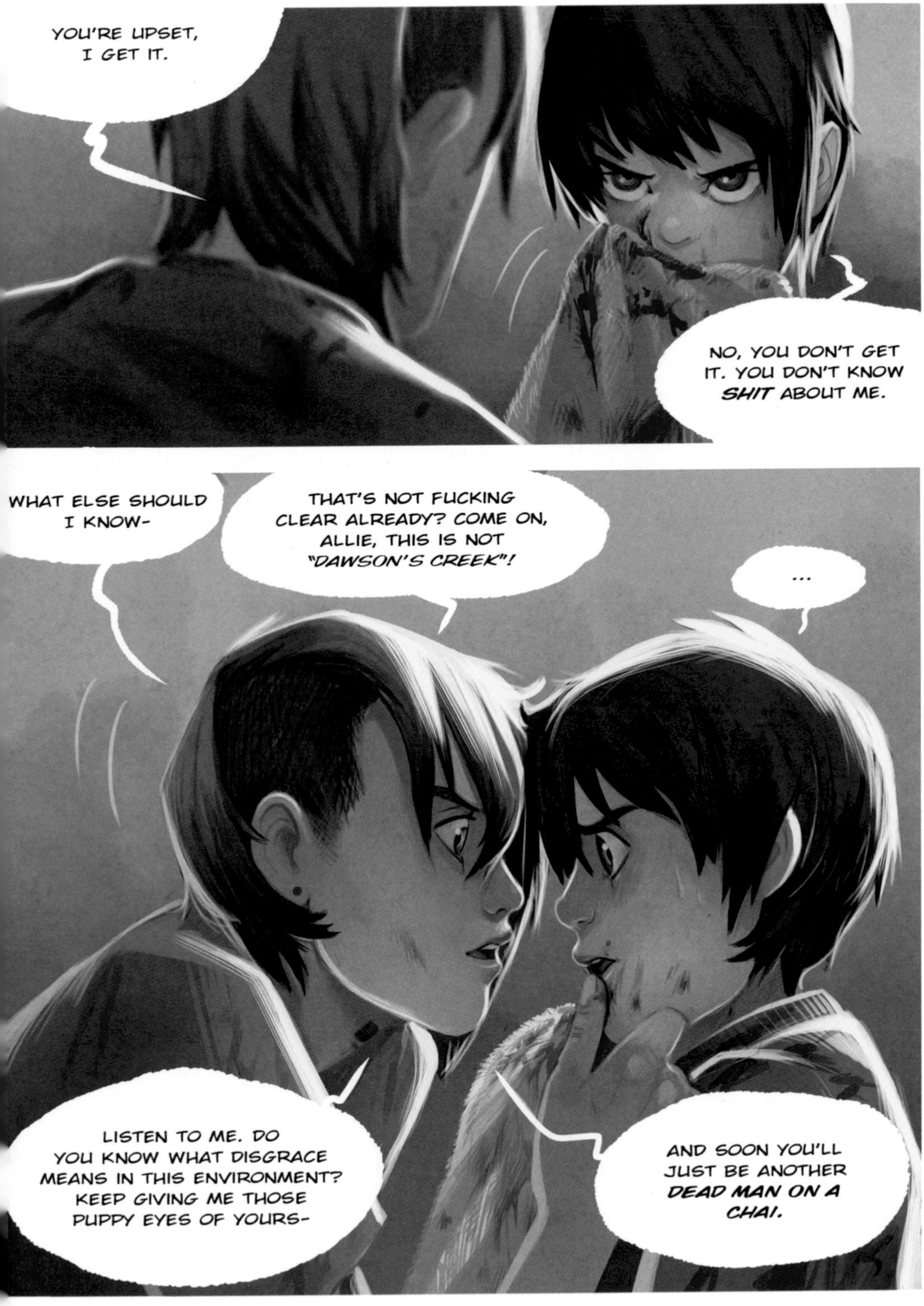
YOU'RE UPSET, I GET IT.
NO, YOU DON'T GET IT. YOU DON'T KNOW *SHIT* ABOUT ME.
WHAT ELSE SHOULD I KNOW-
THAT'S NOT FUCKING CLEAR ALREADY? COME ON, ALLIE, THIS IS NOT *"DAWSON'S CREEK"*!
...
LISTEN TO ME. DO YOU KNOW WHAT DISGRACE MEANS IN THIS ENVIRONMENT? KEEP GIVING ME THOSE PUPPY EYES OF YOURS-
AND SOON YOU'LL JUST BE ANOTHER ***DEAD MAN ON A CHAI.***

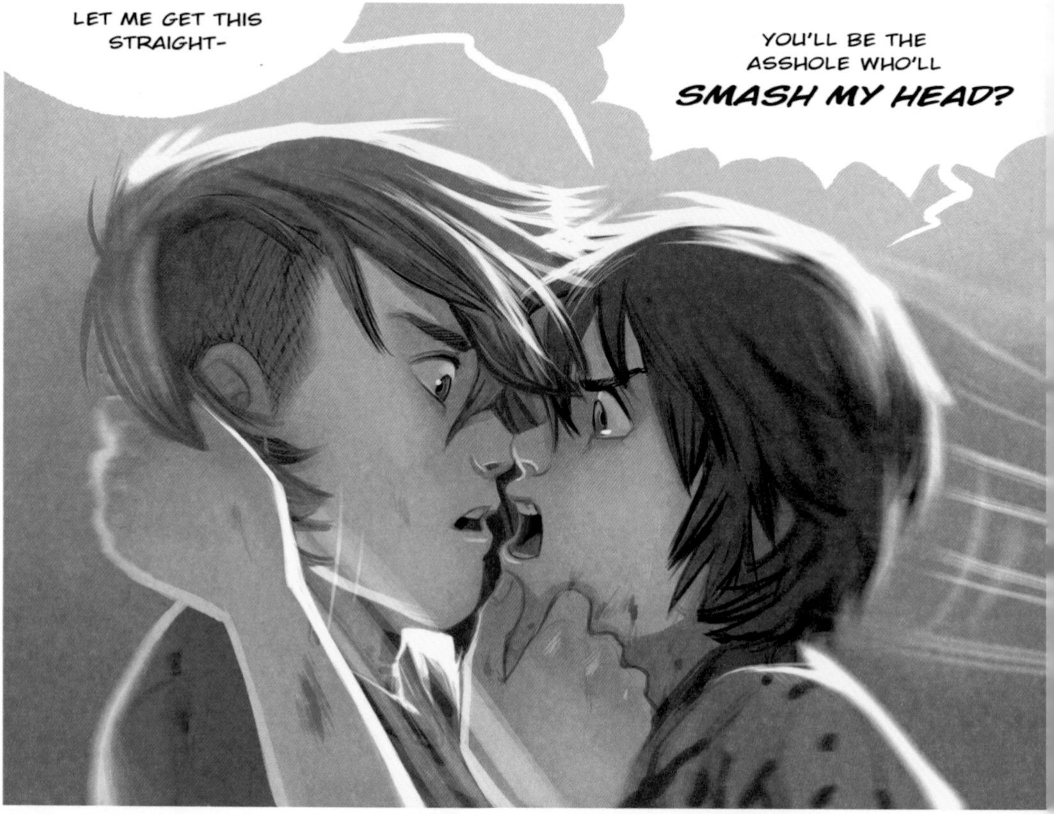
LET ME GET THIS STRAIGHT-
YOU'LL BE THE ASSHOLE WHO'LL SMASH MY HEAD?

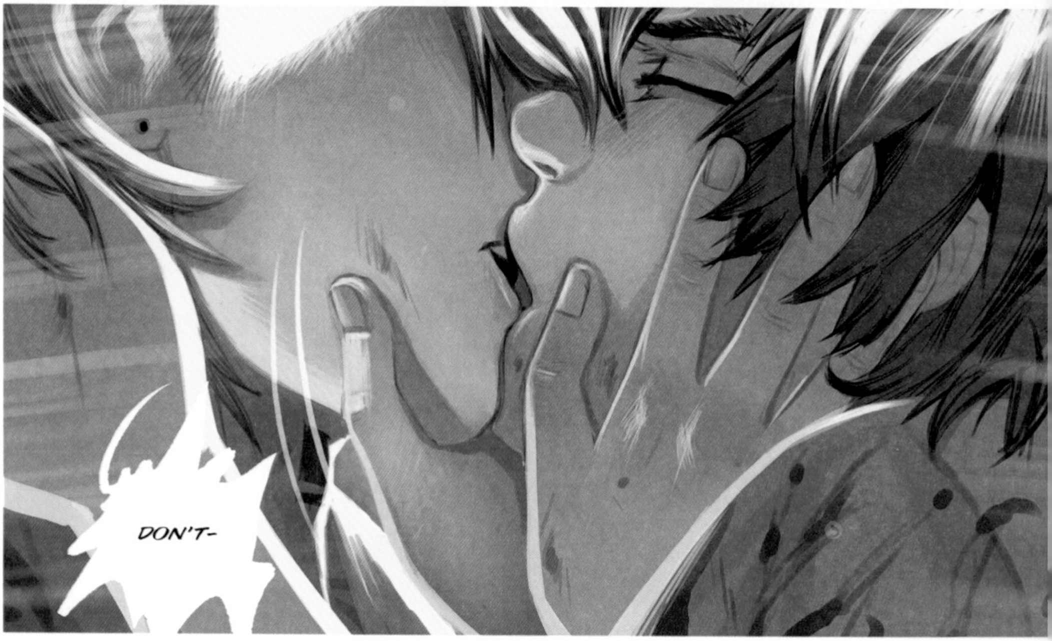
DON'T-

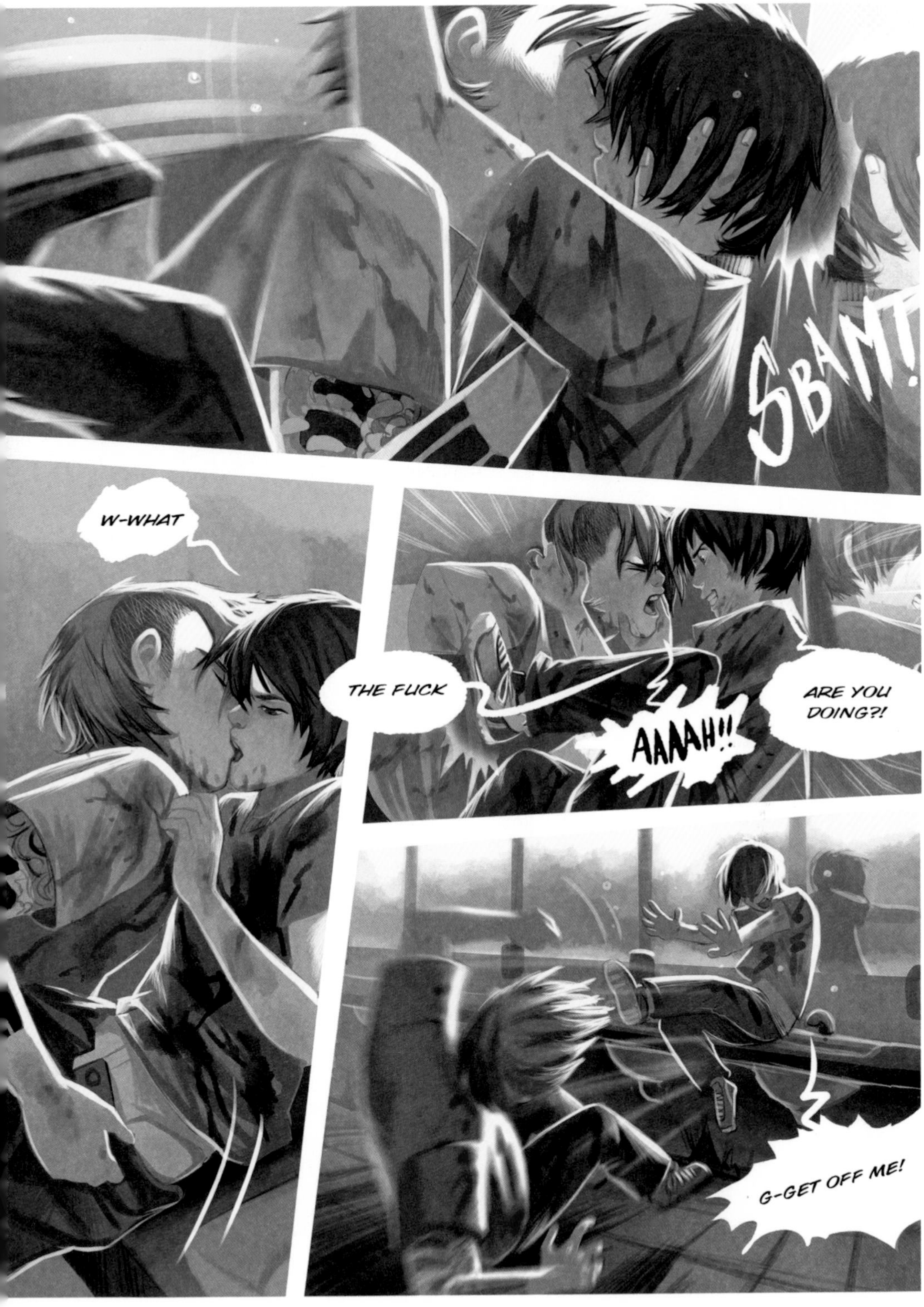
SBAM!
W-WHAT
THE FUCK
AAAAH!!
ARE YOU DOING?!
G-GET OFF ME!

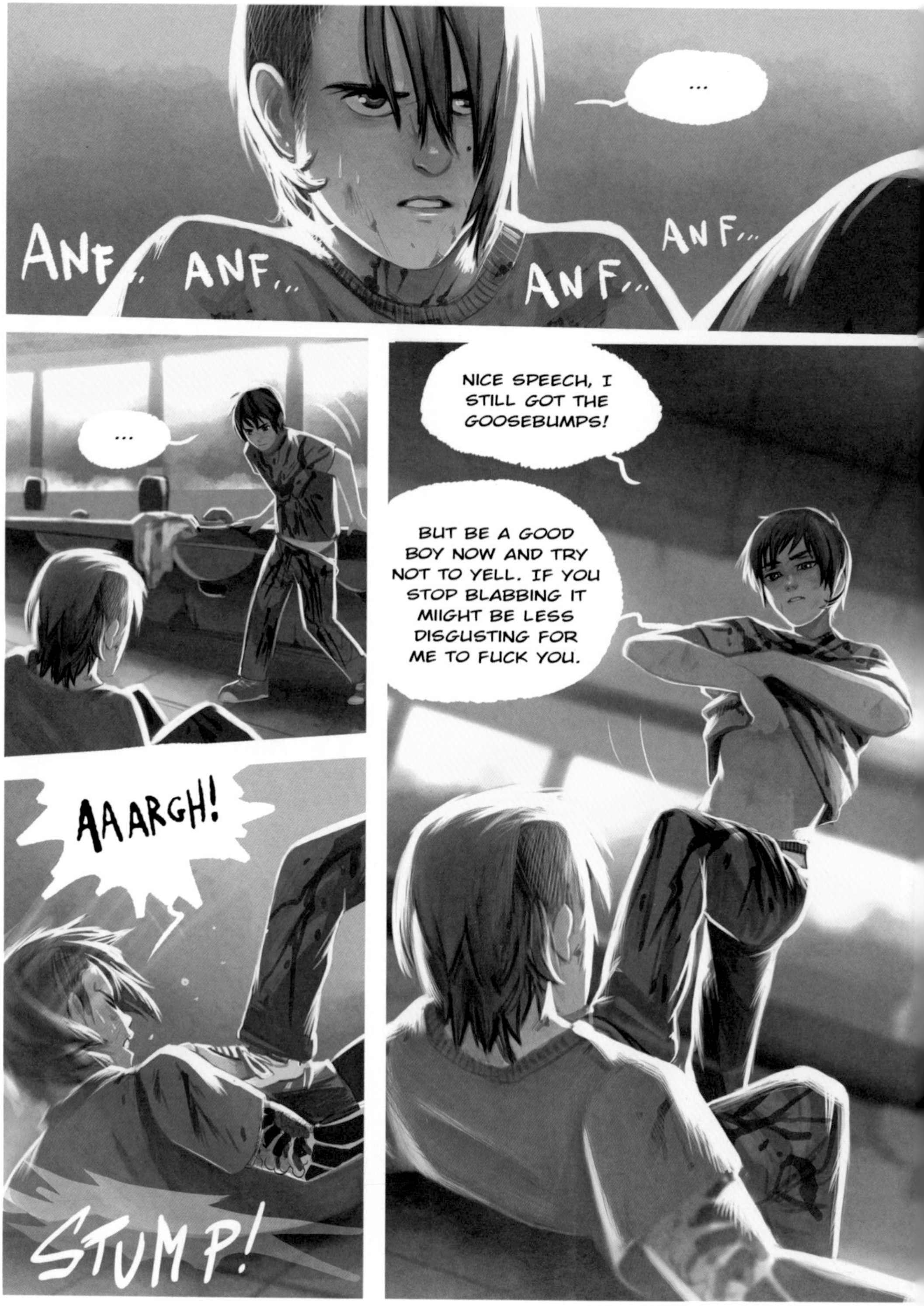
...
ANF... ANF... ANF... ANF...
...
NICE SPEECH, I STILL GOT THE GOOSEBUMPS!
BUT BE A GOOD BOY NOW AND TRY NOT TO YELL. IF YOU STOP BLABBING IT MIIGHT BE LESS DISGUSTING FOR ME TO FUCK YOU.
AAARGH!
STUMP!

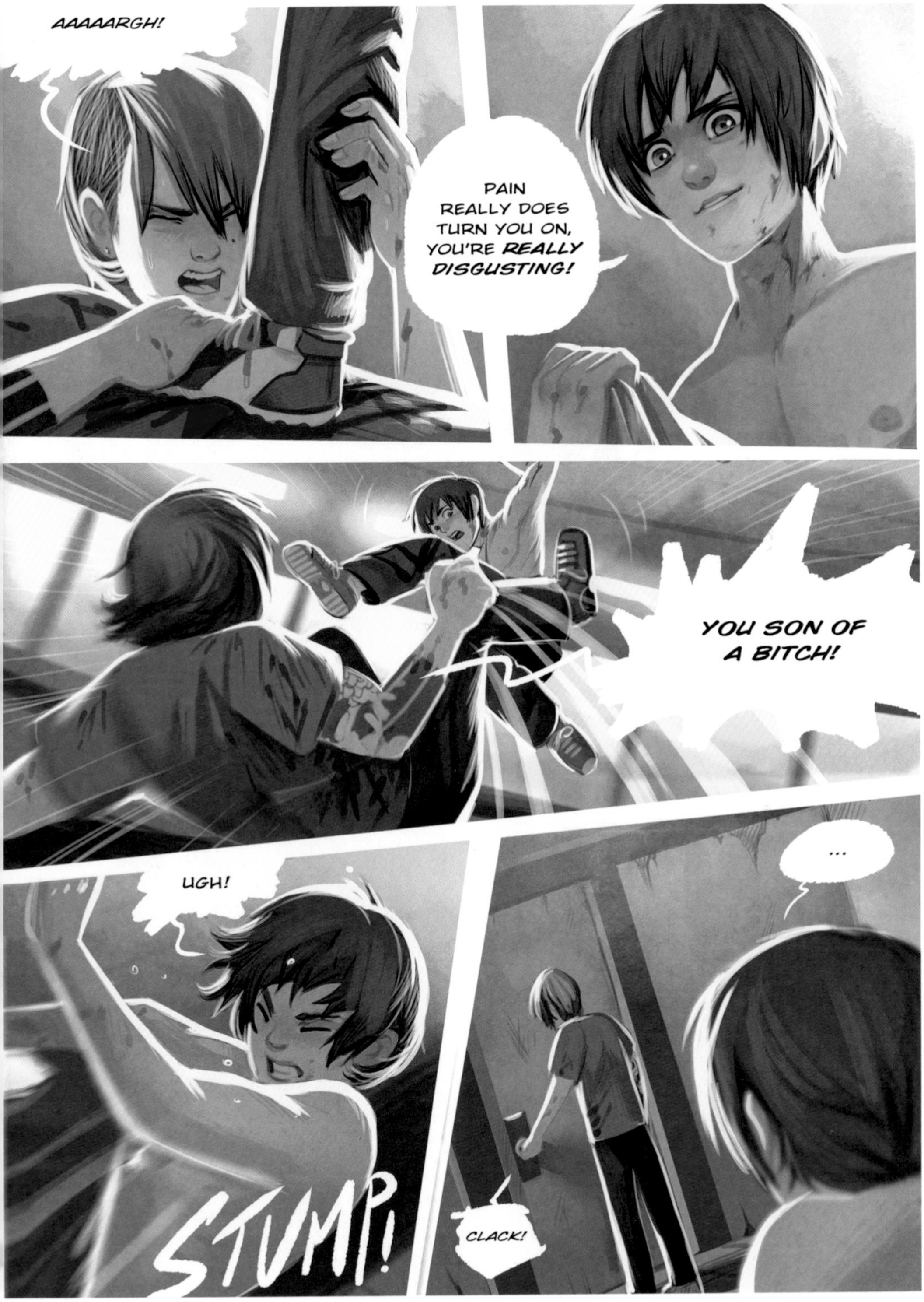
AAAAARGH!
PAIN REALLY DOES TURN YOU ON, YOU'RE **REALLY DISGUSTING!**
YOU SON OF A BITCH!
UGH!
STUMP!
CLACK!
...

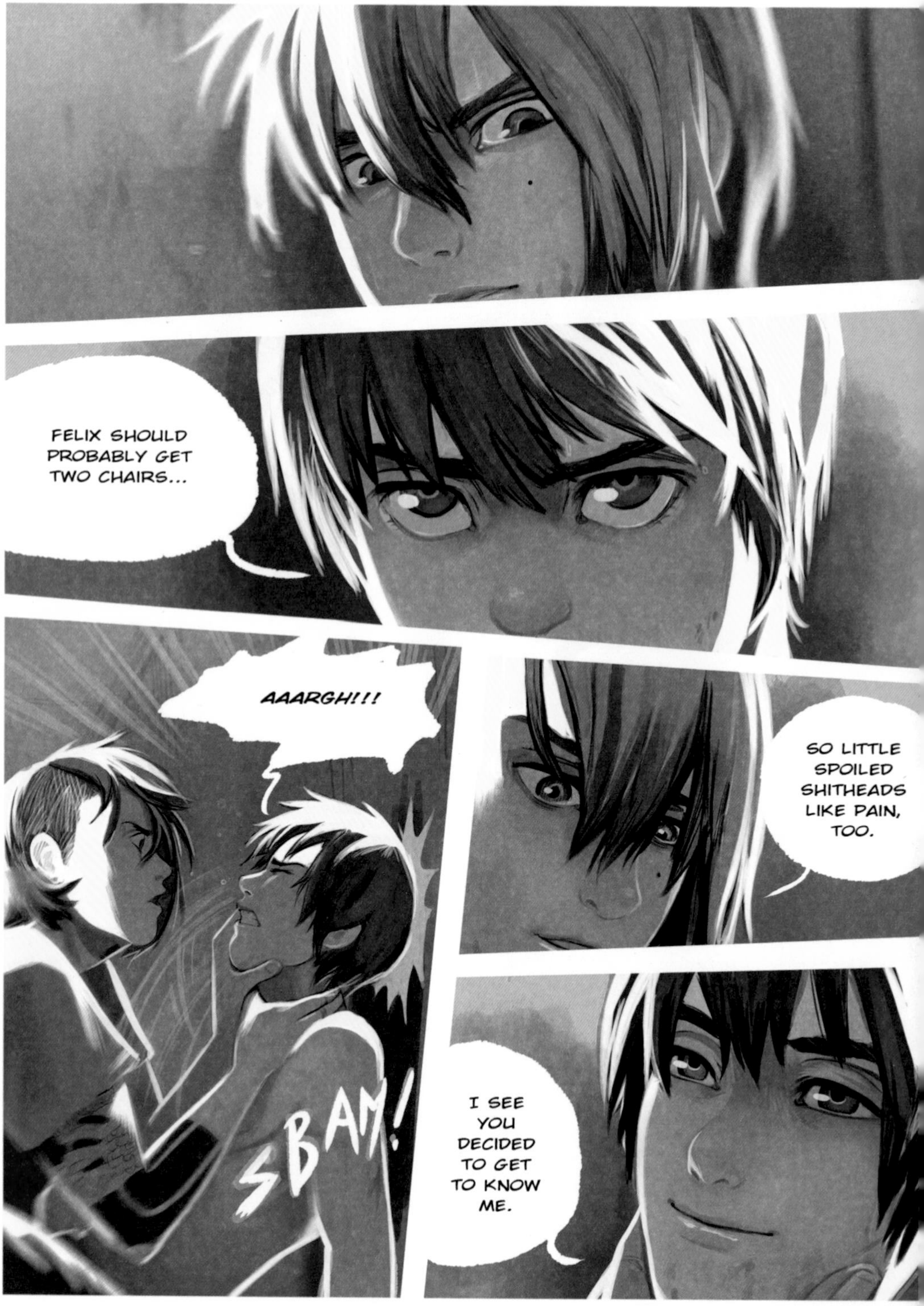
FELIX SHOULD PROBABLY GET TWO CHAIRS...
AAARGH!!!
SBAM!
SO LITTLE SPOILED SHITHEADS LIKE PAIN, TOO.
I SEE YOU DECIDED TO GET TO KNOW ME.

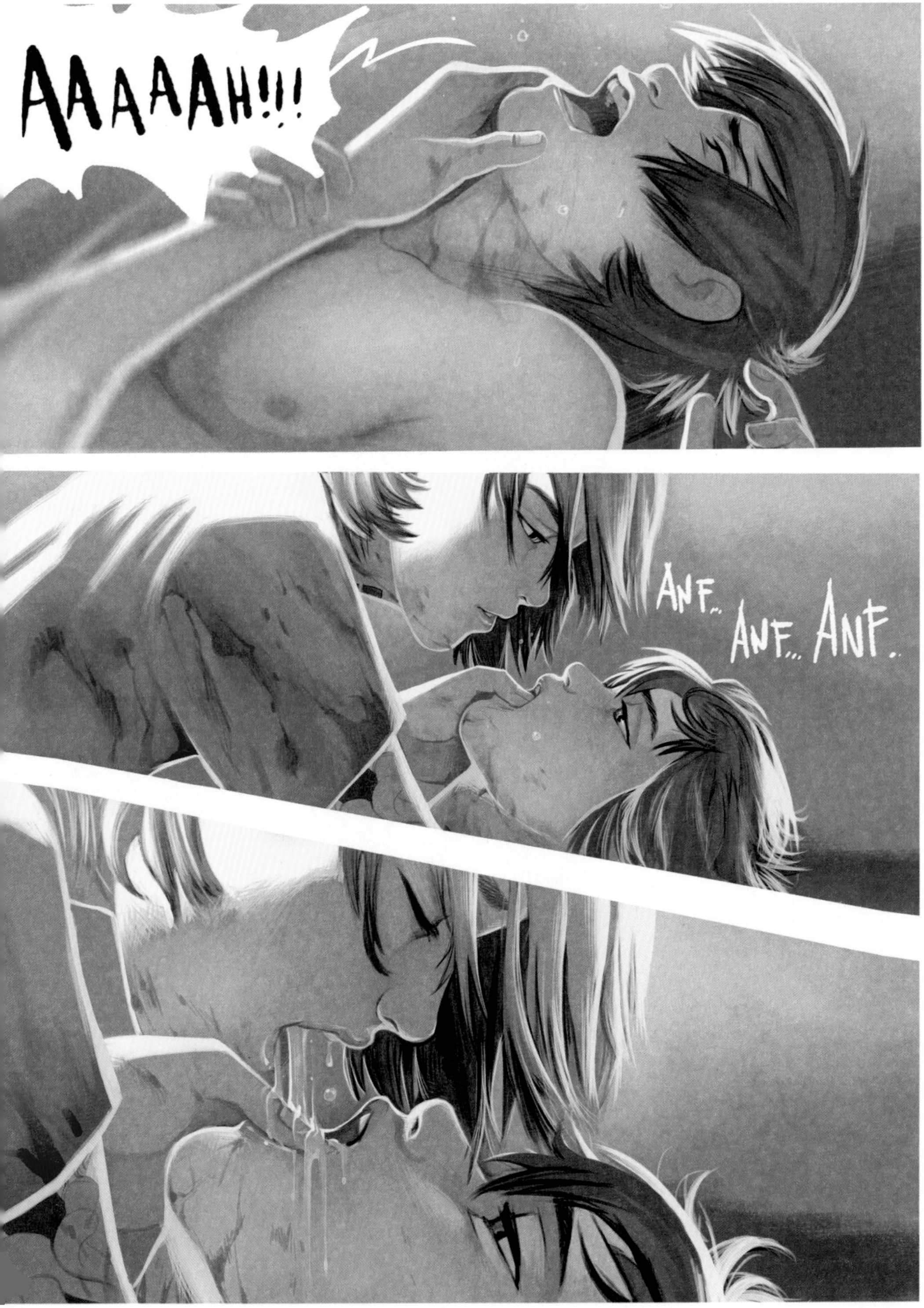
AAAAAH!!!
ANF... ANF.... ANF..

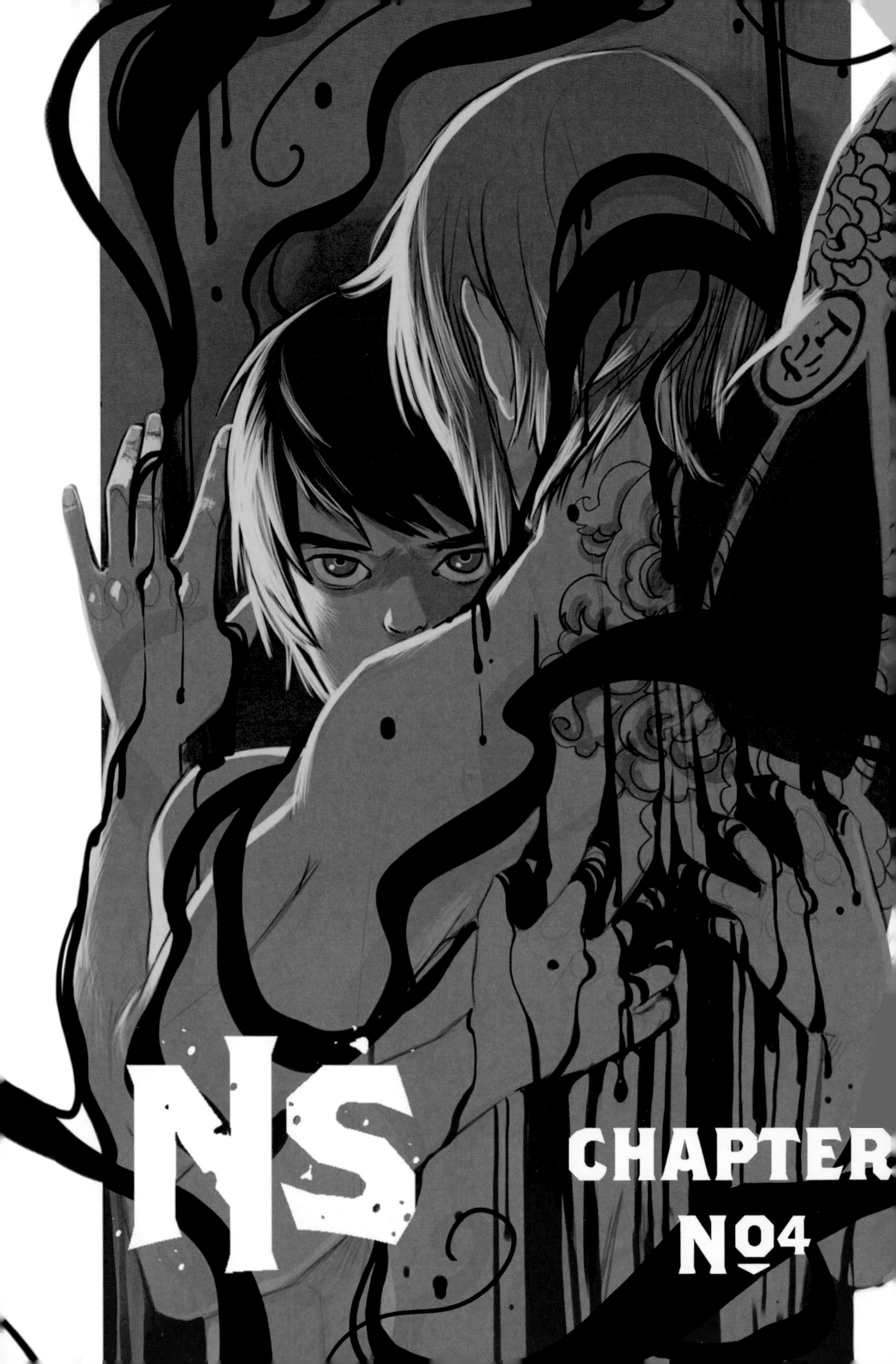
NS
CHAPTER
№4

FORGET.

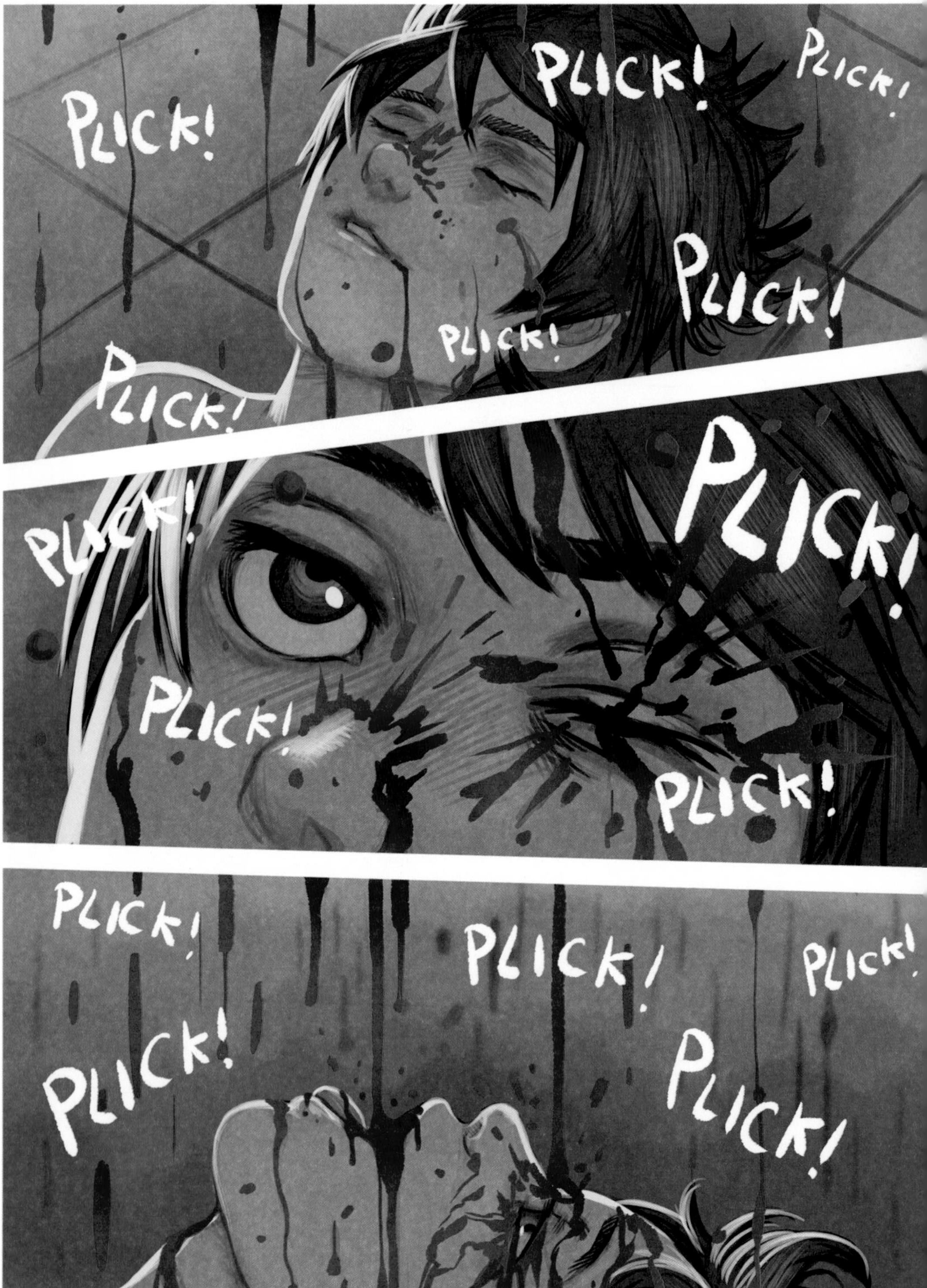
PLICK!
PLICK!
PLICK!
PLICK!
PLICK!
PLICK!
PLICK!
PLICK!
PLICK!
PLICK!
PLICK!
PLICK!
PLICK!
PLICK!
PLICK!

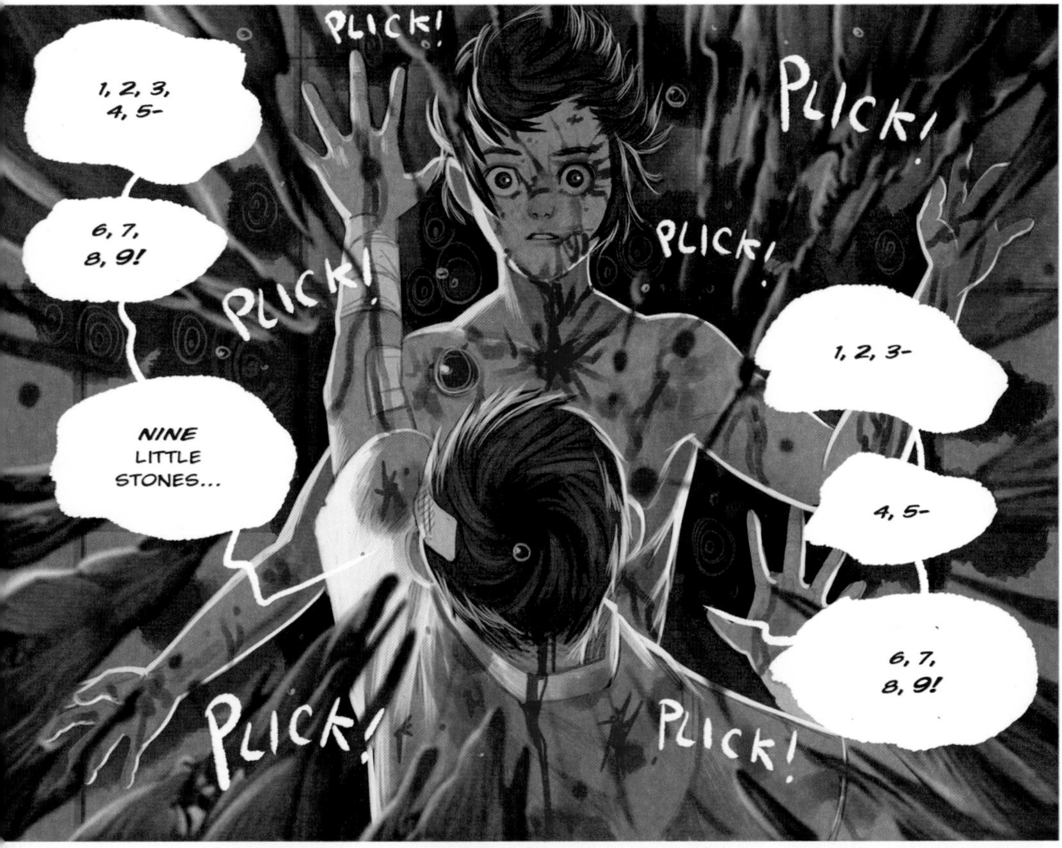
PLICK!
1, 2, 3,
4, 5-
PLICK!
6, 7,
8, 9!
PLICK!
PLICK!
NINE
LITTLE
STONES...
1, 2, 3-
4, 5-
6, 7,
8, 9!
PLICK!
PLICK!

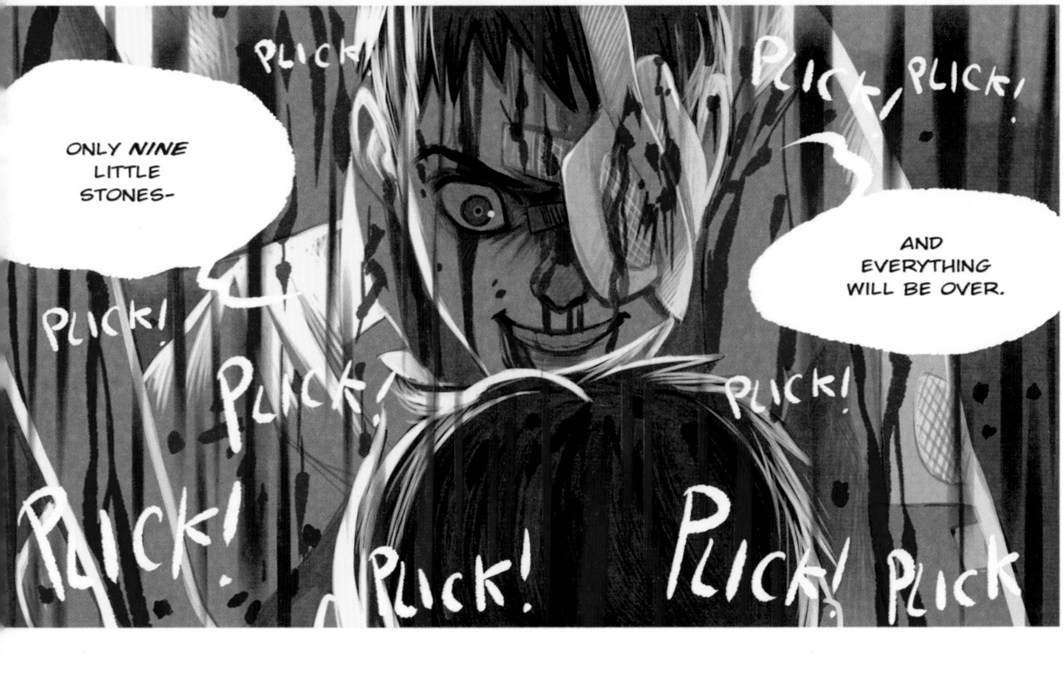
PLICK!
PLICK! PLICK!
ONLY NINE
LITTLE
STONES-
AND
EVERYTHING
WILL BE OVER.
PLICK!
PLICK!
PLICK!
PLICK!
PLICK!
PLICK! PLICK

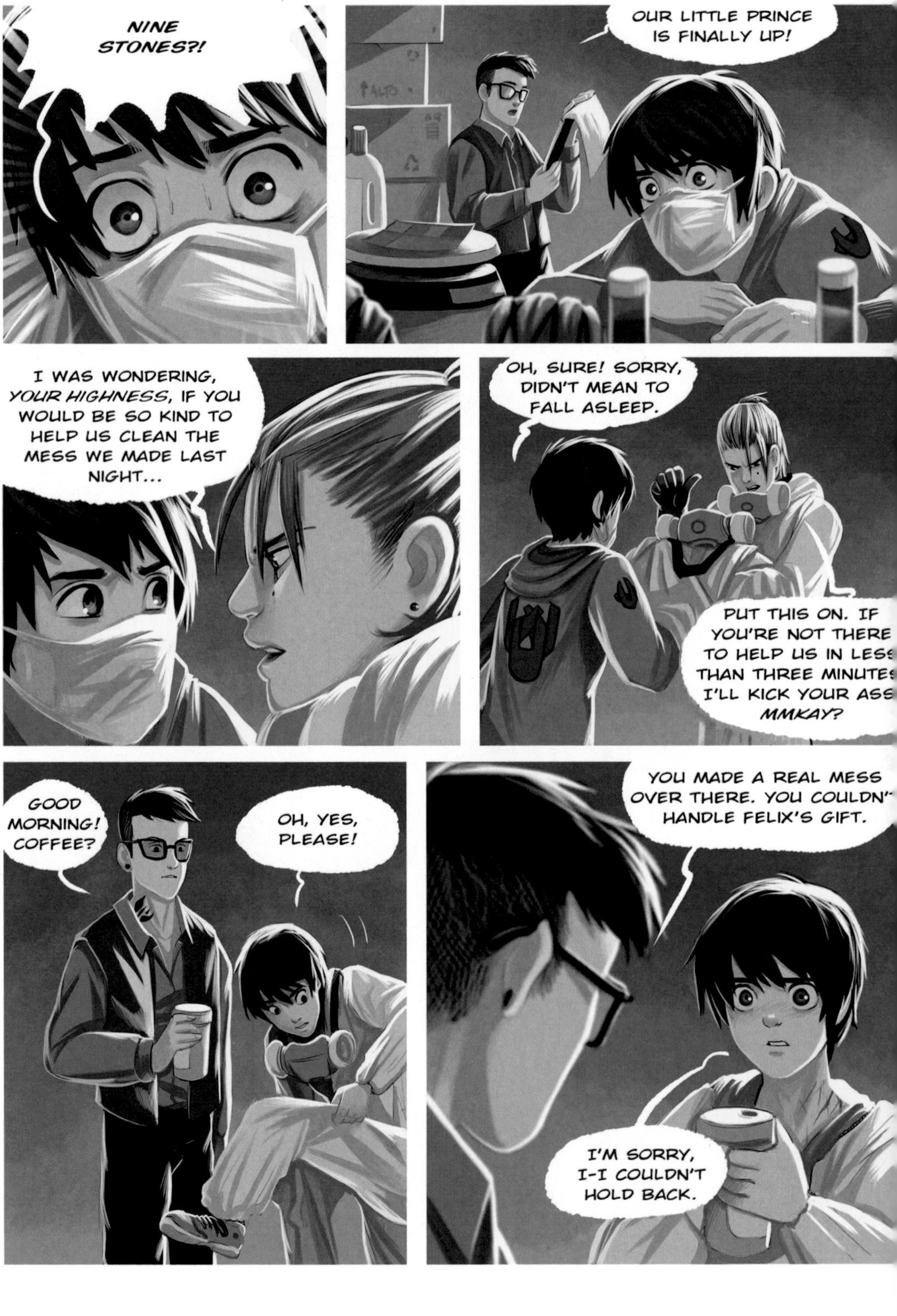
NINE STONES?!
OUR LITTLE PRINCE IS FINALLY UP!
I WAS WONDERING, YOUR HIGHNESS, IF YOU WOULD BE SO KIND TO HELP US CLEAN THE MESS WE MADE LAST NIGHT...
OH, SURE! SORRY, DIDN'T MEAN TO FALL ASLEEP.
PUT THIS ON. IF YOU'RE NOT THERE TO HELP US IN LESS THAN THREE MINUTES I'LL KICK YOUR ASS MMKAY?
GOOD MORNING! COFFEE?
OH, YES, PLEASE!
YOU MADE A REAL MESS OVER THERE. YOU COULDN'T HANDLE FELIX'S GIFT.
I'M SORRY, I-I COULDN'T HOLD BACK.

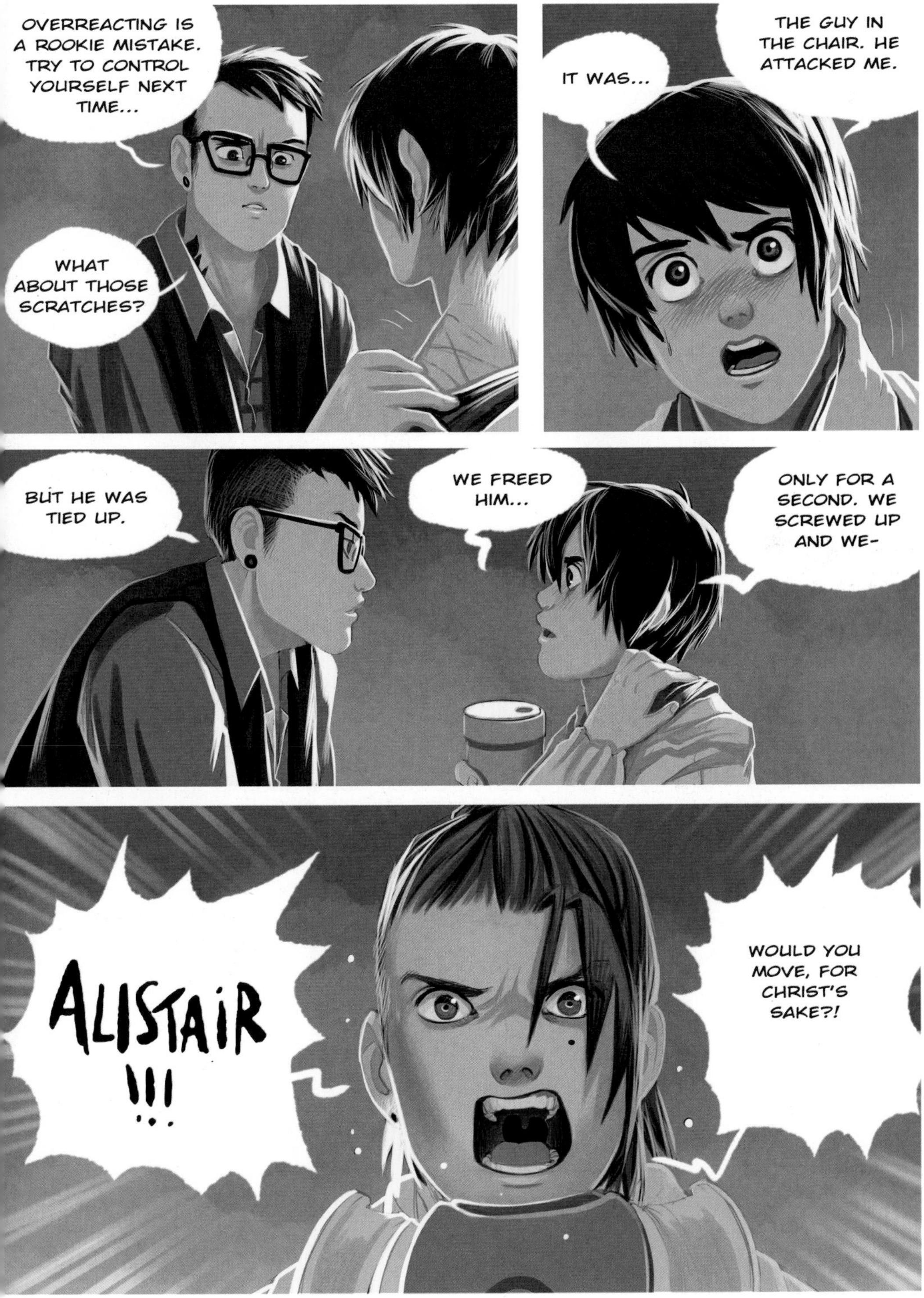
OVERREACTING IS A ROOKIE MISTAKE. TRY TO CONTROL YOURSELF NEXT TIME...
WHAT ABOUT THOSE SCRATCHES?
IT WAS...
THE GUY IN THE CHAIR. HE ATTACKED ME.
BUT HE WAS TIED UP.
WE FREED HIM...
ONLY FOR A SECOND. WE SCREWED UP AND WE-
ALISTAIR!!!
WOULD YOU MOVE, FOR CHRIST'S SAKE?!

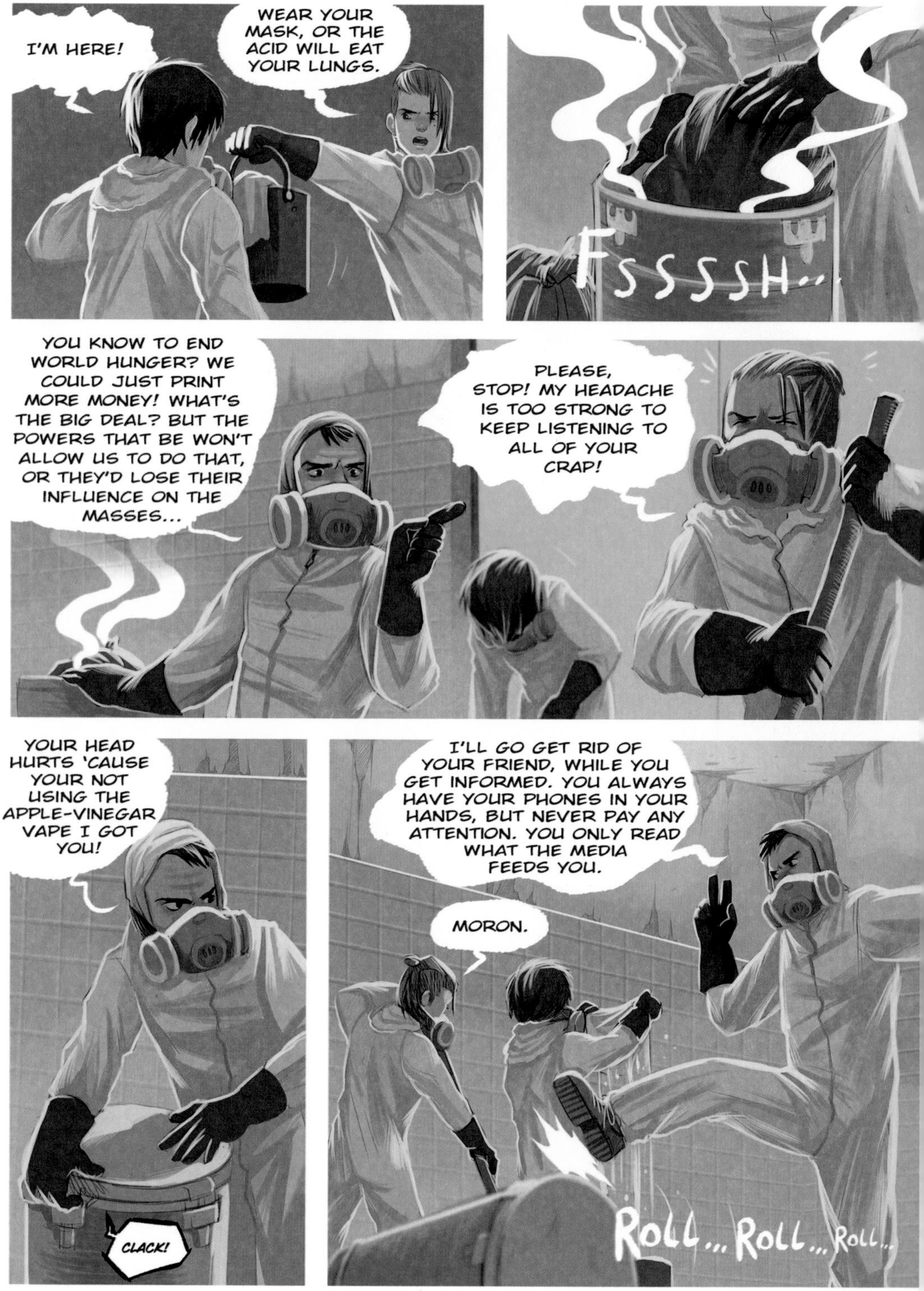
I'M HERE!
WEAR YOUR MASK, OR THE ACID WILL EAT YOUR LUNGS.
FSSSSH...
YOU KNOW TO END WORLD HUNGER? WE COULD JUST PRINT MORE MONEY! WHAT'S THE BIG DEAL? BUT THE POWERS THAT BE WON'T ALLOW US TO DO THAT, OR THEY'D LOSE THEIR INFLUENCE ON THE MASSES...
PLEASE, STOP! MY HEADACHE IS TOO STRONG TO KEEP LISTENING TO ALL OF YOUR CRAP!
YOUR HEAD HURTS 'CAUSE YOUR NOT USING THE APPLE-VINEGAR VAPE I GOT YOU!
CLACK!
I'LL GO GET RID OF YOUR FRIEND, WHILE YOU GET INFORMED. YOU ALWAYS HAVE YOUR PHONES IN YOUR HANDS, BUT NEVER PAY ANY ATTENTION. YOU ONLY READ WHAT THE MEDIA FEEDS YOU.
MORON.
ROLL... ROLL... ROLL...

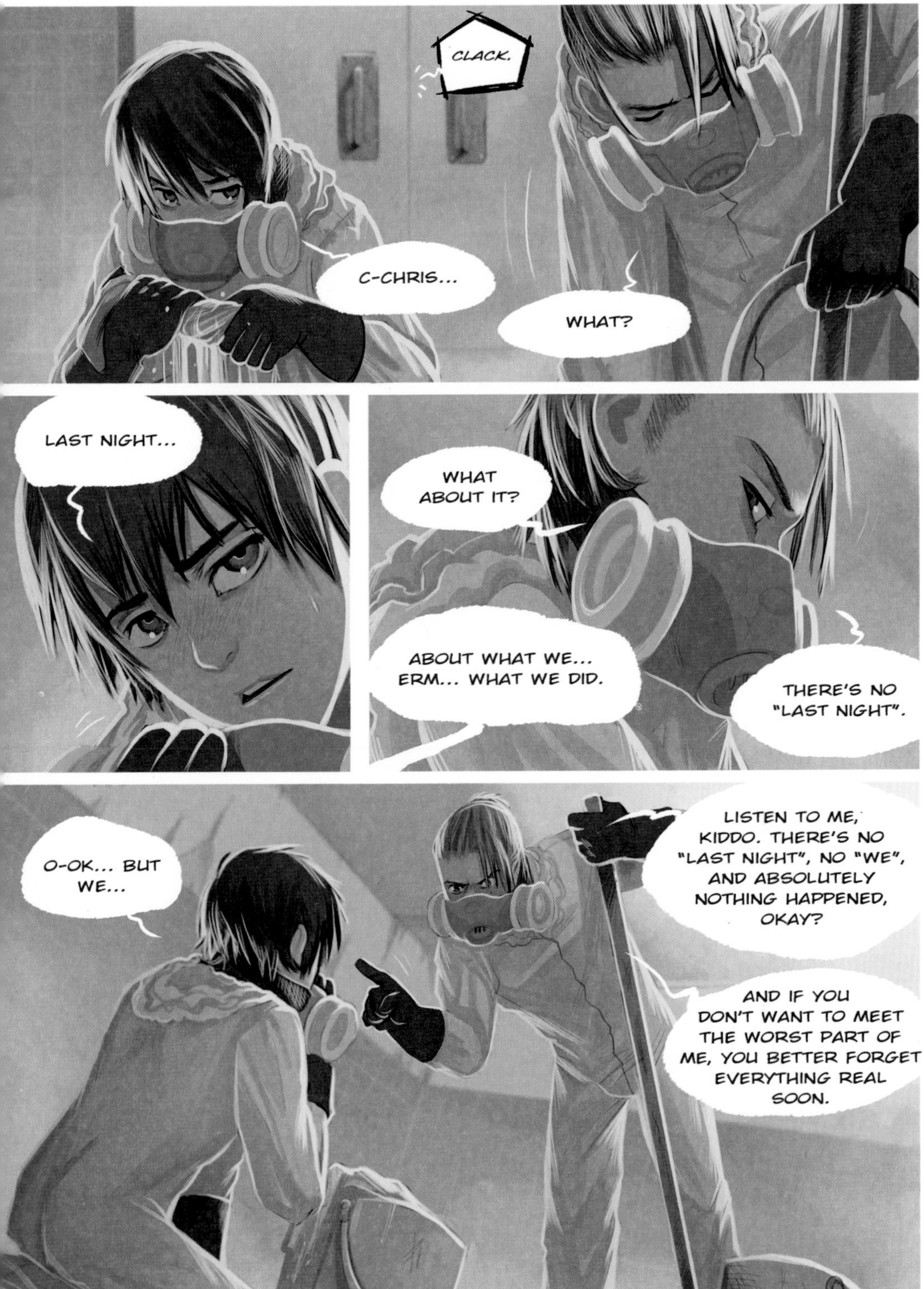
CLACK.
C-CHRIS...
WHAT?
LAST NIGHT...
WHAT ABOUT IT?
ABOUT WHAT WE... ERM... WHAT WE DID.
THERE'S NO "LAST NIGHT".
O-OK... BUT WE...
LISTEN TO ME, KIDDO. THERE'S NO "LAST NIGHT", NO "WE", AND ABSOLUTELY NOTHING HAPPENED, OKAY?
AND IF YOU DON'T WANT TO MEET THE WORST PART OF ME, YOU BETTER FORGET EVERYTHING REAL SOON.

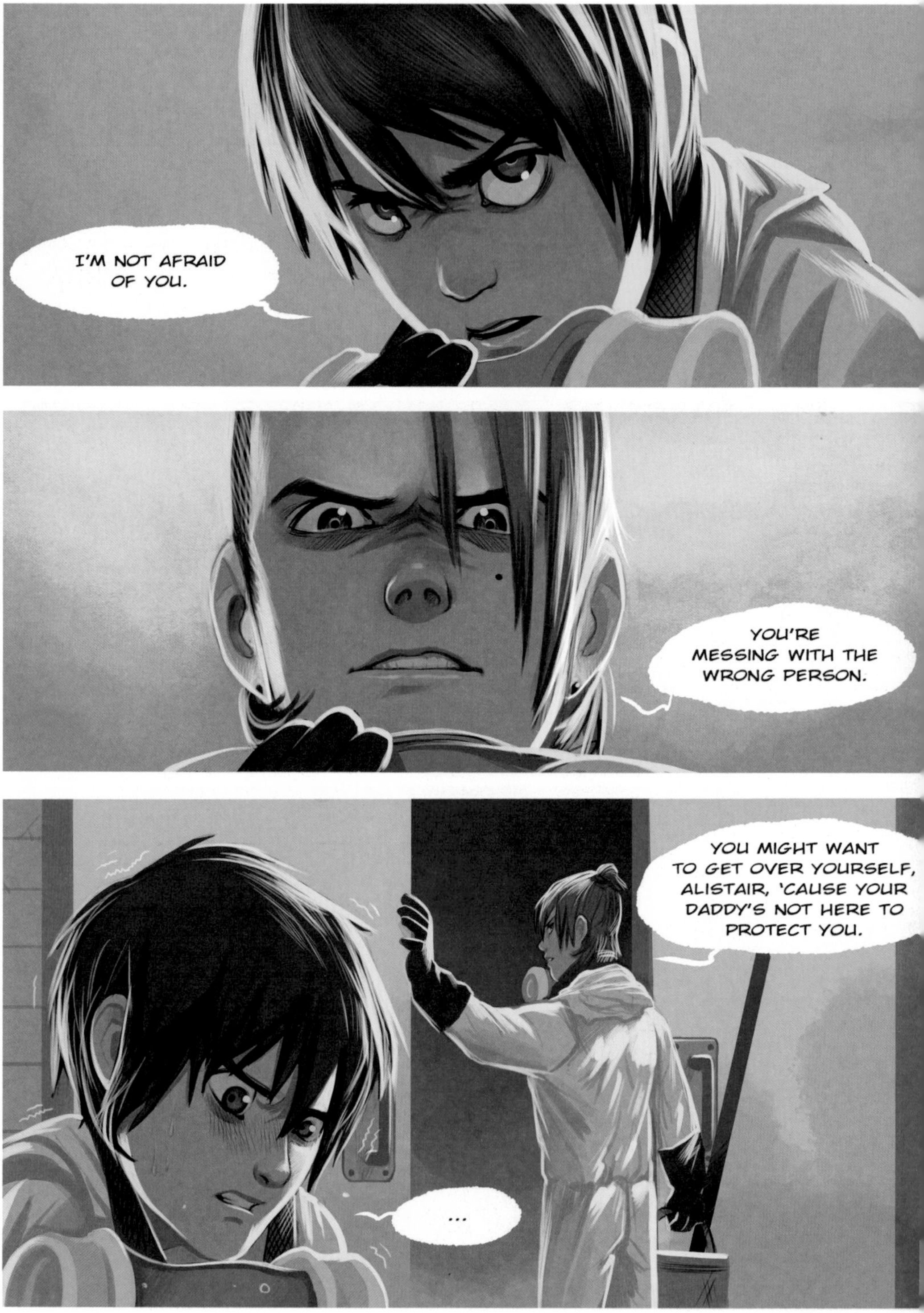
I'M NOT AFRAID OF YOU.
YOU'RE MESSING WITH THE WRONG PERSON.
YOU MIGHT WANT TO GET OVER YOURSELF, ALISTAIR, 'CAUSE YOUR DADDY'S NOT HERE TO PROTECT YOU.
...

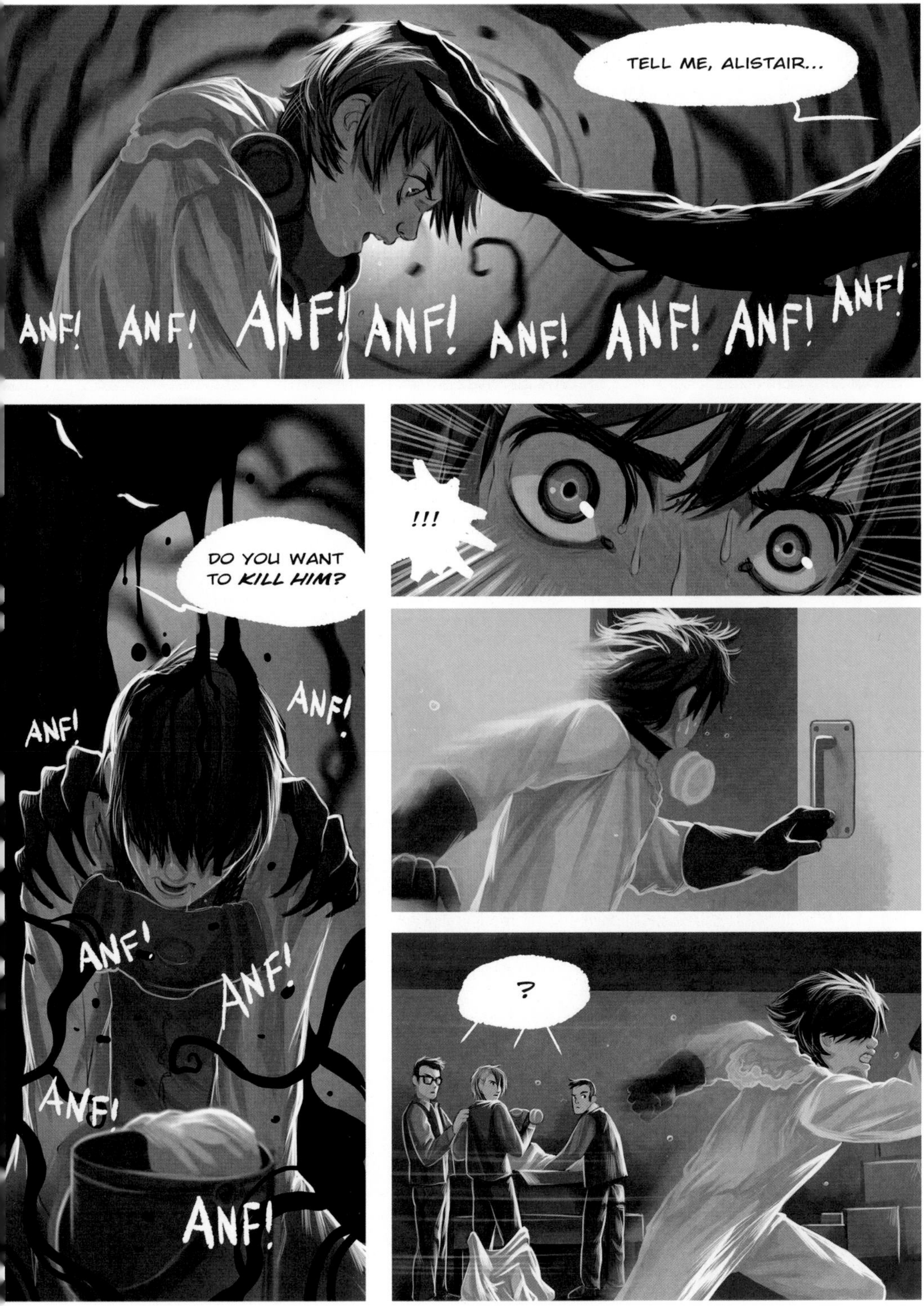

TELL ME, ALISTAIR...
ANF! ANF! ANF! ANF! ANF! ANF! ANF! ANF!
DO YOU WANT TO KILL HIM?
ANF! ANF!
ANF! ANF!
ANF!
ANF!
!!!
?

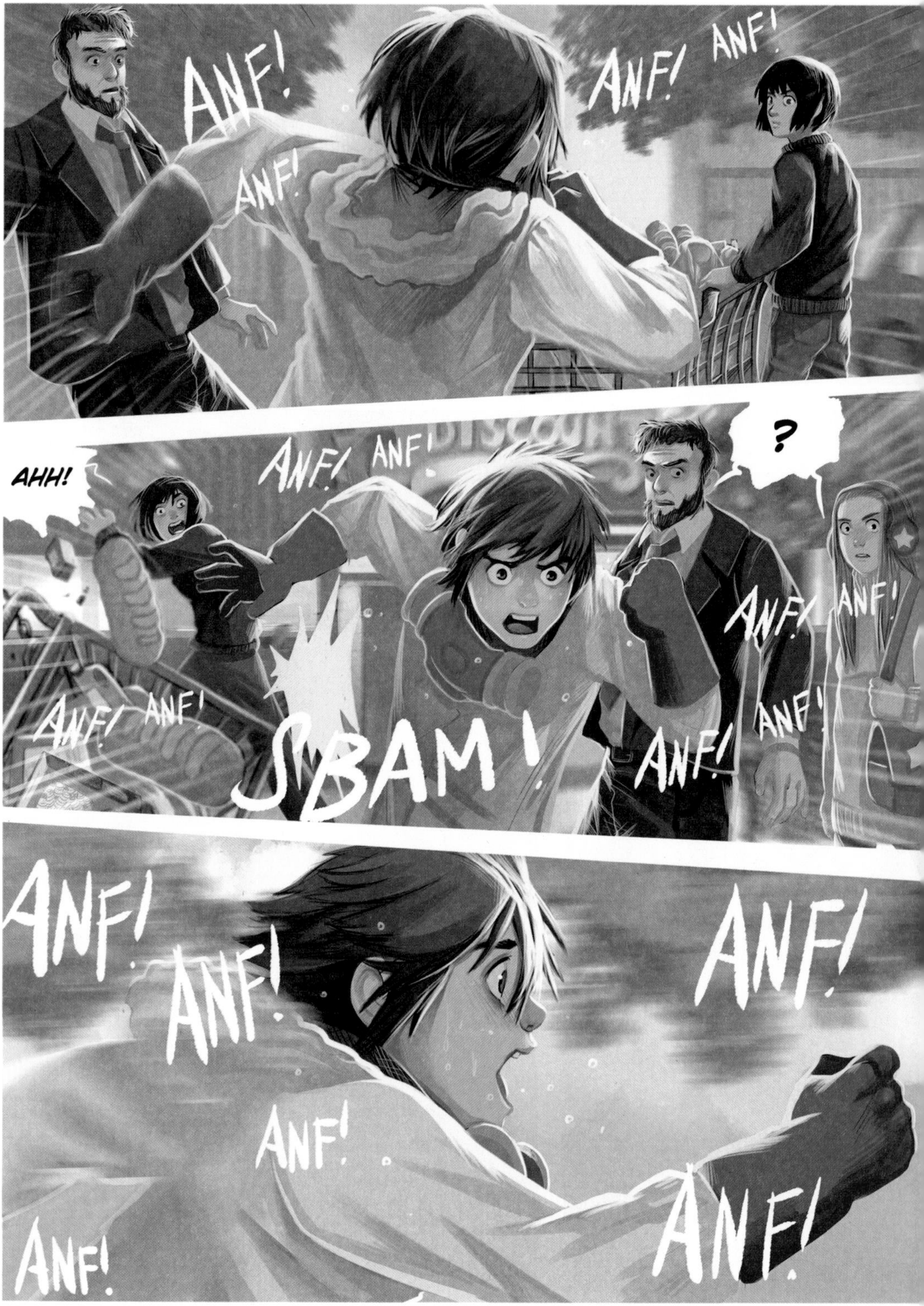

ANF!
ANF!
ANF!
ANF!
ANF! ANF!
AHH!
?
ANF! ANF!
ANF! ANF!
SBAM!
ANF! ANF!
ANF!
ANF!
ANF!
ANF!
ANF!
ANF!

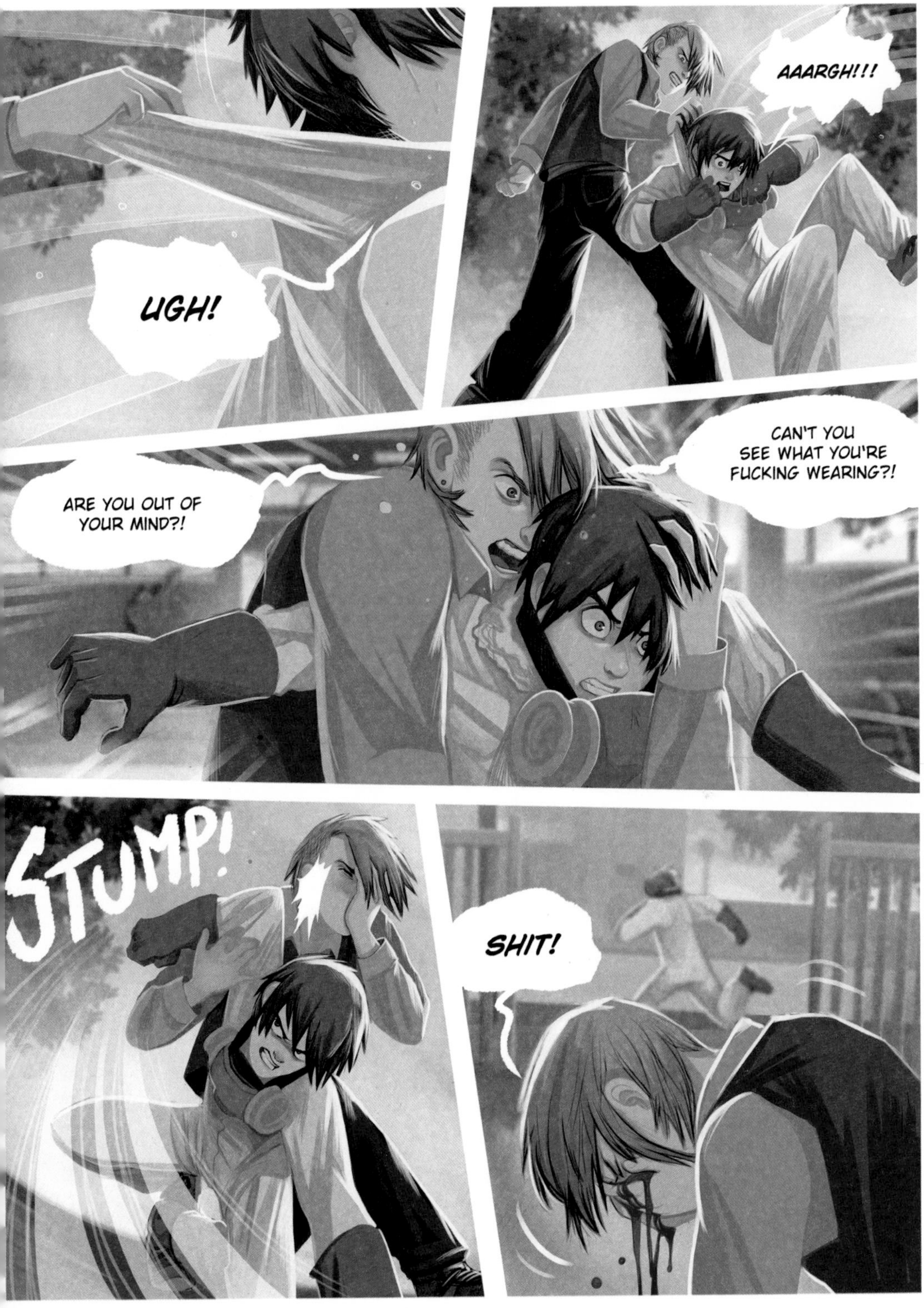
UGH!
AAARGH!!!
ARE YOU OUT OF YOUR MIND?!
CAN'T YOU SEE WHAT YOU'RE FUCKING WEARING?!
STUMP!
SHIT!

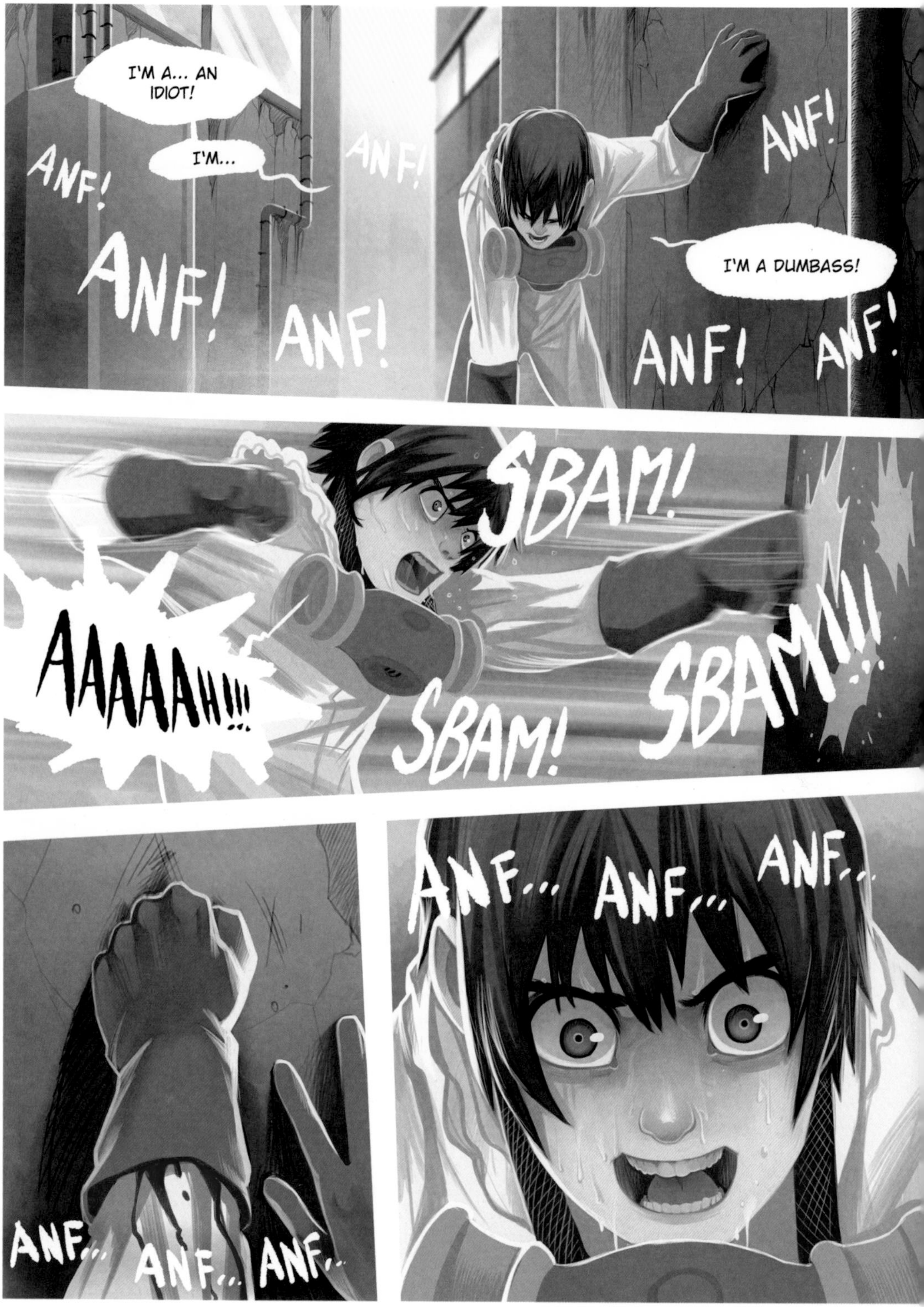
I'M A... AN IDIOT!
I'M...
ANF!
ANF!
ANF!
ANF!
ANF!
I'M A DUMBASS!
ANF!
ANF!
SBAM!
AAAAAH!!!
SBAM!
SBAM!!!
ANF... ANF... ANF...
ANF... ANF... ANF...

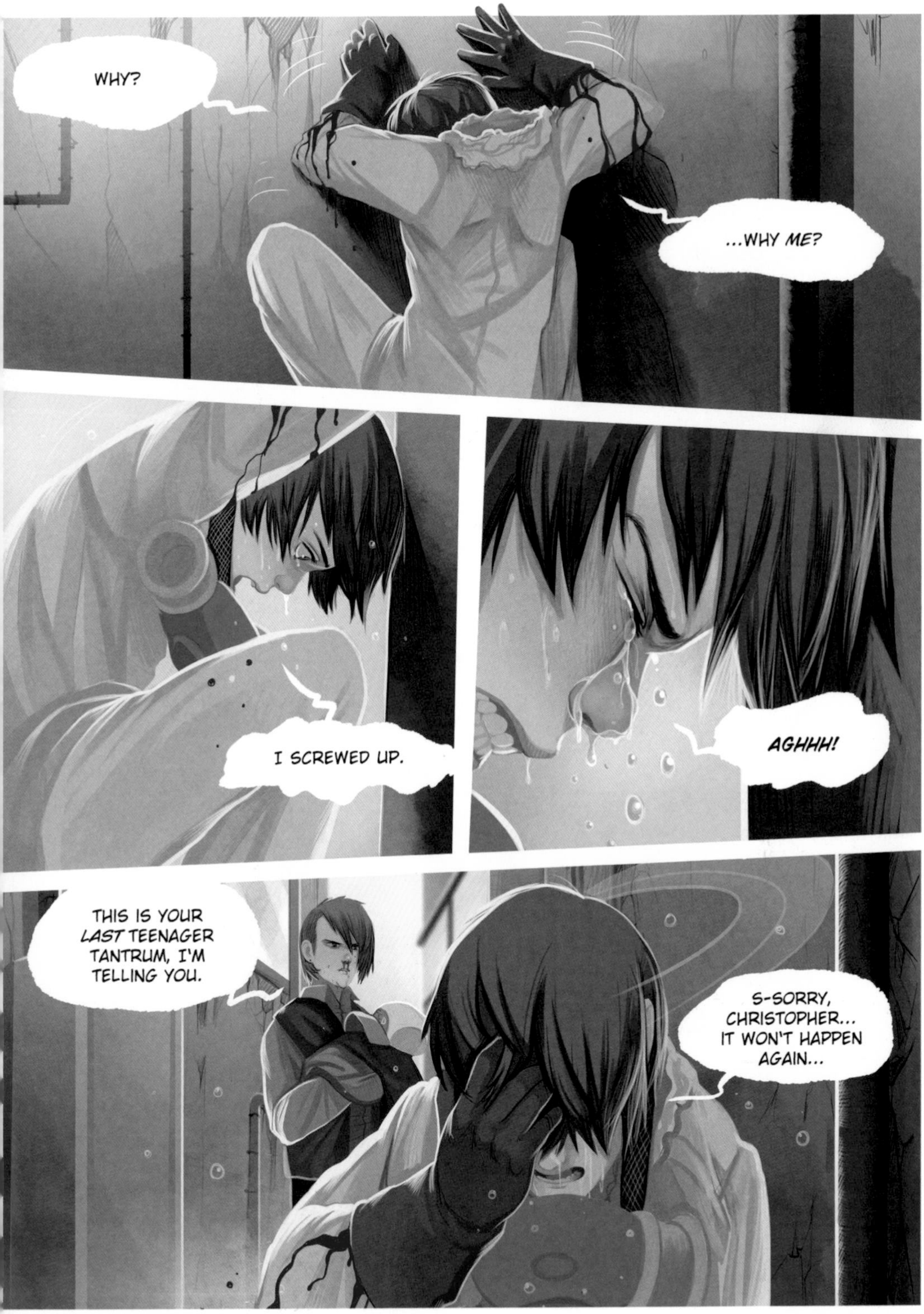
WHY?
...WHY *ME*?
I SCREWED UP.
AGHHH!
THIS IS YOUR *LAST* TEENAGER TANTRUM, I'M TELLING YOU.
S-SORRY, CHRISTOPHER... IT WON'T HAPPEN AGAIN...

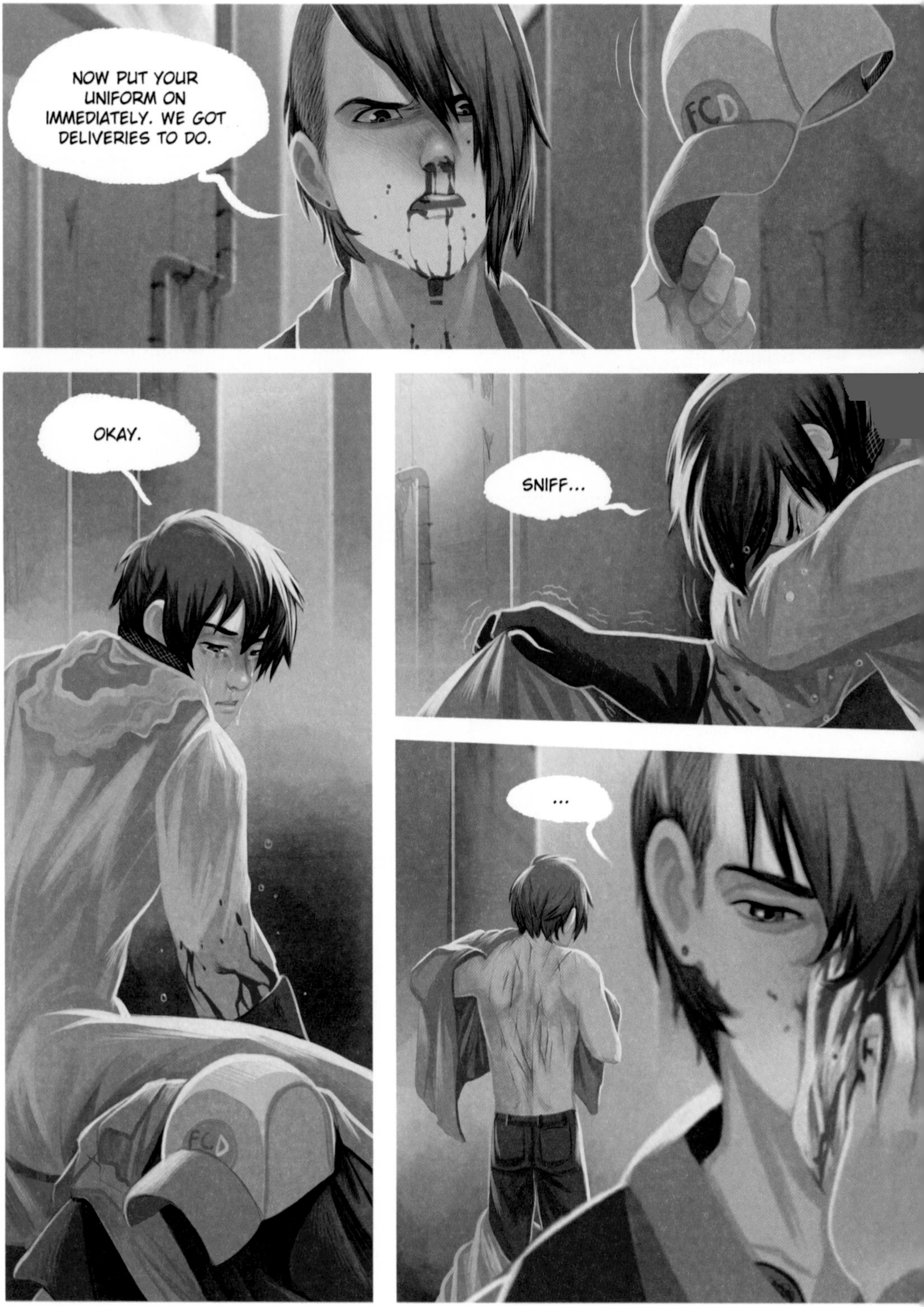
NOW PUT YOUR UNIFORM ON IMMEDIATELY. WE GOT DELIVERIES TO DO.
OKAY.
SNIFF...
...

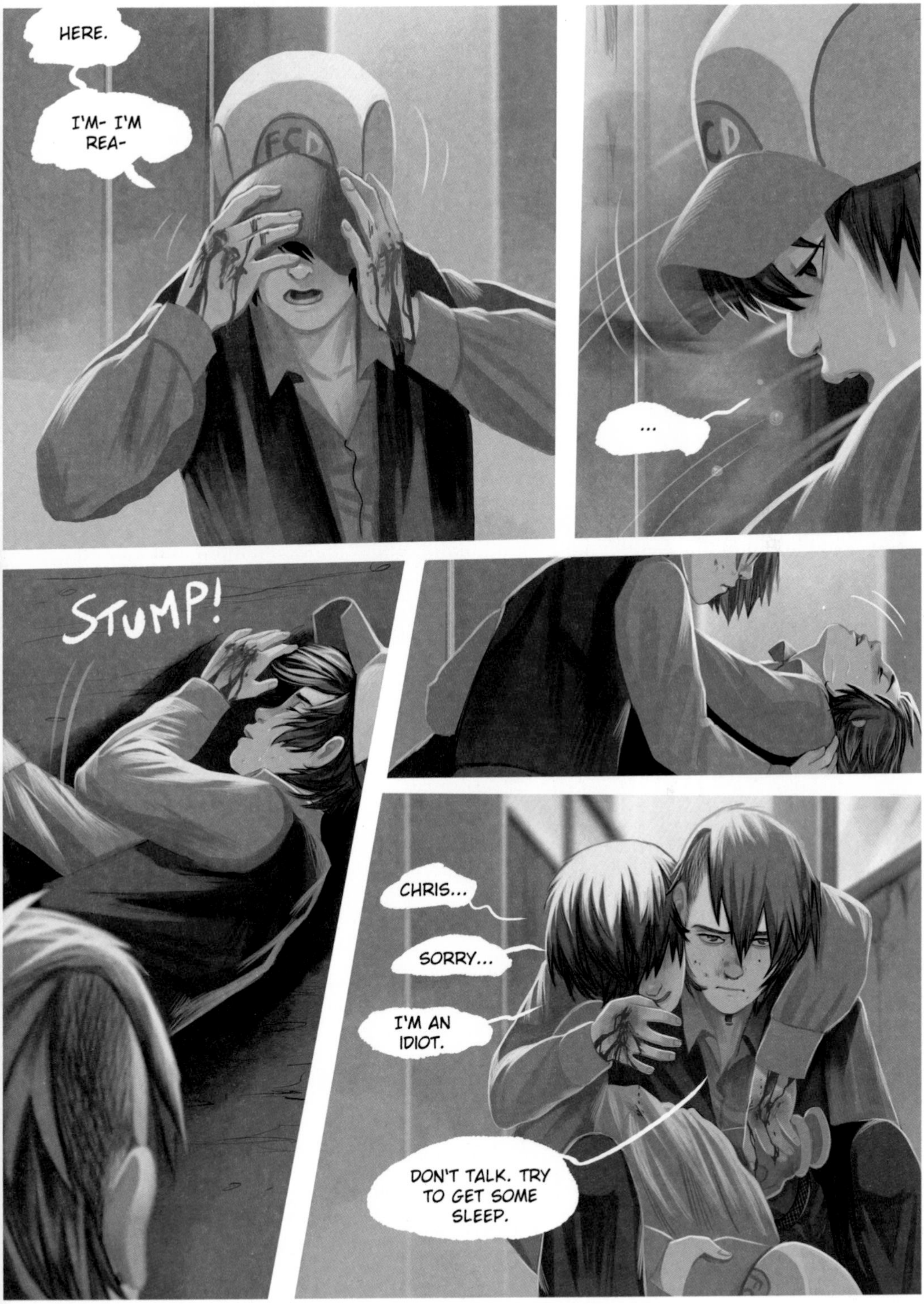
HERE.
I'M- I'M REA-
...
STUMP!
CHRIS...
SORRY...
I'M AN IDIOT.
DON'T TALK. TRY TO GET SOME SLEEP.

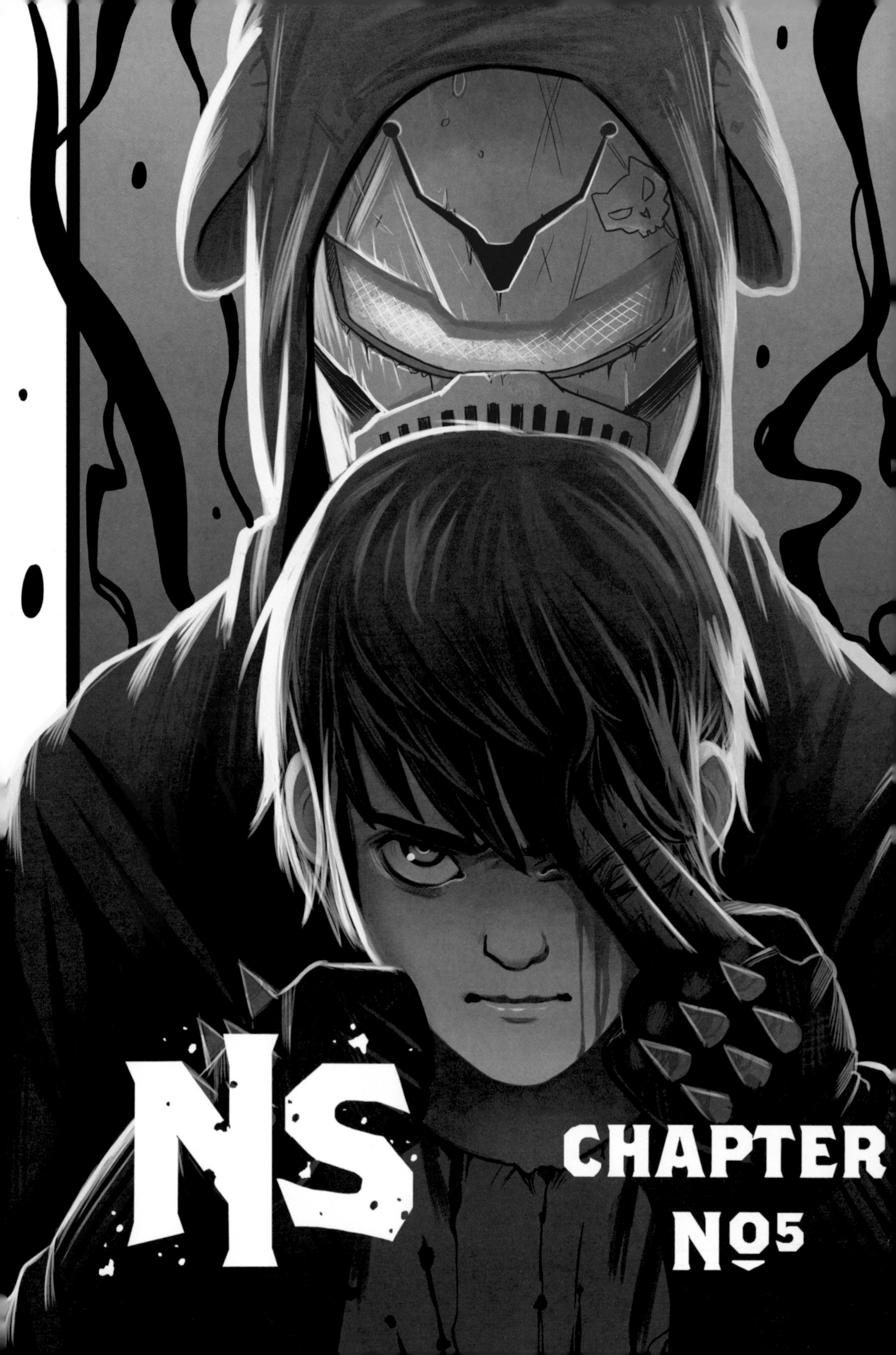
NS
CHAPTER
No5

IN PIECES.

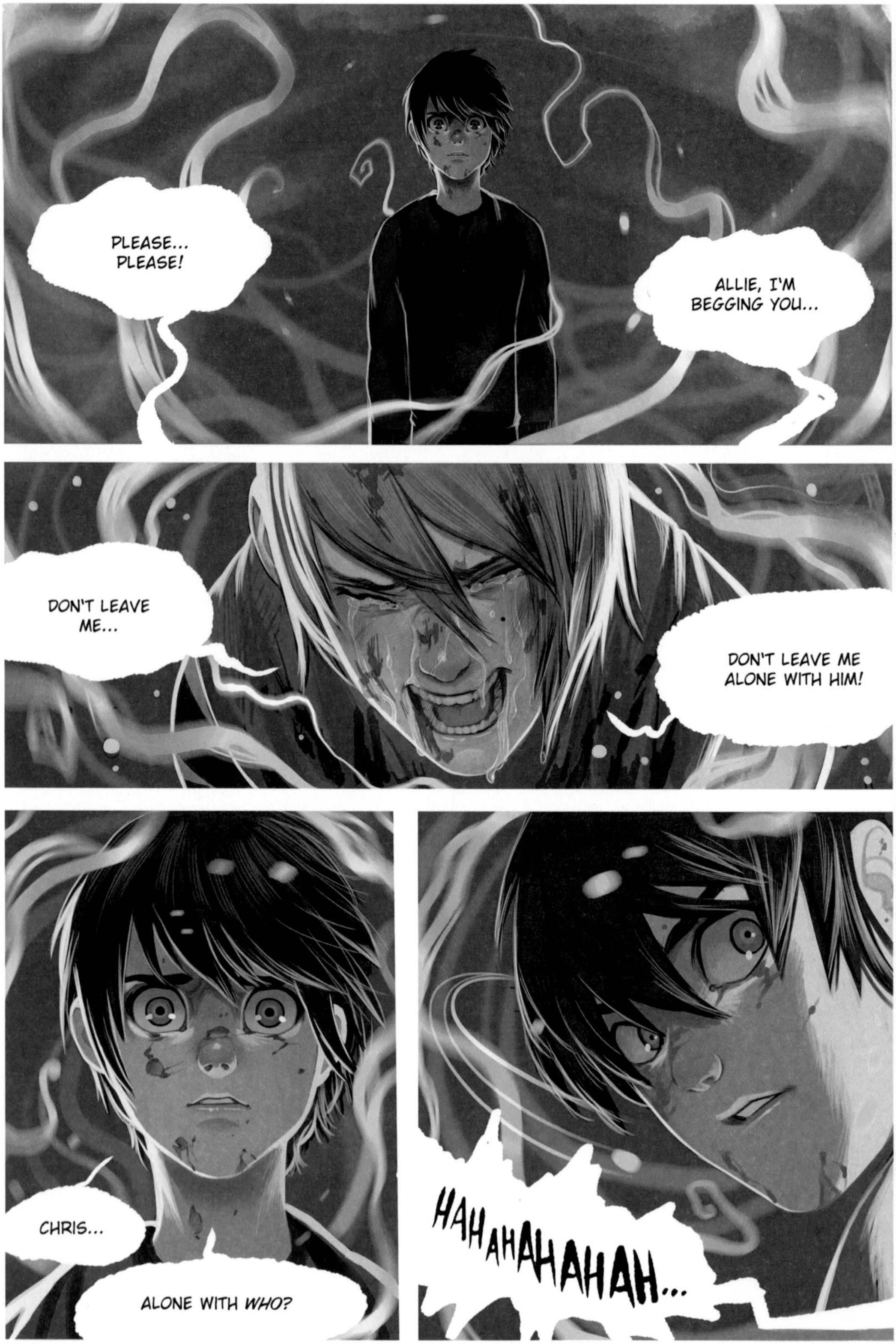
PLEASE...
PLEASE!
ALLIE, I'M
BEGGING YOU...
DON'T LEAVE
ME...
DON'T LEAVE ME
ALONE WITH HIM!
CHRIS...
ALONE WITH *WHO?*
HAHAHAHAHAH...

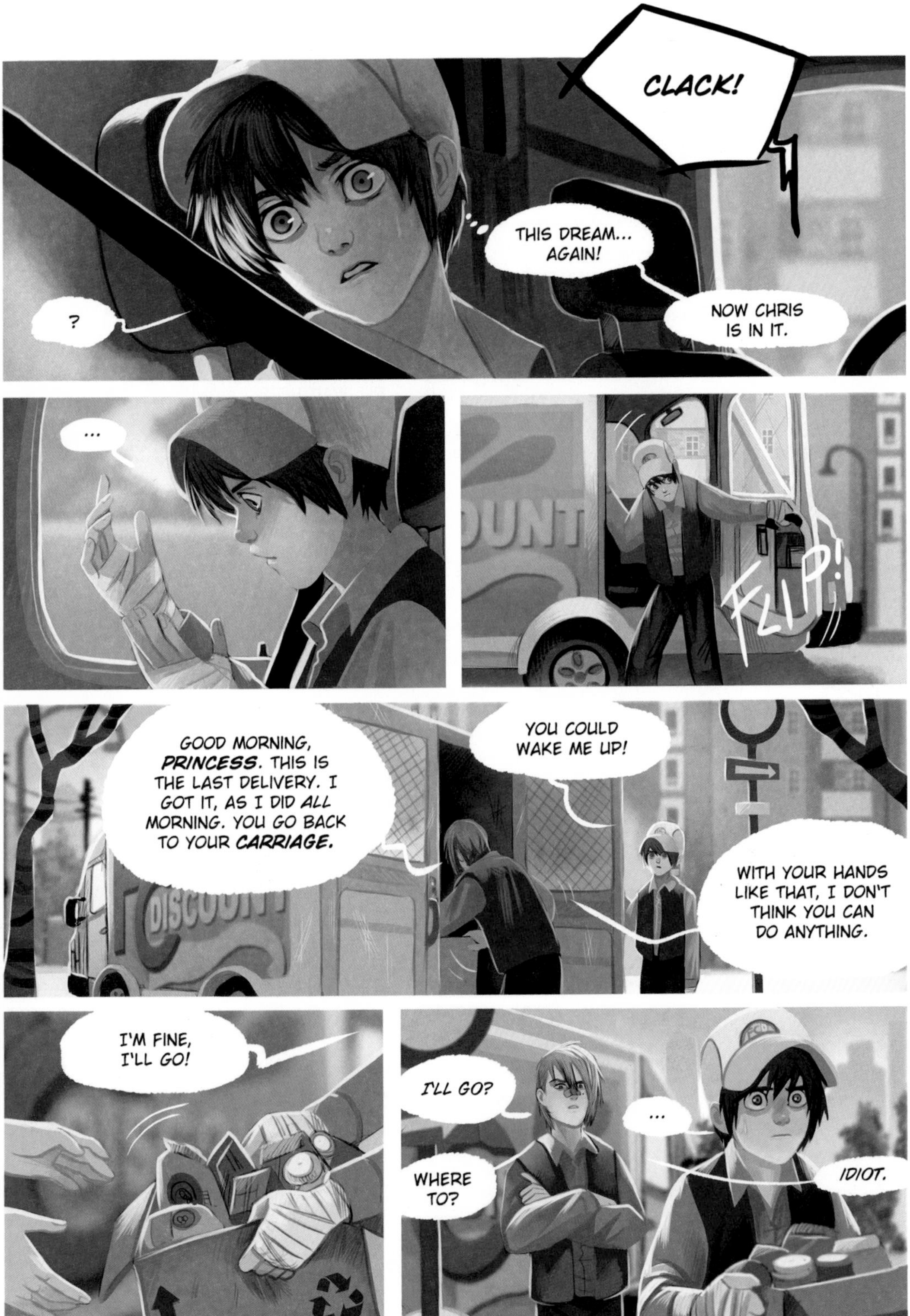
CLACK!
THIS DREAM... AGAIN!
?
NOW CHRIS IS IN IT.
...
FLIP!
GOOD MORNING, PRINCESS. THIS IS THE LAST DELIVERY. I GOT IT, AS I DID ALL MORNING. YOU GO BACK TO YOUR CARRIAGE.
YOU COULD WAKE ME UP!
WITH YOUR HANDS LIKE THAT, I DON'T THINK YOU CAN DO ANYTHING.
I'M FINE, I'LL GO!
I'LL GO?
...
WHERE TO?
IDIOT.

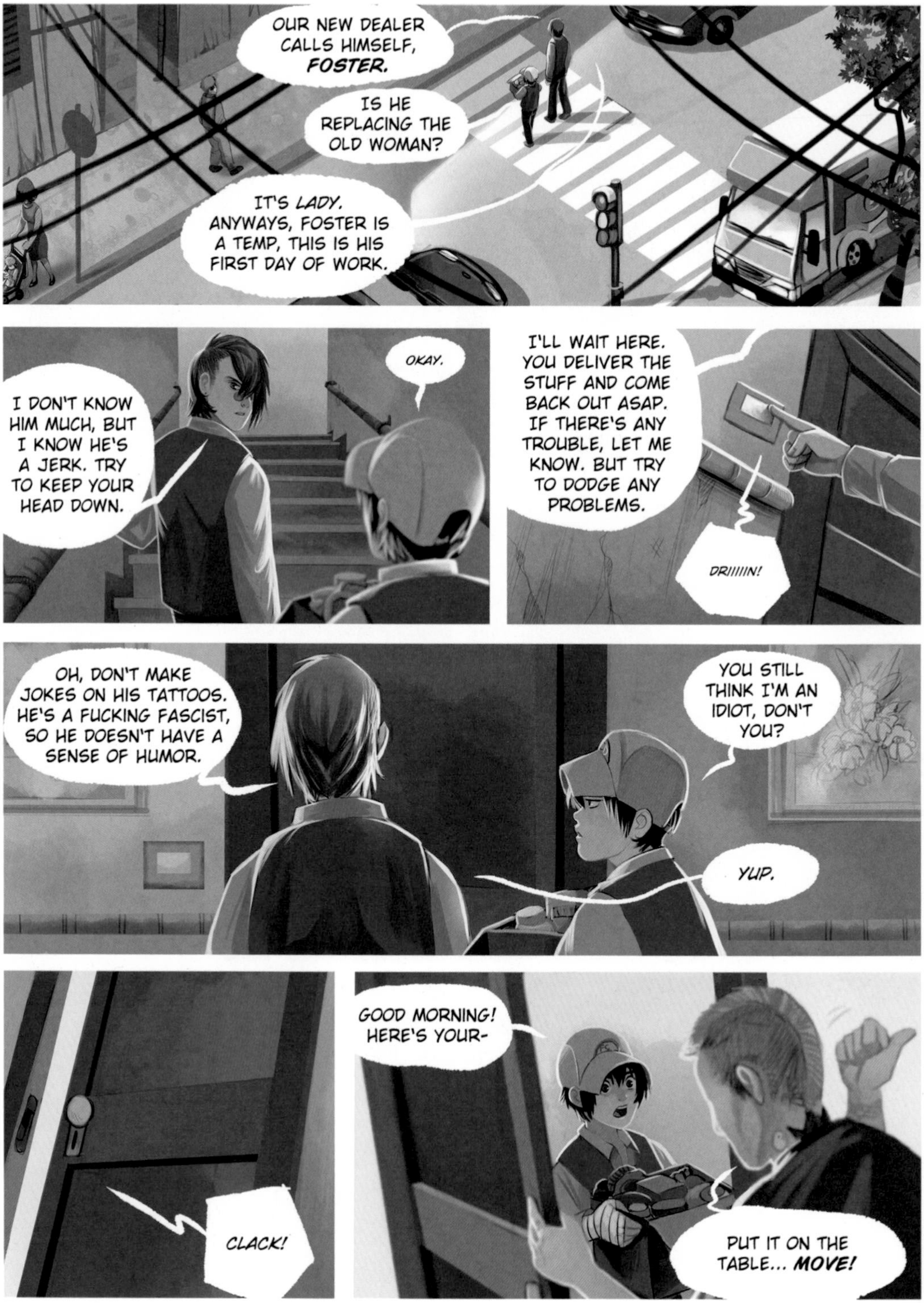
OUR NEW DEALER CALLS HIMSELF, ***FOSTER.***
IS HE REPLACING THE OLD WOMAN?
IT'S *LADY.* ANYWAYS, FOSTER IS A TEMP, THIS IS HIS FIRST DAY OF WORK.
I DON'T KNOW HIM MUCH, BUT I KNOW HE'S A JERK. TRY TO KEEP YOUR HEAD DOWN.
OKAY.
I'LL WAIT HERE. YOU DELIVER THE STUFF AND COME BACK OUT ASAP. IF THERE'S ANY TROUBLE, LET ME KNOW. BUT TRY TO DODGE ANY PROBLEMS.
DRIIIIIN!
OH, DON'T MAKE JOKES ON HIS TATTOOS. HE'S A FUCKING FASCIST, SO HE DOESN'T HAVE A SENSE OF HUMOR.
YOU STILL THINK I'M AN IDIOT, DON'T YOU?
YUP.
CLACK!
GOOD MORNING! HERE'S YOUR-
PUT IT ON THE TABLE... ***MOVE!***

CLACK!

...

I'LL GO THEN! AND YOU PEOPLE SAY: *HAIL HYDRA!*

WAIT.

LET ME CHECK FIRST.

THIS ISN'T THE RIGHT DOSE!

HUH?

ARE YOU DEAF, YOU SHITTY *FAGGOT?* I SAID THIS ISN'T THE RIGHT DOSE, I WAS EXPECTING MORE!

I-I DON'T...

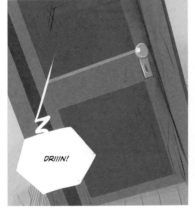

DRIIIN!

WHAT THE FUCK?

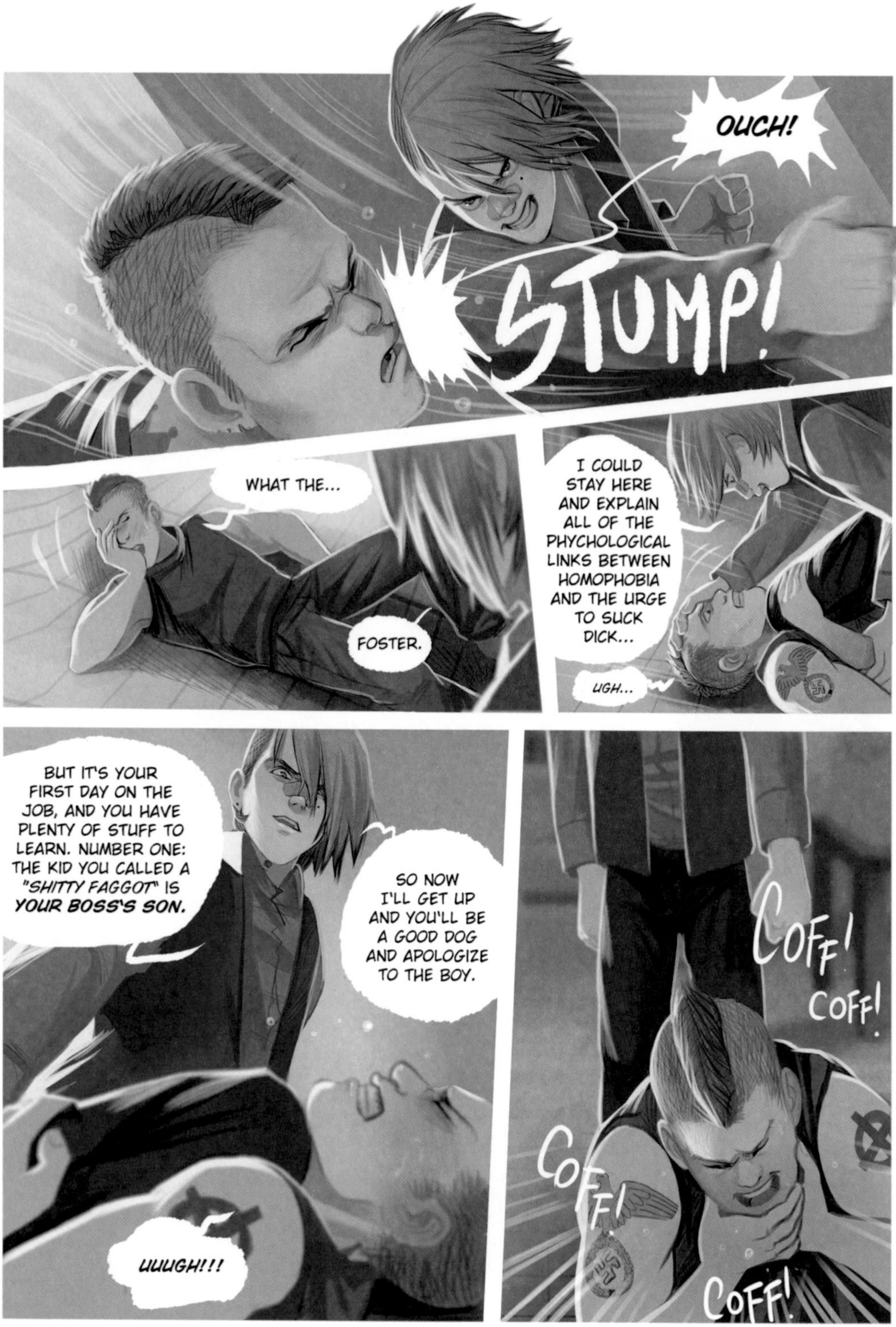
OUCH!
STUMP!
WHAT THE...
FOSTER.
I COULD STAY HERE AND EXPLAIN ALL OF THE PHYCHOLOGICAL LINKS BETWEEN HOMOPHOBIA AND THE URGE TO SUCK DICK...
UGH...
BUT IT'S YOUR FIRST DAY ON THE JOB, AND YOU HAVE PLENTY OF STUFF TO LEARN. NUMBER ONE: THE KID YOU CALLED A "SHITTY FAGGOT" IS YOUR BOSS'S SON.
SO NOW I'LL GET UP AND YOU'LL BE A GOOD DOG AND APOLOGIZE TO THE BOY.
UUUGH!!!
COFF! COFF!
COFF!
COFF!

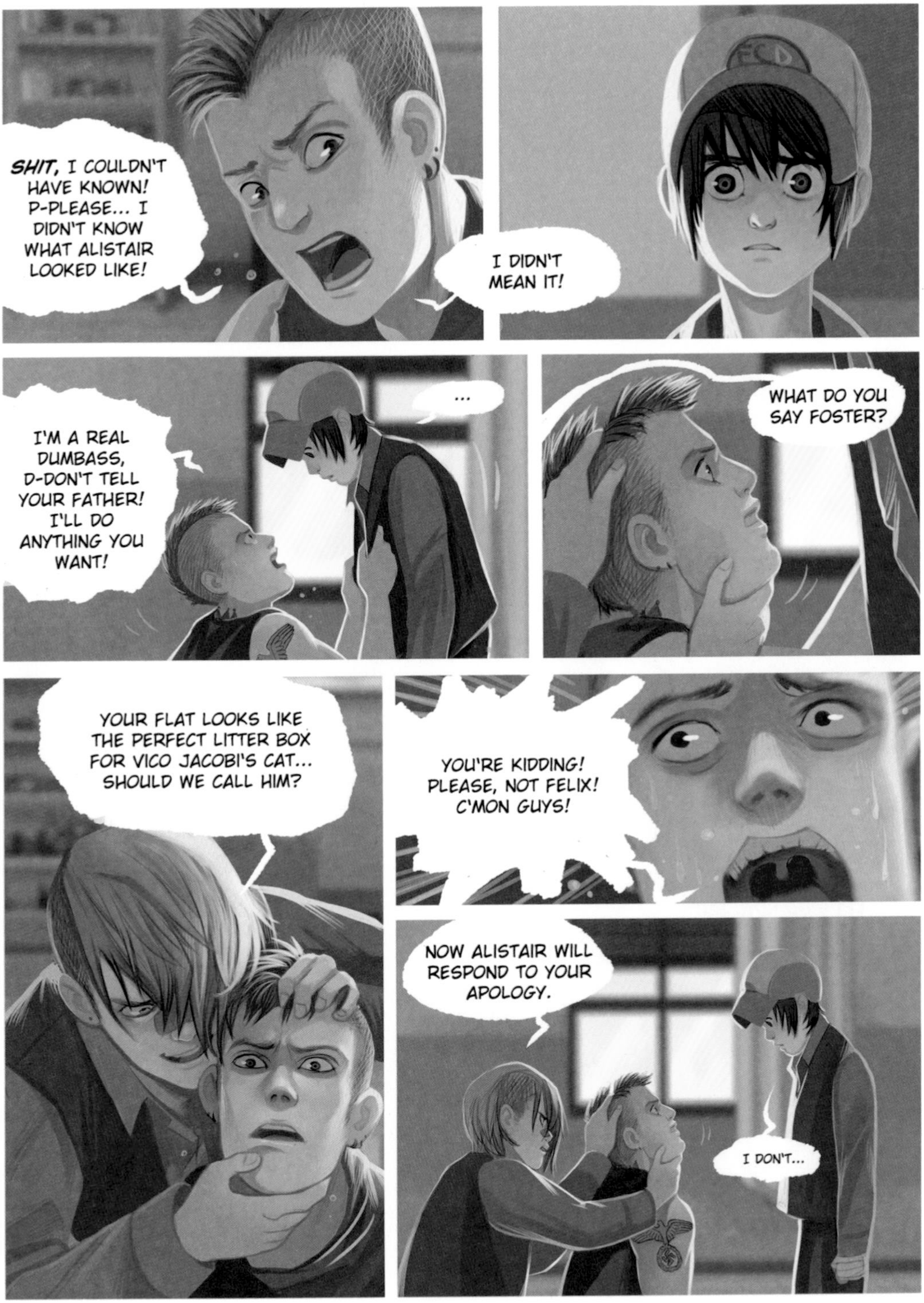
SHIT, I COULDN'T HAVE KNOWN! P-PLEASE... I DIDN'T KNOW WHAT ALISTAIR LOOKED LIKE!
I DIDN'T MEAN IT!
I'M A REAL DUMBASS, D-DON'T TELL YOUR FATHER! I'LL DO ANYTHING YOU WANT!
...
WHAT DO YOU SAY FOSTER?
YOUR FLAT LOOKS LIKE THE PERFECT LITTER BOX FOR VICO JACOBI'S CAT... SHOULD WE CALL HIM?
YOU'RE KIDDING! PLEASE, NOT FELIX! C'MON GUYS!
NOW ALISTAIR WILL RESPOND TO YOUR APOLOGY.
I DON'T...

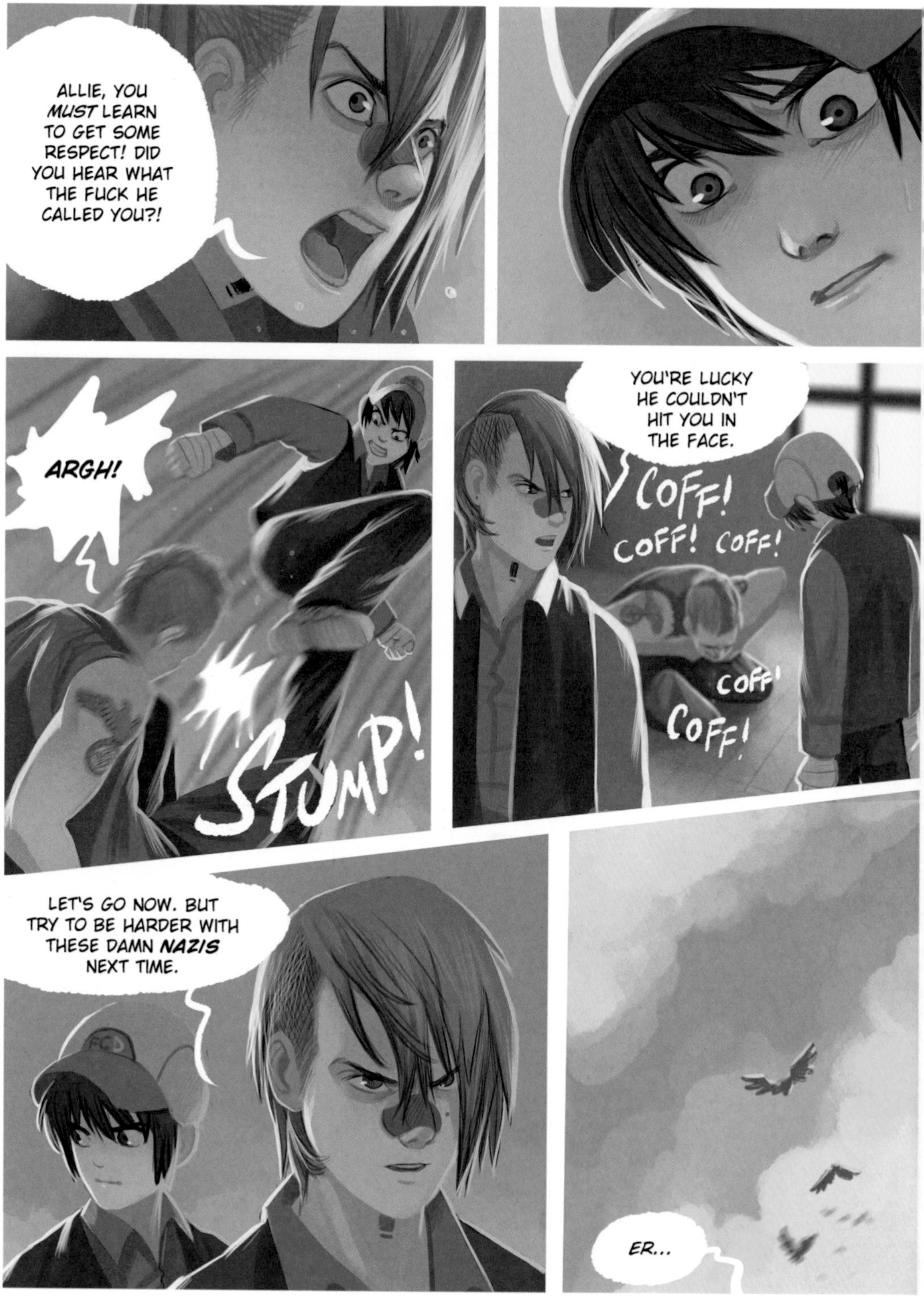
ALLIE, YOU *MUST* LEARN TO GET SOME RESPECT! DID YOU HEAR WHAT THE FUCK HE CALLED YOU?!
ARGH!
STUMP!
YOU'RE LUCKY HE COULDN'T HIT YOU IN THE FACE.
COFF! COFF! COFF!
COFF! COFF!
LET'S GO NOW. BUT TRY TO BE HARDER WITH THESE DAMN *NAZIS* NEXT TIME.
ER...

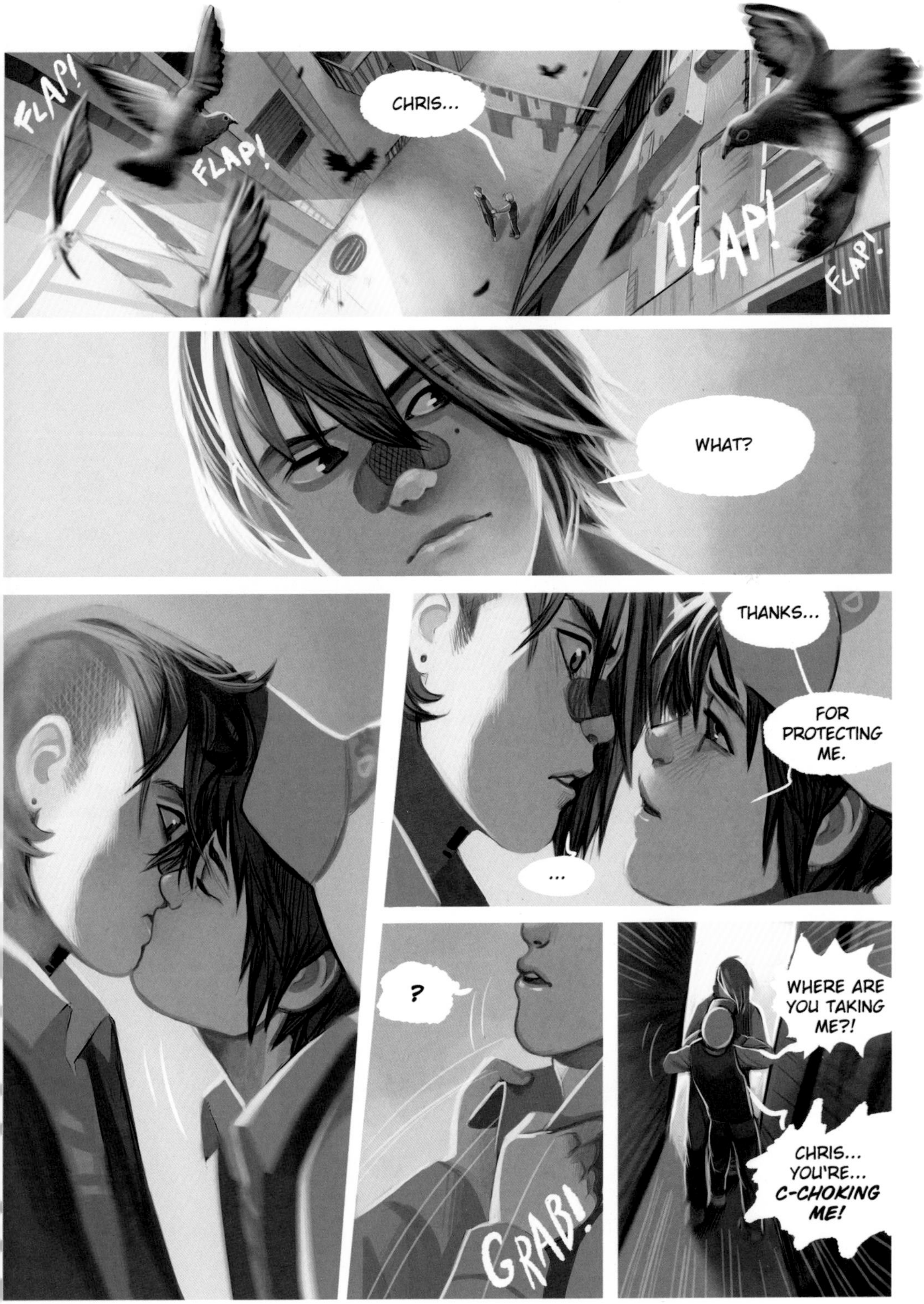
FLAP!
FLAP!
CHRIS...
FLAP!
FLAP!
WHAT?
THANKS...
FOR PROTECTING ME.
...
?
GRAB!
WHERE ARE YOU TAKING ME?!
CHRIS... YOU'RE... C-CHOKING ME!

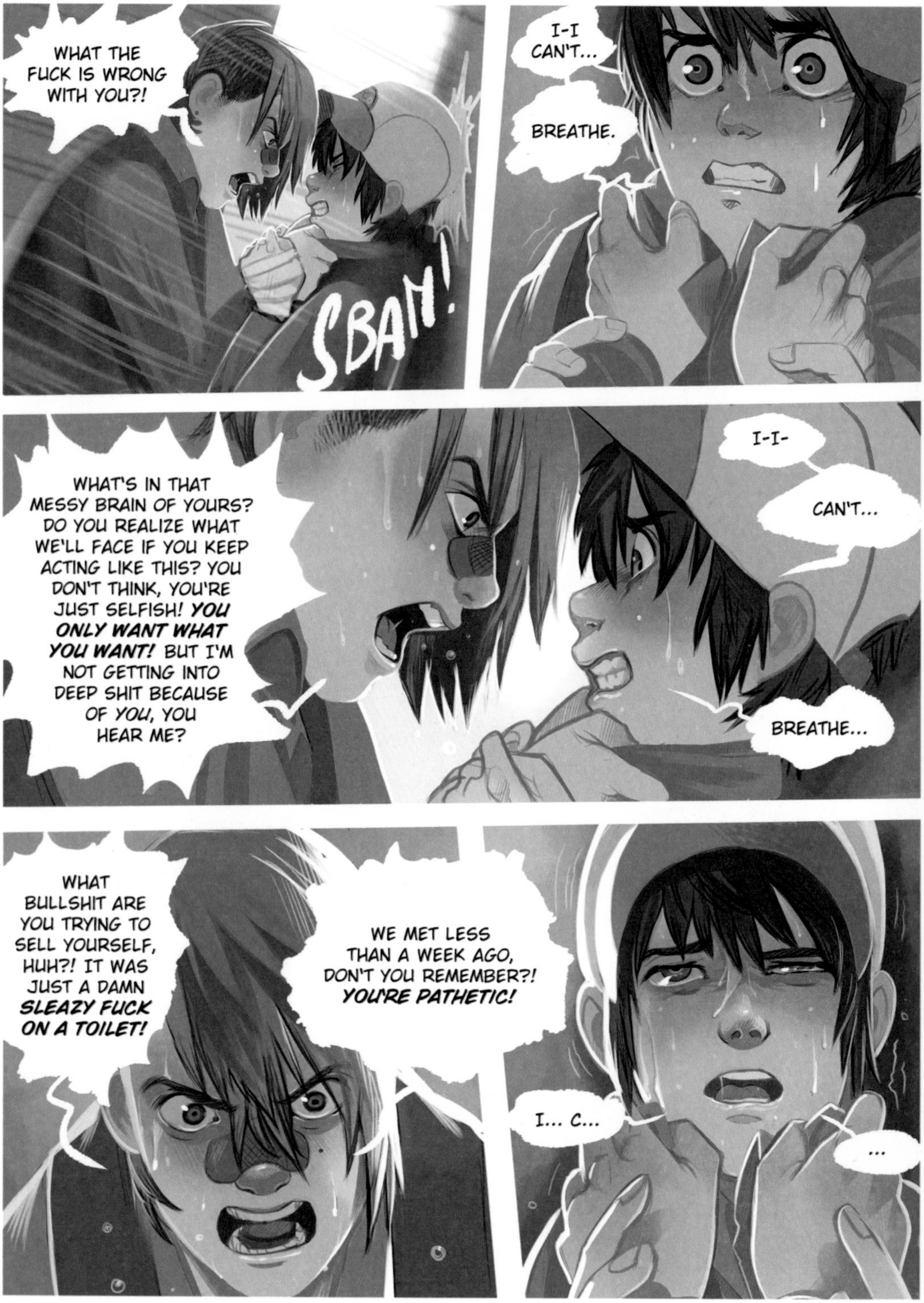
WHAT THE FUCK IS WRONG WITH YOU?!
SBAM!
I-I CAN'T...
BREATHE.
WHAT'S IN THAT MESSY BRAIN OF YOURS? DO YOU REALIZE WHAT WE'LL FACE IF YOU KEEP ACTING LIKE THIS? YOU DON'T THINK, YOU'RE JUST SELFISH! ***YOU ONLY WANT WHAT YOU WANT!*** BUT I'M NOT GETTING INTO DEEP SHIT BECAUSE OF *YOU*, YOU HEAR ME?
I-I-
CAN'T...
BREATHE...
WHAT BULLSHIT ARE YOU TRYING TO SELL YOURSELF, HUH?! IT WAS JUST A DAMN ***SLEAZY FUCK ON A TOILET!***
WE MET LESS THAN A WEEK AGO, DON'T YOU REMEMBER?! ***YOU'RE PATHETIC!***
I... C...
...

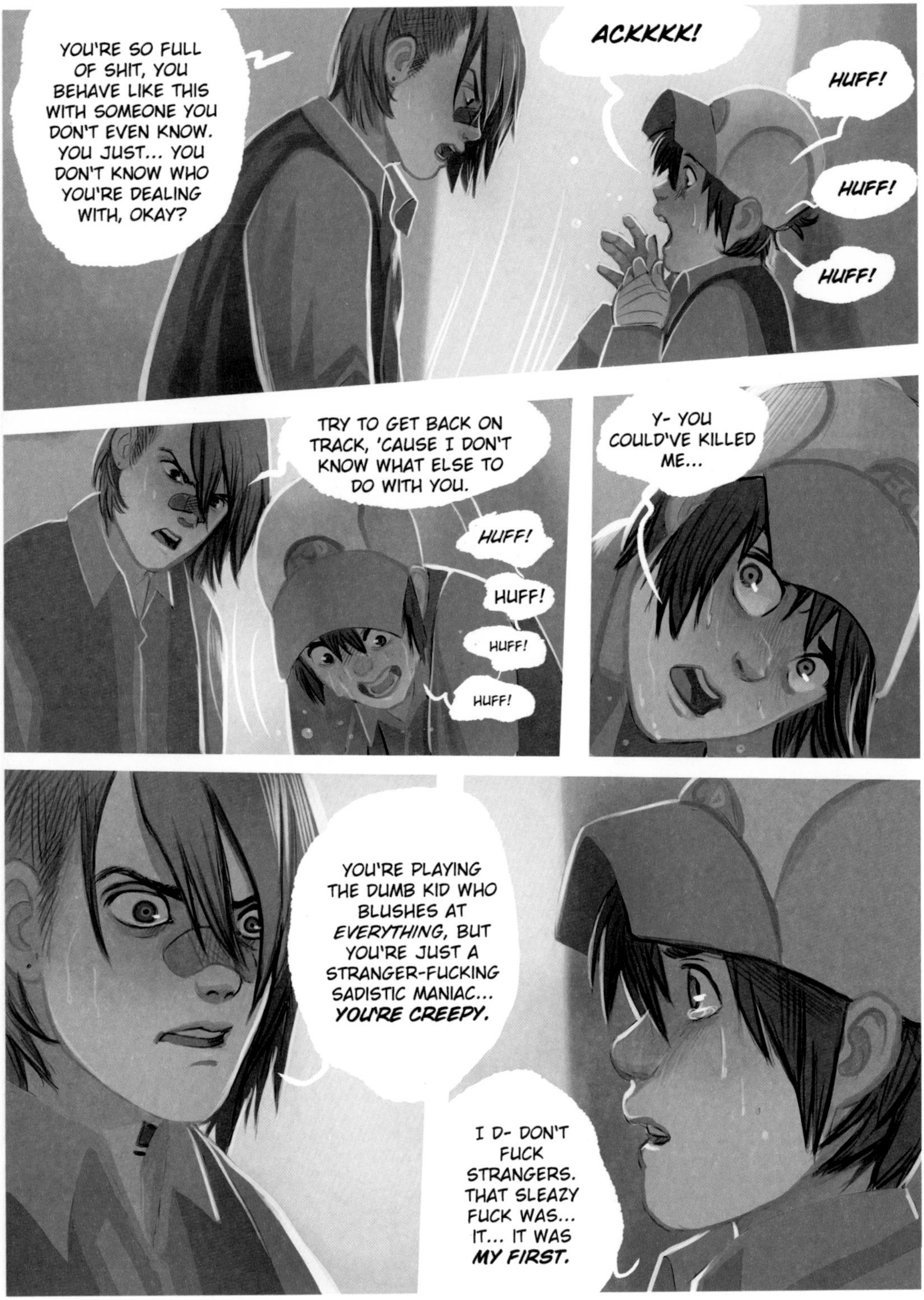
YOU'RE SO FULL OF SHIT, YOU BEHAVE LIKE THIS WITH SOMEONE YOU DON'T EVEN KNOW. YOU JUST... YOU DON'T KNOW WHO YOU'RE DEALING WITH, OKAY?
ACKKKK!
HUFF!
HUFF!
HUFF!
TRY TO GET BACK ON TRACK, 'CAUSE I DON'T KNOW WHAT ELSE TO DO WITH YOU.
HUFF!
HUFF!
HUFF!
HUFF!
Y- YOU COULD'VE KILLED ME...
YOU'RE PLAYING THE DUMB KID WHO BLUSHES AT *EVERYTHING*, BUT YOU'RE JUST A STRANGER-FUCKING SADISTIC MANIAC... ***YOU'RE CREEPY.***
I D- DON'T FUCK STRANGERS. THAT SLEAZY FUCK WAS... IT... IT WAS ***MY FIRST.***

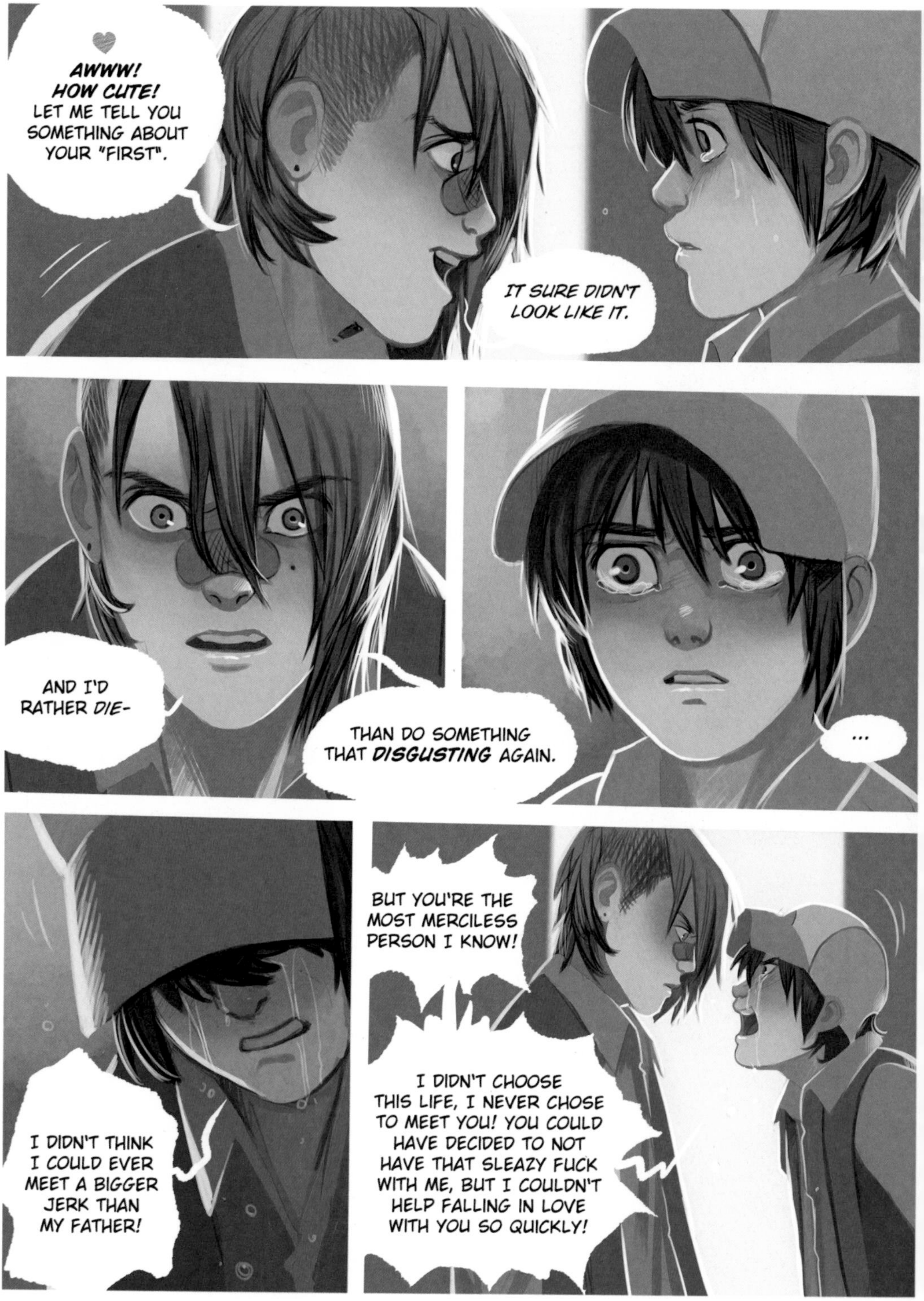
AWWW!
HOW CUTE!
LET ME TELL YOU SOMETHING ABOUT YOUR "FIRST".
IT SURE DIDN'T LOOK LIKE IT.
AND I'D RATHER DIE-
THAN DO SOMETHING THAT DISGUSTING AGAIN.
...
I DIDN'T THINK I COULD EVER MEET A BIGGER JERK THAN MY FATHER!
BUT YOU'RE THE MOST MERCILESS PERSON I KNOW!
I DIDN'T CHOOSE THIS LIFE, I NEVER CHOSE TO MEET YOU! YOU COULD HAVE DECIDED TO NOT HAVE THAT SLEAZY FUCK WITH ME, BUT I COULDN'T HELP FALLING IN LOVE WITH YOU SO QUICKLY!

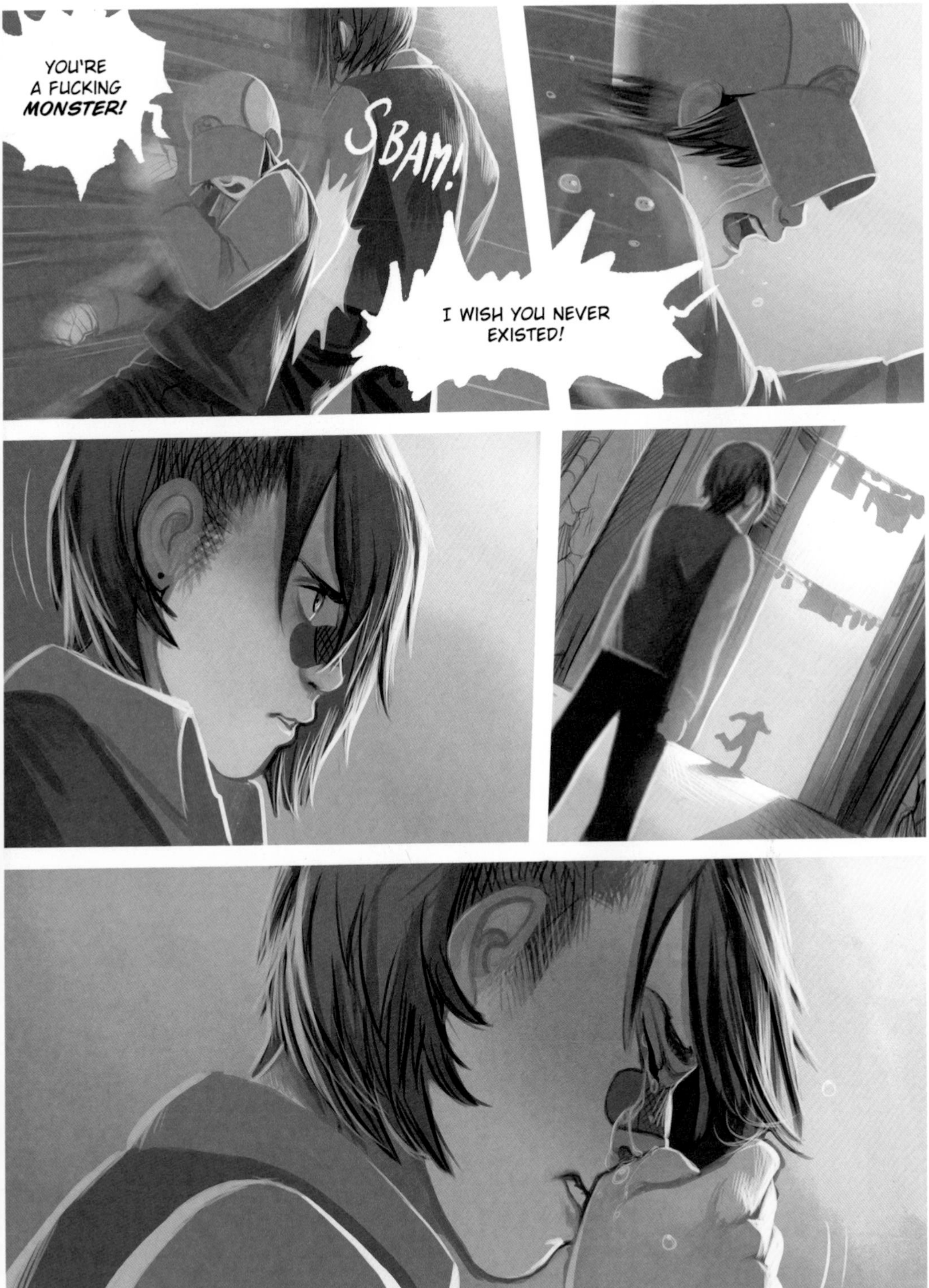
YOU'RE A FUCKING **MONSTER!**
SBAM!
I WISH YOU NEVER EXISTED!

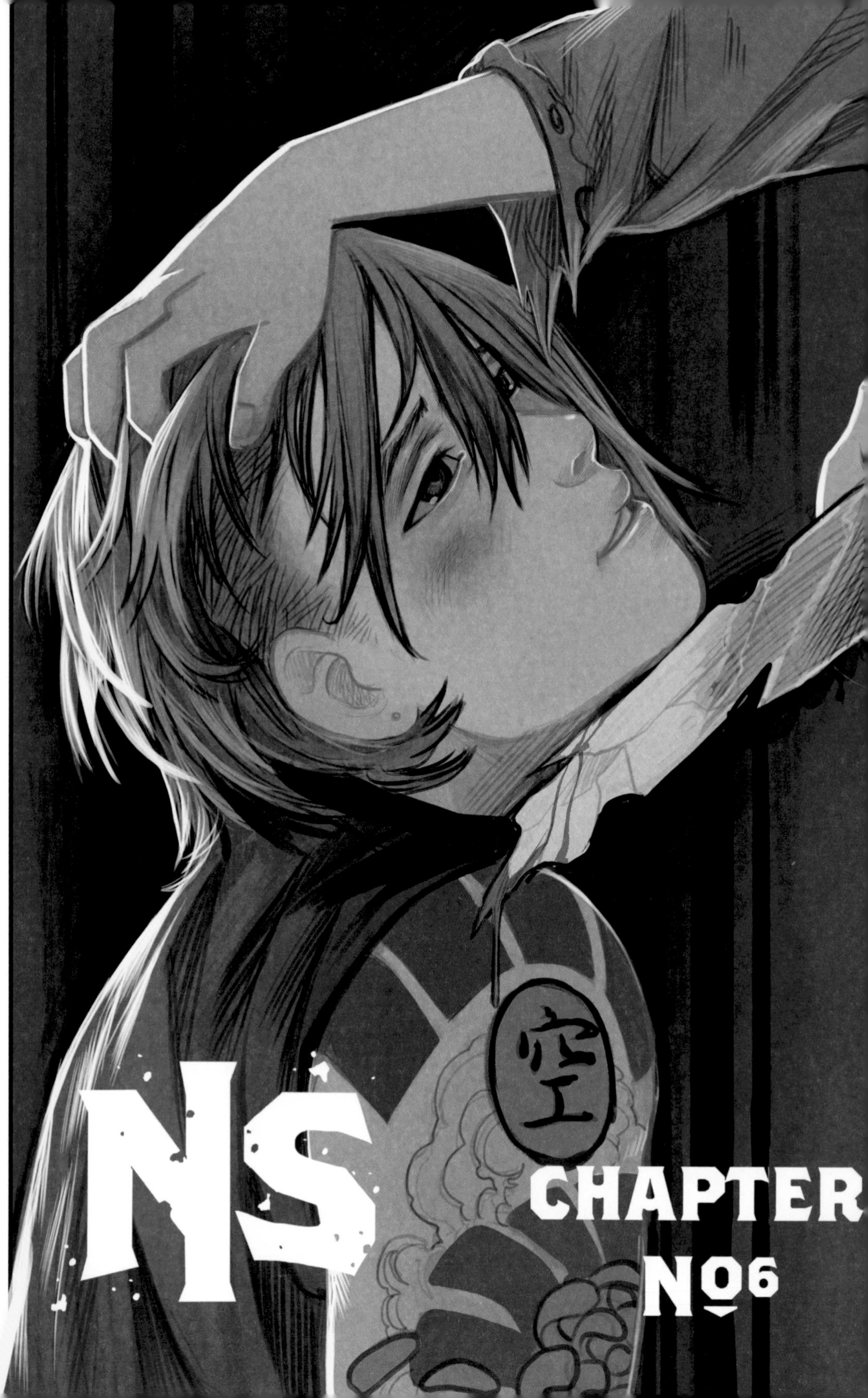
空
NS
CHAPTER
Nº6

DOG.

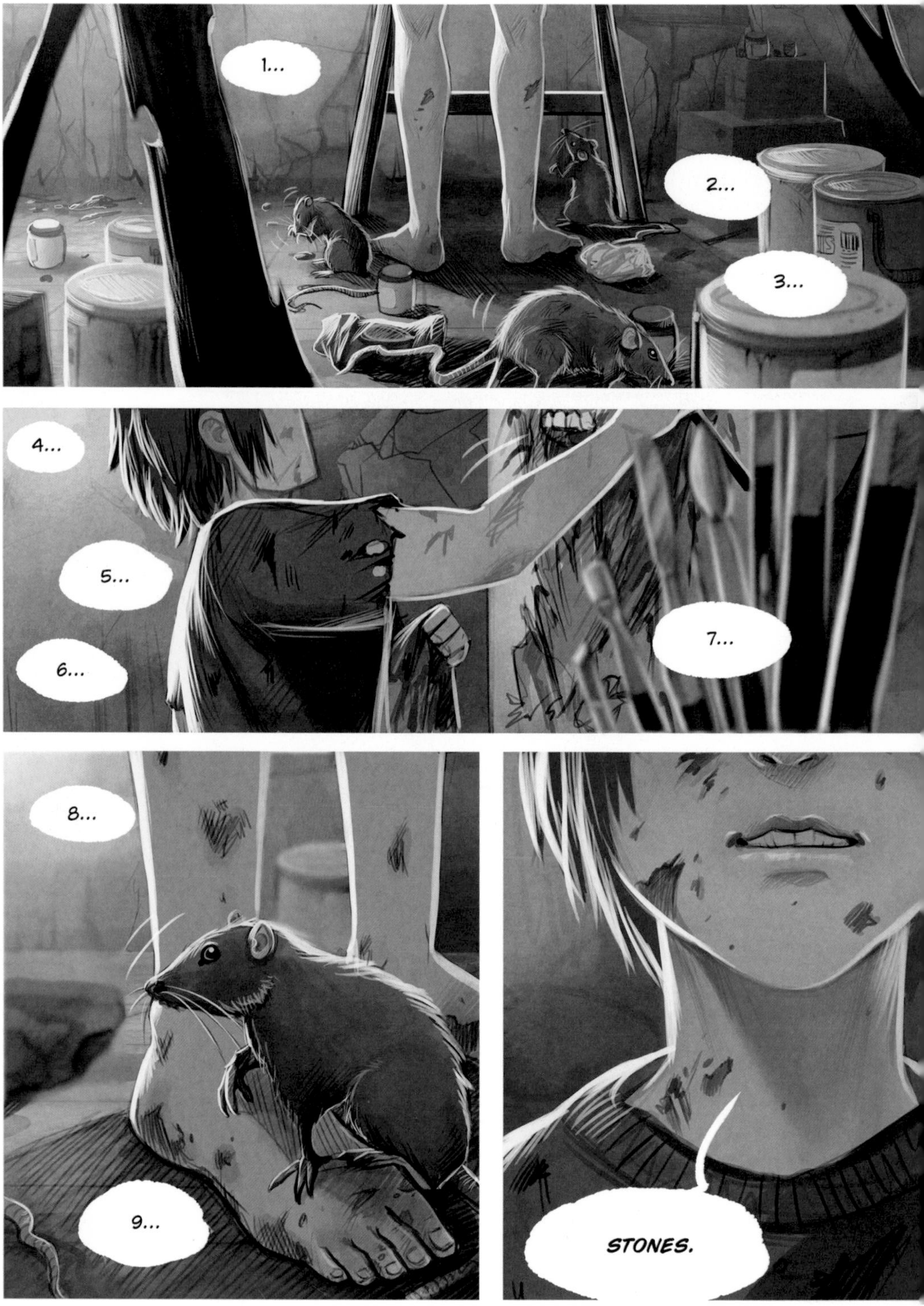
1...
2...
3...
4...
5...
6...
7...
8...
9...
STONES.

ALISTAIR...

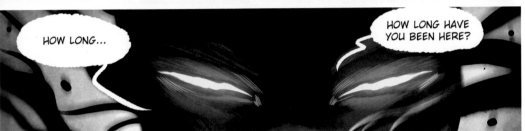

HOW LONG...

HOW LONG HAVE YOU BEEN HERE?

I

HAVE

NO IDEA!

HAVE YOU EVER BEEN FAR FROM HOME FOR SO LONG?

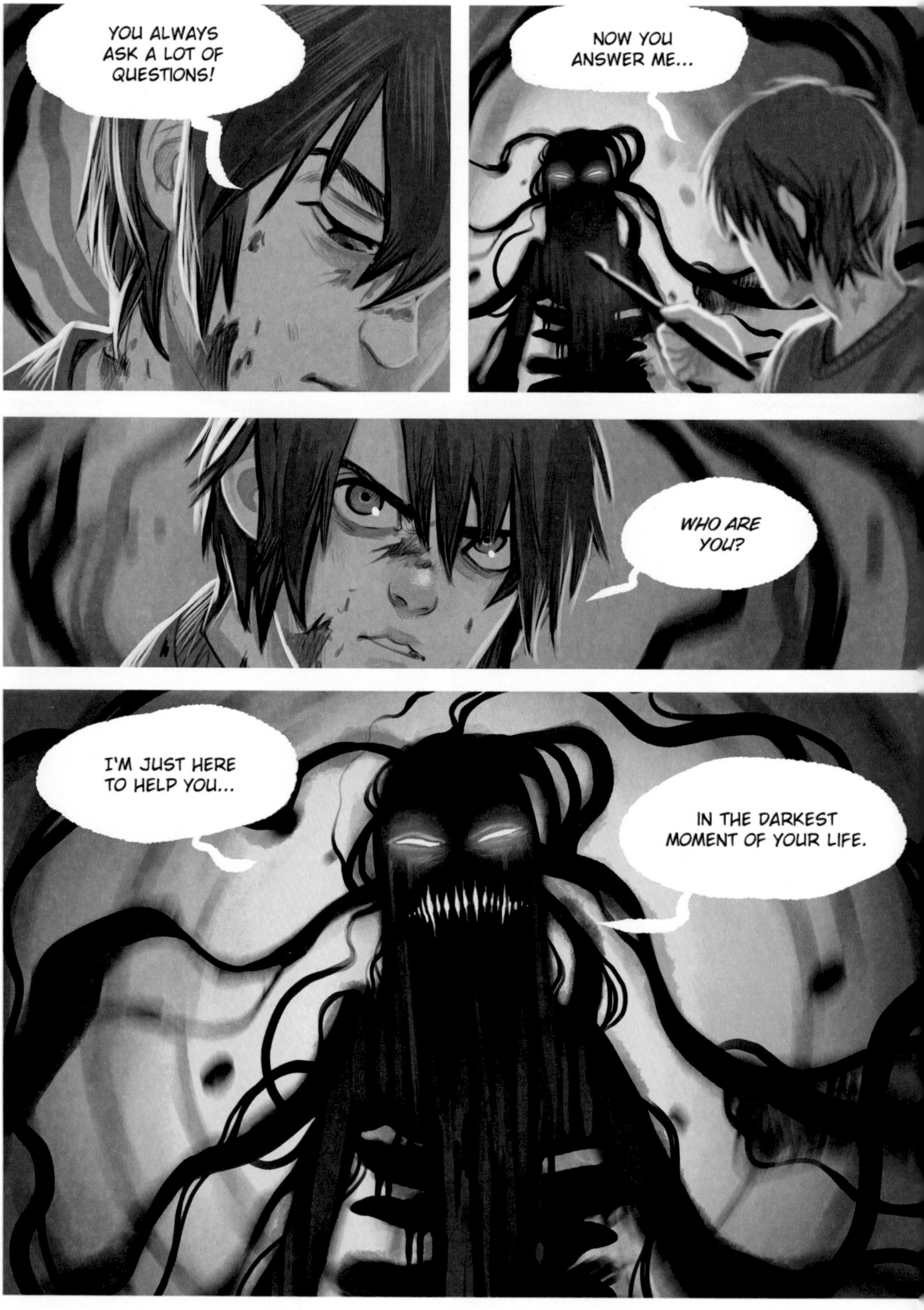
YOU ALWAYS ASK A LOT OF QUESTIONS!
NOW YOU ANSWER ME...
WHO ARE YOU?
I'M JUST HERE TO HELP YOU...
IN THE DARKEST MOMENT OF YOUR LIFE.

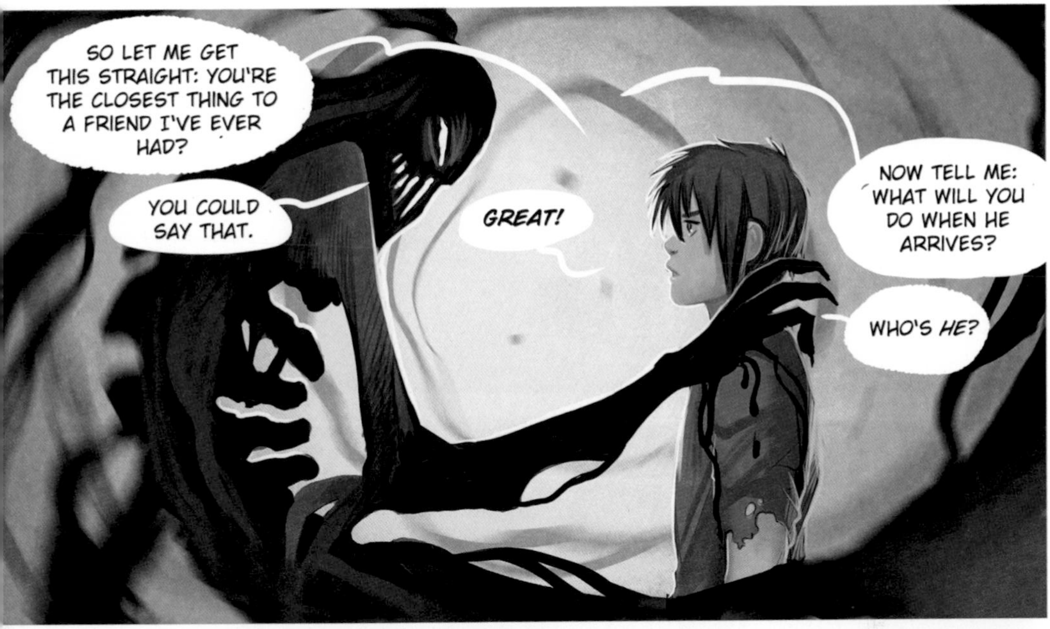
SO LET ME GET THIS STRAIGHT: YOU'RE THE CLOSEST THING TO A FRIEND I'VE EVER HAD?
YOU COULD SAY THAT.
GREAT!
NOW TELL ME: WHAT WILL YOU DO WHEN HE ARRIVES?
WHO'S HE?

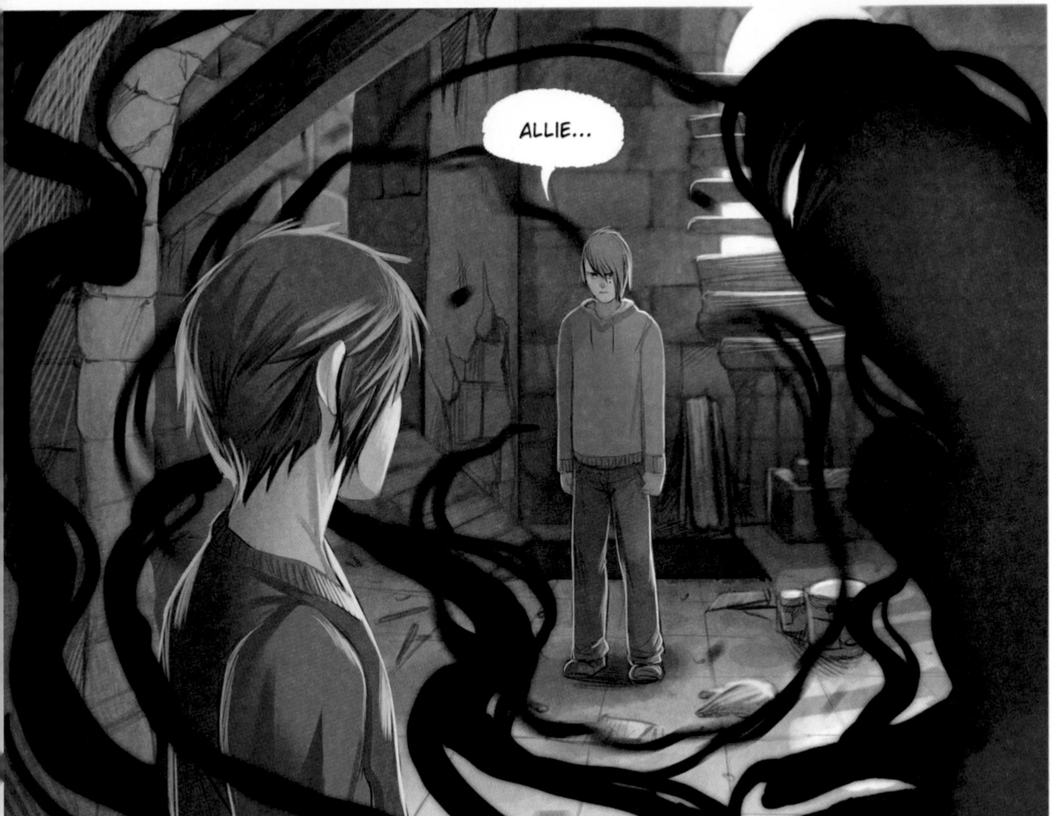
ALLIE...

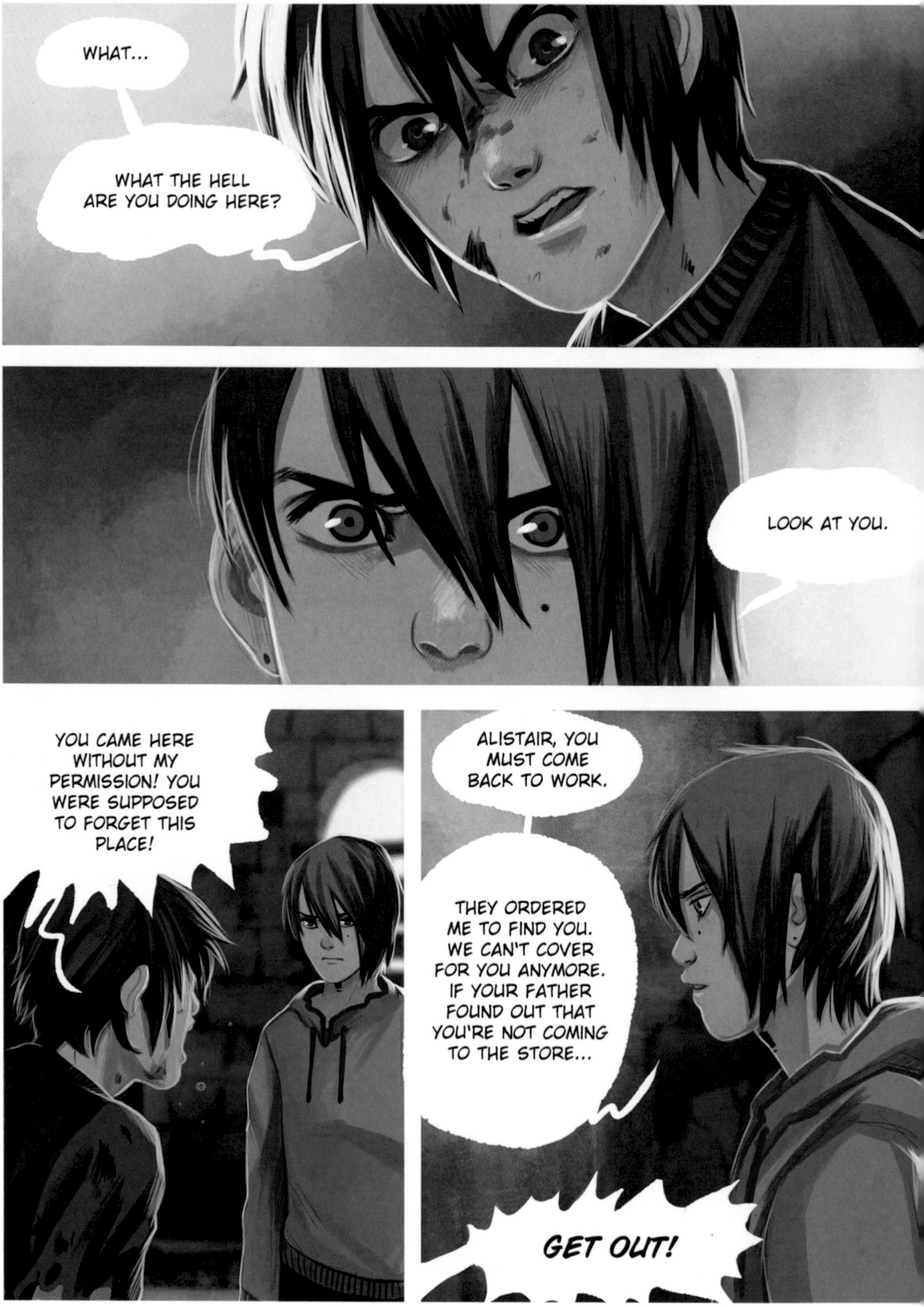
WHAT...
WHAT THE HELL ARE YOU DOING HERE?
LOOK AT YOU.
YOU CAME HERE WITHOUT MY PERMISSION! YOU WERE SUPPOSED TO FORGET THIS PLACE!
ALISTAIR, YOU MUST COME BACK TO WORK.
THEY ORDERED ME TO FIND YOU. WE CAN'T COVER FOR YOU ANYMORE. IF YOUR FATHER FOUND OUT THAT YOU'RE NOT COMING TO THE STORE...
GET OUT!

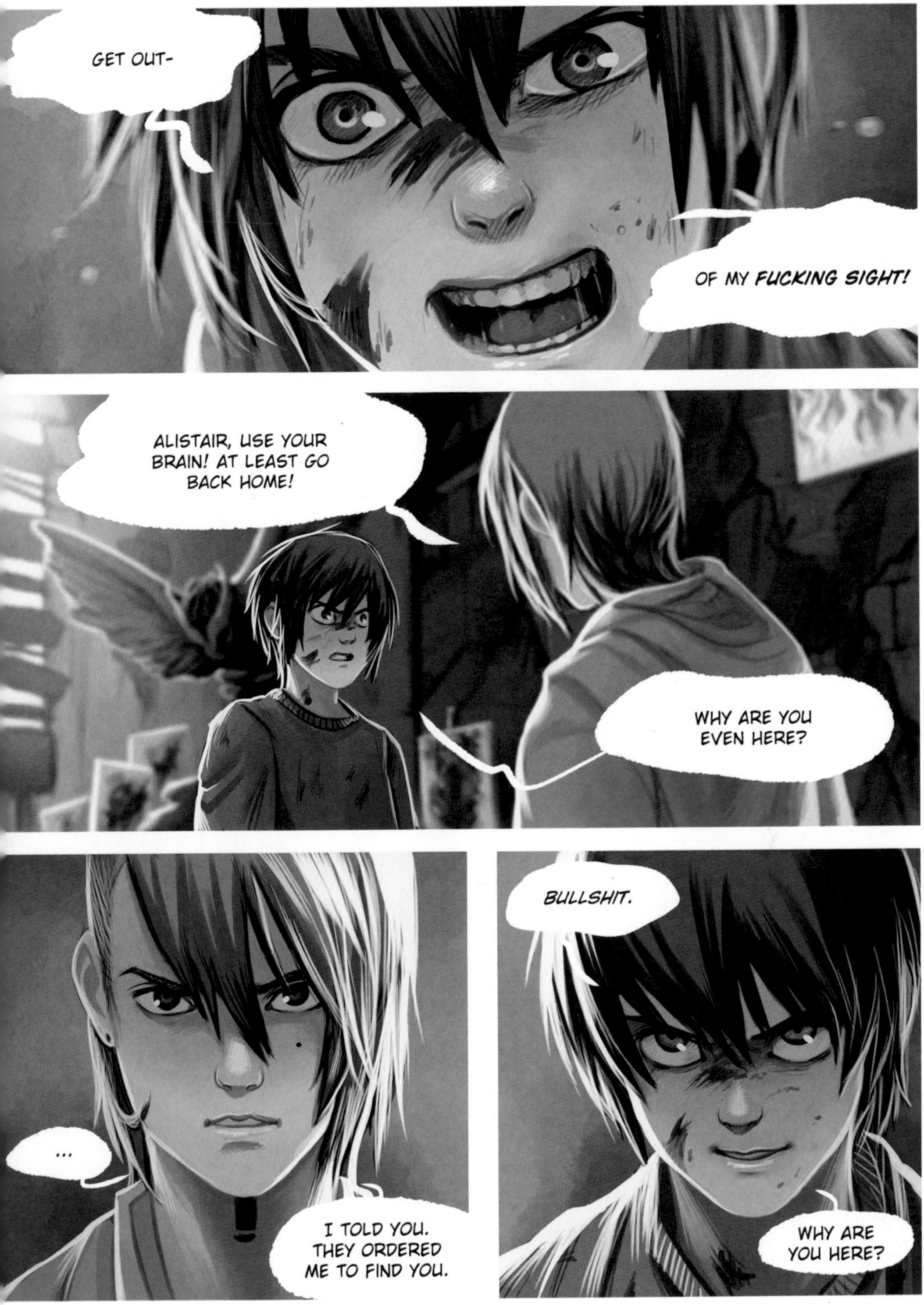
GET OUT-
OF MY FUCKING SIGHT!
ALISTAIR, USE YOUR BRAIN! AT LEAST GO BACK HOME!
WHY ARE YOU EVEN HERE?
...
I TOLD YOU. THEY ORDERED ME TO FIND YOU.
BULLSHIT.
WHY ARE YOU HERE?

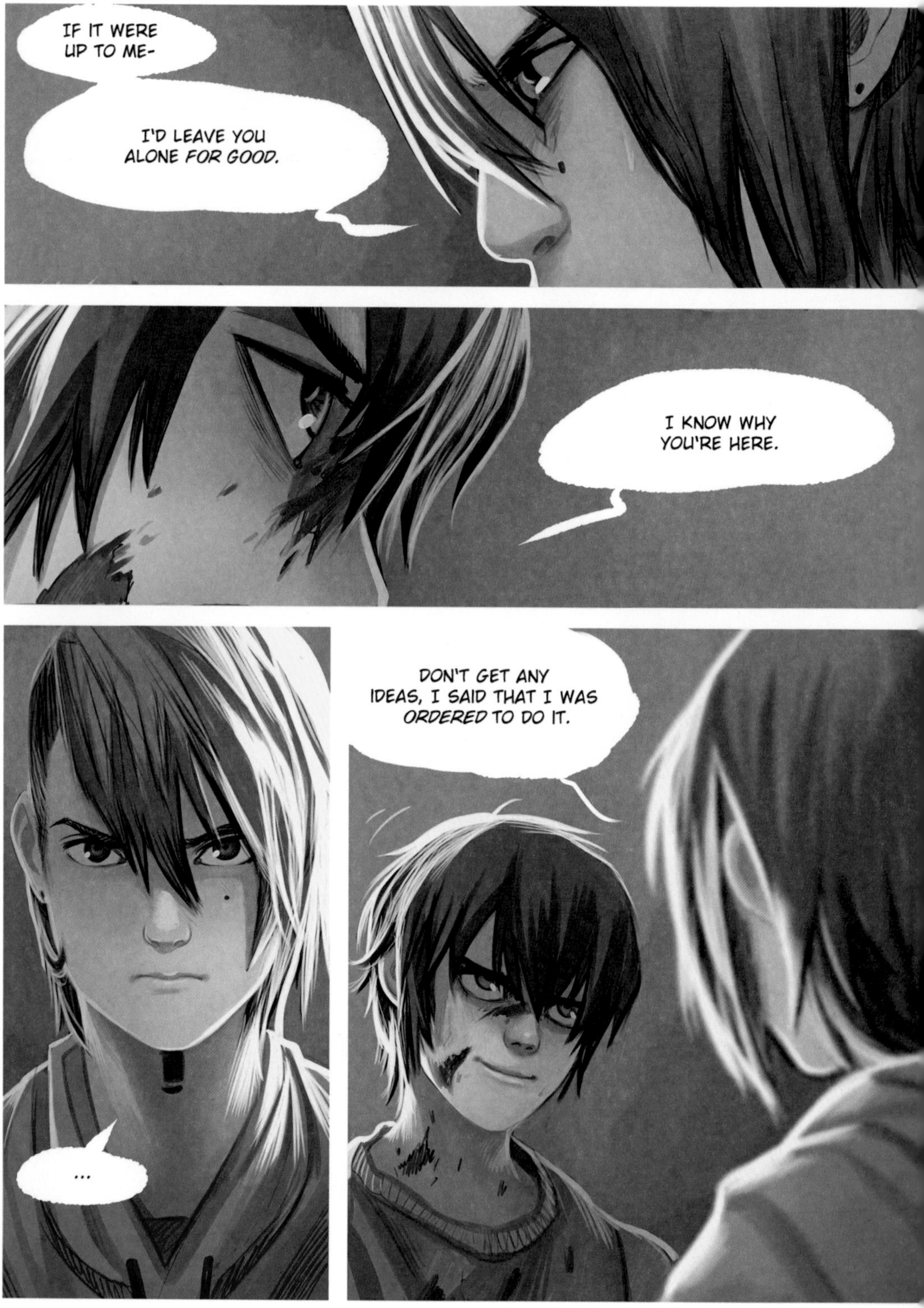
IF IT WERE UP TO ME-
I'D LEAVE YOU ALONE FOR GOOD.
I KNOW WHY YOU'RE HERE.
...
DON'T GET ANY IDEAS, I SAID THAT I WAS ORDERED TO DO IT.

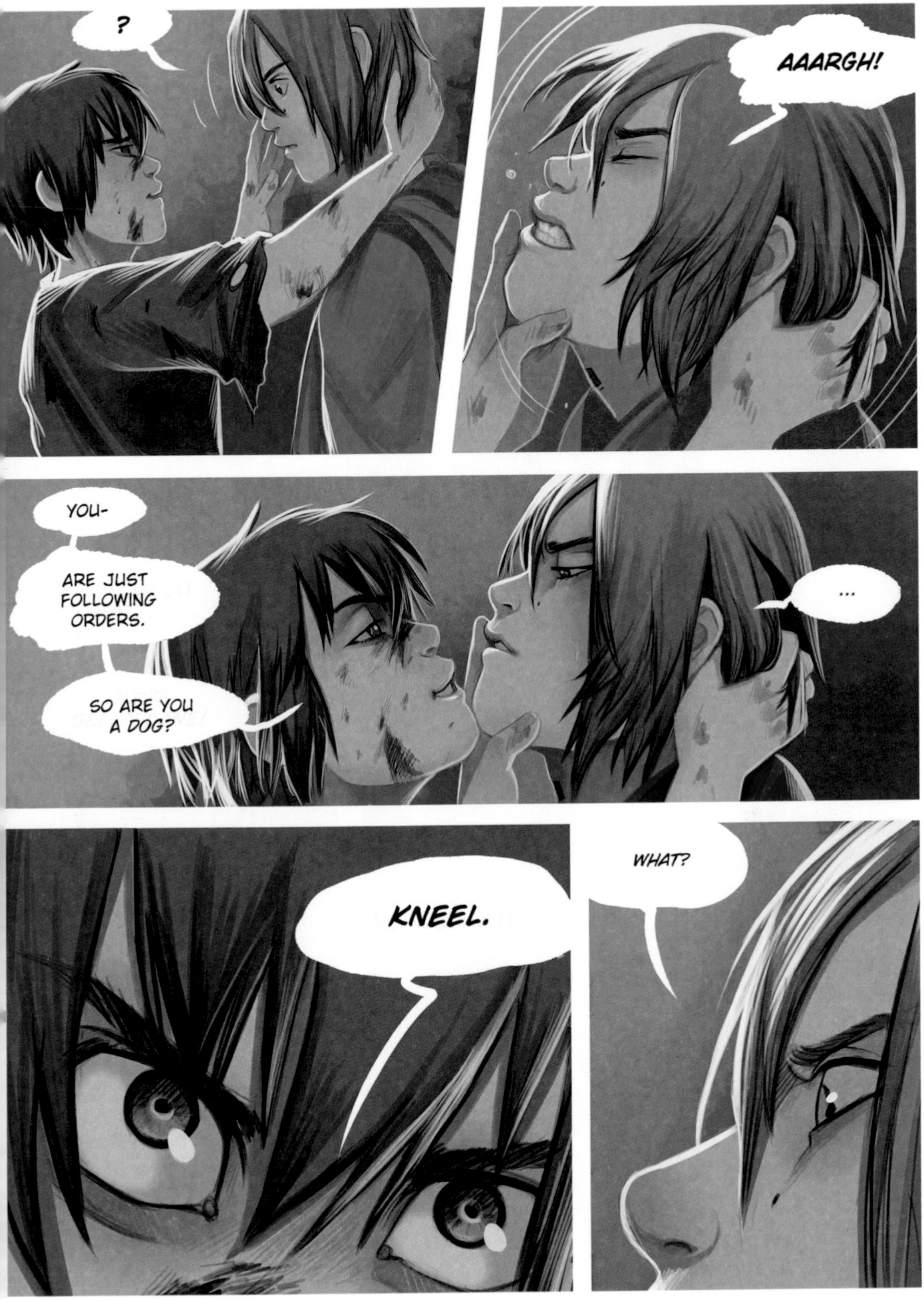
?
AAARGH!
YOU-
ARE JUST FOLLOWING ORDERS.
SO ARE YOU A DOG?
...
KNEEL.
WHAT?

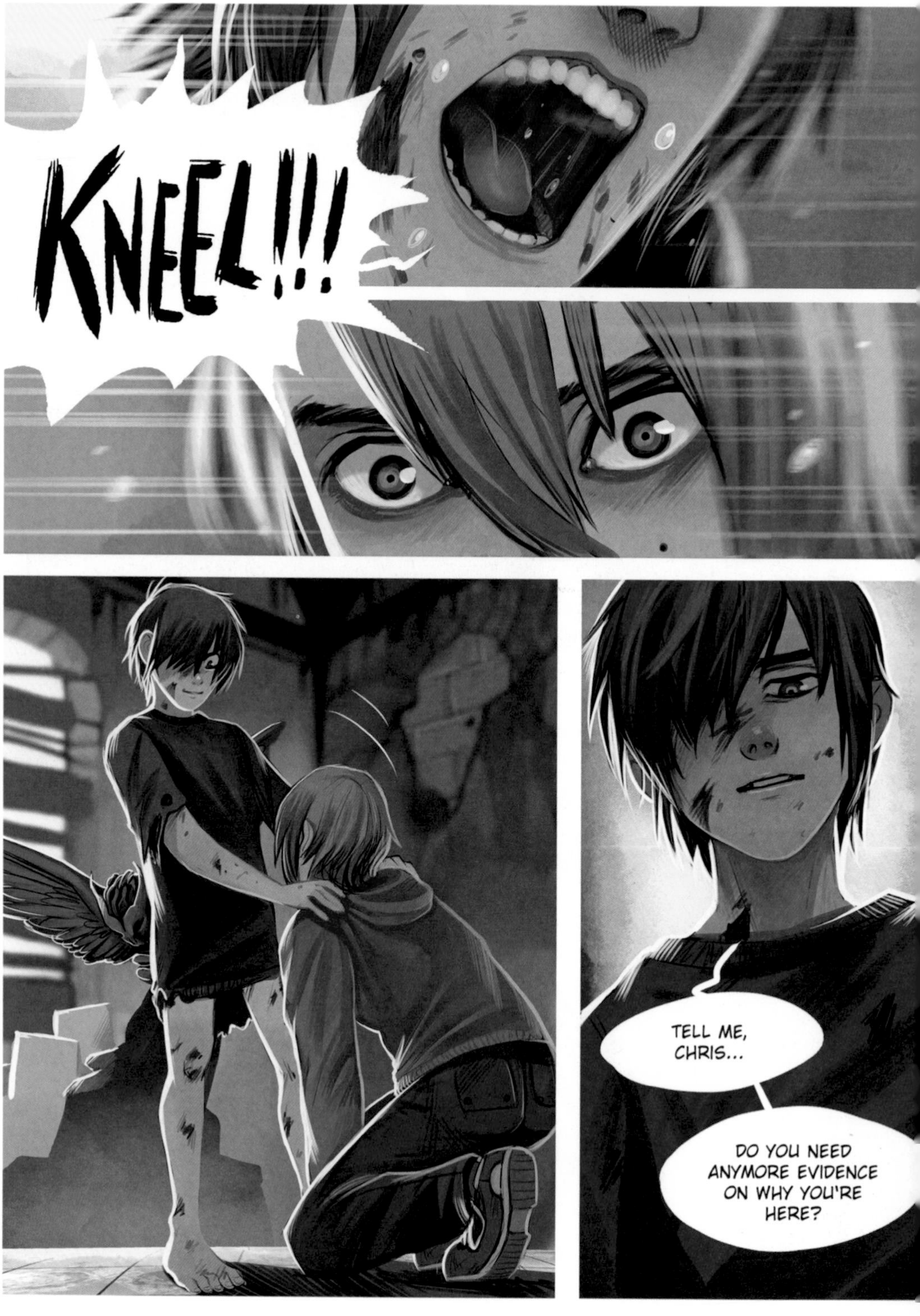
KNEEL!!!
TELL ME, CHRIS...
DO YOU NEED ANYMORE EVIDENCE ON WHY YOU'RE HERE?

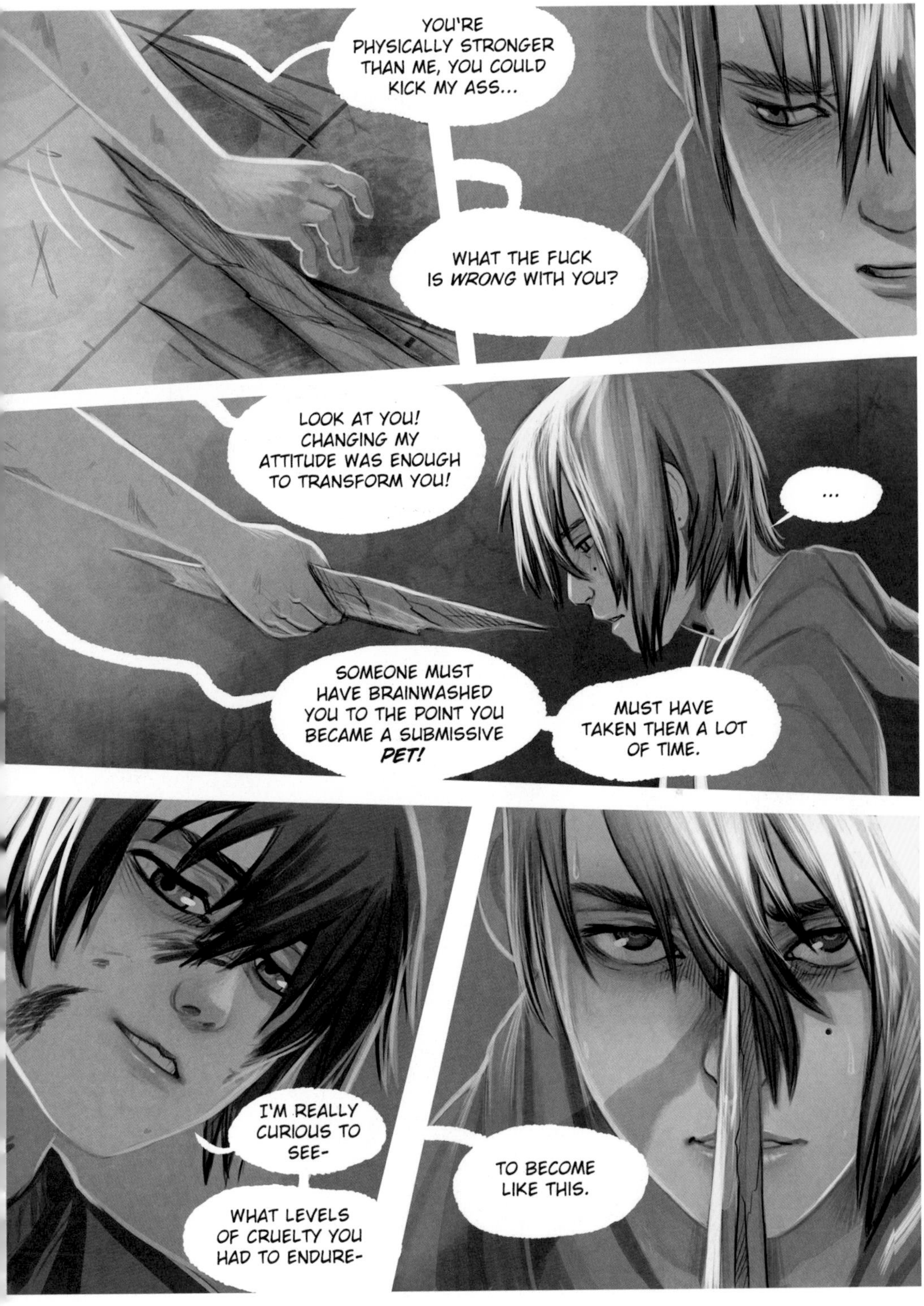
YOU'RE PHYSICALLY STRONGER THAN ME, YOU COULD KICK MY ASS...
WHAT THE FUCK IS *WRONG* WITH YOU?
LOOK AT YOU! CHANGING MY ATTITUDE WAS ENOUGH TO TRANSFORM YOU!
...
SOMEONE MUST HAVE BRAINWASHED YOU TO THE POINT YOU BECAME A SUBMISSIVE ***PET!***
MUST HAVE TAKEN THEM A LOT OF TIME.
I'M REALLY CURIOUS TO SEE-
WHAT LEVELS OF CRUELTY YOU HAD TO ENDURE-
TO BECOME LIKE THIS.

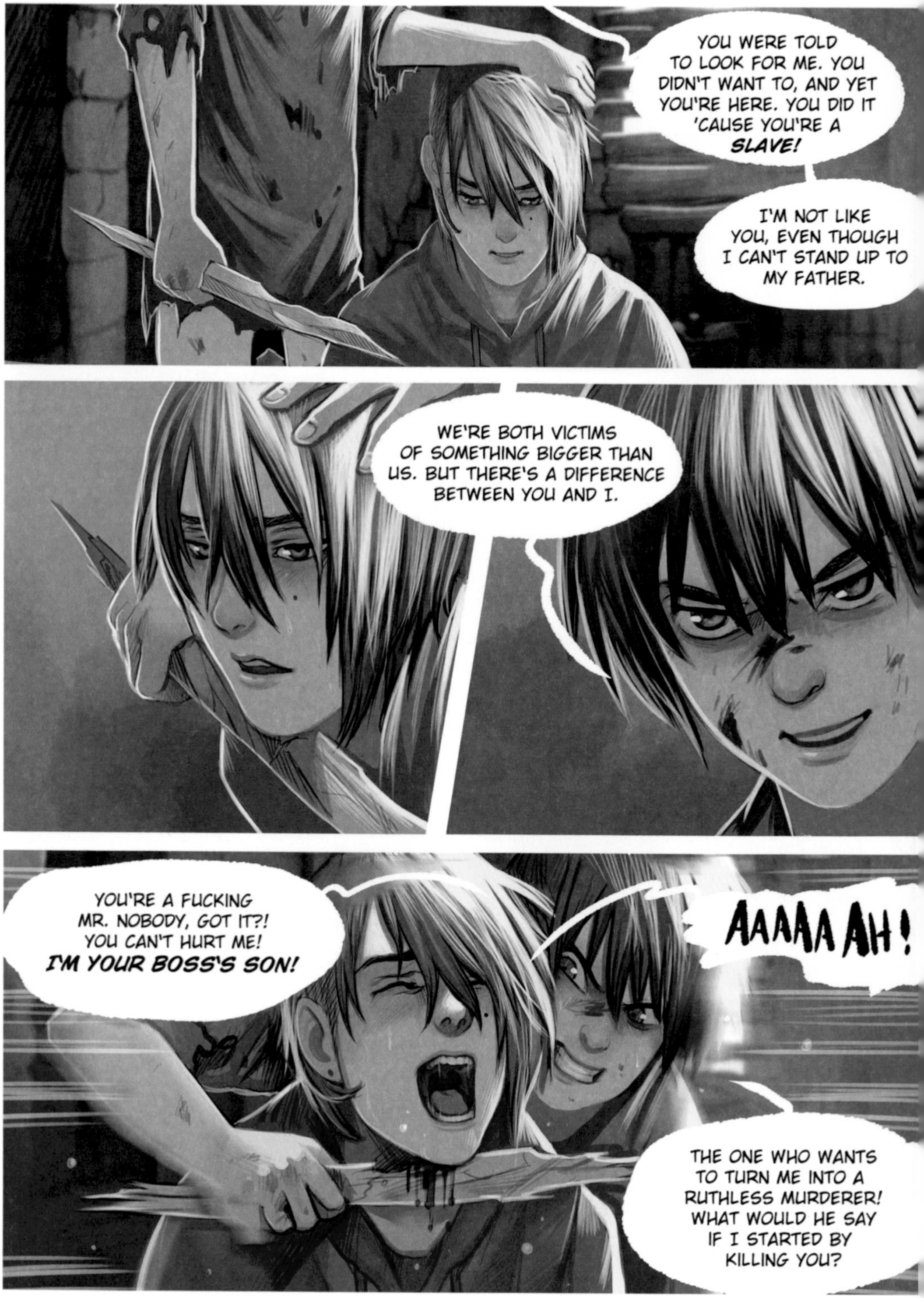
YOU WERE TOLD TO LOOK FOR ME. YOU DIDN'T WANT TO, AND YET YOU'RE HERE. YOU DID IT 'CAUSE YOU'RE A **SLAVE!**
I'M NOT LIKE YOU, EVEN THOUGH I CAN'T STAND UP TO MY FATHER.
WE'RE BOTH VICTIMS OF SOMETHING BIGGER THAN US. BUT THERE'S A DIFFERENCE BETWEEN YOU AND I.
YOU'RE A FUCKING MR. NOBODY, GOT IT?! YOU CAN'T HURT ME! ***I'M YOUR BOSS'S SON!***
AAAAA AH!
THE ONE WHO WANTS TO TURN ME INTO A RUTHLESS MURDERER! WHAT WOULD HE SAY IF I STARTED BY KILLING YOU?

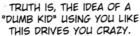
TRUTH IS, THE IDEA OF A "DUMB KID" USING YOU LIKE THIS DRIVES YOU CRAZY.

AAAH!

ALLIE...

AAAAH!

A-ALLIE... PLEASE... LISTEN... TO ME...

YOU DON'T UNDERSTAND...

SHUT UP!

STUMP!

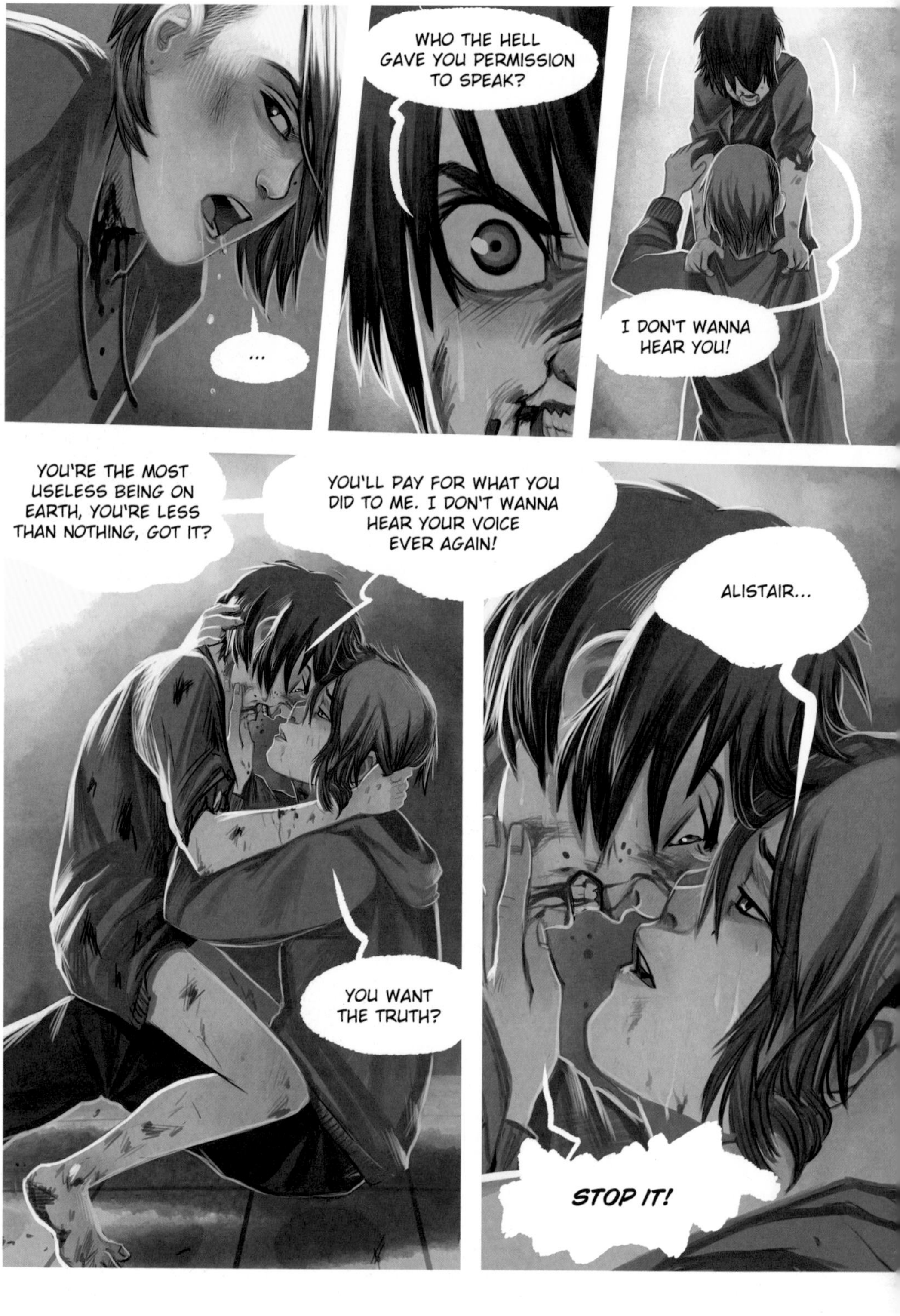
...
WHO THE HELL GAVE YOU PERMISSION TO SPEAK?
I DON'T WANNA HEAR YOU!
YOU'RE THE MOST USELESS BEING ON EARTH, YOU'RE LESS THAN NOTHING, GOT IT?
YOU'LL PAY FOR WHAT YOU DID TO ME. I DON'T WANNA HEAR YOUR VOICE EVER AGAIN!
YOU WANT THE TRUTH?
ALISTAIR...
STOP IT!

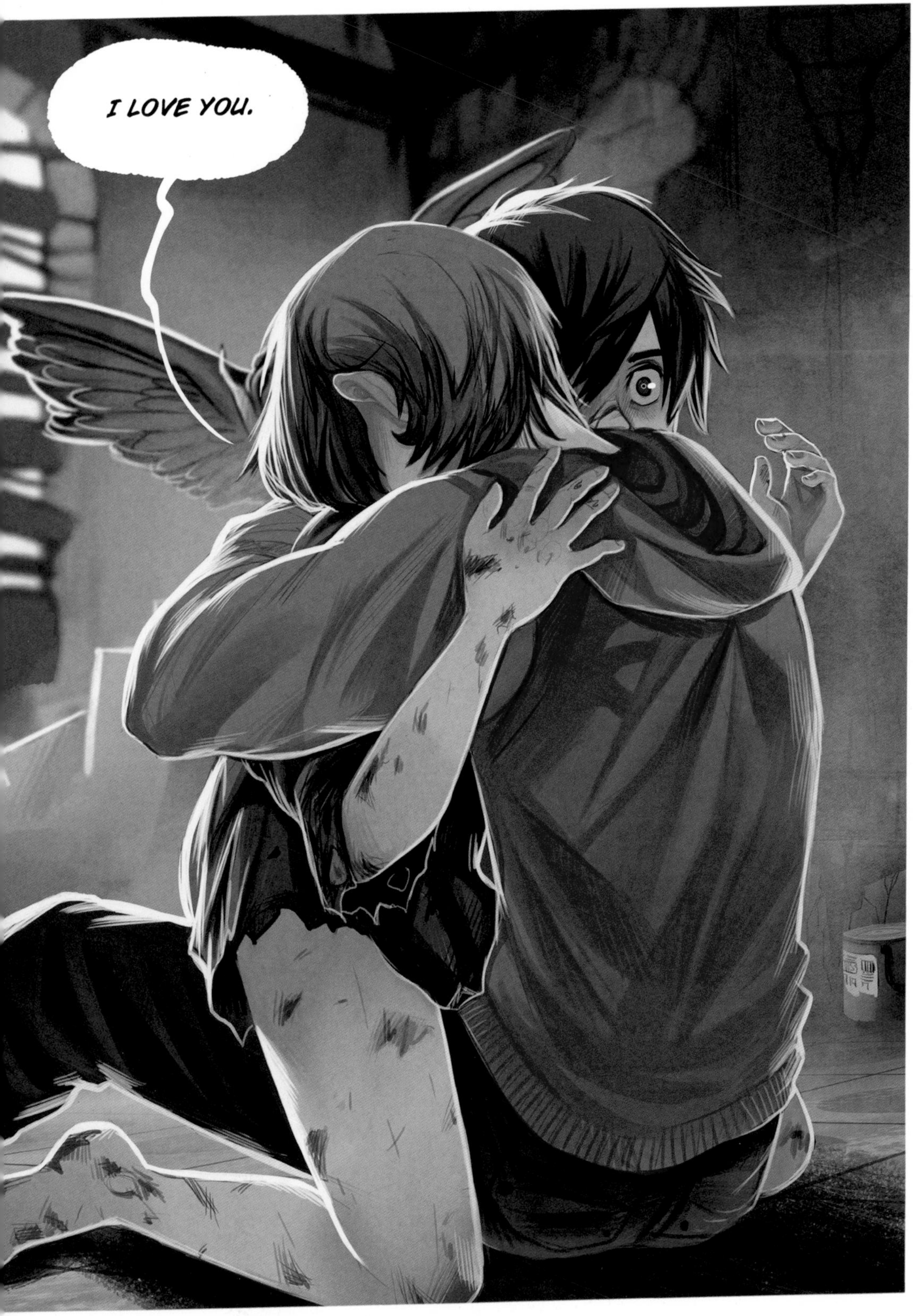
I LOVE YOU.

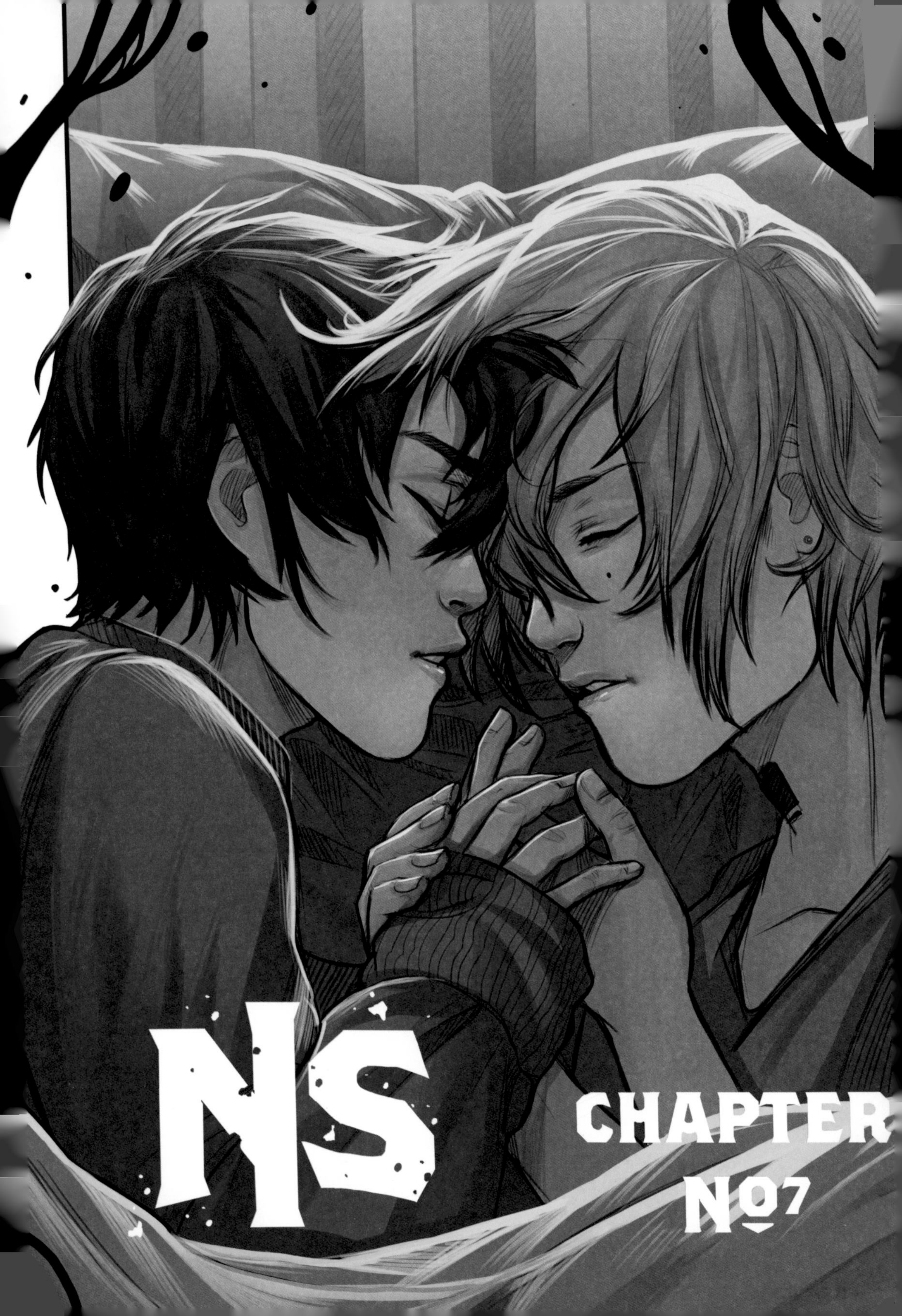
NS
CHAPTER
№7

MOUSE KING.

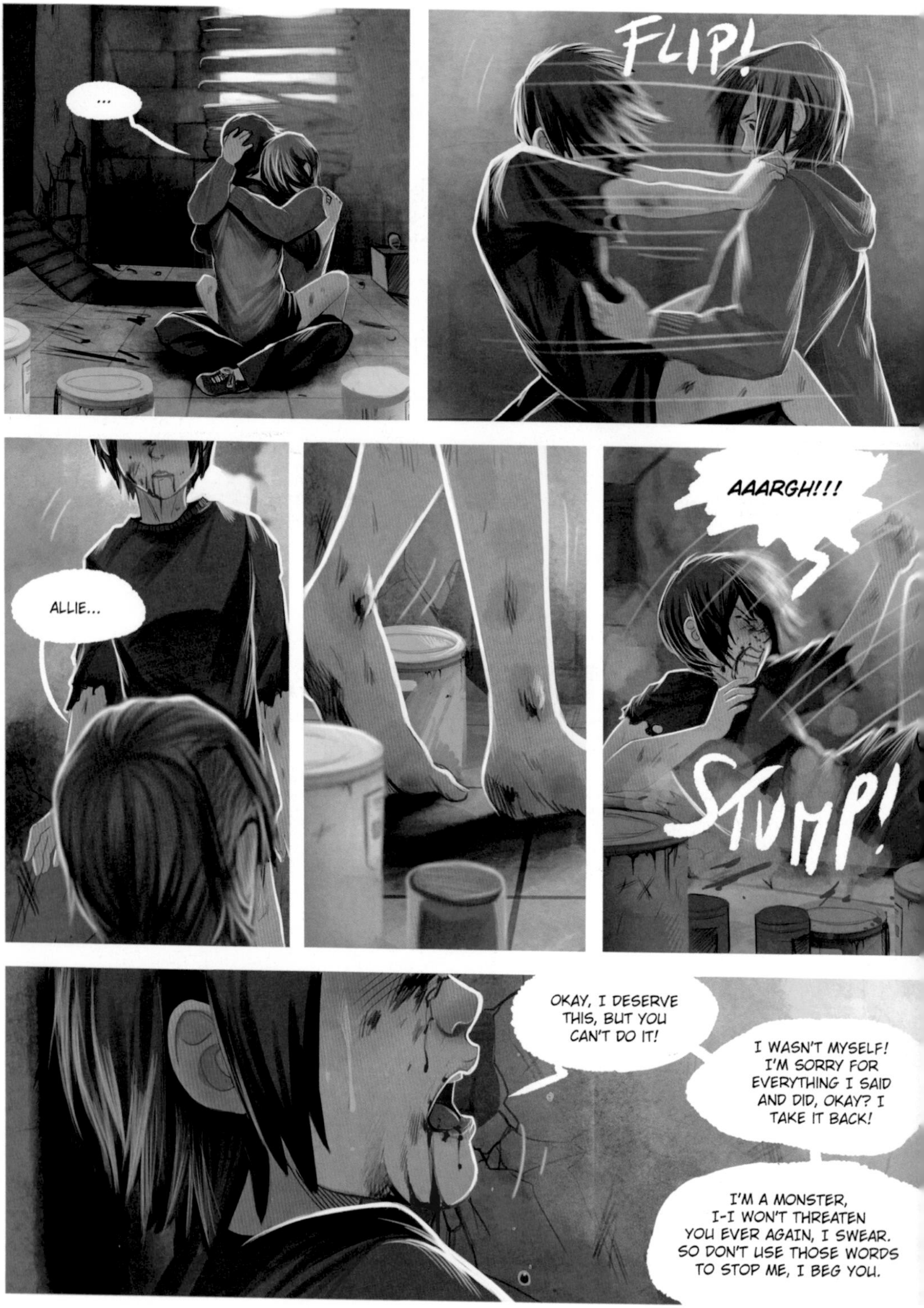
...
FLIP!
ALLIE...
AAARGH!!!
STUMP!
OKAY, I DESERVE THIS, BUT YOU CAN'T DO IT!
I WASN'T MYSELF! I'M SORRY FOR EVERYTHING I SAID AND DID, OKAY? I TAKE IT BACK!
I'M A MONSTER, I-I WON'T THREATEN YOU EVER AGAIN, I SWEAR. SO DON'T USE THOSE WORDS TO STOP ME, I BEG YOU.

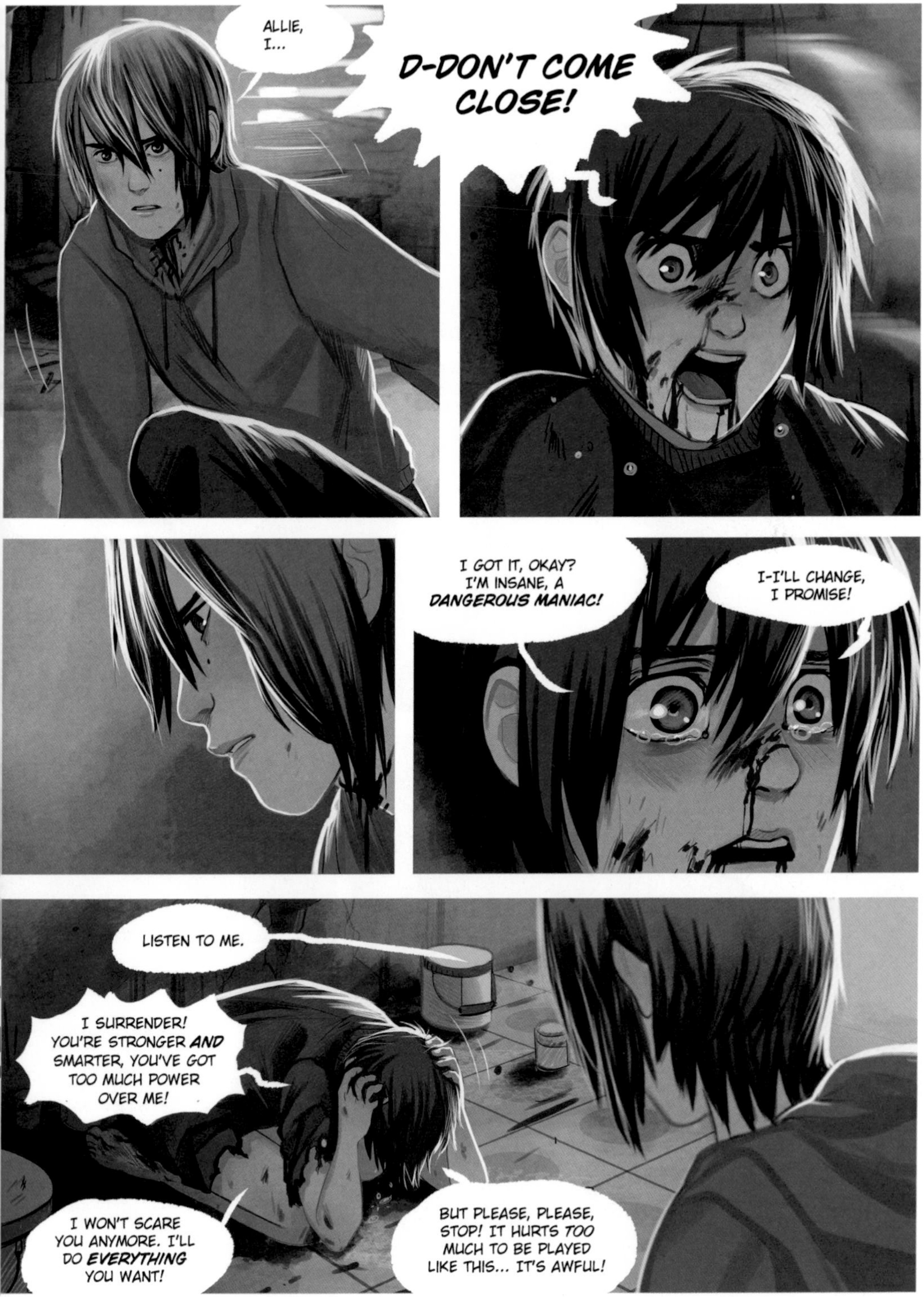
ALLIE, I...
D-DON'T COME CLOSE!
I GOT IT, OKAY? I'M INSANE, A DANGEROUS MANIAC!
I-I'LL CHANGE, I PROMISE!
LISTEN TO ME.
I SURRENDER! YOU'RE STRONGER AND SMARTER, YOU'VE GOT TOO MUCH POWER OVER ME!
I WON'T SCARE YOU ANYMORE. I'LL DO EVERYTHING YOU WANT!
BUT PLEASE, PLEASE, STOP! IT HURTS TOO MUCH TO BE PLAYED LIKE THIS... IT'S AWFUL!

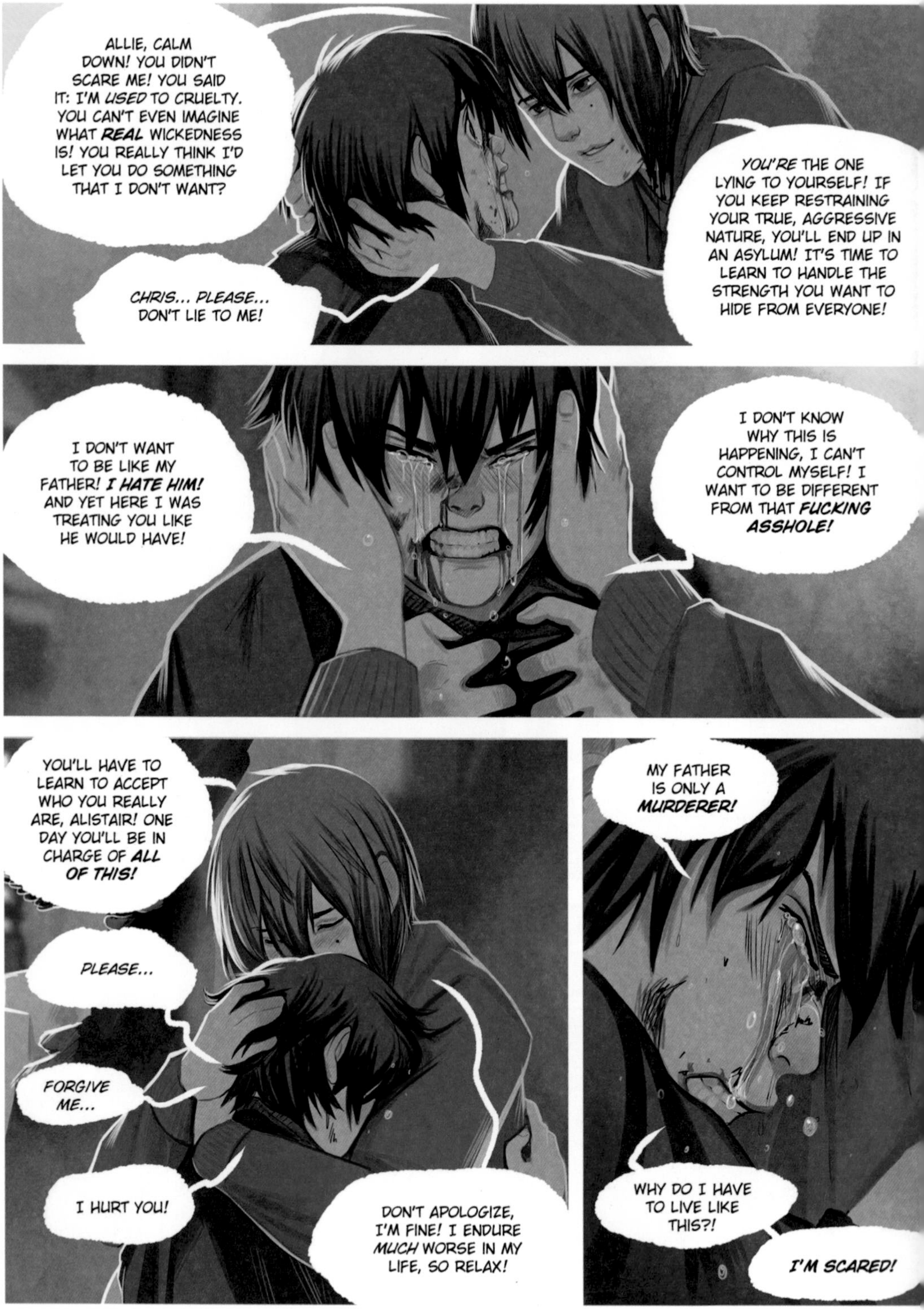
ALLIE, CALM DOWN! YOU DIDN'T SCARE ME! YOU SAID IT: I'M USED TO CRUELTY. YOU CAN'T EVEN IMAGINE WHAT REAL WICKEDNESS IS! YOU REALLY THINK I'D LET YOU DO SOMETHING THAT I DON'T WANT?
CHRIS... PLEASE... DON'T LIE TO ME!
YOU'RE THE ONE LYING TO YOURSELF! IF YOU KEEP RESTRAINING YOUR TRUE, AGGRESSIVE NATURE, YOU'LL END UP IN AN ASYLUM! IT'S TIME TO LEARN TO HANDLE THE STRENGTH YOU WANT TO HIDE FROM EVERYONE!
I DON'T WANT TO BE LIKE MY FATHER! I HATE HIM! AND YET HERE I WAS TREATING YOU LIKE HE WOULD HAVE!
I DON'T KNOW WHY THIS IS HAPPENING, I CAN'T CONTROL MYSELF! I WANT TO BE DIFFERENT FROM THAT FUCKING ASSHOLE!
YOU'LL HAVE TO LEARN TO ACCEPT WHO YOU REALLY ARE, ALISTAIR! ONE DAY YOU'LL BE IN CHARGE OF ALL OF THIS!
PLEASE...
FORGIVE ME...
I HURT YOU!
DON'T APOLOGIZE, I'M FINE! I ENDURE MUCH WORSE IN MY LIFE, SO RELAX!
MY FATHER IS ONLY A MURDERER!
WHY DO I HAVE TO LIVE LIKE THIS?!
I'M SCARED!

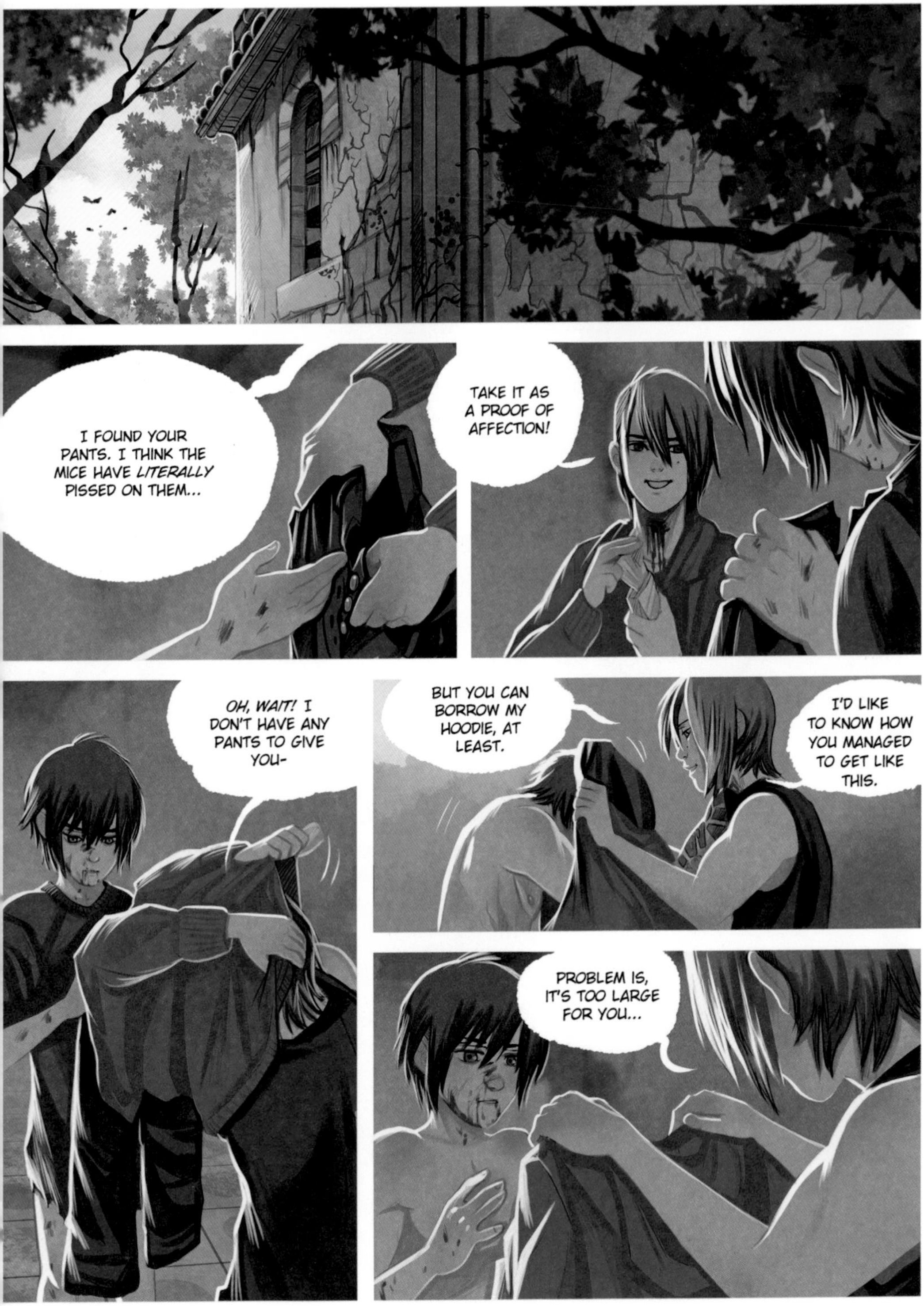
I FOUND YOUR PANTS. I THINK THE MICE HAVE *LITERALLY* PISSED ON THEM...
TAKE IT AS A PROOF OF AFFECTION!
OH, WAIT! I DON'T HAVE ANY PANTS TO GIVE YOU-
BUT YOU CAN BORROW MY HOODIE, AT LEAST.
I'D LIKE TO KNOW HOW YOU MANAGED TO GET LIKE THIS.
PROBLEM IS, IT'S TOO LARGE FOR YOU...

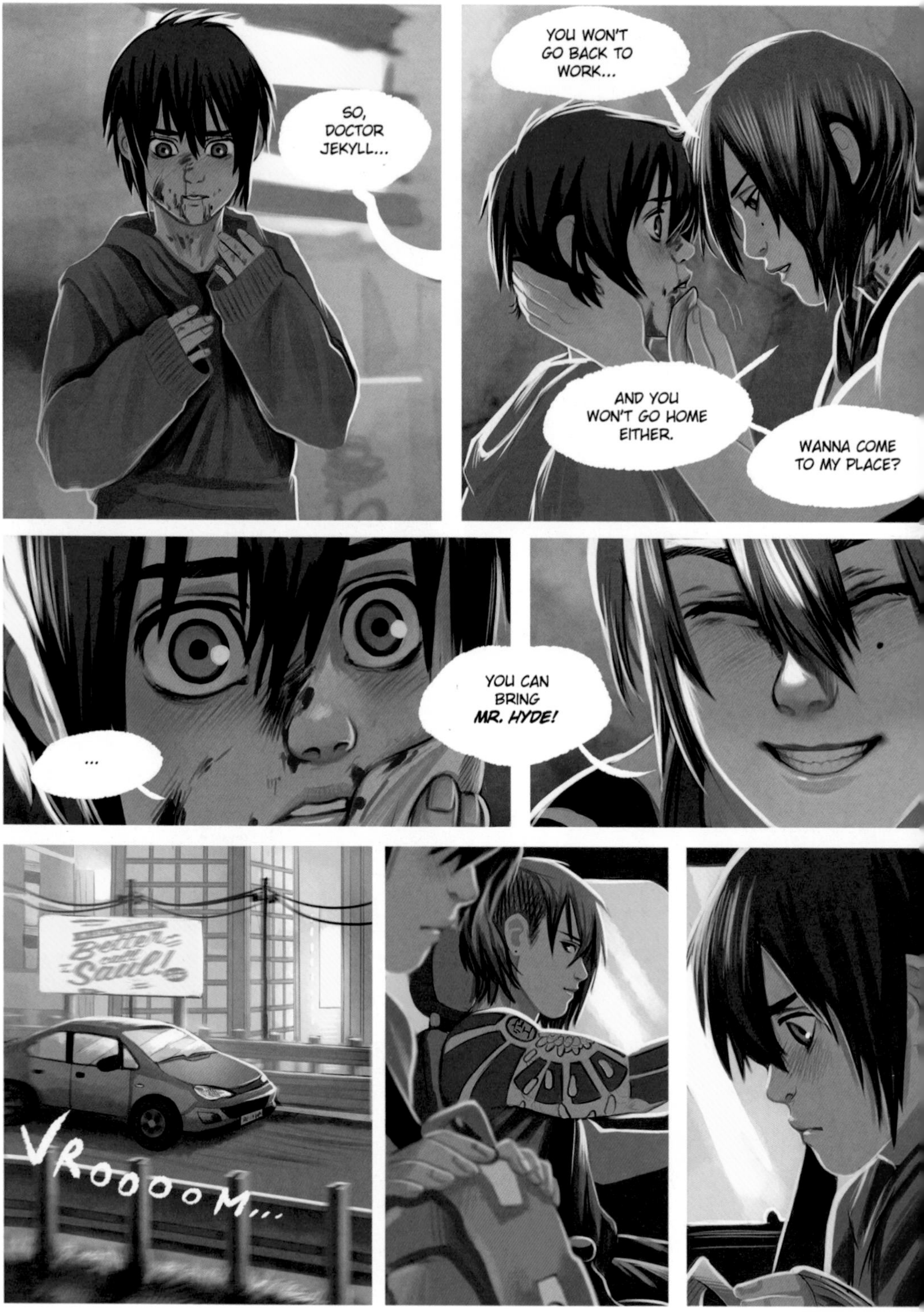
SO, DOCTOR JEKYLL...
YOU WON'T GO BACK TO WORK...
AND YOU WON'T GO HOME EITHER.
WANNA COME TO MY PLACE?
...
YOU CAN BRING ***MR. HYDE!***
Better call Saul!
VROOOOOM...

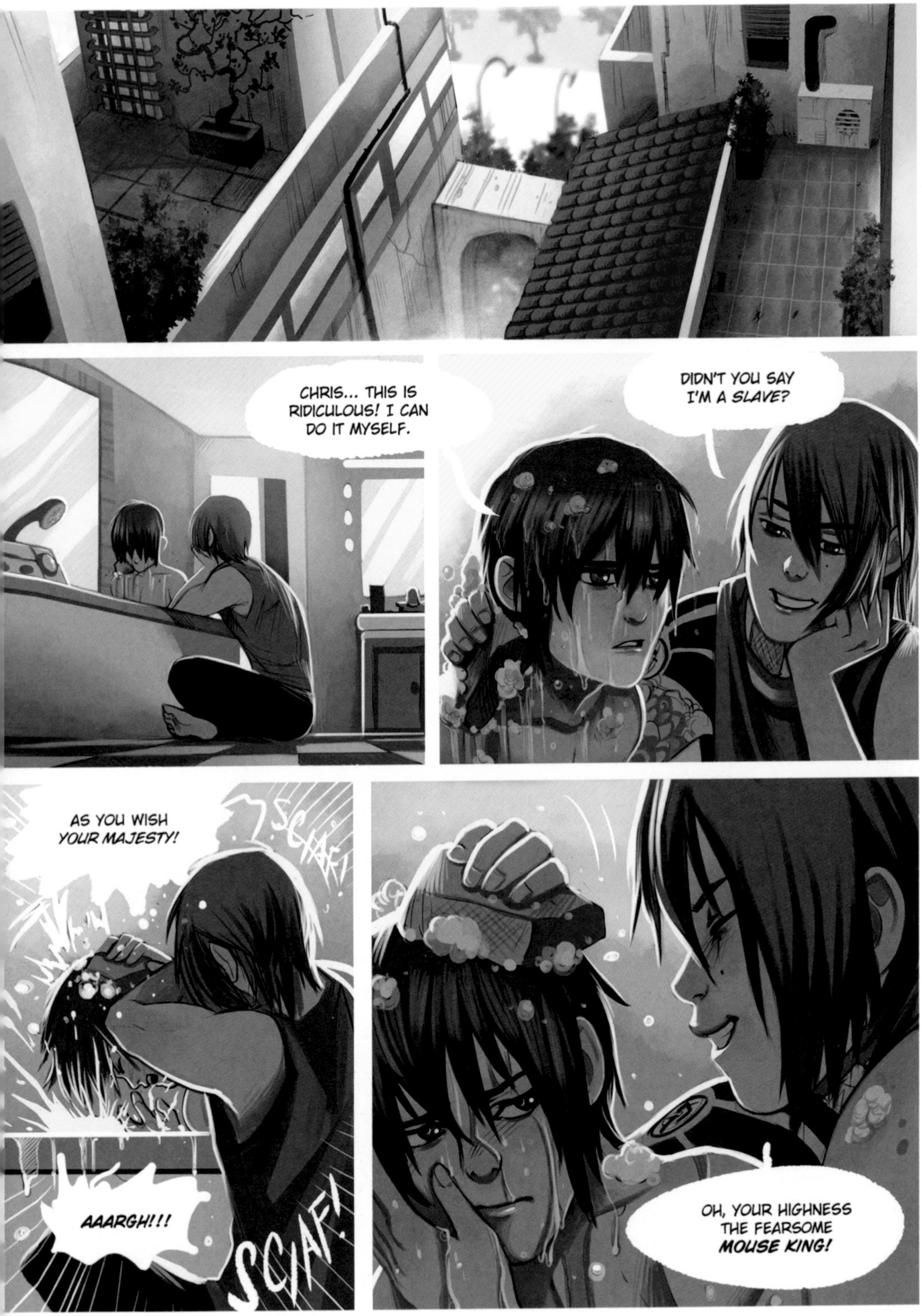
CHRIS... THIS IS RIDICULOUS! I CAN DO IT MYSELF.
DIDN'T YOU SAY I'M A *SLAVE*?
AS YOU WISH *YOUR MAJESTY!*
SCIAF!
AAARGH!!!
SCIAF!
OH, YOUR HIGHNESS THE FEARSOME ***MOUSE KING!***

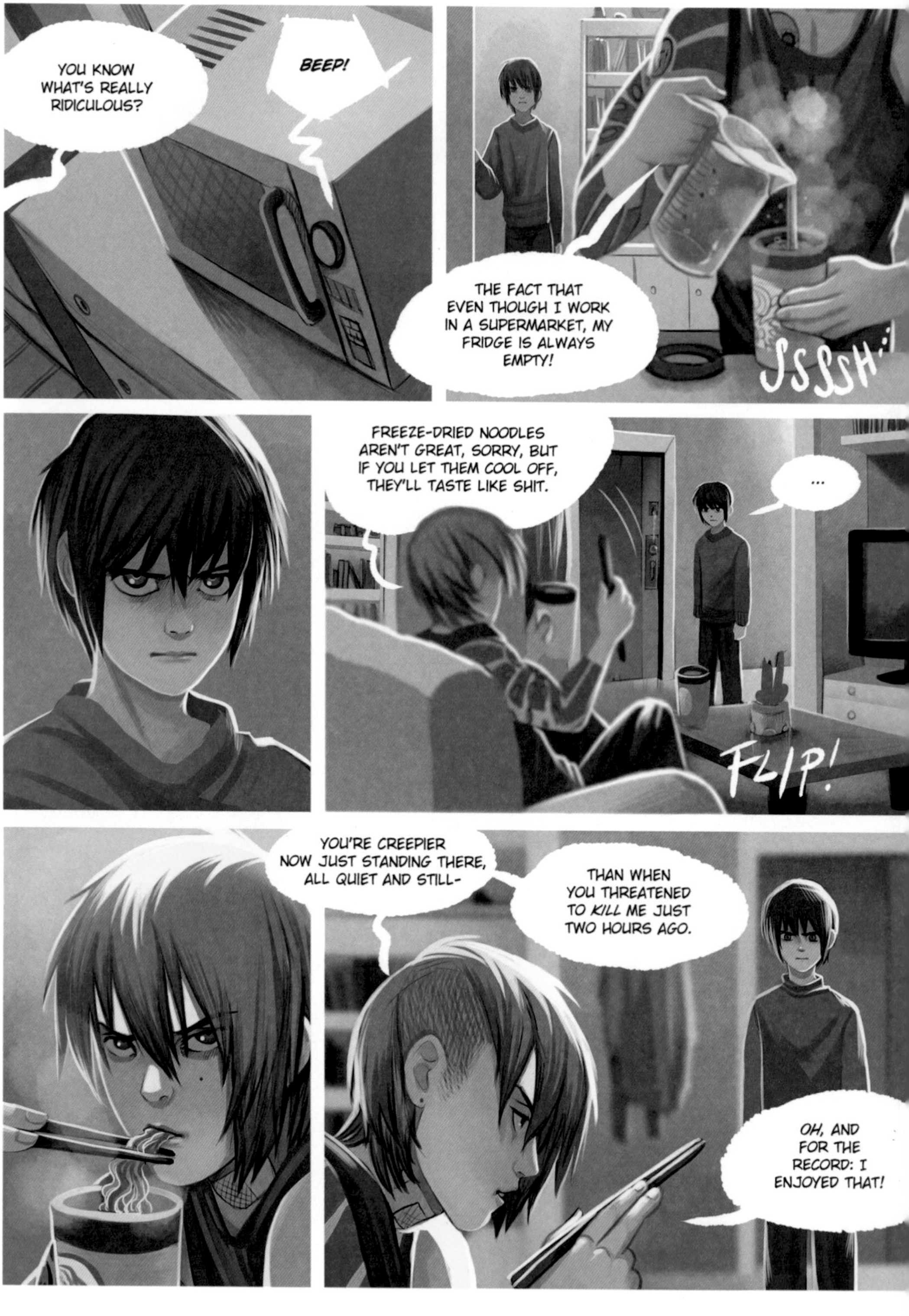
YOU KNOW WHAT'S REALLY RIDICULOUS?
BEEP!
THE FACT THAT EVEN THOUGH I WORK IN A SUPERMARKET, MY FRIDGE IS ALWAYS EMPTY!
SSSSH...
FREEZE-DRIED NOODLES AREN'T GREAT, SORRY, BUT IF YOU LET THEM COOL OFF, THEY'LL TASTE LIKE SHIT.
...
FLIP!
YOU'RE CREEPIER NOW JUST STANDING THERE, ALL QUIET AND STILL-
THAN WHEN YOU THREATENED TO *KILL* ME JUST TWO HOURS AGO.
OH, AND FOR THE RECORD: I ENJOYED THAT!

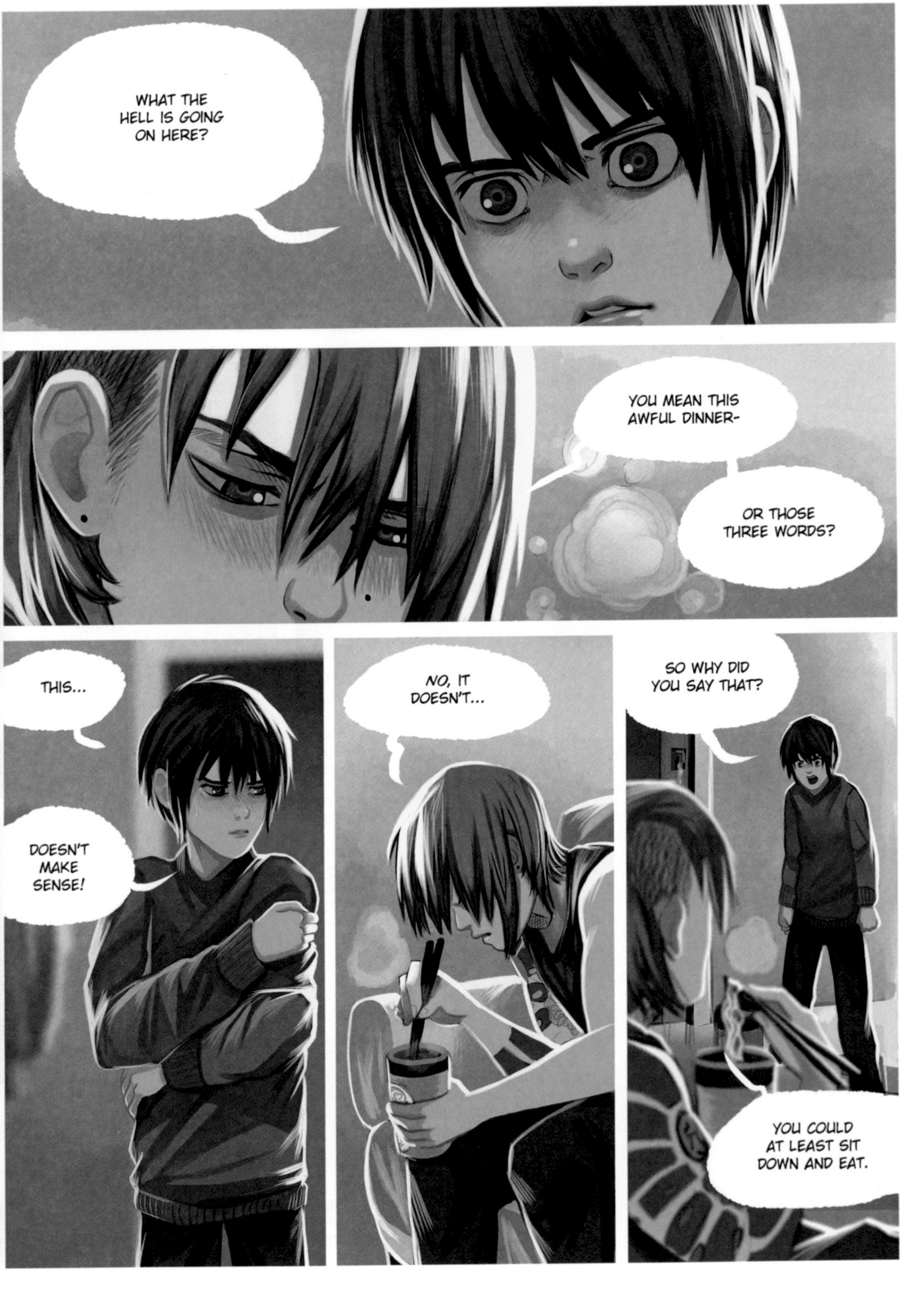
WHAT THE HELL IS GOING ON HERE?
YOU MEAN THIS AWFUL DINNER-
OR THOSE THREE WORDS?
THIS...
DOESN'T MAKE SENSE!
NO, IT DOESN'T...
SO WHY DID YOU SAY THAT?
YOU COULD AT LEAST SIT DOWN AND EAT.

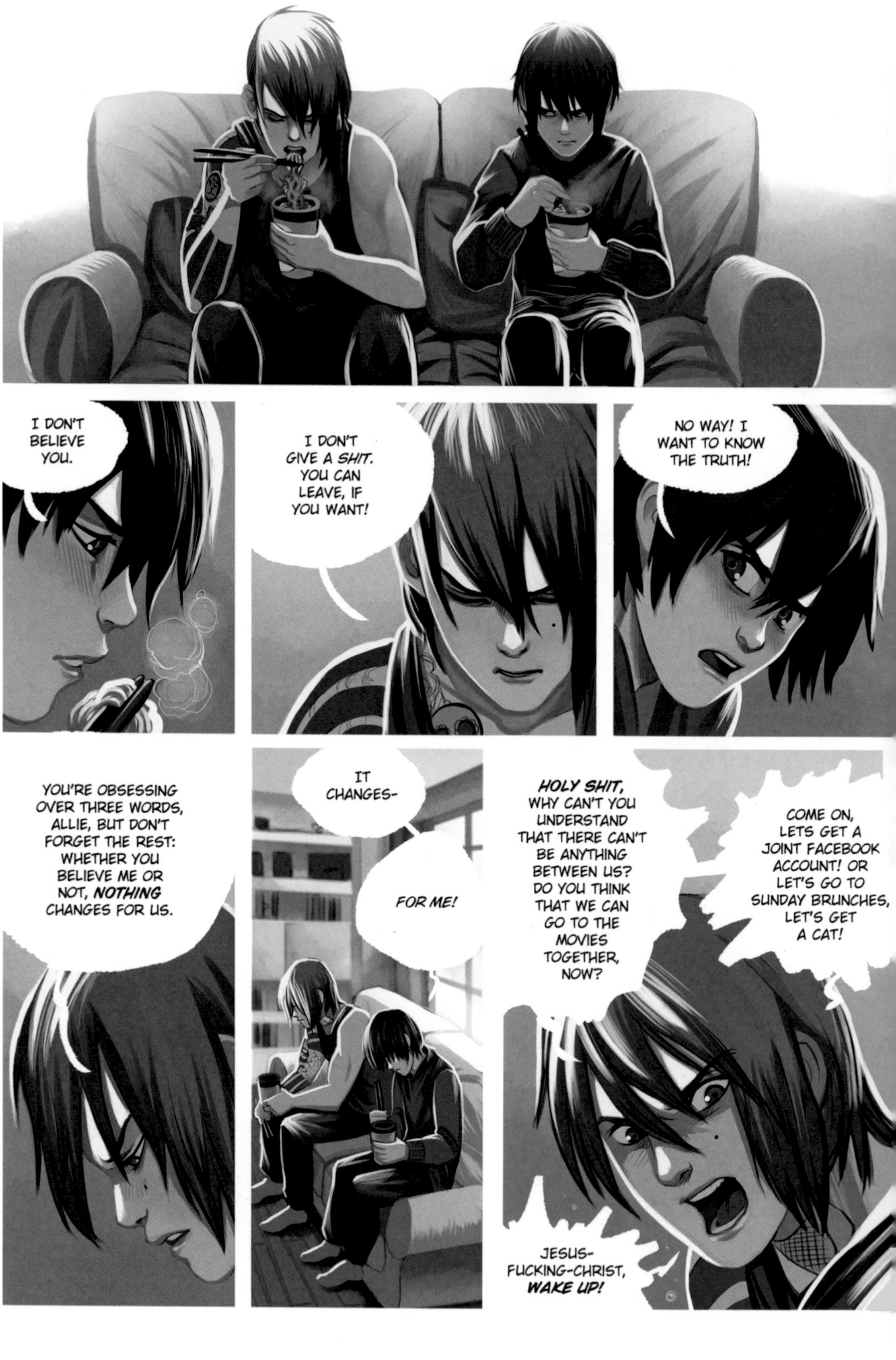
I DON'T BELIEVE YOU.
I DON'T GIVE A *SHIT*. YOU CAN LEAVE, IF YOU WANT!
NO WAY! I WANT TO KNOW THE TRUTH!
YOU'RE OBSESSING OVER THREE WORDS, ALLIE, BUT DON'T FORGET THE REST: WHETHER YOU BELIEVE ME OR NOT, ***NOTHING*** CHANGES FOR US.
IT CHANGES-
FOR ME!
HOLY SHIT, WHY CAN'T YOU UNDERSTAND THAT THERE CAN'T BE ANYTHING BETWEEN US? DO YOU THINK THAT WE CAN GO TO THE MOVIES TOGETHER, NOW?
COME ON, LETS GET A JOINT FACEBOOK ACCOUNT! OR LET'S GO TO SUNDAY BRUNCHES, LET'S GET A CAT!
JESUS-FUCKING-CHRIST, ***WAKE UP!***

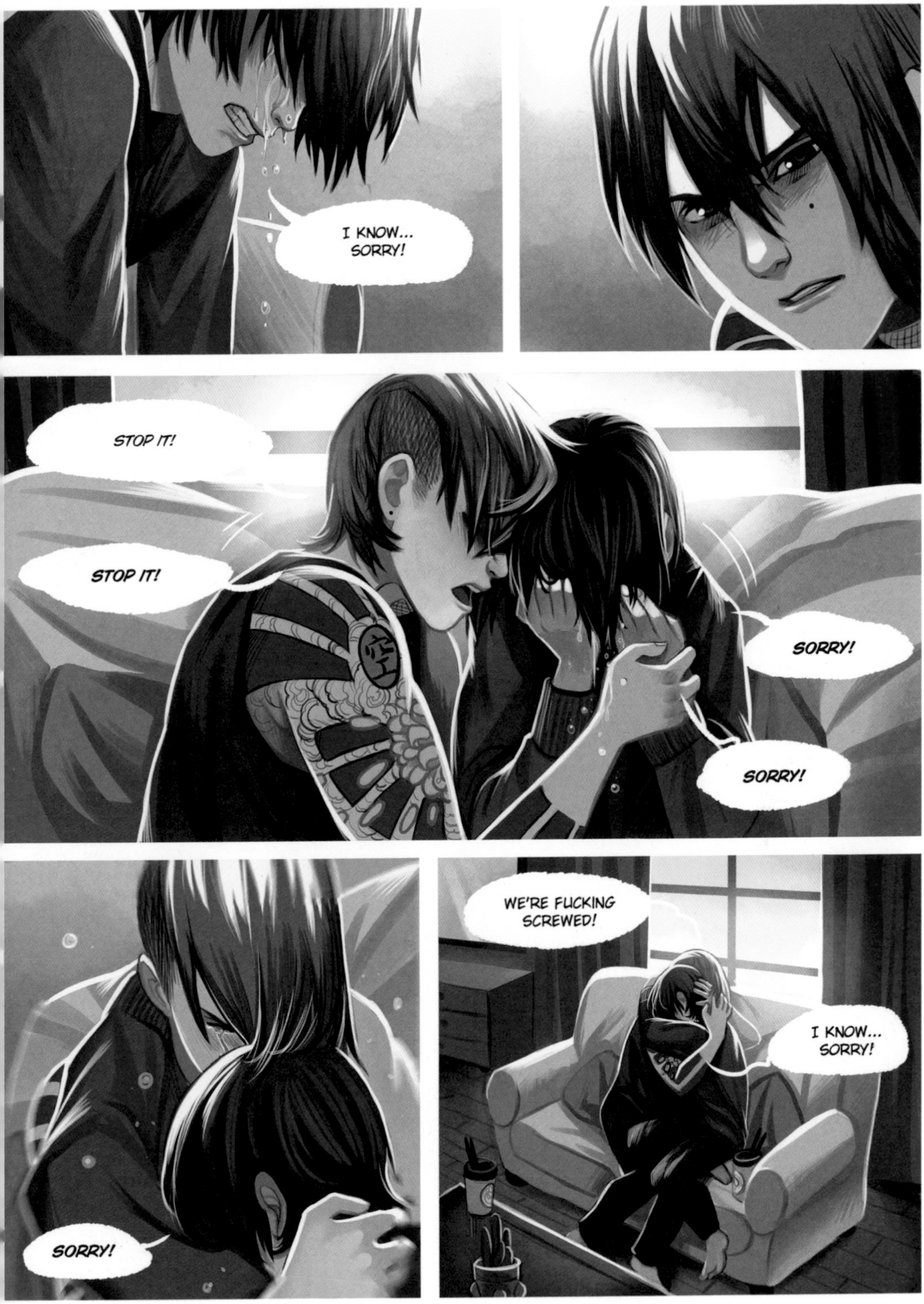
I KNOW... SORRY!
STOP IT!
STOP IT!
SORRY!
SORRY!
SORRY!
WE'RE FUCKING SCREWED!
I KNOW... SORRY!

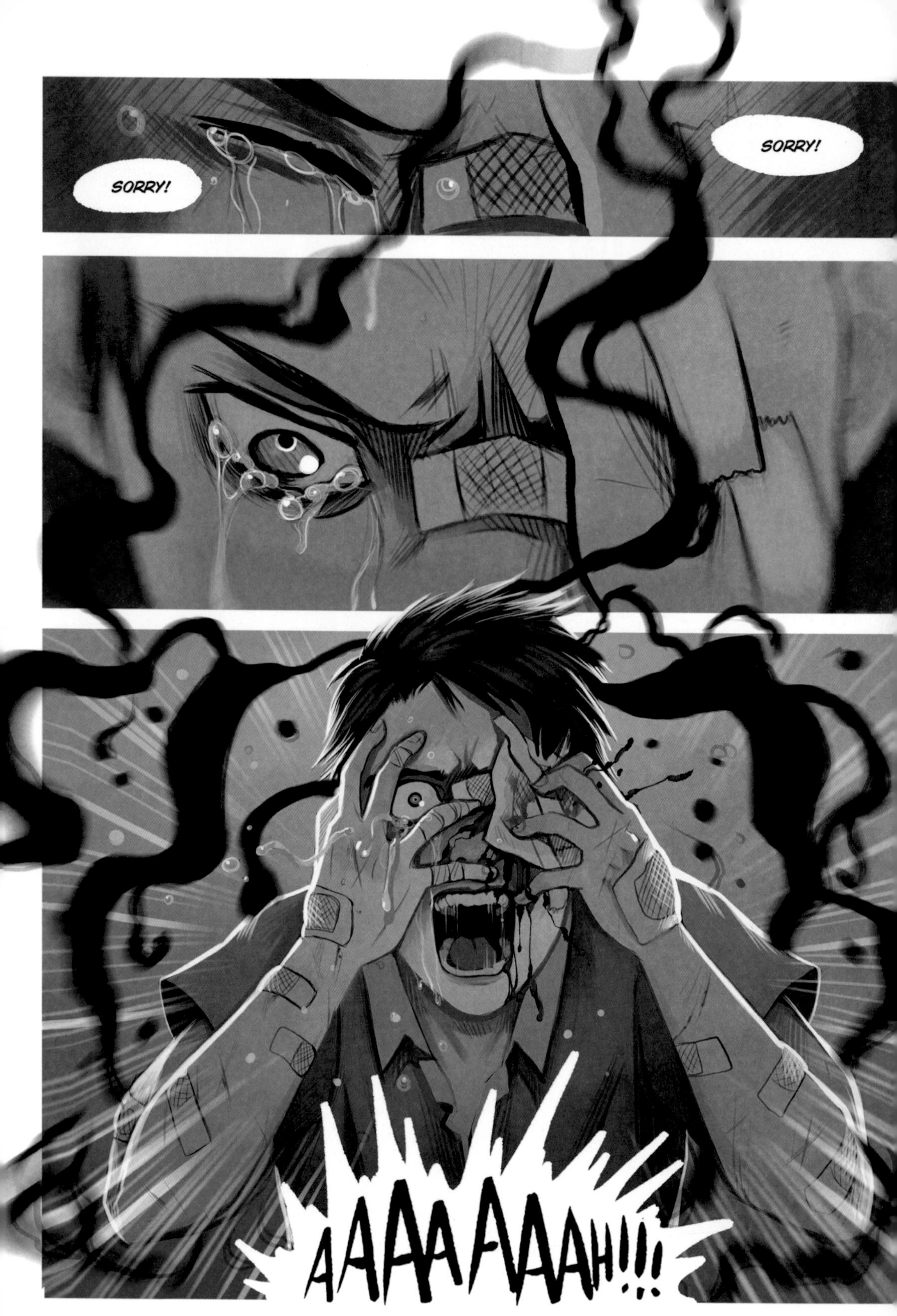
SORRY!
SORRY!
AAAAAAAH!!!

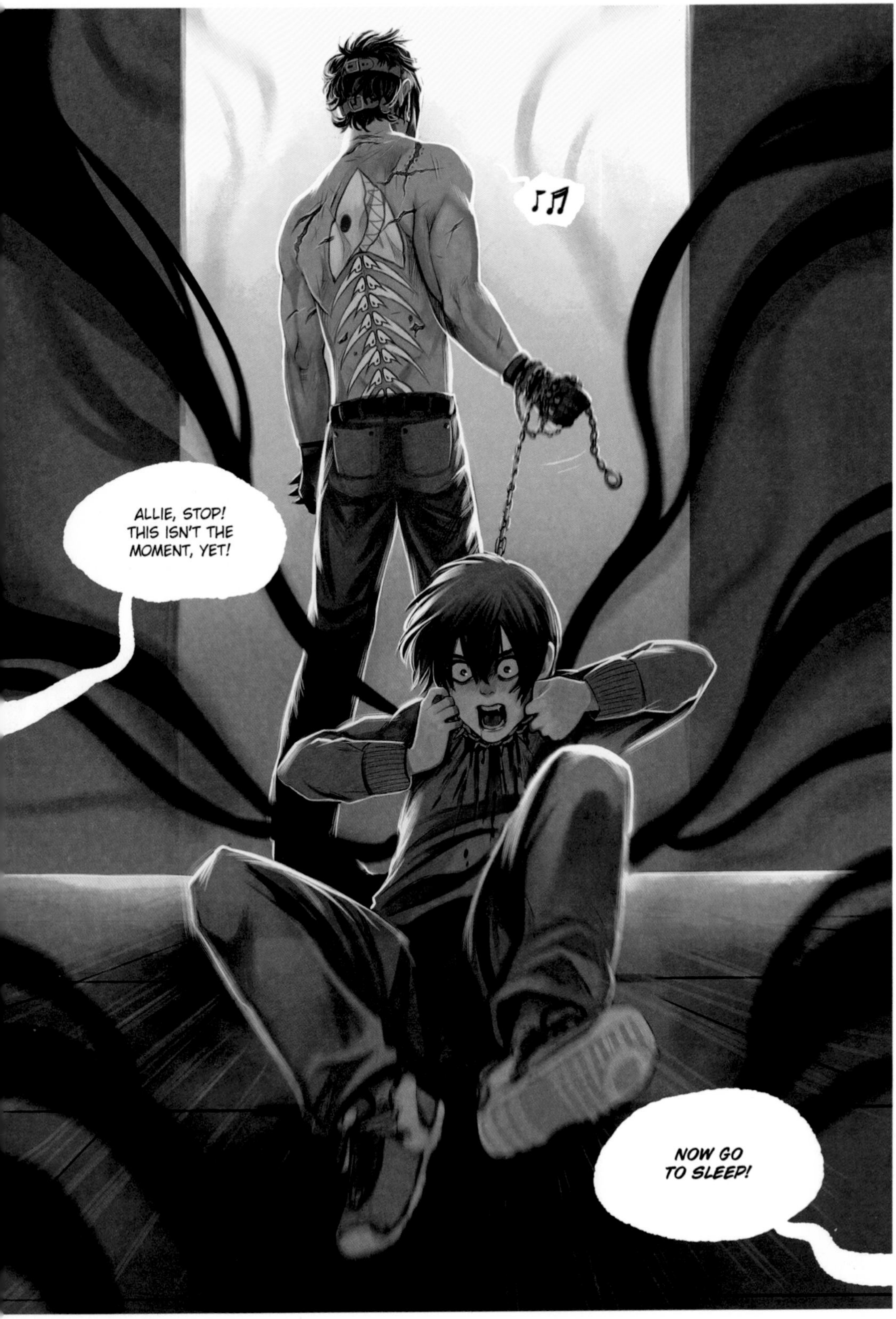
ALLIE, STOP! THIS ISN'T THE MOMENT, YET!
NOW GO TO SLEEP!

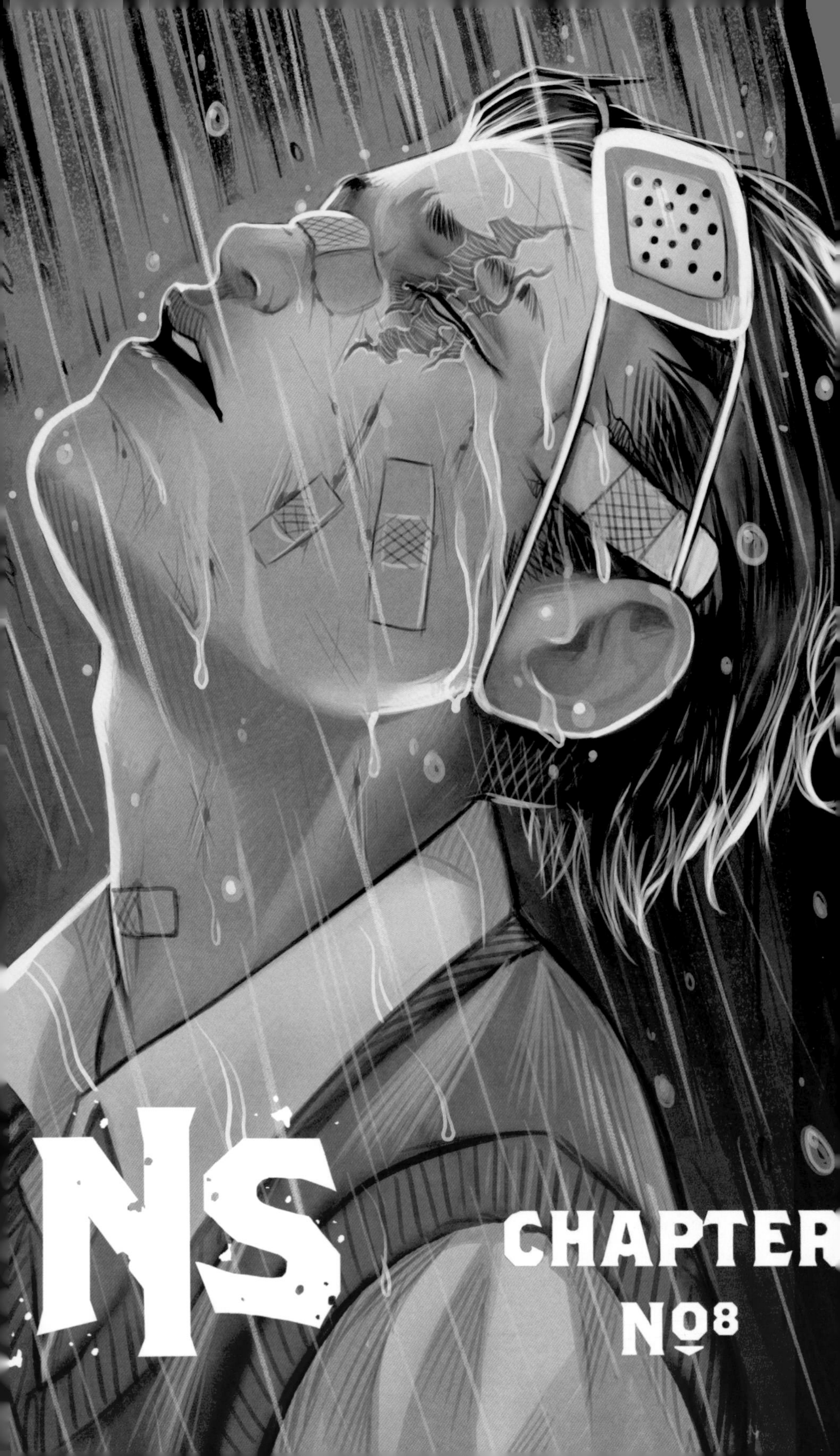
NS
CHAPTER
№8

MUSIC CLASS.

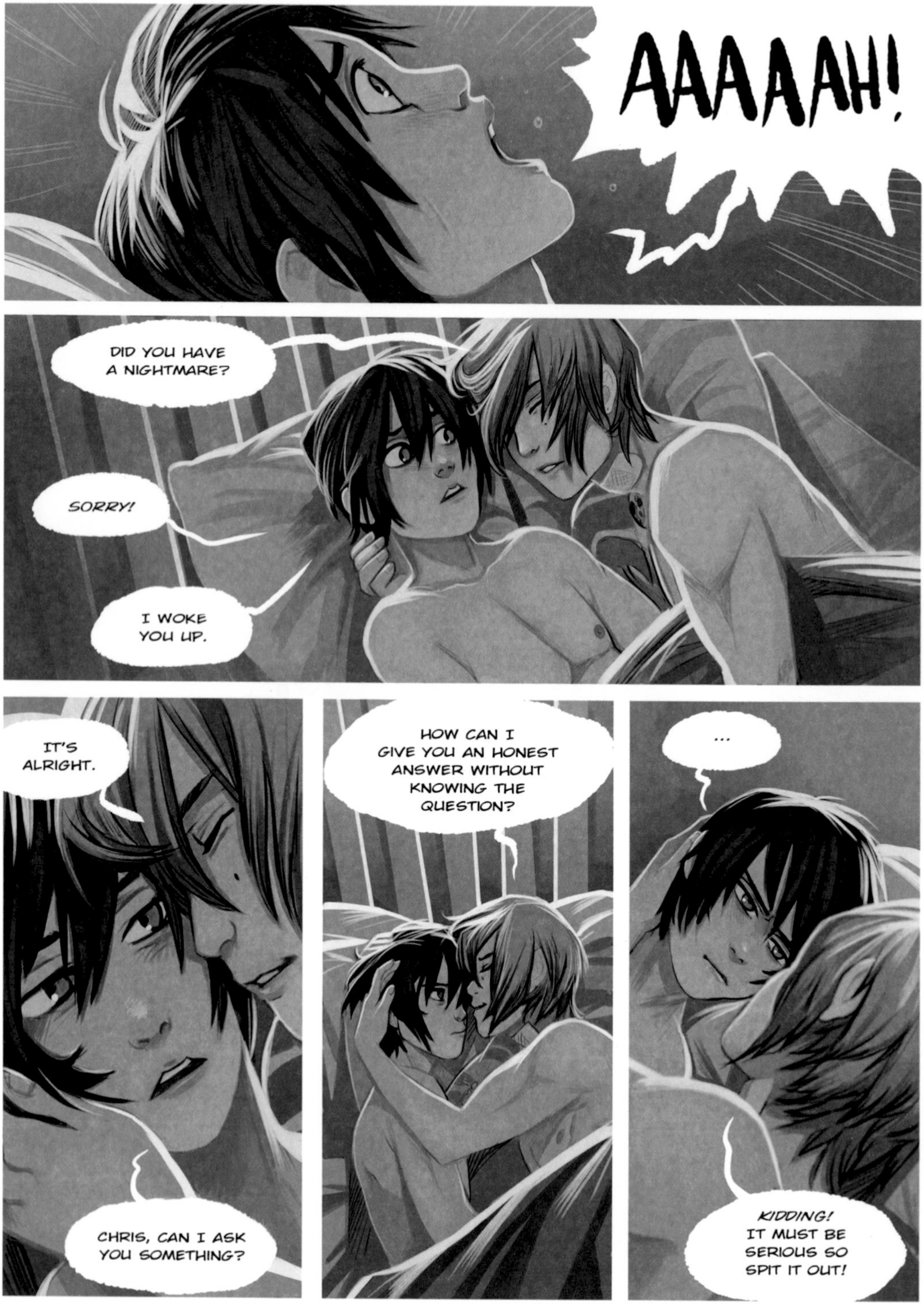
AAAAAH!
DID YOU HAVE A NIGHTMARE?
SORRY!
I WOKE YOU UP.
IT'S ALRIGHT.
CHRIS, CAN I ASK YOU SOMETHING?
HOW CAN I GIVE YOU AN HONEST ANSWER WITHOUT KNOWING THE QUESTION?
...
KIDDING! IT MUST BE SERIOUS SO SPIT IT OUT!

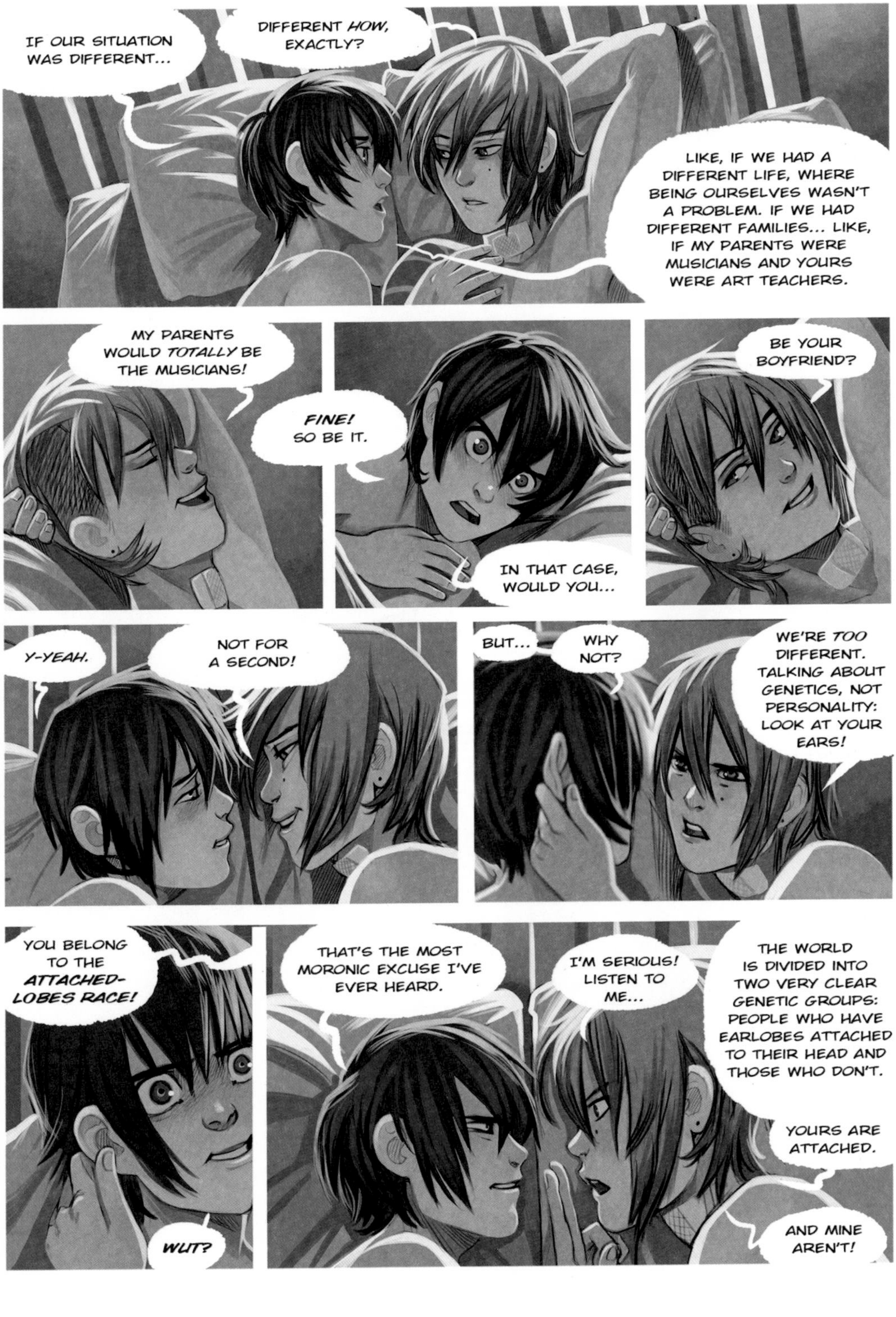
IF OUR SITUATION WAS DIFFERENT...
DIFFERENT *HOW,* EXACTLY?
LIKE, IF WE HAD A DIFFERENT LIFE, WHERE BEING OURSELVES WASN'T A PROBLEM. IF WE HAD DIFFERENT FAMILIES... LIKE, IF MY PARENTS WERE MUSICIANS AND YOURS WERE ART TEACHERS.
MY PARENTS WOULD *TOTALLY* BE THE MUSICIANS!
FINE! SO BE IT.
IN THAT CASE, WOULD YOU...
BE YOUR BOYFRIEND?
Y-YEAH.
NOT FOR A SECOND!
BUT...
WHY NOT?
WE'RE *TOO* DIFFERENT. TALKING ABOUT GENETICS, NOT PERSONALITY: LOOK AT YOUR EARS!
YOU BELONG TO THE *ATTACHED-LOBES RACE!*
WUT?
THAT'S THE MOST MORONIC EXCUSE I'VE EVER HEARD.
I'M SERIOUS! LISTEN TO ME...
THE WORLD IS DIVIDED INTO TWO VERY CLEAR GENETIC GROUPS: PEOPLE WHO HAVE EARLOBES ATTACHED TO THEIR HEAD AND THOSE WHO DON'T.
YOURS ARE ATTACHED.
AND MINE AREN'T!

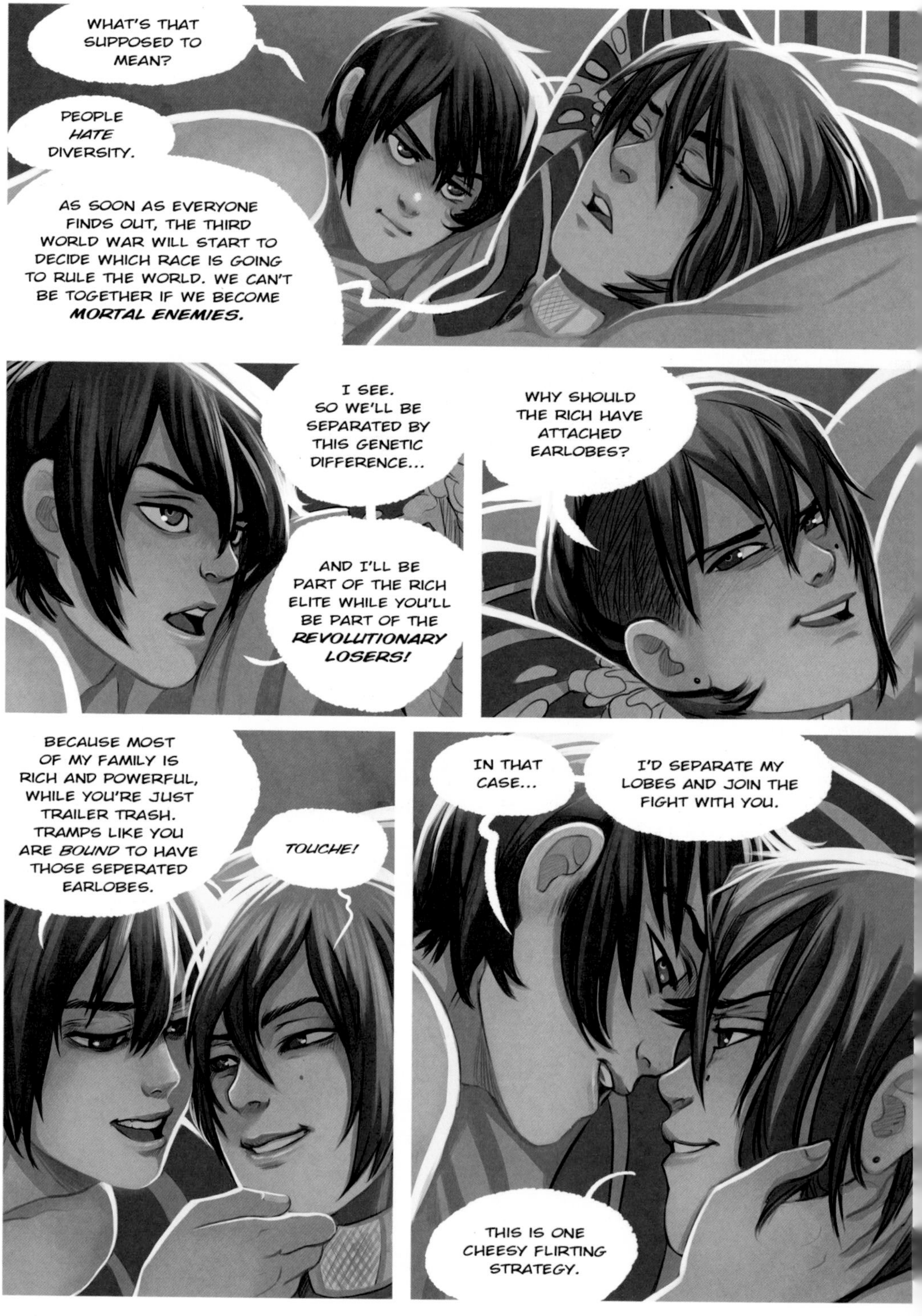
WHAT'S THAT SUPPOSED TO MEAN?
PEOPLE *HATE* DIVERSITY.
AS SOON AS EVERYONE FINDS OUT, THE THIRD WORLD WAR WILL START TO DECIDE WHICH RACE IS GOING TO RULE THE WORLD. WE CAN'T BE TOGETHER IF WE BECOME ***MORTAL ENEMIES.***
I SEE. SO WE'LL BE SEPARATED BY THIS GENETIC DIFFERENCE...
AND I'LL BE PART OF THE RICH ELITE WHILE YOU'LL BE PART OF THE ***REVOLUTIONARY LOSERS!***
WHY SHOULD THE RICH HAVE ATTACHED EARLOBES?
BECAUSE MOST OF MY FAMILY IS RICH AND POWERFUL, WHILE YOU'RE JUST TRAILER TRASH. TRAMPS LIKE YOU ARE *BOUND* TO HAVE THOSE SEPERATED EARLOBES.
TOUCHE!
IN THAT CASE...
I'D SEPARATE MY LOBES AND JOIN THE FIGHT WITH YOU.
THIS IS ONE CHEESY FLIRTING STRATEGY.

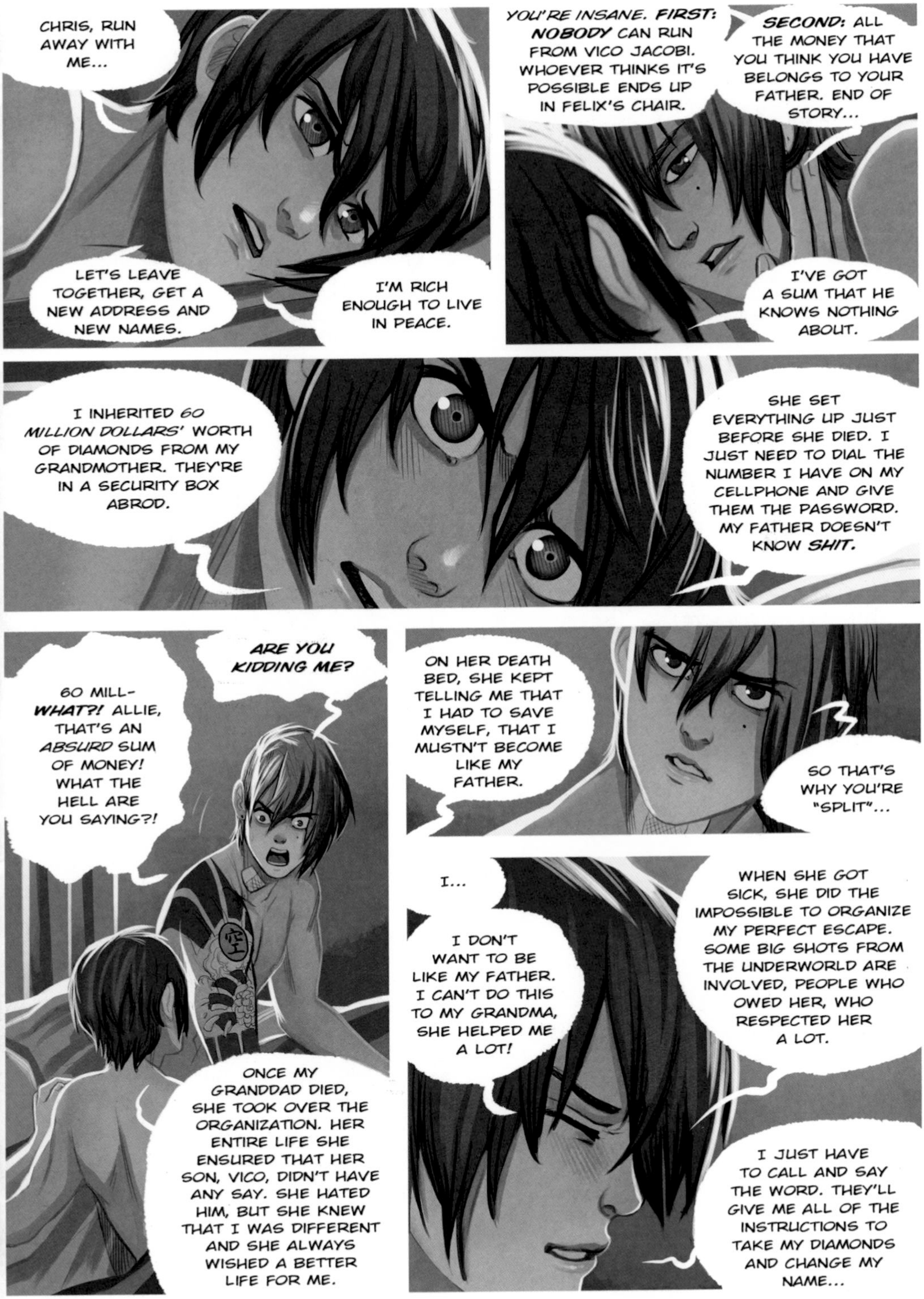
CHRIS, RUN AWAY WITH ME...
LET'S LEAVE TOGETHER, GET A NEW ADDRESS AND NEW NAMES.
I'M RICH ENOUGH TO LIVE IN PEACE.
YOU'RE INSANE. FIRST: NOBODY CAN RUN FROM VICO JACOBI. WHOEVER THINKS IT'S POSSIBLE ENDS UP IN FELIX'S CHAIR.
SECOND: ALL THE MONEY THAT YOU THINK YOU HAVE BELONGS TO YOUR FATHER. END OF STORY...
I'VE GOT A SUM THAT HE KNOWS NOTHING ABOUT.
I INHERITED 60 MILLION DOLLARS' WORTH OF DIAMONDS FROM MY GRANDMOTHER. THEY'RE IN A SECURITY BOX ABROD.
SHE SET EVERYTHING UP JUST BEFORE SHE DIED. I JUST NEED TO DIAL THE NUMBER I HAVE ON MY CELLPHONE AND GIVE THEM THE PASSWORD. MY FATHER DOESN'T KNOW SHIT.
60 MILL- WHAT?! ALLIE, THAT'S AN ABSURD SUM OF MONEY! WHAT THE HELL ARE YOU SAYING?!
ARE YOU KIDDING ME?
ONCE MY GRANDDAD DIED, SHE TOOK OVER THE ORGANIZATION. HER ENTIRE LIFE SHE ENSURED THAT HER SON, VICO, DIDN'T HAVE ANY SAY. SHE HATED HIM, BUT SHE KNEW THAT I WAS DIFFERENT AND SHE ALWAYS WISHED A BETTER LIFE FOR ME.
ON HER DEATH BED, SHE KEPT TELLING ME THAT I HAD TO SAVE MYSELF, THAT I MUSTN'T BECOME LIKE MY FATHER.
SO THAT'S WHY YOU'RE "SPLIT"...
I...
I DON'T WANT TO BE LIKE MY FATHER. I CAN'T DO THIS TO MY GRANDMA, SHE HELPED ME A LOT!
WHEN SHE GOT SICK, SHE DID THE IMPOSSIBLE TO ORGANIZE MY PERFECT ESCAPE. SOME BIG SHOTS FROM THE UNDERWORLD ARE INVOLVED, PEOPLE WHO OWED HER, WHO RESPECTED HER A LOT.
I JUST HAVE TO CALL AND SAY THE WORD. THEY'LL GIVE ME ALL OF THE INSTRUCTIONS TO TAKE MY DIAMONDS AND CHANGE MY NAME...

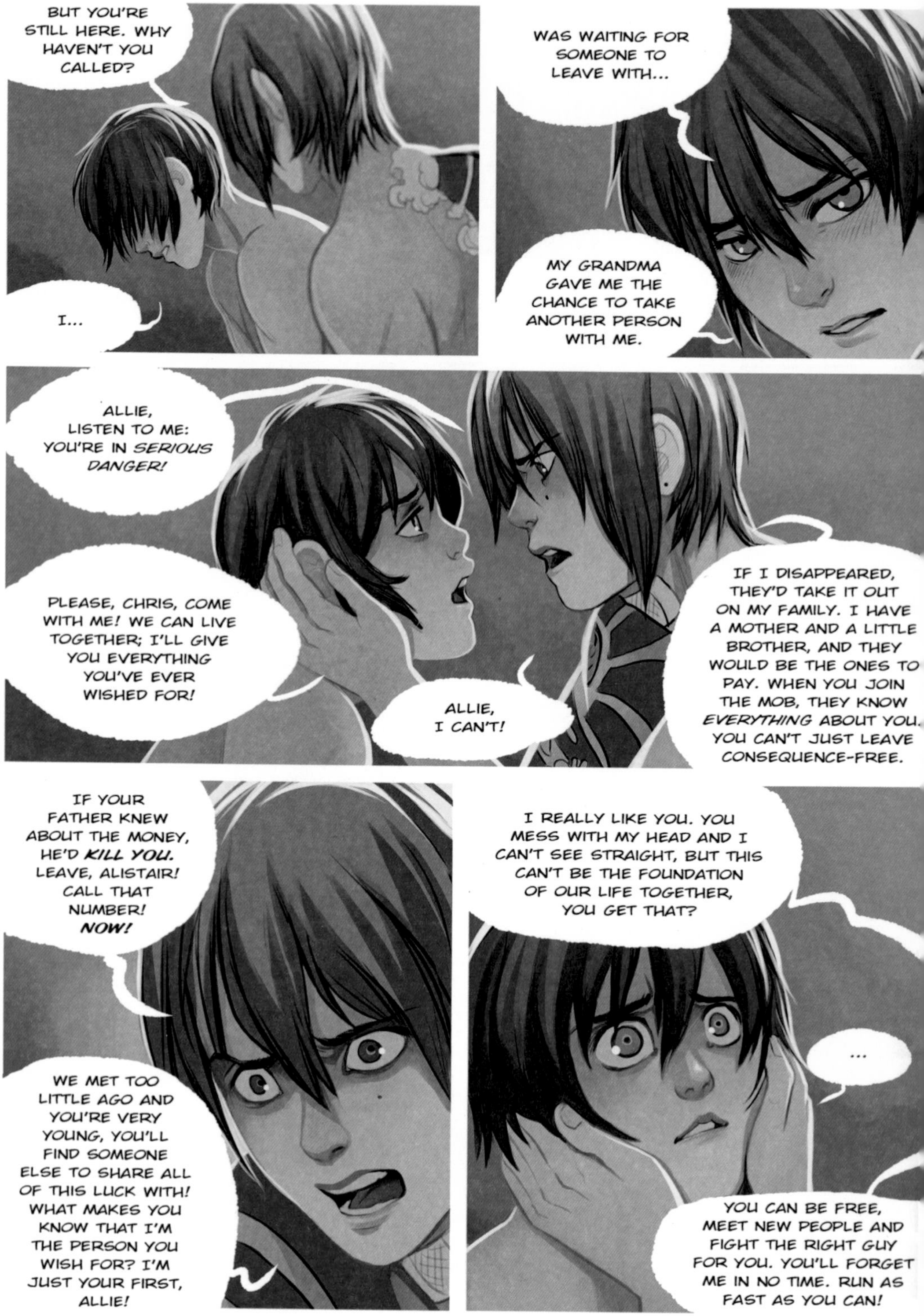
BUT YOU'RE STILL HERE. WHY HAVEN'T YOU CALLED?
I...
WAS WAITING FOR SOMEONE TO LEAVE WITH...
MY GRANDMA GAVE ME THE CHANCE TO TAKE ANOTHER PERSON WITH ME.
ALLIE, LISTEN TO ME: YOU'RE IN *SERIOUS DANGER!*
PLEASE, CHRIS, COME WITH ME! WE CAN LIVE TOGETHER; I'LL GIVE YOU EVERYTHING YOU'VE EVER WISHED FOR!
ALLIE, I CAN'T!
IF I DISAPPEARED, THEY'D TAKE IT OUT ON MY FAMILY. I HAVE A MOTHER AND A LITTLE BROTHER, AND THEY WOULD BE THE ONES TO PAY. WHEN YOU JOIN THE MOB, THEY KNOW *EVERYTHING* ABOUT YOU. YOU CAN'T JUST LEAVE CONSEQUENCE-FREE.
IF YOUR FATHER KNEW ABOUT THE MONEY, HE'D ***KILL YOU.*** LEAVE, ALISTAIR! CALL THAT NUMBER! ***NOW!***
WE MET TOO LITTLE AGO AND YOU'RE VERY YOUNG, YOU'LL FIND SOMEONE ELSE TO SHARE ALL OF THIS LUCK WITH! WHAT MAKES YOU KNOW THAT I'M THE PERSON YOU WISH FOR? I'M JUST YOUR FIRST, ALLIE!
I REALLY LIKE YOU. YOU MESS WITH MY HEAD AND I CAN'T SEE STRAIGHT, BUT THIS CAN'T BE THE FOUNDATION OF OUR LIFE TOGETHER, YOU GET THAT?
...
YOU CAN BE FREE, MEET NEW PEOPLE AND FIGHT THE RIGHT GUY FOR YOU. YOU'LL FORGET ME IN NO TIME. RUN AS FAST AS YOU CAN!

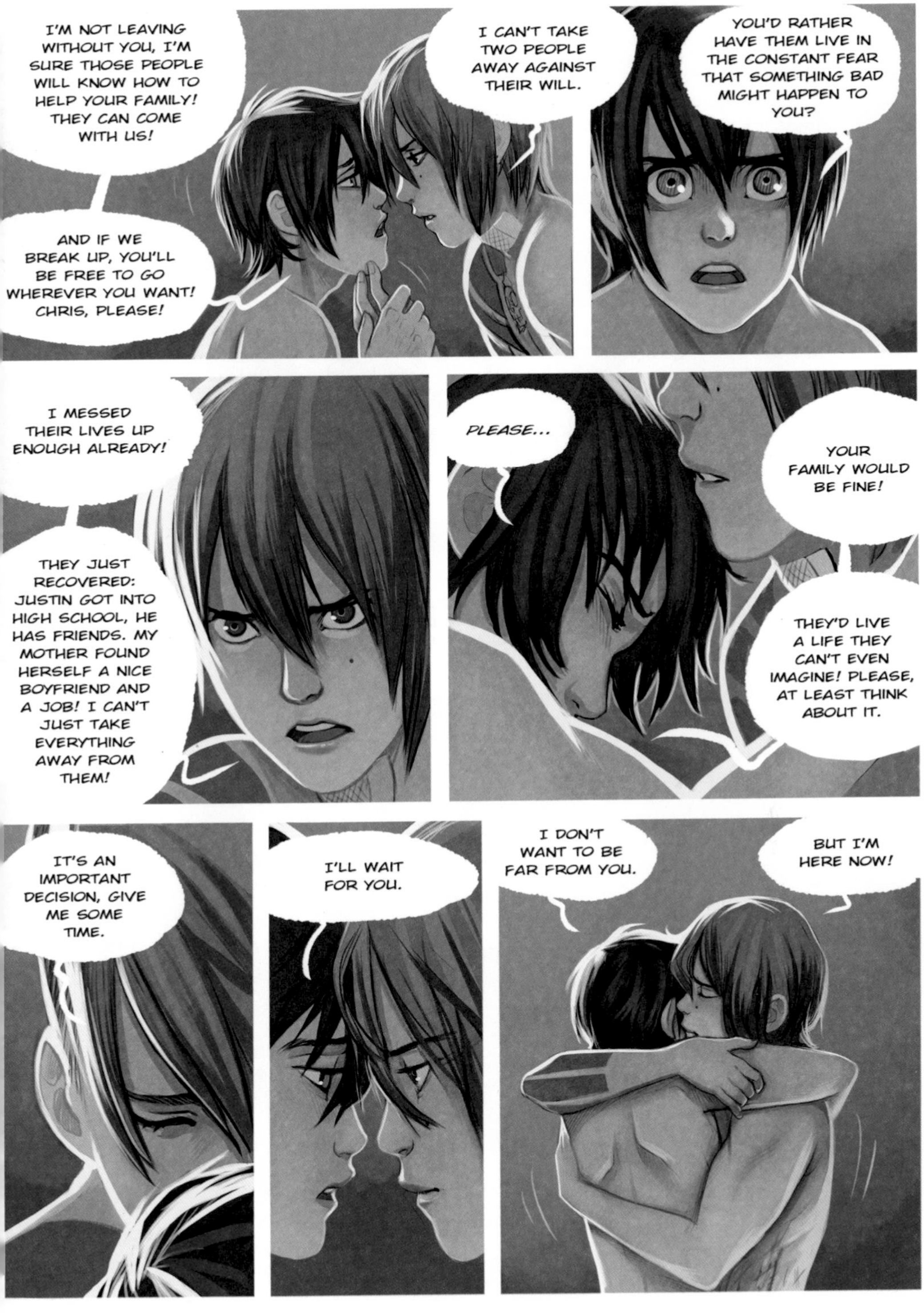
I'M NOT LEAVING WITHOUT YOU, I'M SURE THOSE PEOPLE WILL KNOW HOW TO HELP YOUR FAMILY! THEY CAN COME WITH US!
AND IF WE BREAK UP, YOU'LL BE FREE TO GO WHEREVER YOU WANT! CHRIS, PLEASE!
I CAN'T TAKE TWO PEOPLE AWAY AGAINST THEIR WILL.
YOU'D RATHER HAVE THEM LIVE IN THE CONSTANT FEAR THAT SOMETHING BAD MIGHT HAPPEN TO YOU?
I MESSED THEIR LIVES UP ENOUGH ALREADY!
THEY JUST RECOVERED: JUSTIN GOT INTO HIGH SCHOOL, HE HAS FRIENDS. MY MOTHER FOUND HERSELF A NICE BOYFRIEND AND A JOB! I CAN'T JUST TAKE EVERYTHING AWAY FROM THEM!
PLEASE...
YOUR FAMILY WOULD BE FINE!
THEY'D LIVE A LIFE THEY CAN'T EVEN IMAGINE! PLEASE, AT LEAST THINK ABOUT IT.
IT'S AN IMPORTANT DECISION, GIVE ME SOME TIME.
I'LL WAIT FOR YOU.
I DON'T WANT TO BE FAR FROM YOU.
BUT I'M HERE NOW!

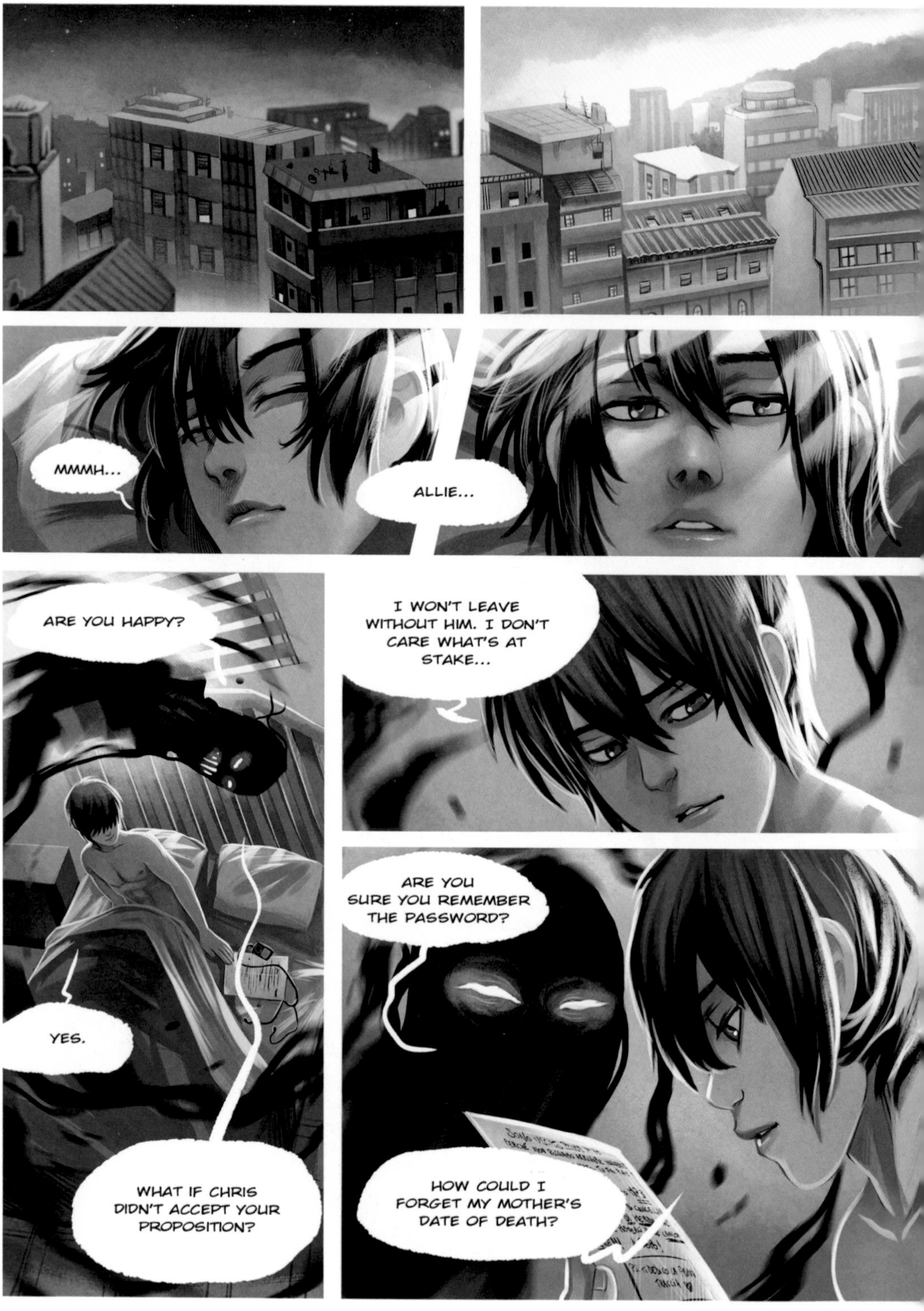
MMMH...
ALLIE...
ARE YOU HAPPY?
YES.
WHAT IF CHRIS DIDN'T ACCEPT YOUR PROPOSITION?
I WON'T LEAVE WITHOUT HIM. I DON'T CARE WHAT'S AT STAKE...
ARE YOU SURE YOU REMEMBER THE PASSWORD?
HOW COULD I FORGET MY MOTHER'S DATE OF DEATH?

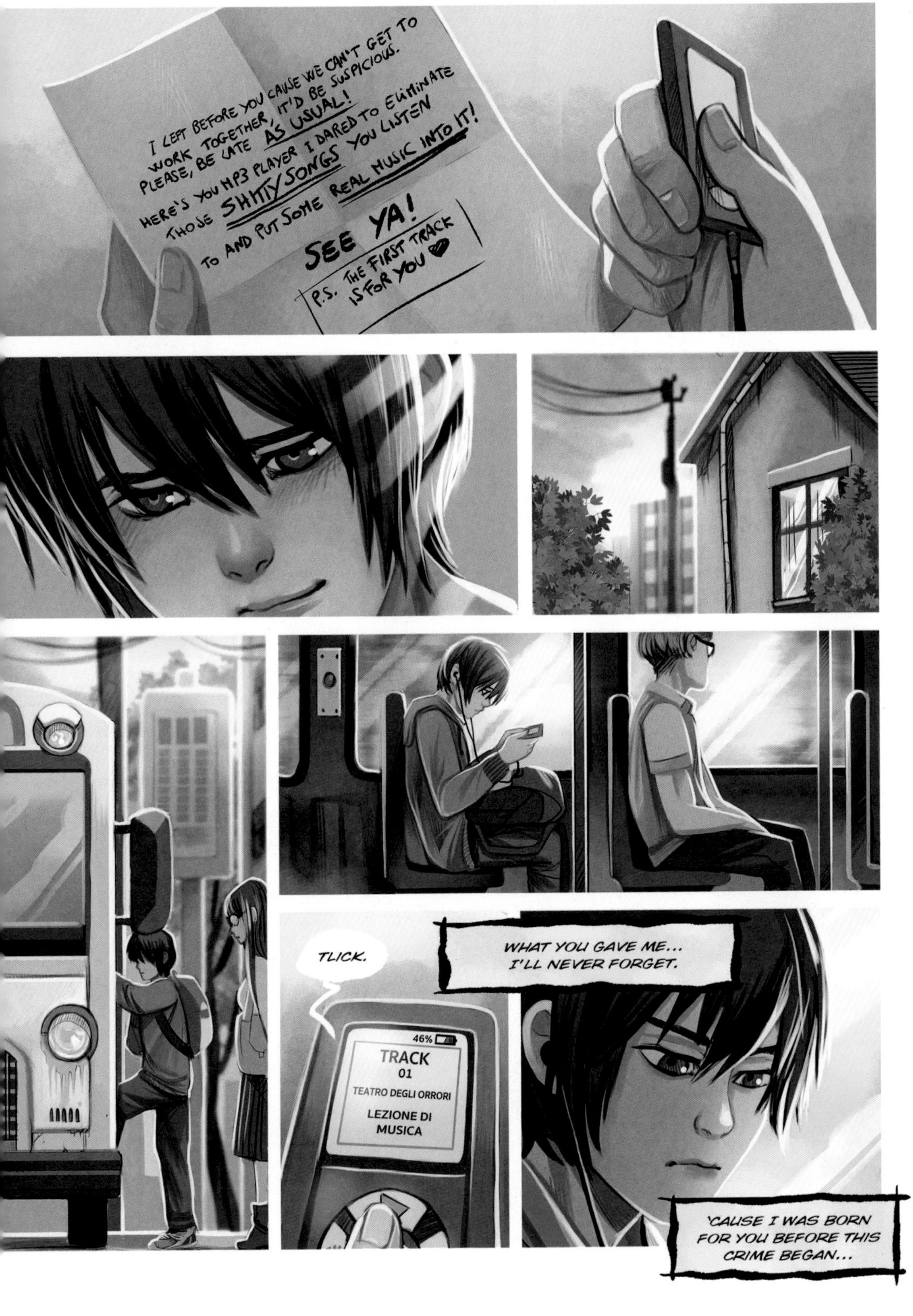
I LEFT BEFORE YOU CAUSE WE CAN'T GET TO WORK TOGETHER, IT'D BE SUSPICIOUS. PLEASE, BE LATE AS USUAL!
HERE'S YOU MP3 PLAYER I DARED TO ELIMINATE THOSE SHITTY SONGS YOU LISTEN TO AND PUT SOME REAL MUSIC INTO IT!
SEE YA!
P.S. THE FIRST TRACK IS FOR YOU
TLICK.
WHAT YOU GAVE ME... I'LL NEVER FORGET.
46%
TRACK 01
TEATRO DEGLI ORRORI
LEZIONE DI MUSICA
'CAUSE I WAS BORN FOR YOU BEFORE THIS CRIME BEGAN...

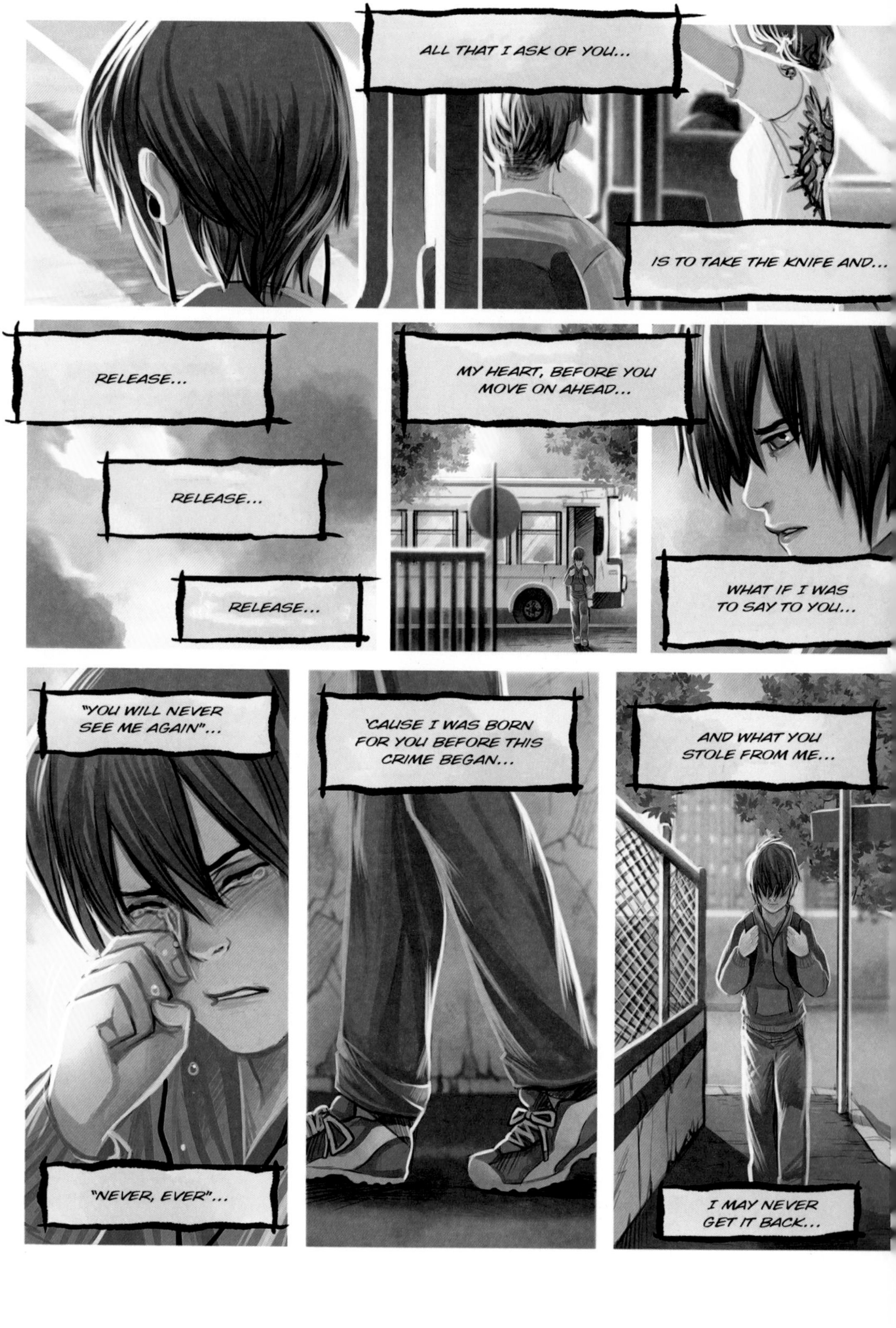
ALL THAT I ASK OF YOU...
IS TO TAKE THE KNIFE AND...
RELEASE...
RELEASE...
RELEASE...
MY HEART, BEFORE YOU MOVE ON AHEAD...
WHAT IF I WAS TO SAY TO YOU...
"YOU WILL NEVER SEE ME AGAIN"...
"NEVER, EVER"...
'CAUSE I WAS BORN FOR YOU BEFORE THIS CRIME BEGAN...
AND WHAT YOU STOLE FROM ME...
I MAY NEVER GET IT BACK...

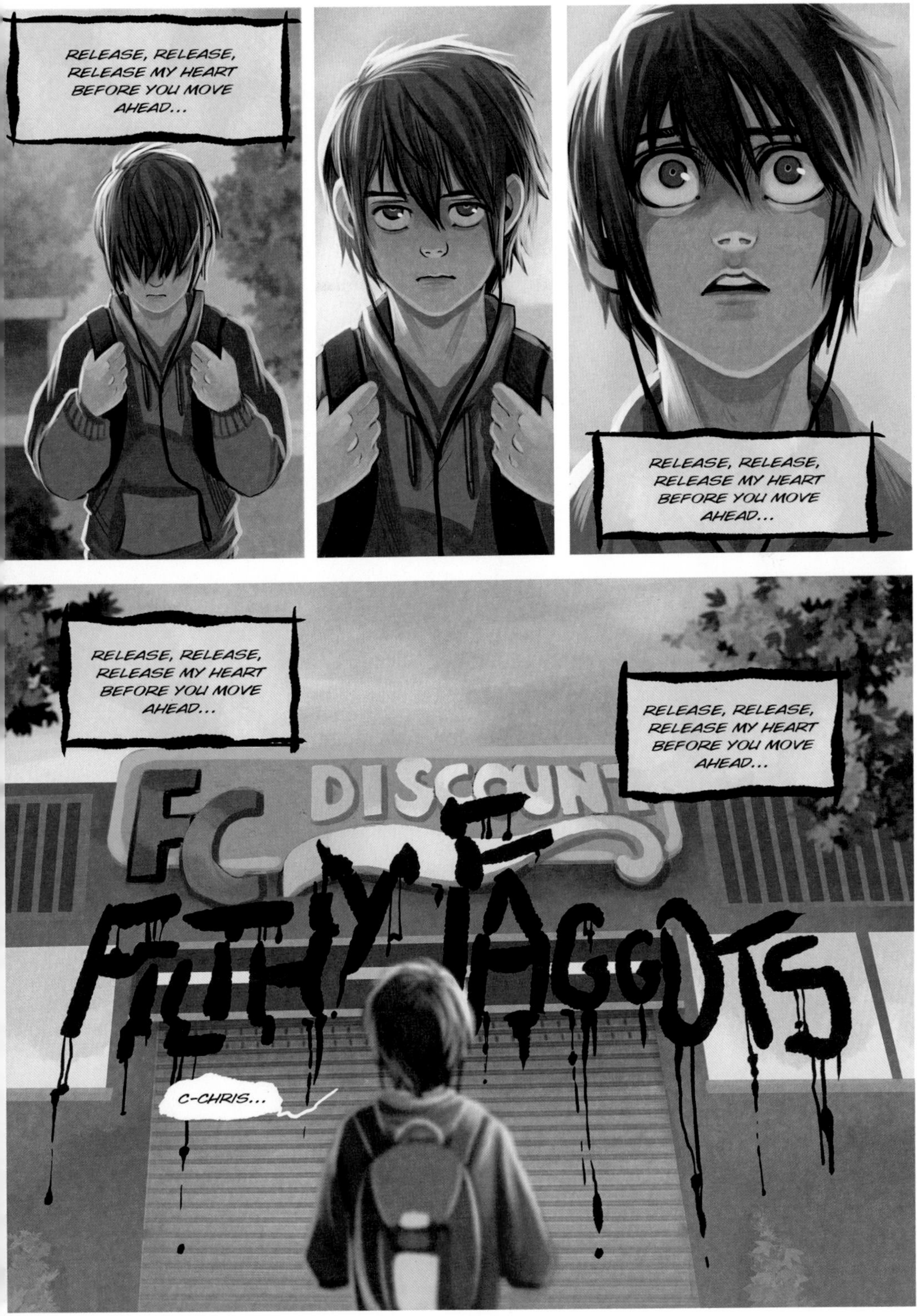
RELEASE, RELEASE, RELEASE MY HEART BEFORE YOU MOVE AHEAD...
RELEASE, RELEASE, RELEASE MY HEART BEFORE YOU MOVE AHEAD...
RELEASE, RELEASE, RELEASE MY HEART BEFORE YOU MOVE AHEAD...
RELEASE, RELEASE, RELEASE MY HEART BEFORE YOU MOVE AHEAD...
FC
FILTHY FAGGOTS
C-CHRIS...

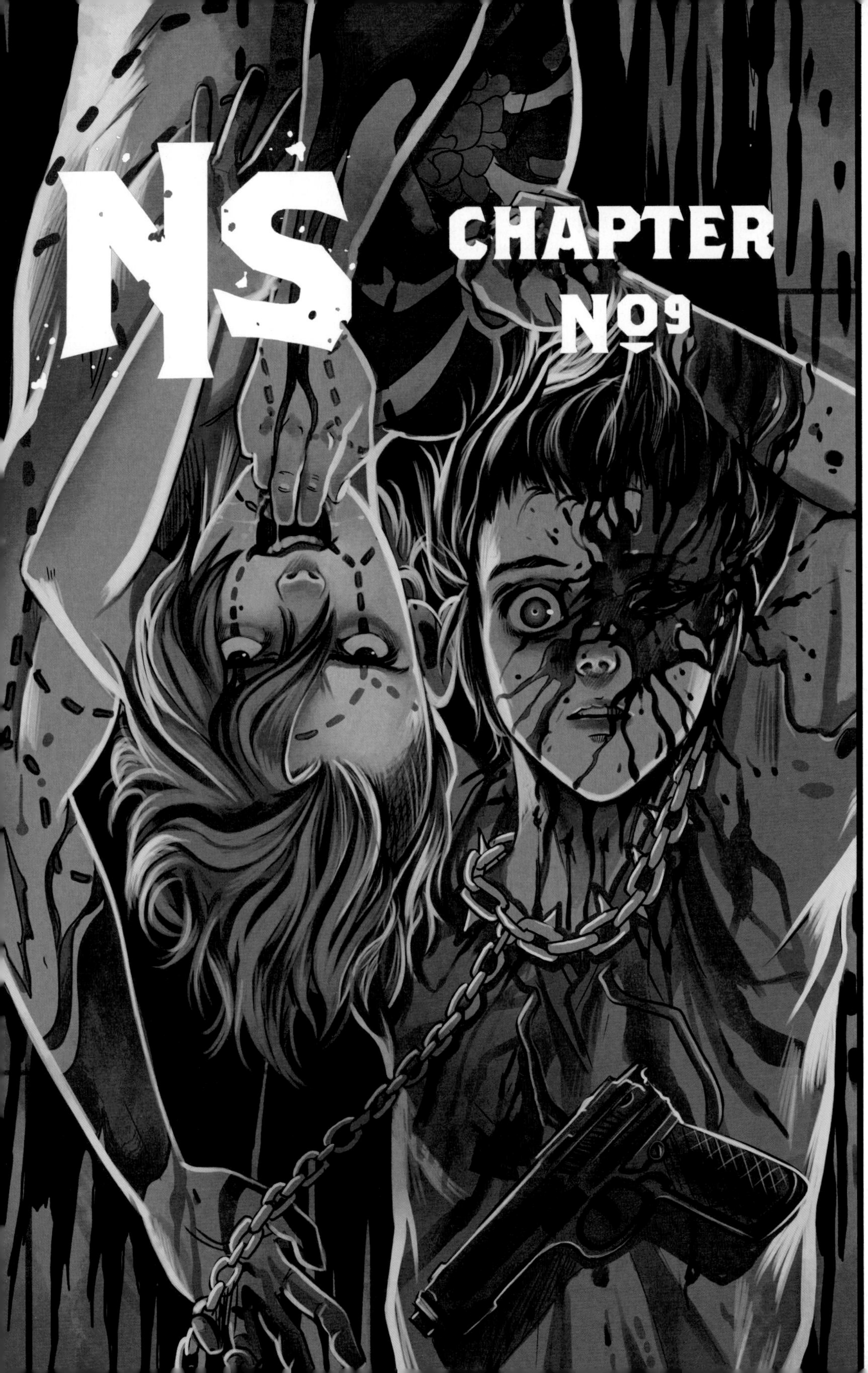
NS
CHAPTER
Nº9

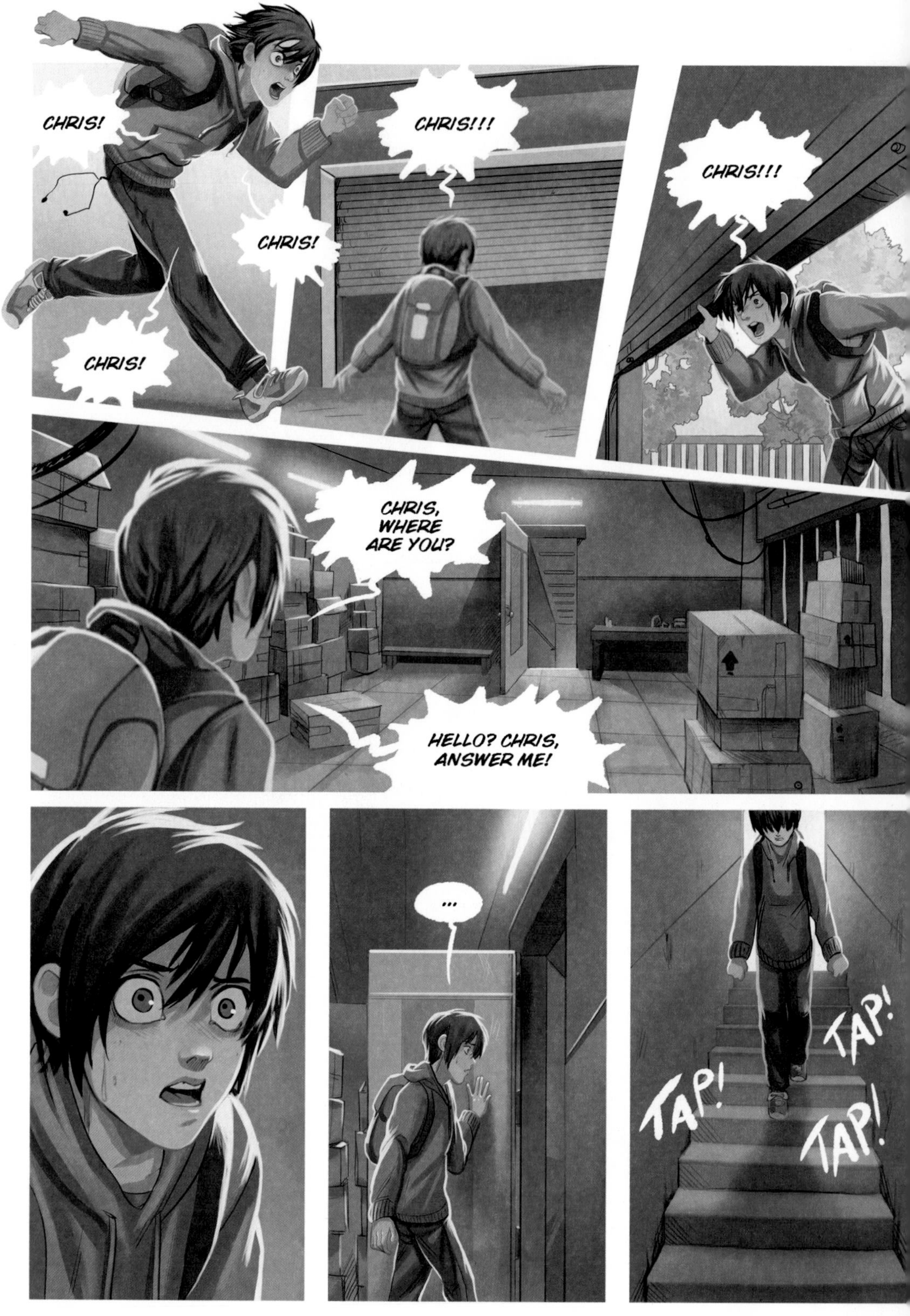
CHRIS!
CHRIS!
CHRIS!
CHRIS!!!
CHRIS!!!
CHRIS, WHERE ARE YOU?
HELLO? CHRIS, ANSWER ME!
...
TAP!
TAP!
TAP!

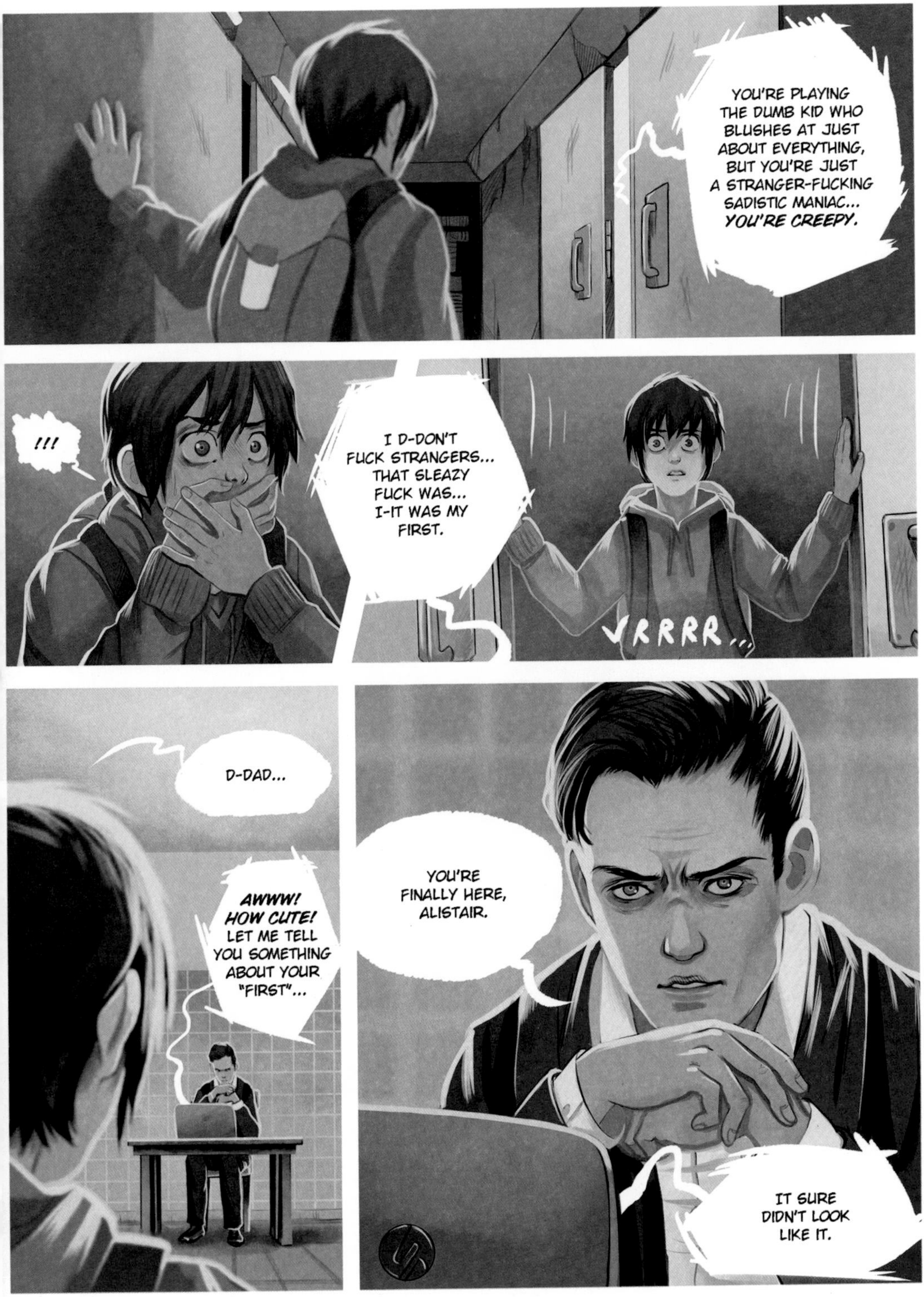
YOU'RE PLAYING THE DUMB KID WHO BLUSHES AT JUST ABOUT EVERYTHING, BUT YOU'RE JUST A STRANGER-FUCKING SADISTIC MANIAC... *YOU'RE CREEPY.*
!!!
I D-DON'T FUCK STRANGERS... THAT SLEAZY FUCK WAS... I-IT WAS MY FIRST.
VRRRR...
D-DAD...
AWWW! HOW CUTE! LET ME TELL YOU SOMETHING ABOUT YOUR "FIRST"...
YOU'RE FINALLY HERE, ALISTAIR.
IT SURE DIDN'T LOOK LIKE IT.

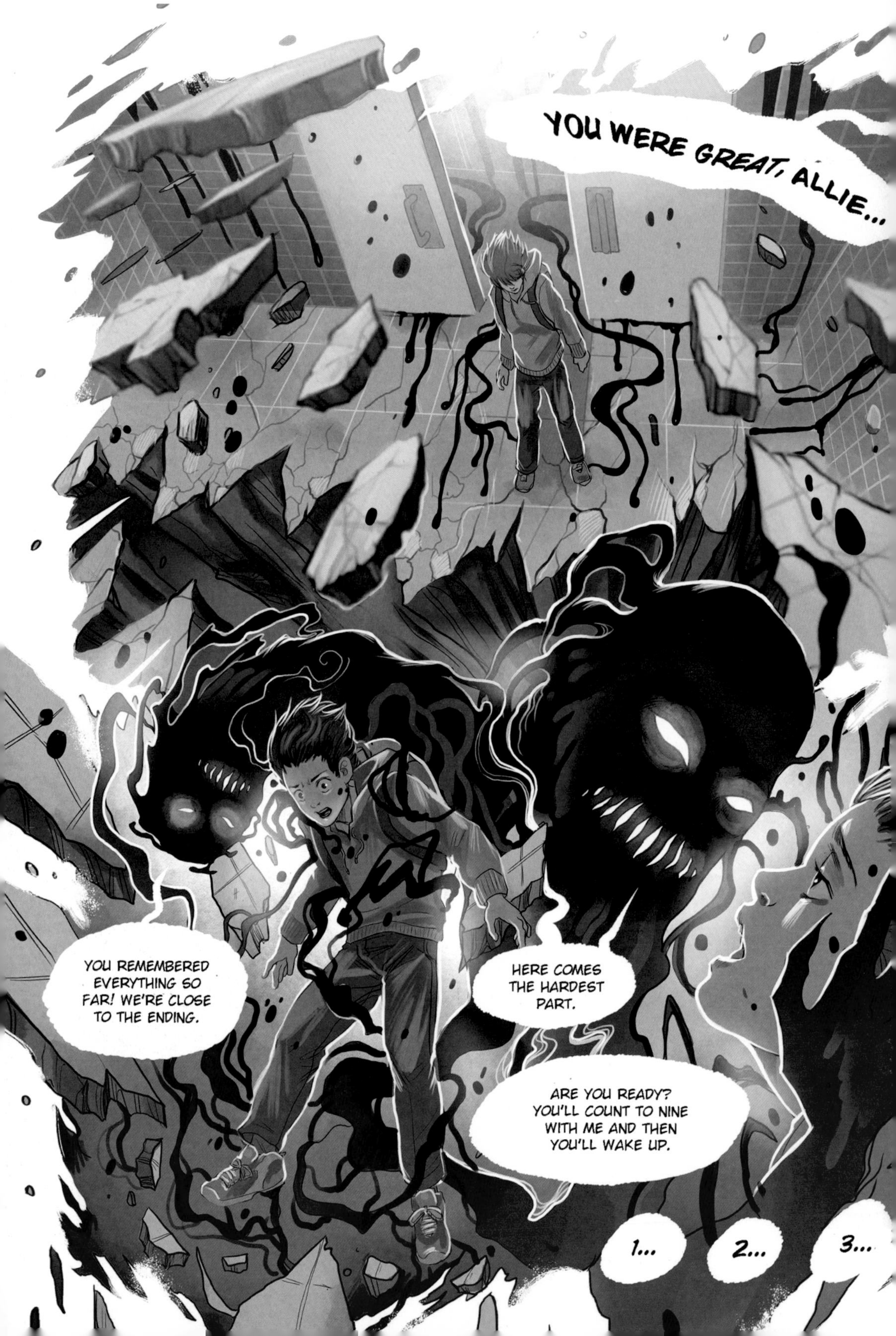
YOU WERE GREAT, ALLIE...
YOU REMEMBERED EVERYTHING SO FAR! WE'RE CLOSE TO THE ENDING.
HERE COMES THE HARDEST PART.
ARE YOU READY? YOU'LL COUNT TO NINE WITH ME AND THEN YOU'LL WAKE UP.
1...
2...
3...

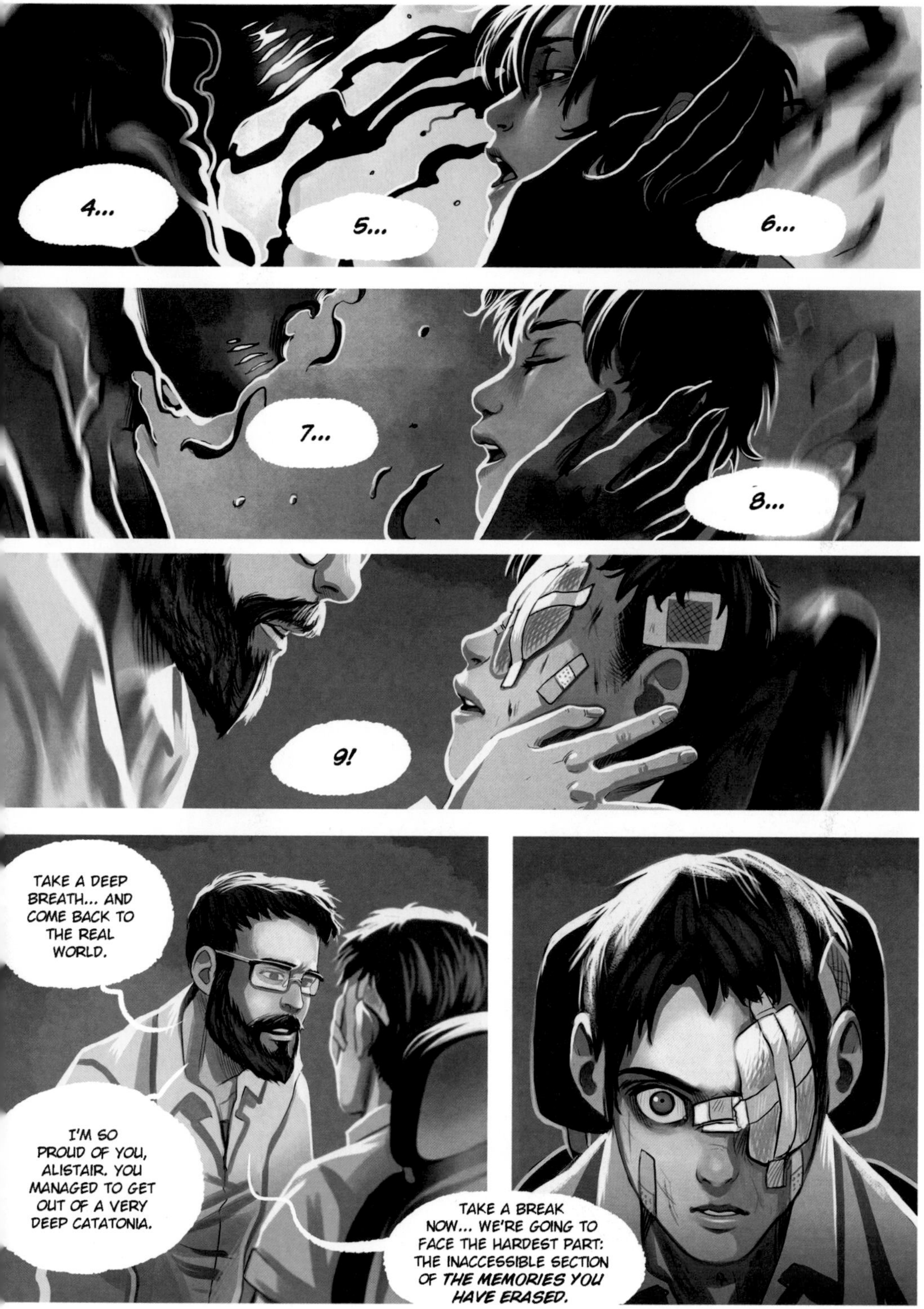
4...
5...
6...
7...
8...
9!
TAKE A DEEP BREATH... AND COME BACK TO THE REAL WORLD.
I'M SO PROUD OF YOU, ALISTAIR. YOU MANAGED TO GET OUT OF A VERY DEEP CATATONIA.
TAKE A BREAK NOW... WE'RE GOING TO FACE THE HARDEST PART: THE INACCESSIBLE SECTION OF *THE MEMORIES YOU HAVE ERASED.*

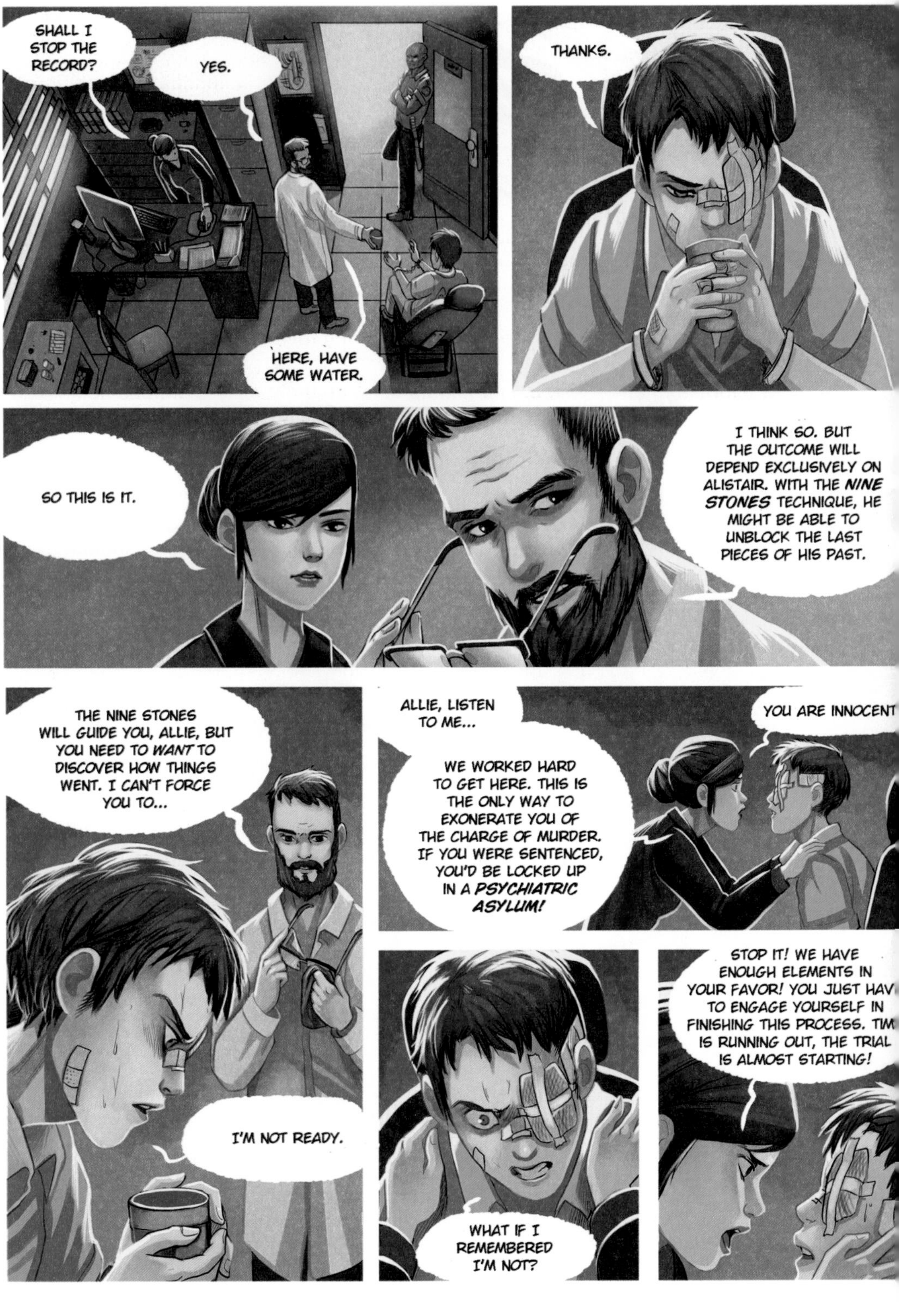
SHALL I STOP THE RECORD?
YES.
HERE, HAVE SOME WATER.
THANKS.
SO THIS IS IT.
I THINK SO. BUT THE OUTCOME WILL DEPEND EXCLUSIVELY ON ALISTAIR. WITH THE *NINE STONES* TECHNIQUE, HE MIGHT BE ABLE TO UNBLOCK THE LAST PIECES OF HIS PAST.
THE NINE STONES WILL GUIDE YOU, ALLIE, BUT YOU NEED TO *WANT* TO DISCOVER HOW THINGS WENT. I CAN'T FORCE YOU TO...
I'M NOT READY.
ALLIE, LISTEN TO ME...
WE WORKED HARD TO GET HERE. THIS IS THE ONLY WAY TO EXONERATE YOU OF THE CHARGE OF MURDER. IF YOU WERE SENTENCED, YOU'D BE LOCKED UP IN A ***PSYCHIATRIC ASYLUM!***
YOU ARE INNOCENT
WHAT IF I REMEMBERED I'M NOT?
STOP IT! WE HAVE ENOUGH ELEMENTS IN YOUR FAVOR! YOU JUST HAV TO ENGAGE YOURSELF IN FINISHING THIS PROCESS. TIM IS RUNNING OUT, THE TRIAL IS ALMOST STARTING!

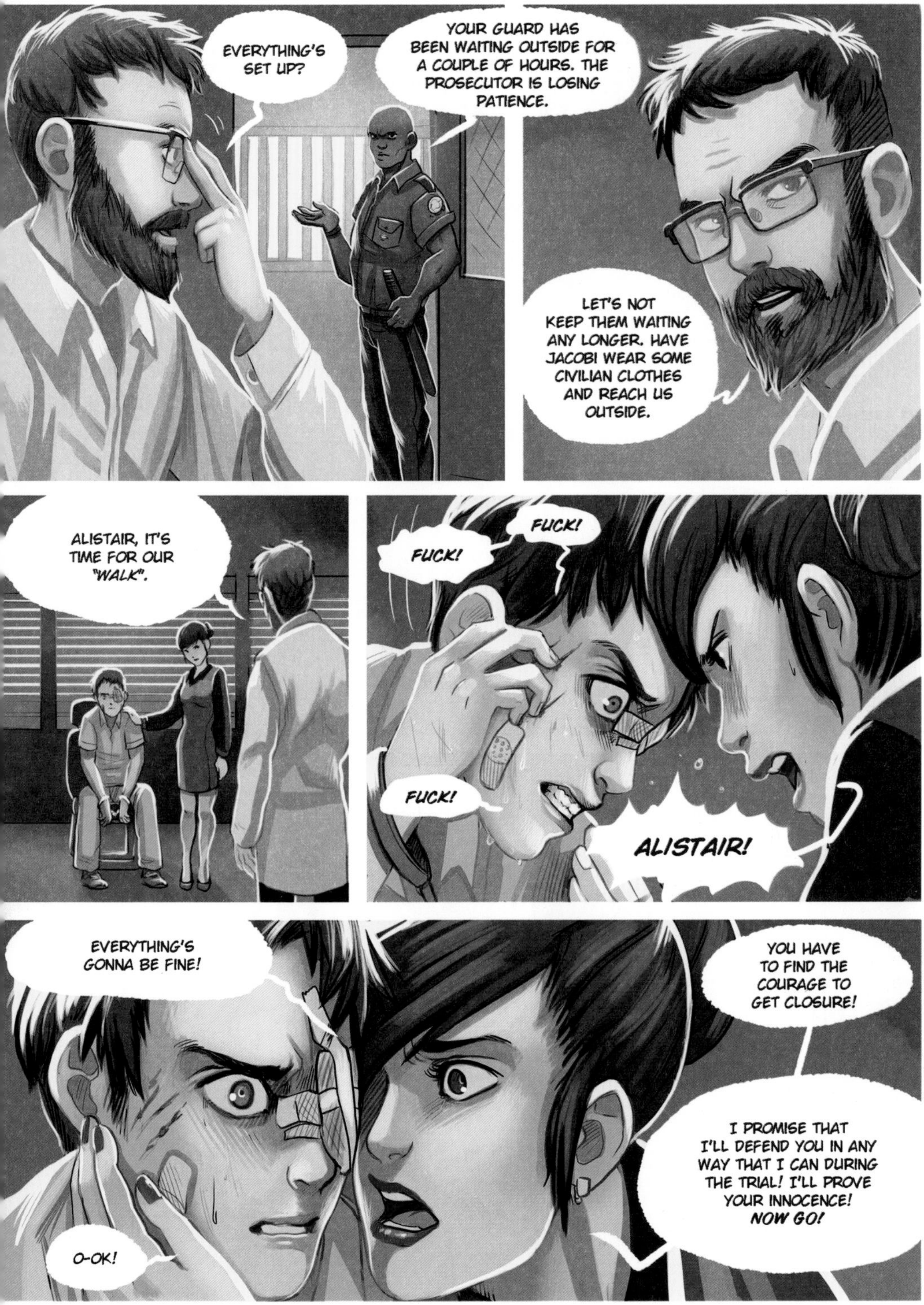
EVERYTHING'S SET UP?
YOUR GUARD HAS BEEN WAITING OUTSIDE FOR A COUPLE OF HOURS. THE PROSECUTOR IS LOSING PATIENCE.
LET'S NOT KEEP THEM WAITING ANY LONGER. HAVE JACOBI WEAR SOME CIVILIAN CLOTHES AND REACH US OUTSIDE.
ALISTAIR, IT'S TIME FOR OUR "WALK".
FUCK!
FUCK!
FUCK!
ALISTAIR!
EVERYTHING'S GONNA BE FINE!
YOU HAVE TO FIND THE COURAGE TO GET CLOSURE!
I PROMISE THAT I'LL DEFEND YOU IN ANY WAY THAT I CAN DURING THE TRIAL! I'LL PROVE YOUR INNOCENCE! NOW GO!
O-OK!

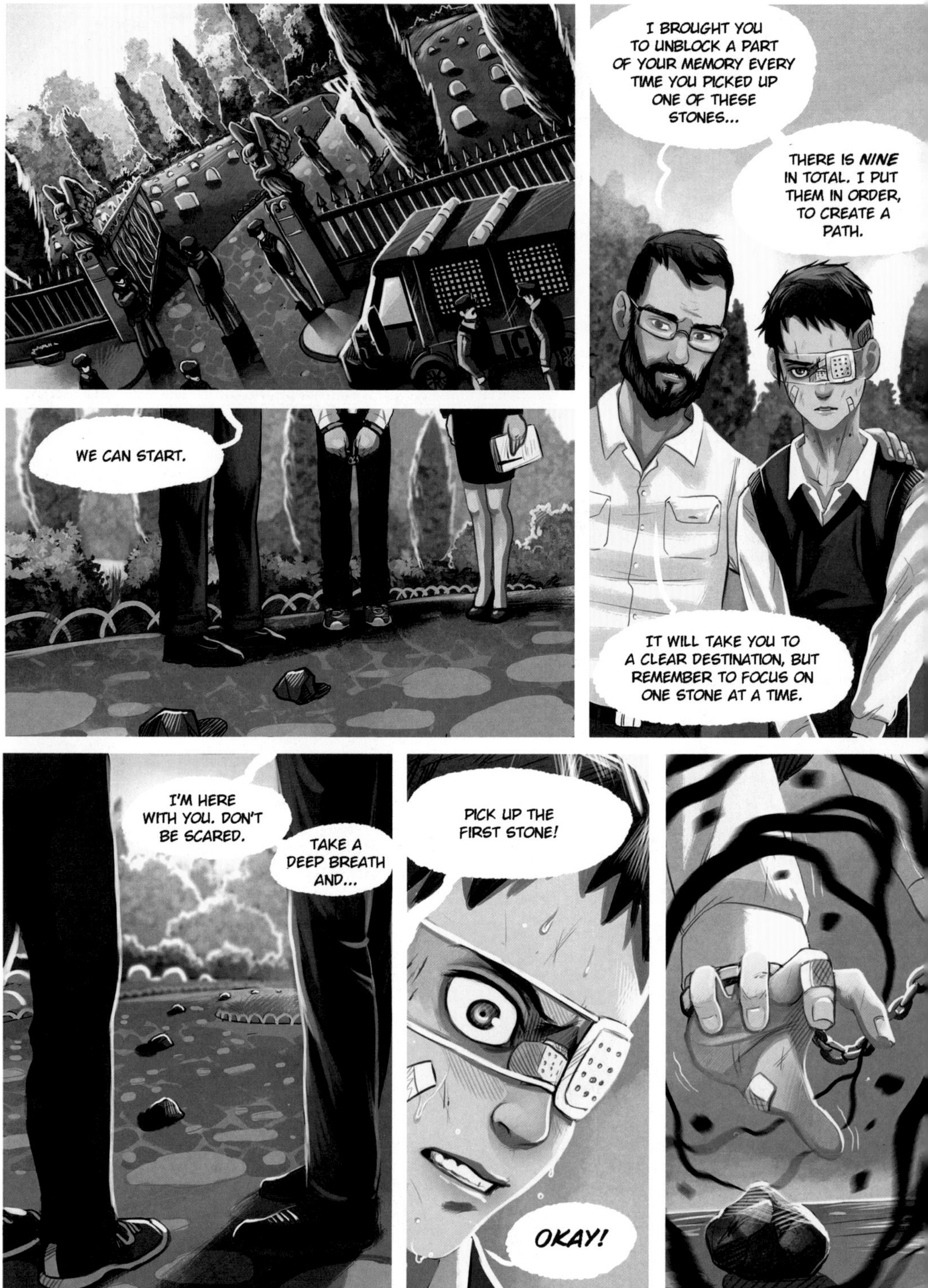
I BROUGHT YOU TO UNBLOCK A PART OF YOUR MEMORY EVERY TIME YOU PICKED UP ONE OF THESE STONES...
THERE IS *NINE* IN TOTAL. I PUT THEM IN ORDER, TO CREATE A PATH.
WE CAN START.
IT WILL TAKE YOU TO A CLEAR DESTINATION, BUT REMEMBER TO FOCUS ON ONE STONE AT A TIME.
I'M HERE WITH YOU. DON'T BE SCARED.
TAKE A DEEP BREATH AND...
PICK UP THE FIRST STONE!
OKAY!

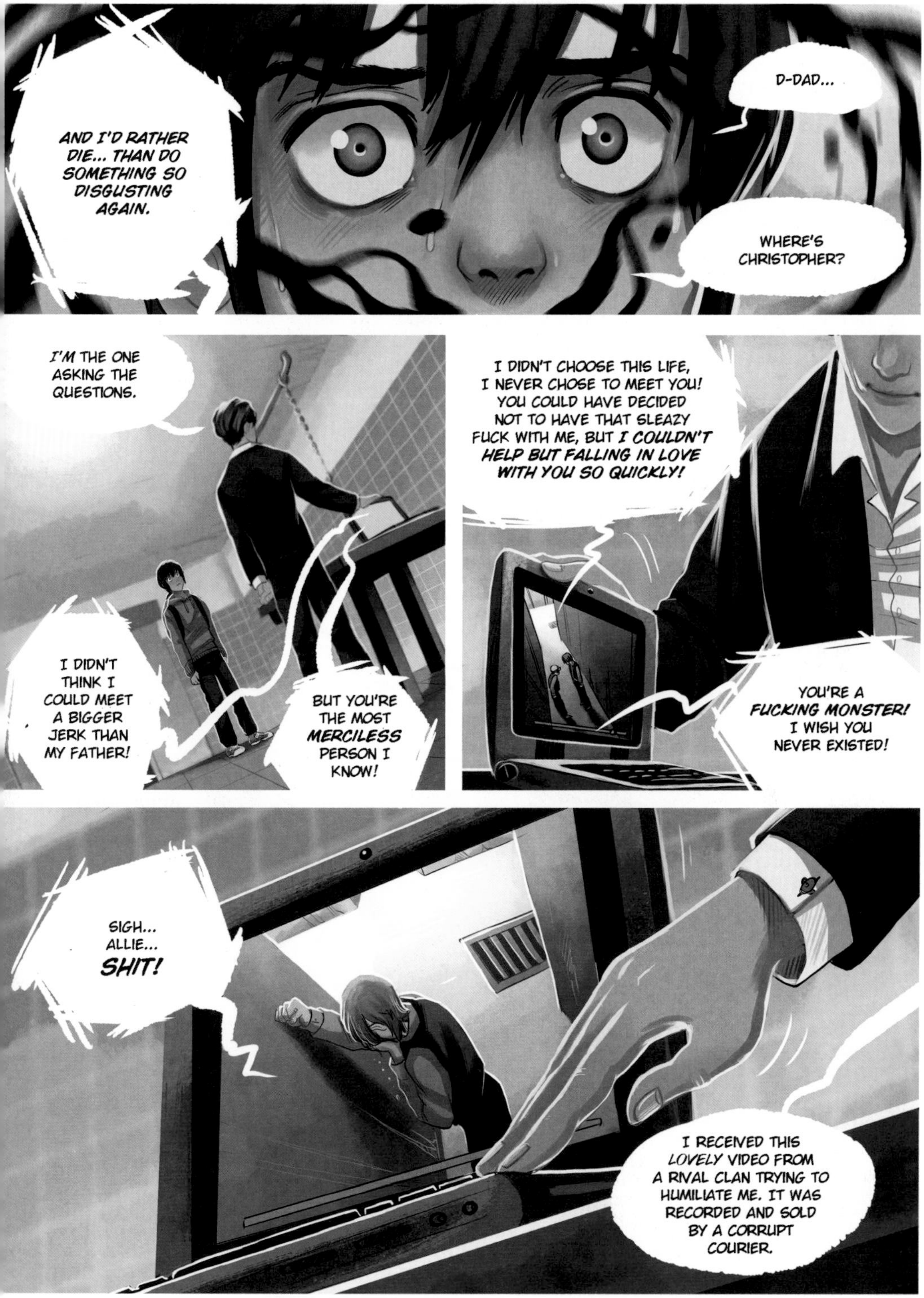
AND I'D RATHER DIE... THAN DO SOMETHING SO DISGUSTING AGAIN.
D-DAD...
WHERE'S CHRISTOPHER?
I'M THE ONE ASKING THE QUESTIONS.
I DIDN'T THINK I COULD MEET A BIGGER JERK THAN MY FATHER!
BUT YOU'RE THE MOST MERCILESS PERSON I KNOW!
I DIDN'T CHOOSE THIS LIFE, I NEVER CHOSE TO MEET YOU! YOU COULD HAVE DECIDED NOT TO HAVE THAT SLEAZY FUCK WITH ME, BUT I COULDN'T HELP BUT FALLING IN LOVE WITH YOU SO QUICKLY!
YOU'RE A FUCKING MONSTER! I WISH YOU NEVER EXISTED!
SIGH... ALLIE... SHIT!
I RECEIVED THIS LOVELY VIDEO FROM A RIVAL CLAN TRYING TO HUMILIATE ME. IT WAS RECORDED AND SOLD BY A CORRUPT COURIER.

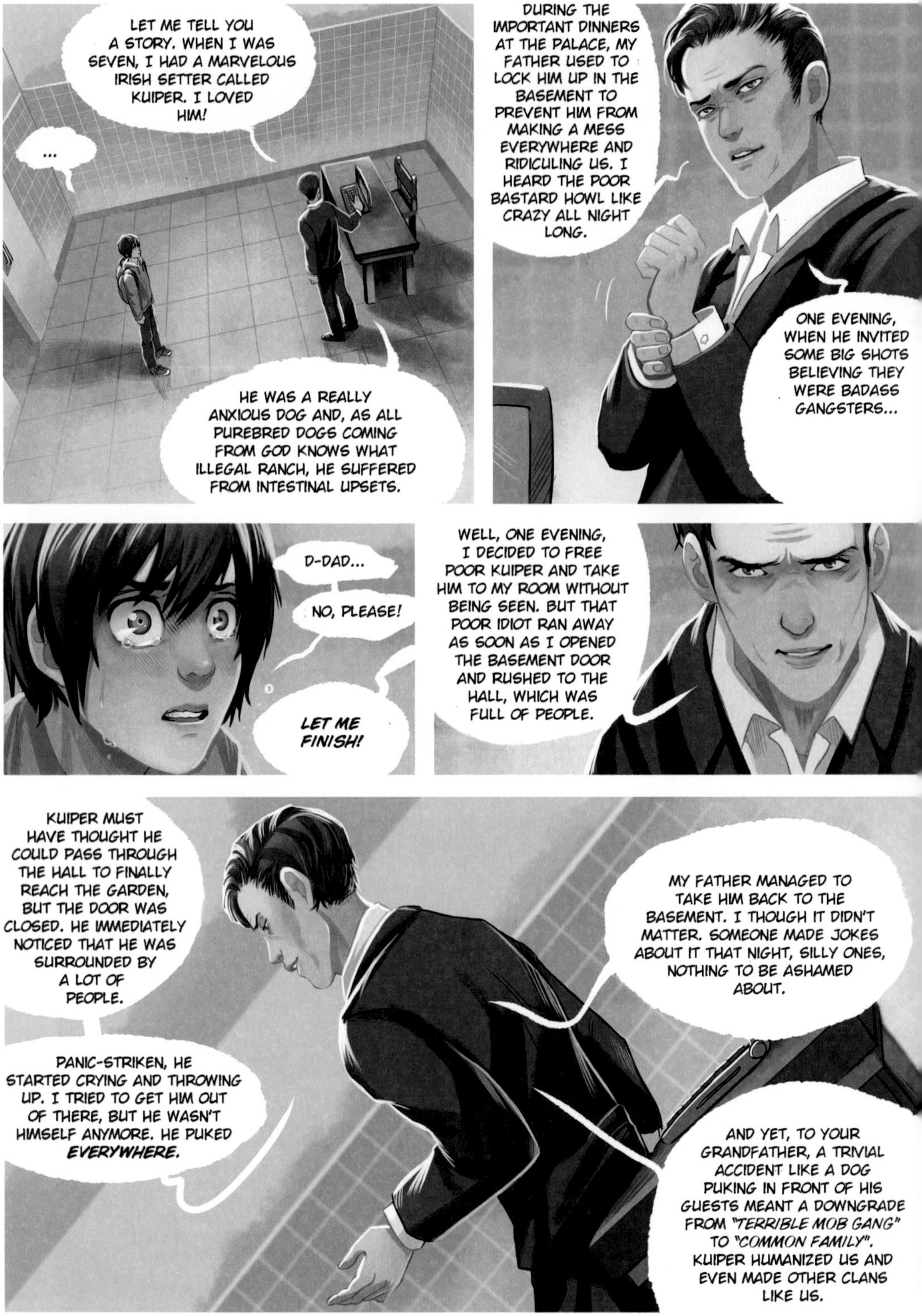
LET ME TELL YOU A STORY. WHEN I WAS SEVEN, I HAD A MARVELOUS IRISH SETTER CALLED KUIPER. I LOVED HIM!
...
HE WAS A REALLY ANXIOUS DOG AND, AS ALL PUREBRED DOGS COMING FROM GOD KNOWS WHAT ILLEGAL RANCH, HE SUFFERED FROM INTESTINAL UPSETS.
DURING THE IMPORTANT DINNERS AT THE PALACE, MY FATHER USED TO LOCK HIM UP IN THE BASEMENT TO PREVENT HIM FROM MAKING A MESS EVERYWHERE AND RIDICULING US. I HEARD THE POOR BASTARD HOWL LIKE CRAZY ALL NIGHT LONG.
ONE EVENING, WHEN HE INVITED SOME BIG SHOTS BELIEVING THEY WERE BADASS GANGSTERS...
D-DAD...
NO, PLEASE!
LET ME FINISH!
WELL, ONE EVENING, I DECIDED TO FREE POOR KUIPER AND TAKE HIM TO MY ROOM WITHOUT BEING SEEN. BUT THAT POOR IDIOT RAN AWAY AS SOON AS I OPENED THE BASEMENT DOOR AND RUSHED TO THE HALL, WHICH WAS FULL OF PEOPLE.
KUIPER MUST HAVE THOUGHT HE COULD PASS THROUGH THE HALL TO FINALLY REACH THE GARDEN, BUT THE DOOR WAS CLOSED. HE IMMEDIATELY NOTICED THAT HE WAS SURROUNDED BY A LOT OF PEOPLE.
PANIC-STRIKEN, HE STARTED CRYING AND THROWING UP. I TRIED TO GET HIM OUT OF THERE, BUT HE WASN'T HIMSELF ANYMORE. HE PUKED EVERYWHERE.
MY FATHER MANAGED TO TAKE HIM BACK TO THE BASEMENT. I THOUGH IT DIDN'T MATTER. SOMEONE MADE JOKES ABOUT IT THAT NIGHT, SILLY ONES, NOTHING TO BE ASHAMED ABOUT.
AND YET, TO YOUR GRANDFATHER, A TRIVIAL ACCIDENT LIKE A DOG PUKING IN FRONT OF HIS GUESTS MEANT A DOWNGRADE FROM "TERRIBLE MOB GANG" TO "COMMON FAMILY". KUIPER HUMANIZED US AND EVEN MADE OTHER CLANS LIKE US.

AFTER THAT, WE HAD ANOTHER PARTY. THAT NIGHT, MY FATHER CAME TO MY ROOM, CALLED ME...

THEN TOOK KUIPER BY HIS COLLAR AND ESCORTED US TO THE HALL. HE GAVE ME A BERETTA .92 – MY FIRST GUN – AND ASKED THE GUESTS TO FOLLOW US IN THE GARDEN.

HE FORCED ME TO SHOOT THAT DOG IN THE HEAD IN FRONT OF EVERYONE.

NOBODY EVER DARED TO MAKE JOKES OR CONSIDER US A NORMAL FAMILY EVER AGAIN. THE FUNNY THING IS THAT MY MOTHER, YOUR BELOVED GRANDMOTHER, ALWAYS TRIED TO PROTECT YOU FROM ME. I WAS NEVER SO LUCKY, NOBODY EVER PROTECTED ME FROM YOUR GRANDFATHER.

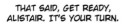

...

THAT SAID, GET READY, ALISTAIR. IT'S YOUR TURN.

FELIX IS GOING TO TAKE YOU TO *CHRISTOPHER*.

WHA-

COME ON, KID...

RELAX, ALISTAIR.

IT'LL BE QUICK.

D-DAD, WAIT! I-I BEG YOU! CHRIS HAS NOTHING TO DO WITH THIS! I PROVOKED HIM, HE DIDN'T WANT TO! YOU HEARD HIM!

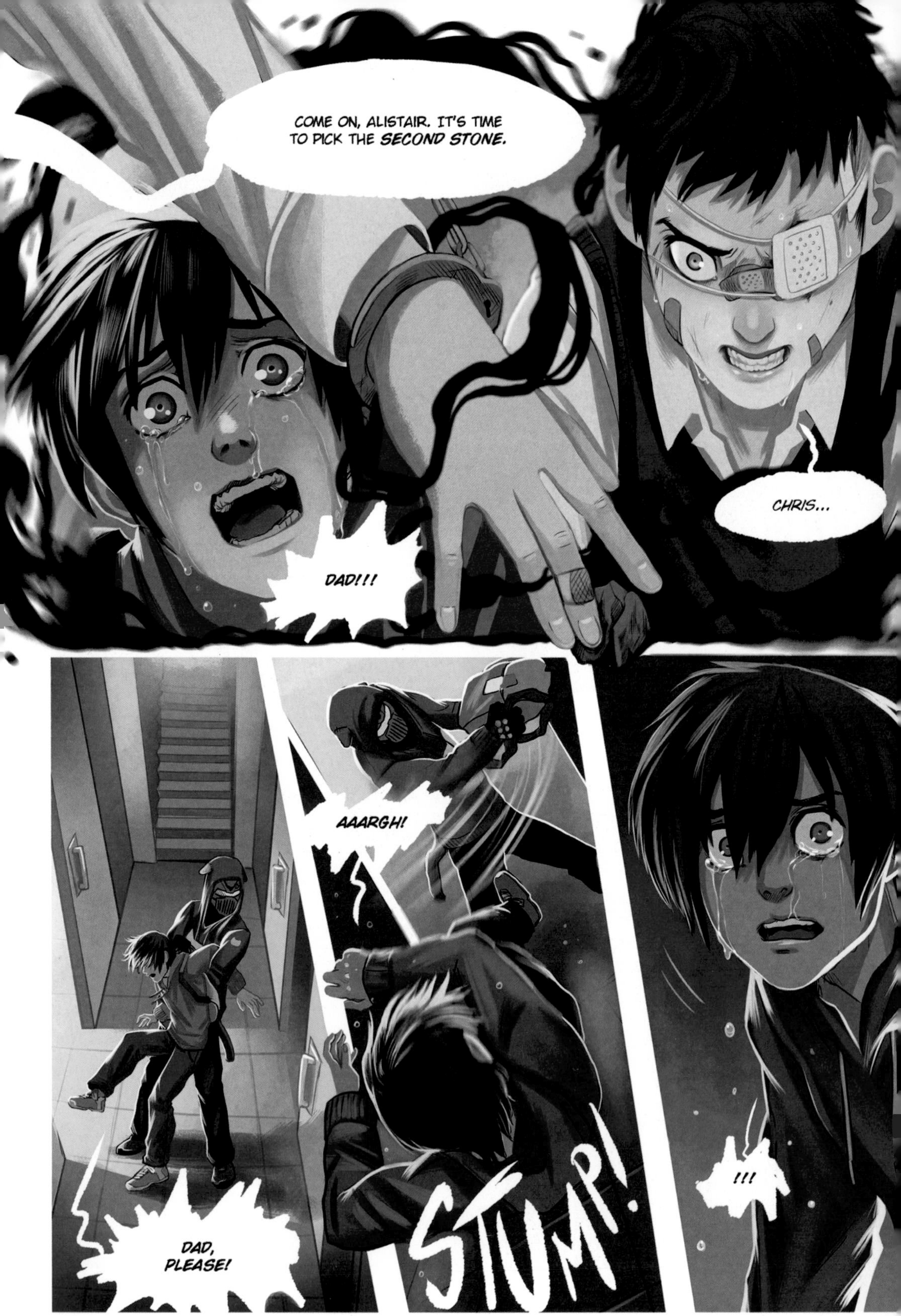
COME ON, ALISTAIR. IT'S TIME TO PICK THE SECOND STONE.
CHRIS...
DAD!!!
AAARGH!
DAD, PLEASE!
STUMP!
!!!

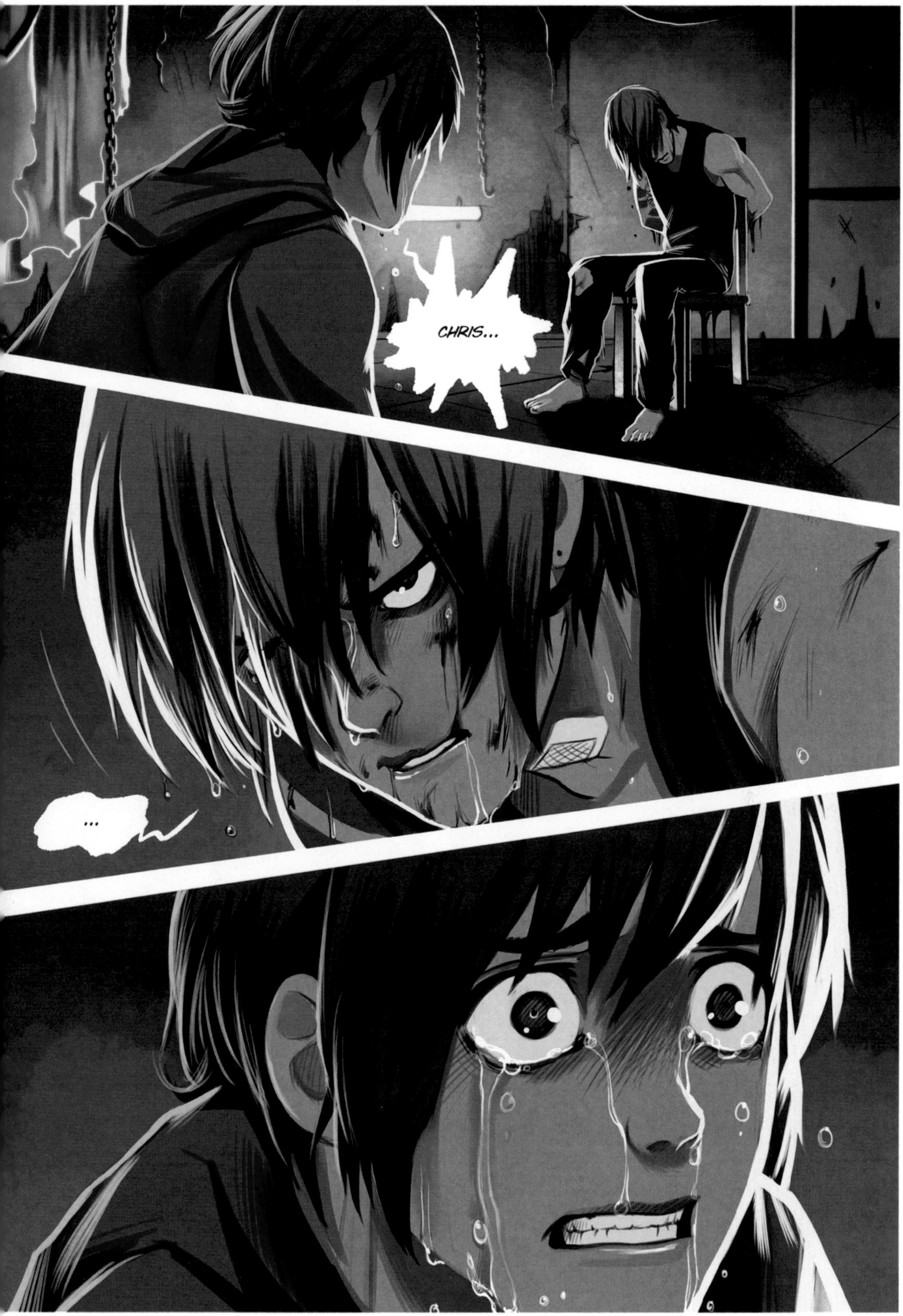
CHRIS...
...

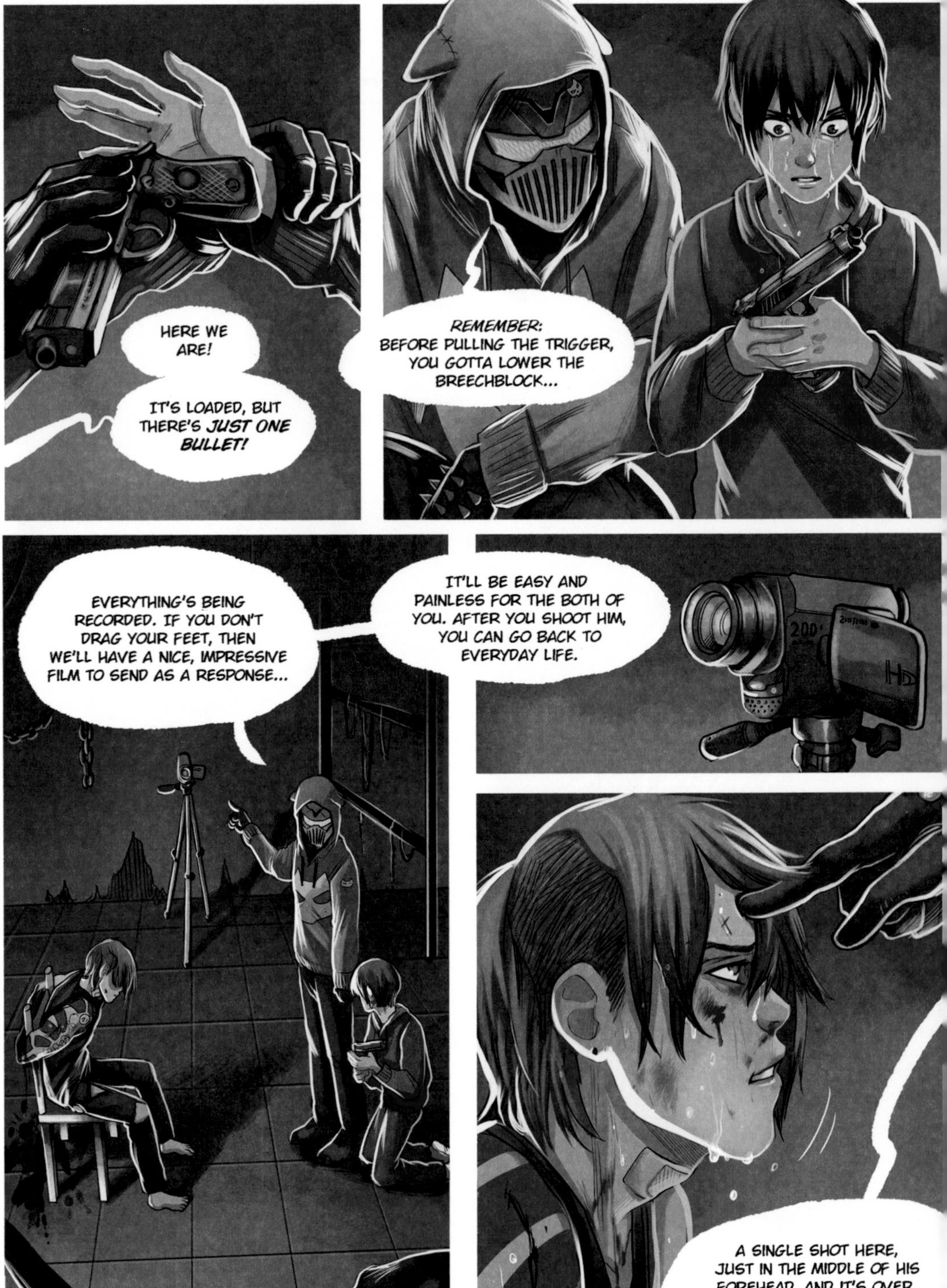
HERE WE ARE!
IT'S LOADED, BUT THERE'S *JUST ONE BULLET!*
REMEMBER: BEFORE PULLING THE TRIGGER, YOU GOTTA LOWER THE BREECHBLOCK...
EVERYTHING'S BEING RECORDED. IF YOU DON'T DRAG YOUR FEET, THEN WE'LL HAVE A NICE, IMPRESSIVE FILM TO SEND AS A RESPONSE...
IT'LL BE EASY AND PAINLESS FOR THE BOTH OF YOU. AFTER YOU SHOOT HIM, YOU CAN GO BACK TO EVERYDAY LIFE.
A SINGLE SHOT HERE, JUST IN THE MIDDLE OF HIS FOREHEAD, AND IT'S OVER, ALISTAIR...

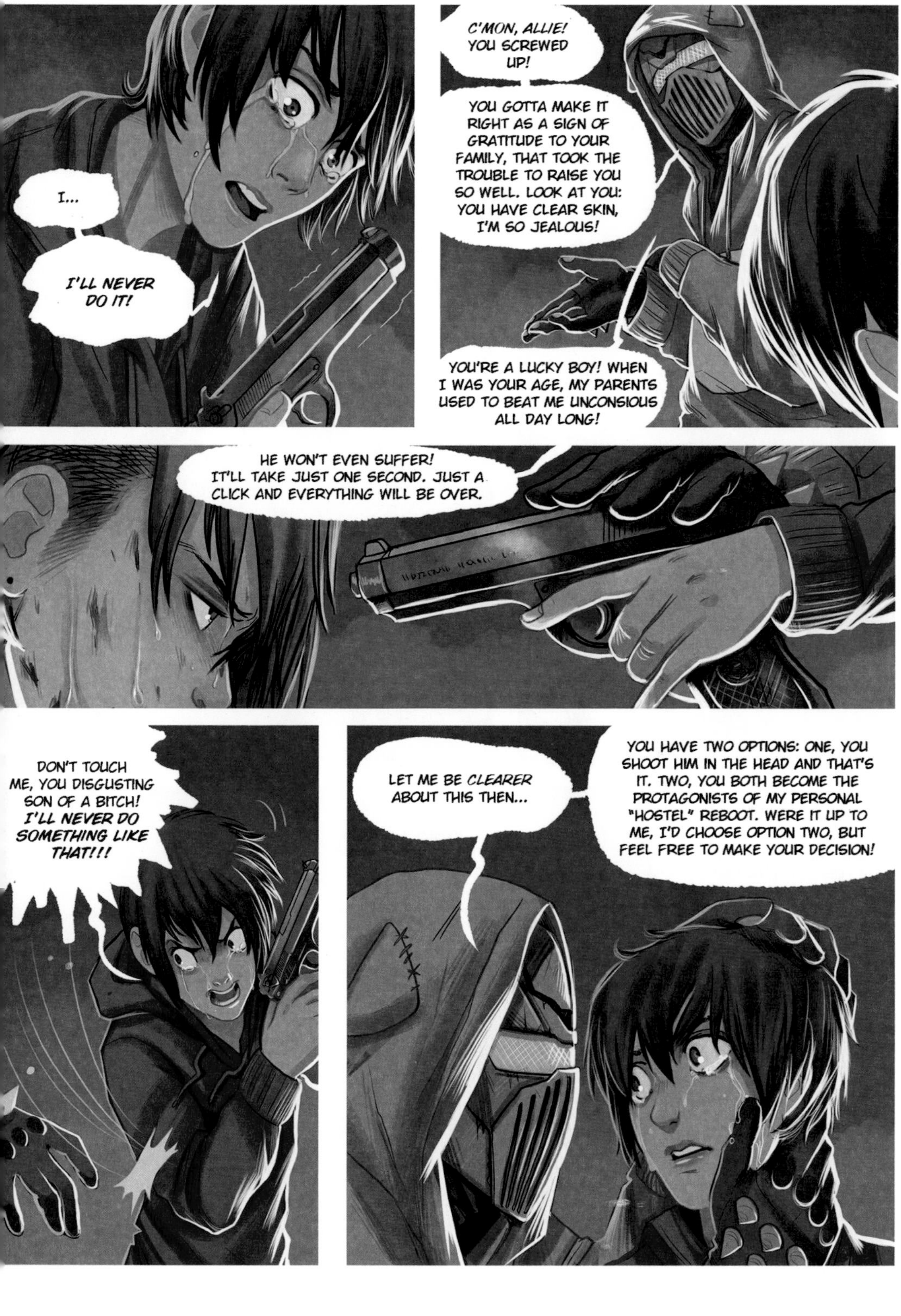
I...
I'LL NEVER DO IT!
C'MON, ALLIE! YOU SCREWED UP!
YOU GOTTA MAKE IT RIGHT AS A SIGN OF GRATITUDE TO YOUR FAMILY, THAT TOOK THE TROUBLE TO RAISE YOU SO WELL. LOOK AT YOU: YOU HAVE CLEAR SKIN, I'M SO JEALOUS!
YOU'RE A LUCKY BOY! WHEN I WAS YOUR AGE, MY PARENTS USED TO BEAT ME UNCONSIOUS ALL DAY LONG!
HE WON'T EVEN SUFFER! IT'LL TAKE JUST ONE SECOND. JUST A CLICK AND EVERYTHING WILL BE OVER.
DON'T TOUCH ME, YOU DISGUSTING SON OF A BITCH! I'LL NEVER DO SOMETHING LIKE THAT!!!
LET ME BE CLEARER ABOUT THIS THEN...
YOU HAVE TWO OPTIONS: ONE, YOU SHOOT HIM IN THE HEAD AND THAT'S IT. TWO, YOU BOTH BECOME THE PROTAGONISTS OF MY PERSONAL "HOSTEL" REBOOT. WERE IT UP TO ME, I'D CHOOSE OPTION TWO, BUT FEEL FREE TO MAKE YOUR DECISION!

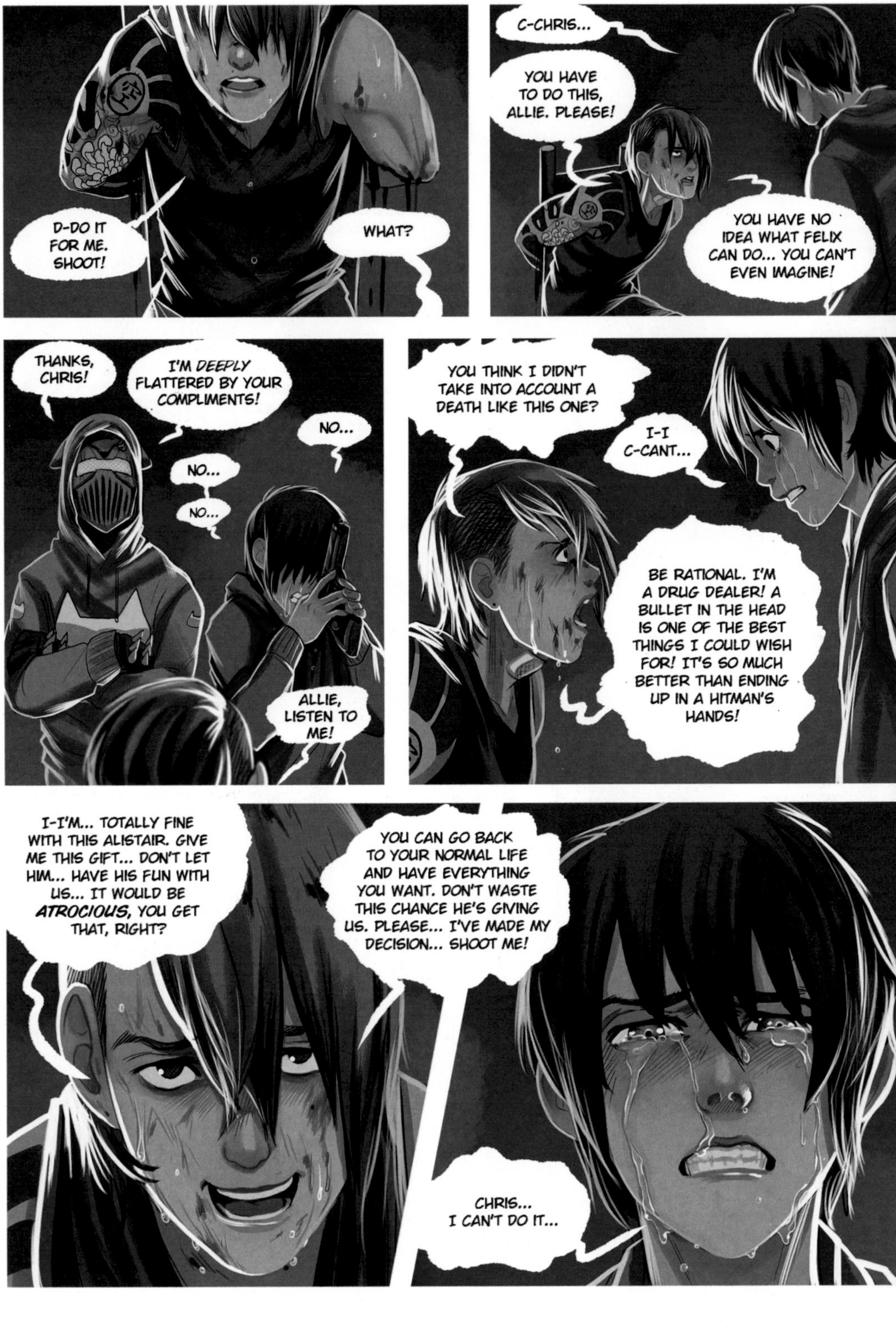
D-DO IT FOR ME. SHOOT!
WHAT?
C-CHRIS...
YOU HAVE TO DO THIS, ALLIE. PLEASE!
YOU HAVE NO IDEA WHAT FELIX CAN DO... YOU CAN'T EVEN IMAGINE!
THANKS, CHRIS!
I'M *DEEPLY* FLATTERED BY YOUR COMPLIMENTS!
NO...
NO...
NO...
ALLIE, LISTEN TO ME!
YOU THINK I DIDN'T TAKE INTO ACCOUNT A DEATH LIKE THIS ONE?
I-I C-CANT...
BE RATIONAL. I'M A DRUG DEALER! A BULLET IN THE HEAD IS ONE OF THE BEST THINGS I COULD WISH FOR! IT'S SO MUCH BETTER THAN ENDING UP IN A HITMAN'S HANDS!
I-I'M... TOTALLY FINE WITH THIS ALISTAIR. GIVE ME THIS GIFT... DON'T LET HIM... HAVE HIS FUN WITH US... IT WOULD BE ***ATROCIOUS***, YOU GET THAT, RIGHT?
YOU CAN GO BACK TO YOUR NORMAL LIFE AND HAVE EVERYTHING YOU WANT. DON'T WASTE THIS CHANCE HE'S GIVING US. PLEASE... I'VE MADE MY DECISION... SHOOT ME!
CHRIS... I CAN'T DO IT...

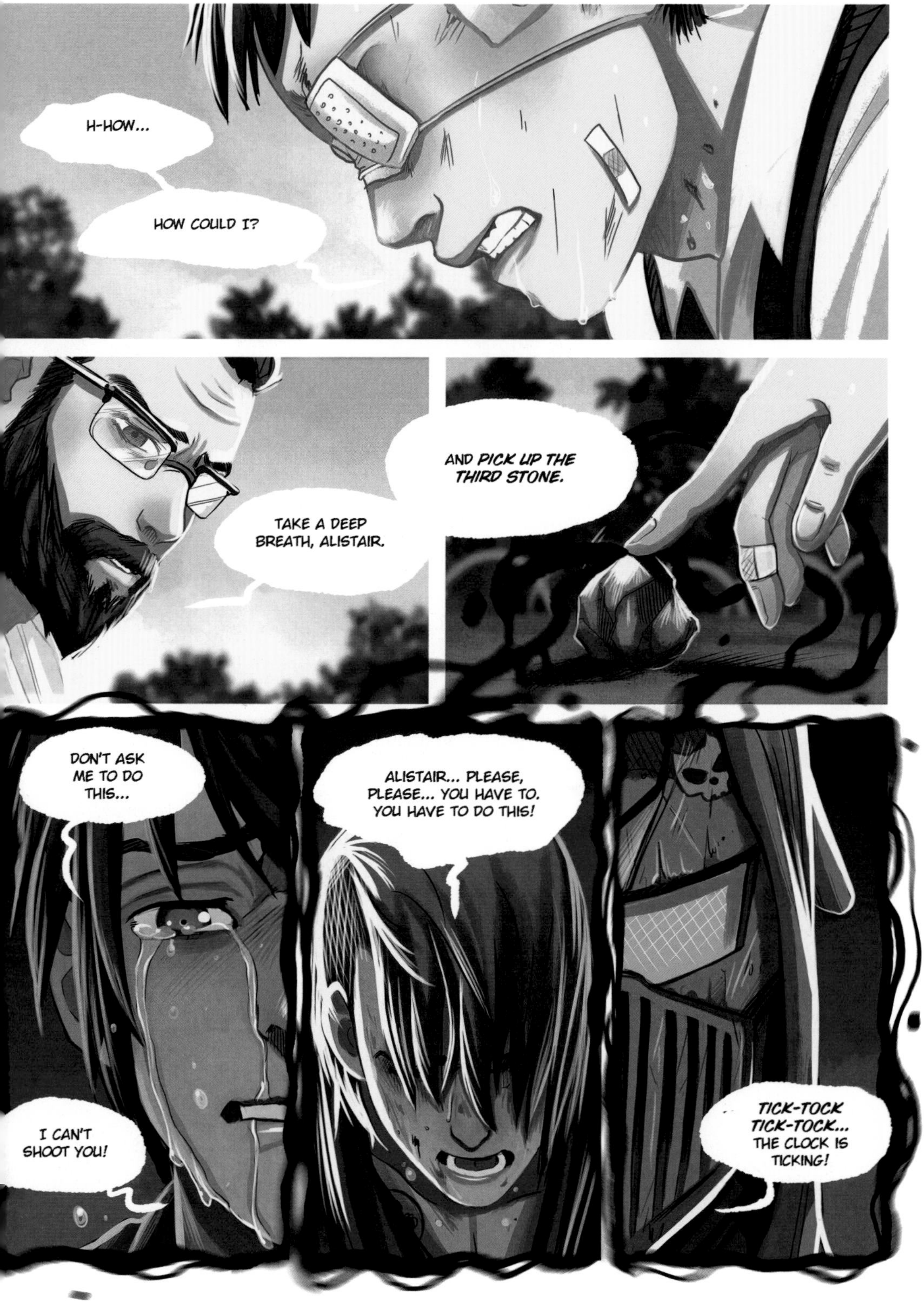
H-HOW...
HOW COULD I?
TAKE A DEEP BREATH, ALISTAIR.
AND PICK UP THE THIRD STONE.
DON'T ASK ME TO DO THIS...
I CAN'T SHOOT YOU!
ALISTAIR... PLEASE, PLEASE... YOU HAVE TO. YOU HAVE TO DO THIS!
TICK-TOCK TICK-TOCK... THE CLOCK IS TICKING!

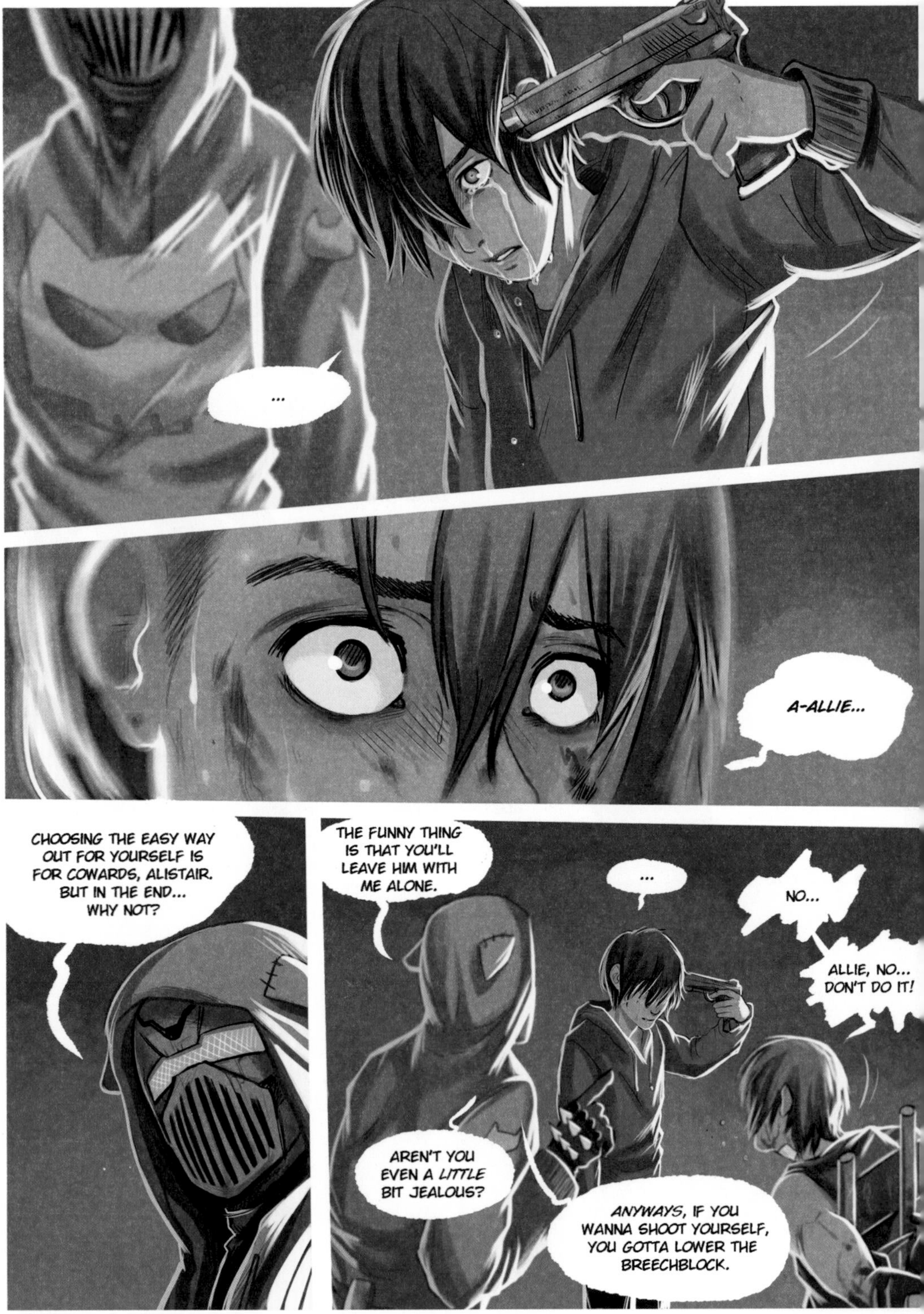
...
A-ALLIE...
CHOOSING THE EASY WAY OUT FOR YOURSELF IS FOR COWARDS, ALISTAIR. BUT IN THE END... WHY NOT?
THE FUNNY THING IS THAT YOU'LL LEAVE HIM WITH ME ALONE.
...
NO...
ALLIE, NO... DON'T DO IT!
AREN'T YOU EVEN A *LITTLE* BIT JEALOUS?
ANYWAYS, IF YOU WANNA SHOOT YOURSELF, YOU GOTTA LOWER THE BREECHBLOCK.

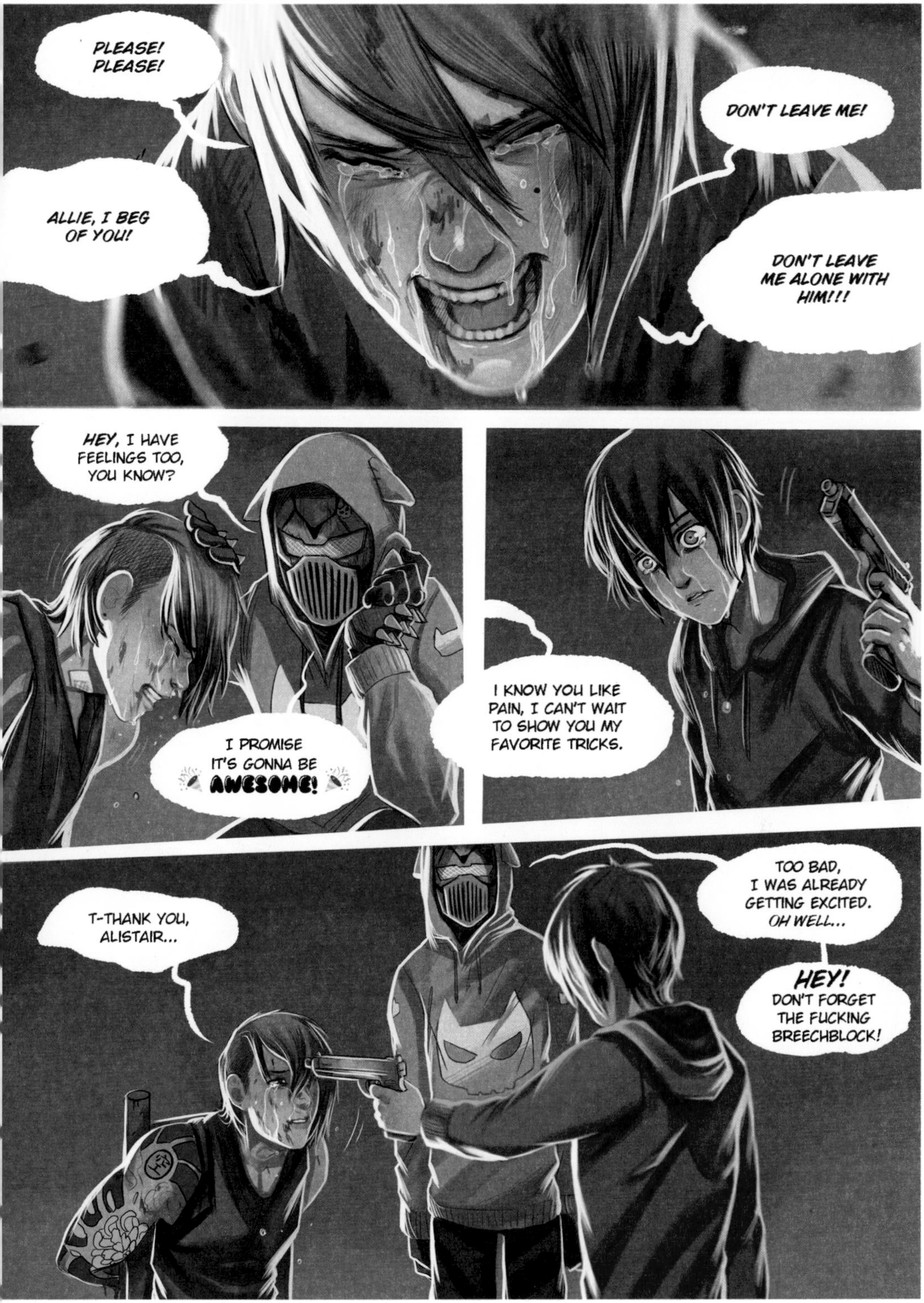
PLEASE! PLEASE!
DON'T LEAVE ME!
ALLIE, I BEG OF YOU!
DON'T LEAVE ME ALONE WITH HIM!!!
HEY, I HAVE FEELINGS TOO, YOU KNOW?
I PROMISE IT'S GONNA BE AWESOME!
I KNOW YOU LIKE PAIN, I CAN'T WAIT TO SHOW YOU MY FAVORITE TRICKS.
T-THANK YOU, ALISTAIR...
TOO BAD, I WAS ALREADY GETTING EXCITED. OH WELL...
HEY! DON'T FORGET THE FUCKING BREECHBLOCK!

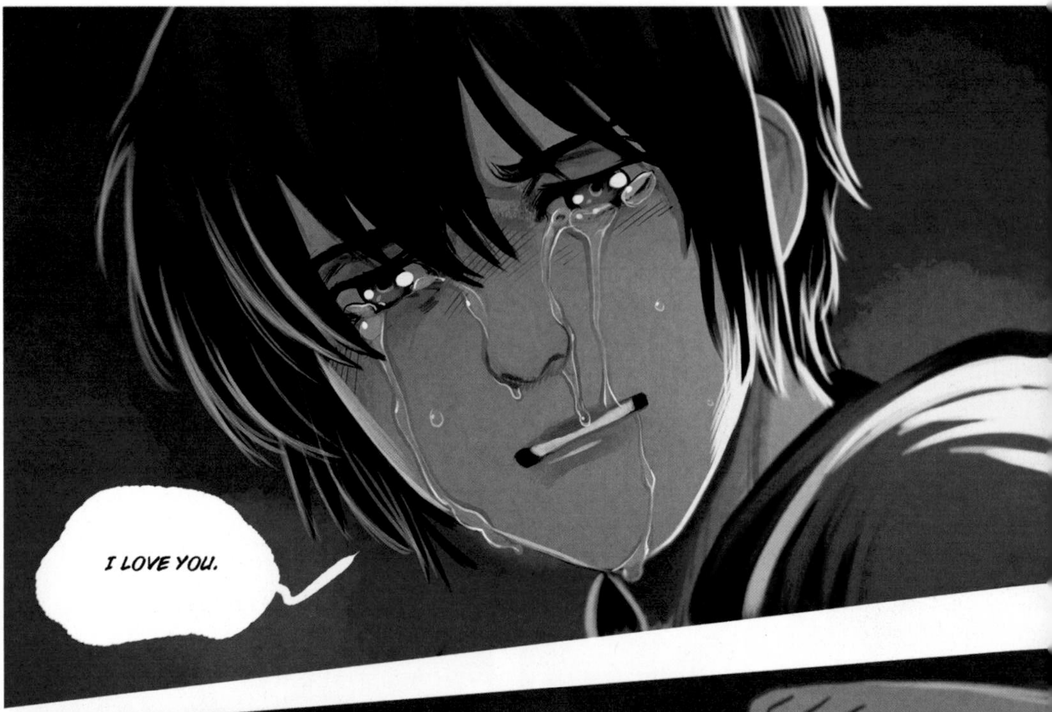
I LOVE YOU.

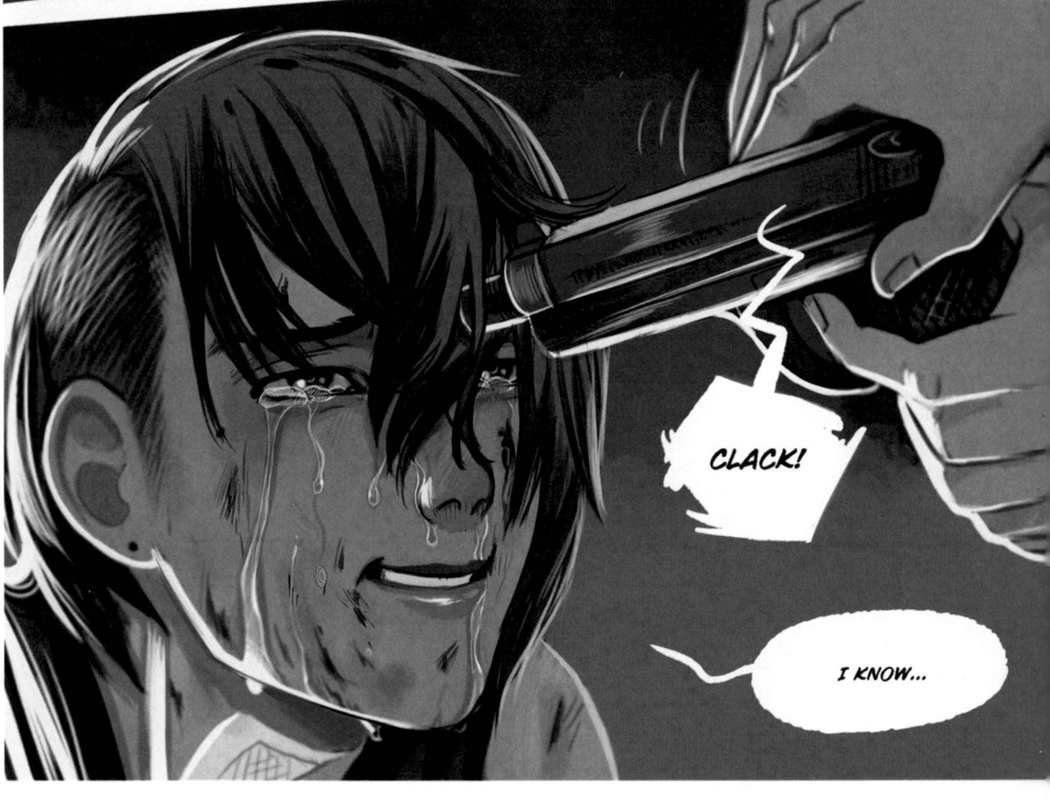
CLACK!
I KNOW...

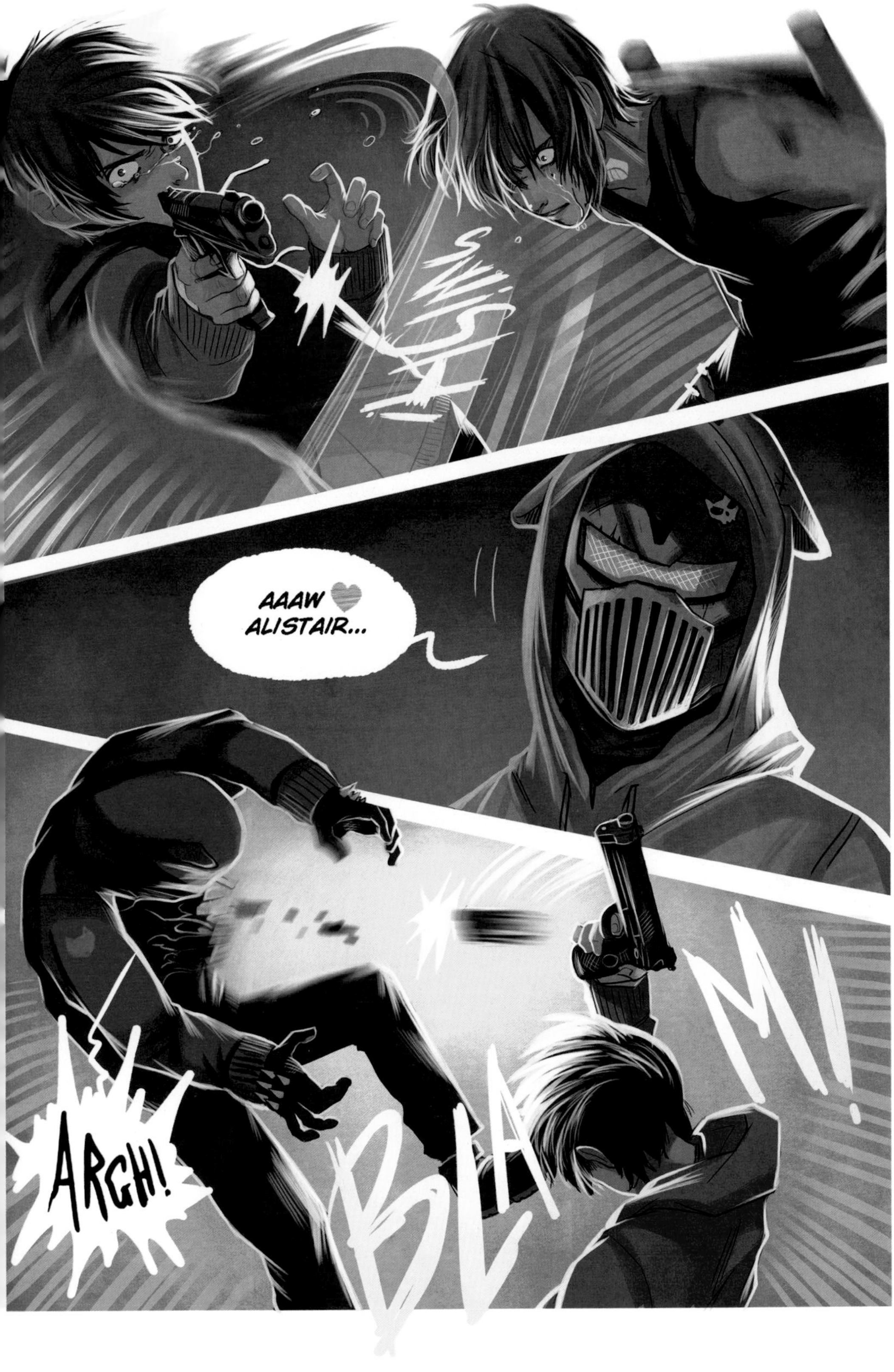

SWISH!
AAAW ♥ ALISTAIR...
ARGH!
BLAM!!

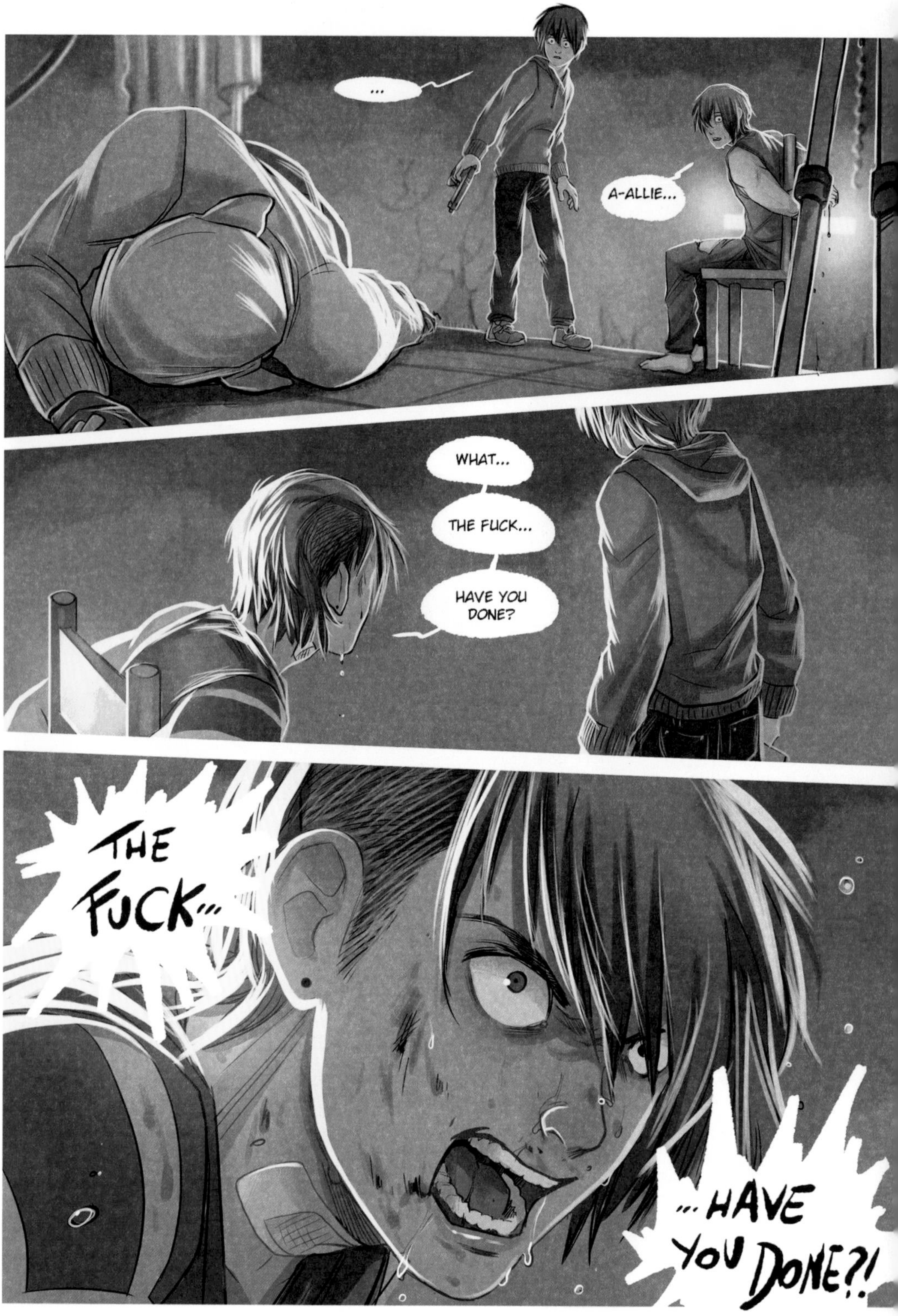
...
A-ALLIE...
WHAT...
THE FUCK...
HAVE YOU DONE?
THE FUCK...
...HAVE YOU DONE?!

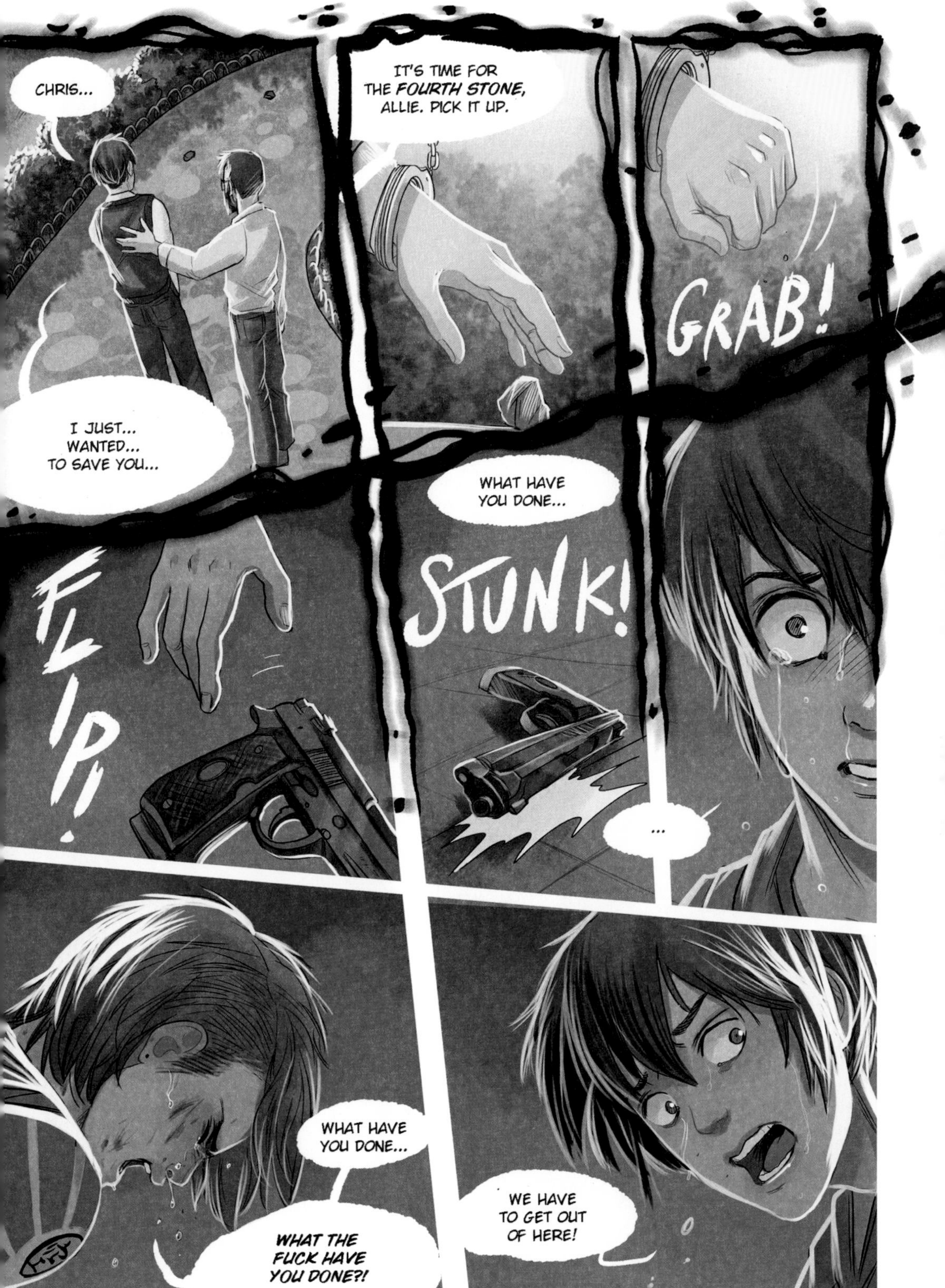
CHRIS...
I JUST... WANTED... TO SAVE YOU...
IT'S TIME FOR THE *FOURTH STONE*, ALLIE. PICK IT UP.
GRAB!
FLIP!
WHAT HAVE YOU DONE...
STUNK!
...
WHAT HAVE YOU DONE...
WHAT THE FUCK HAVE YOU DONE?!
WE HAVE TO GET OUT OF HERE!

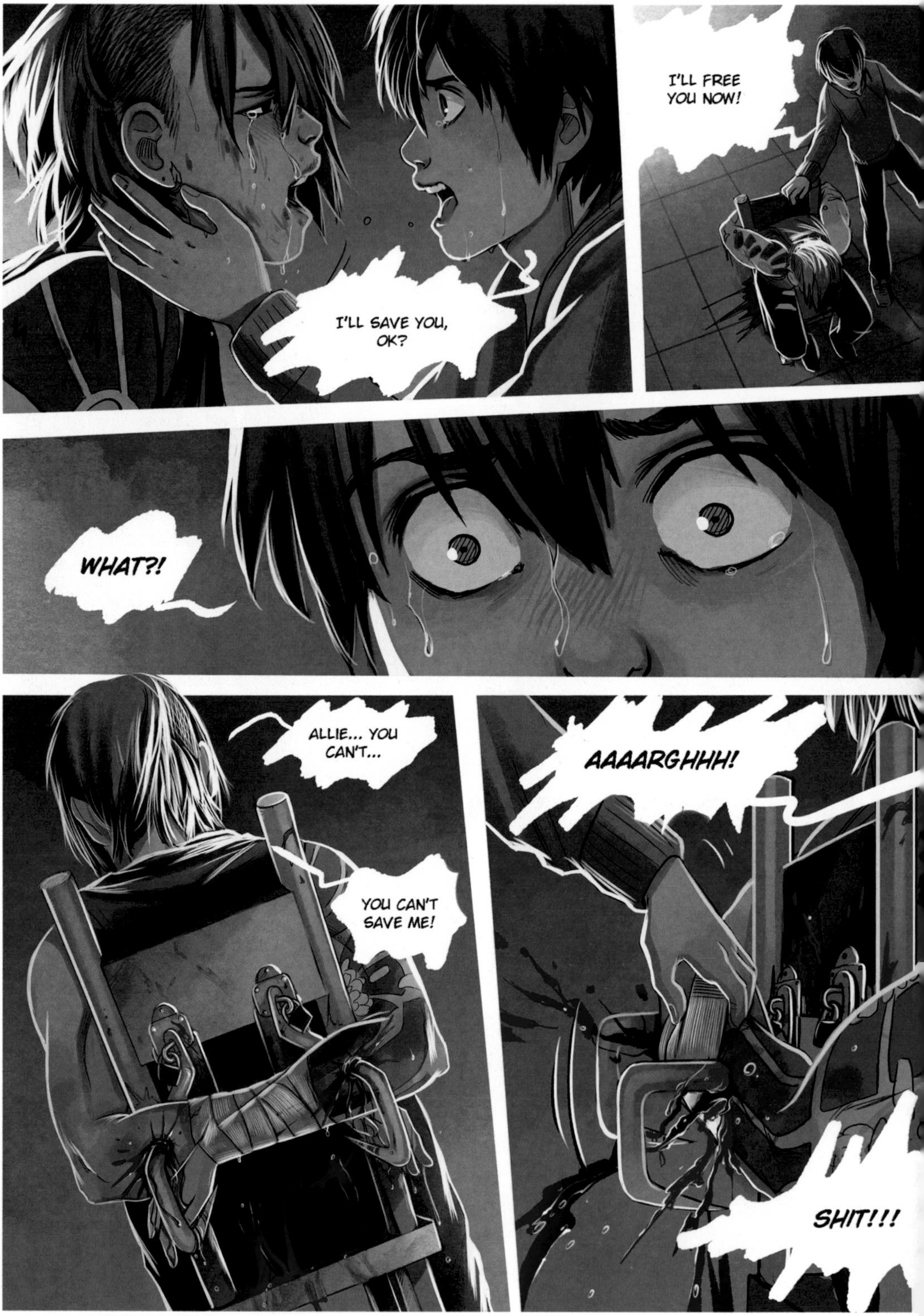
I'LL SAVE YOU, OK?
I'LL FREE YOU NOW!
WHAT?!
ALLIE... YOU CAN'T...
YOU CAN'T SAVE ME!
AAAARGHHH!
SHIT!!!

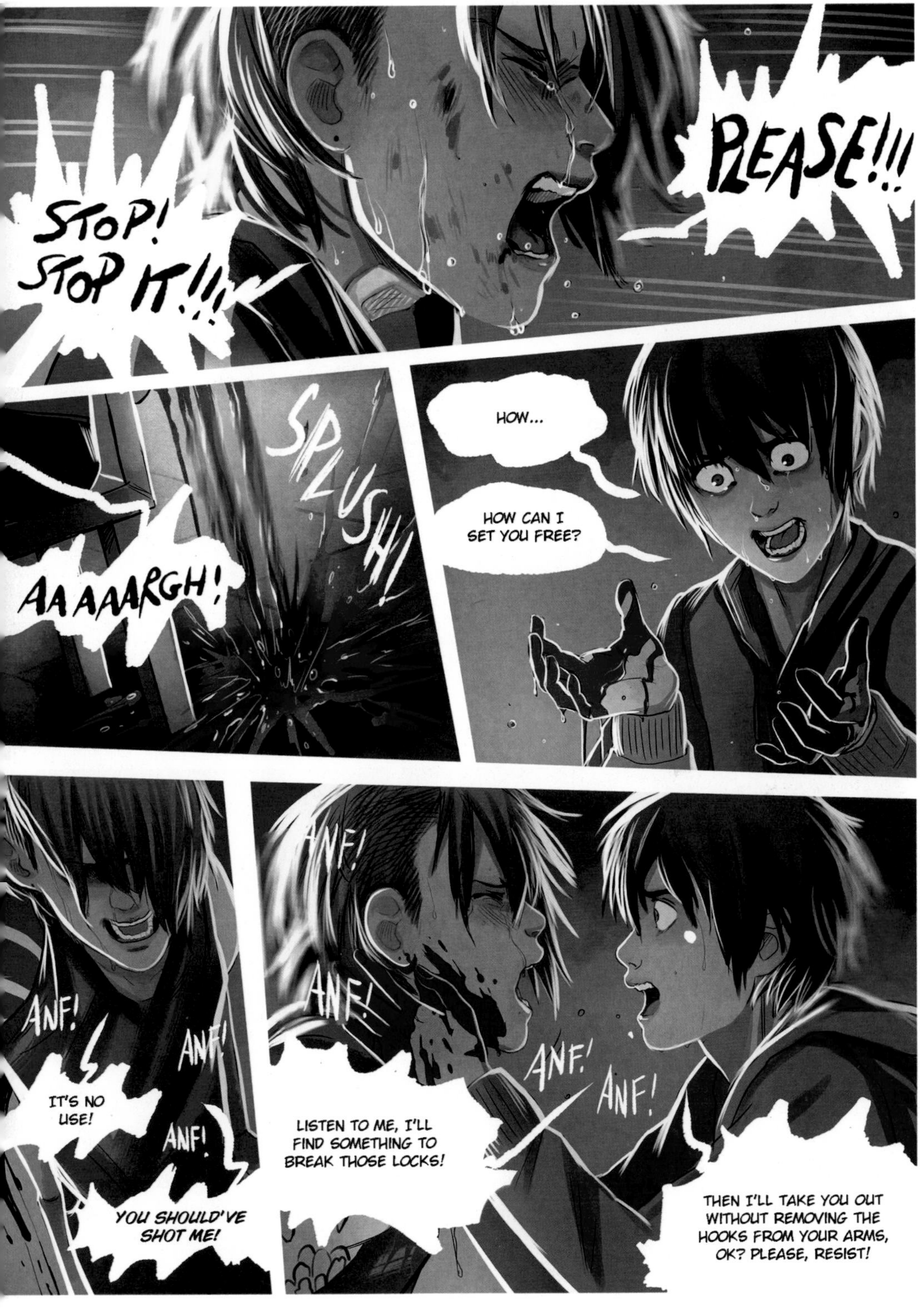
STOP! STOP IT!!!
PLEASE!!!
SPLUSH!
AAAAARGH!
HOW...
HOW CAN I SET YOU FREE?
ANF!
ANF!
IT'S NO USE!
ANF!
YOU SHOULD'VE SHOT ME!
ANF!
ANF!
LISTEN TO ME, I'LL FIND SOMETHING TO BREAK THOSE LOCKS!
ANF!
ANF!
THEN I'LL TAKE YOU OUT WITHOUT REMOVING THE HOOKS FROM YOUR ARMS, OK? PLEASE, RESIST!

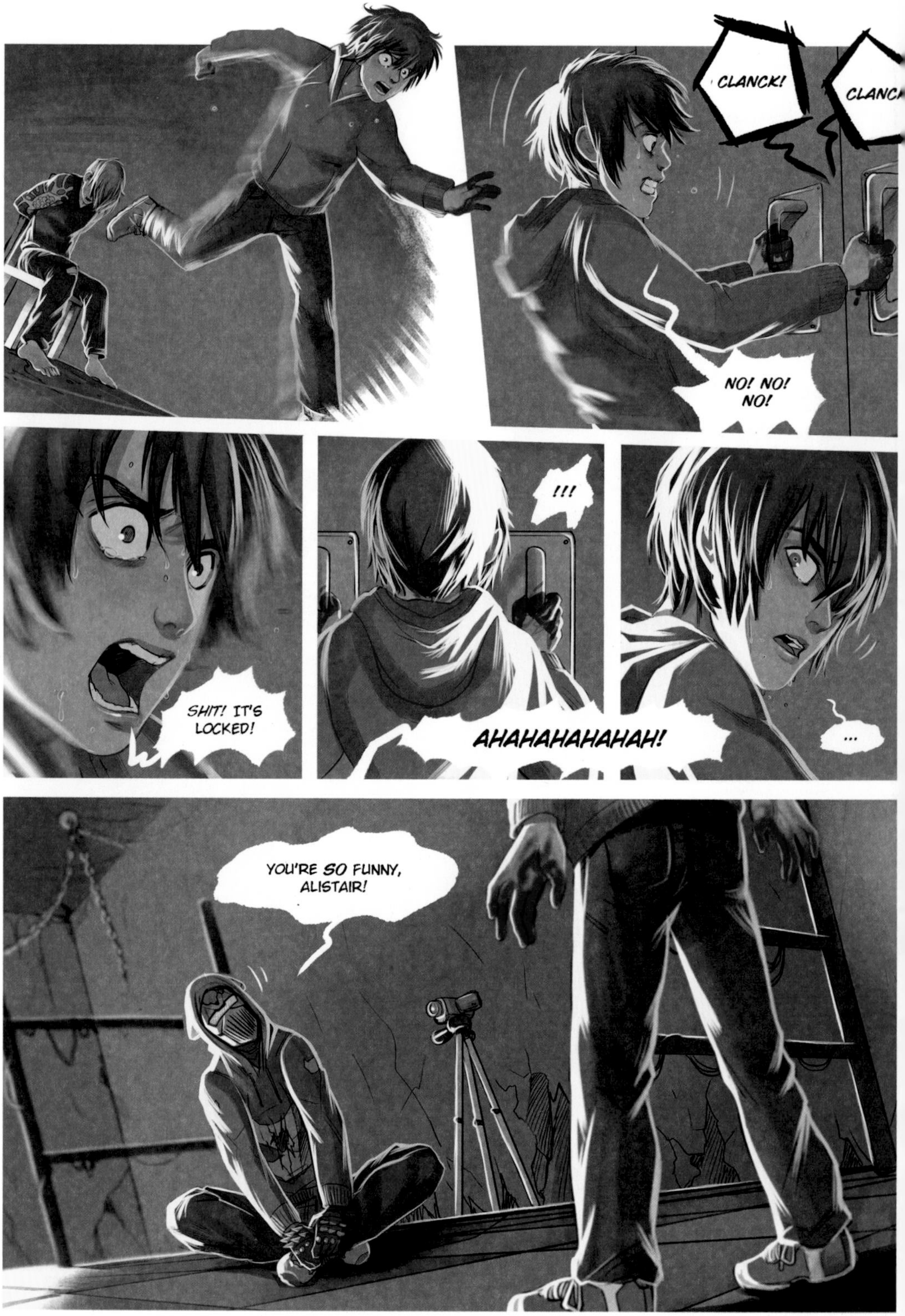
CLANCK!
CLANC
NO! NO! NO!
SHIT! IT'S LOCKED!
!!!
AHAHAHAHAHAH!
...
YOU'RE SO FUNNY, ALISTAIR!

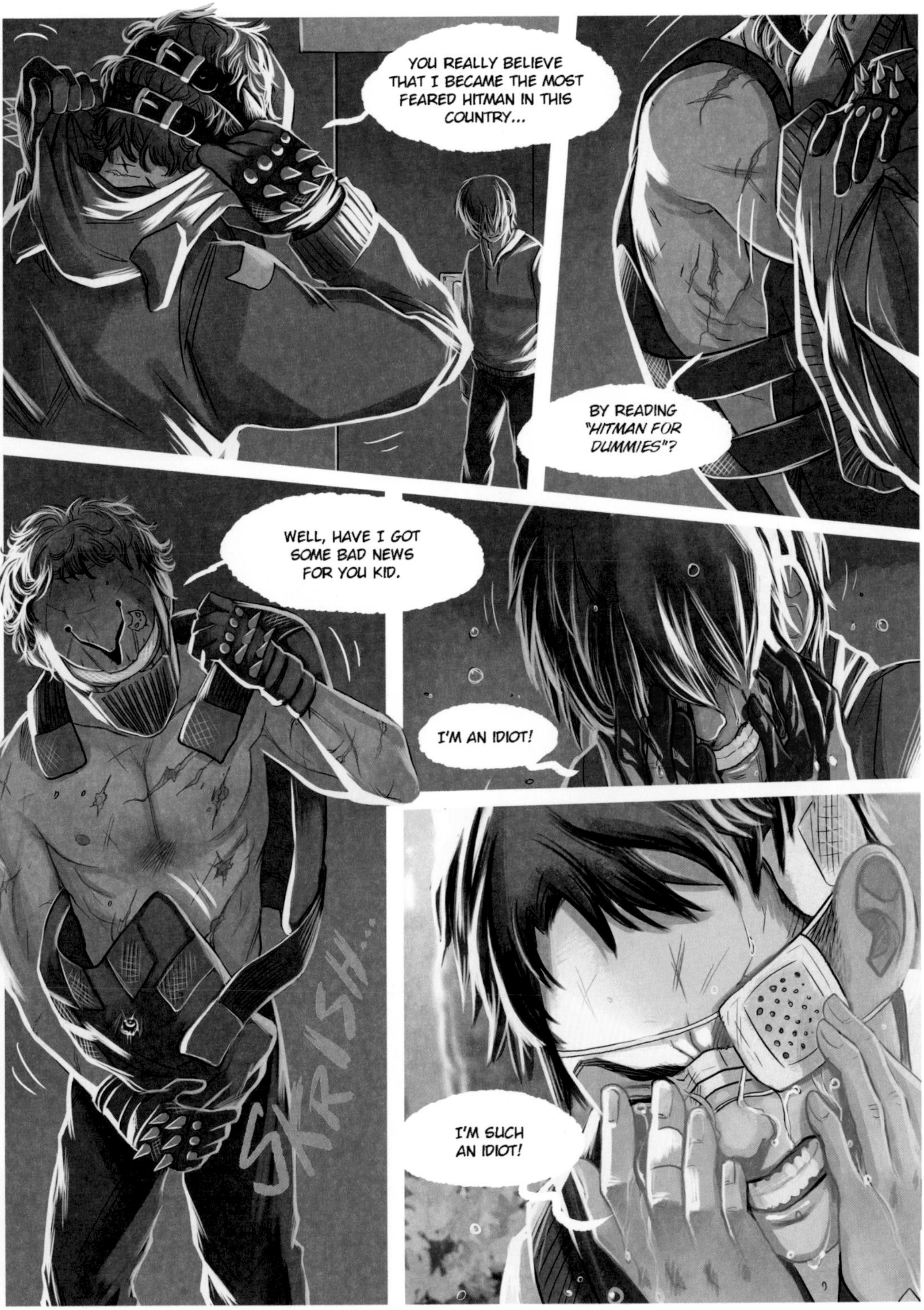

YOU REALLY BELIEVE THAT I BECAME THE MOST FEARED HITMAN IN THIS COUNTRY...
BY READING "HITMAN FOR DUMMIES"?
WELL, HAVE I GOT SOME BAD NEWS FOR YOU KID.
I'M AN IDIOT!
SKRISH...
I'M SUCH AN IDIOT!

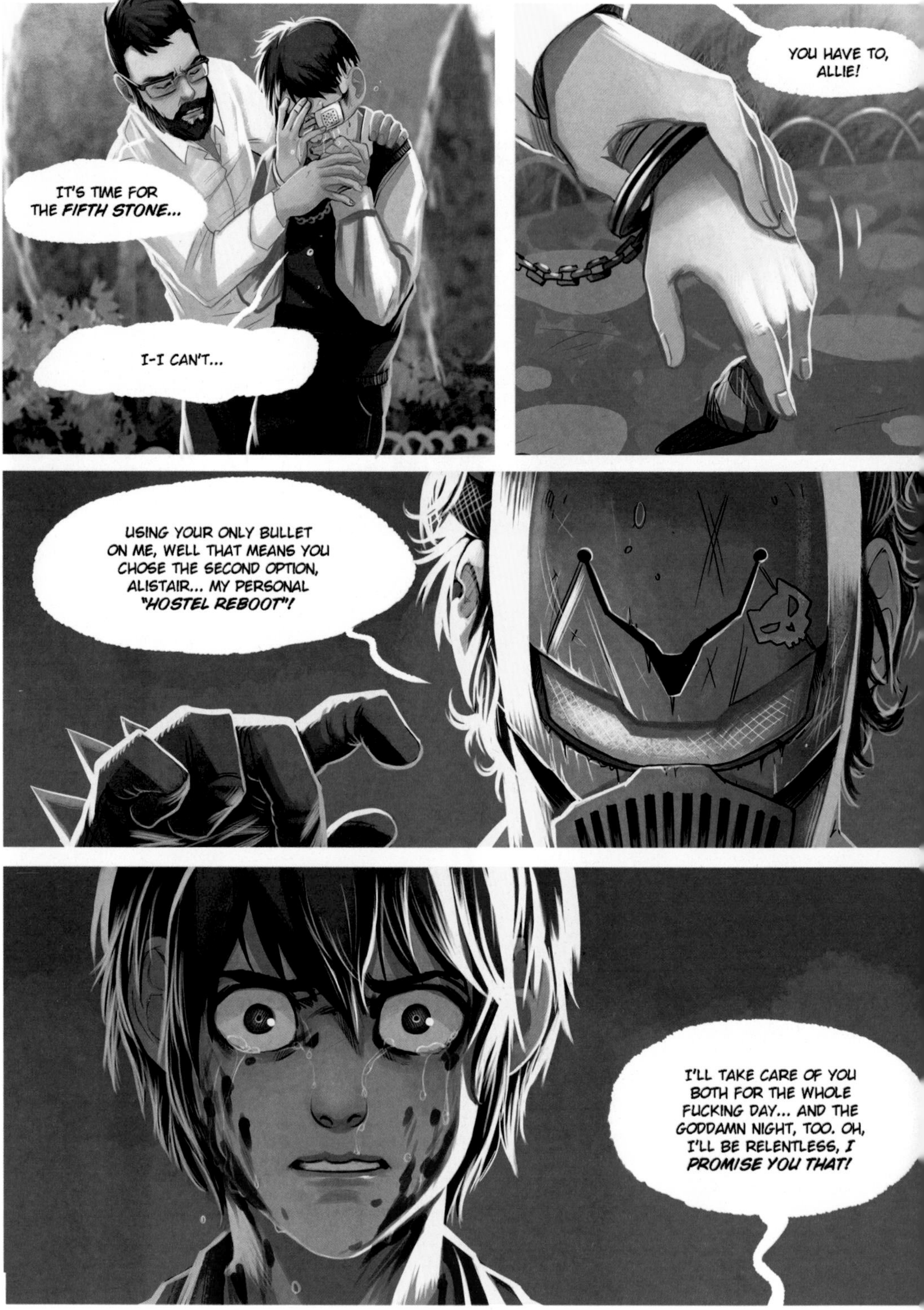
IT'S TIME FOR THE *FIFTH STONE...*
I-I CAN'T...
YOU HAVE TO, ALLIE!
USING YOUR ONLY BULLET ON ME, WELL THAT MEANS YOU CHOSE THE SECOND OPTION, ALISTAIR... MY PERSONAL *"HOSTEL REBOOT"!*
I'LL TAKE CARE OF YOU BOTH FOR THE WHOLE FUCKING DAY... AND THE GODDAMN NIGHT, TOO. OH, I'LL BE RELENTLESS, *I PROMISE YOU THAT!*

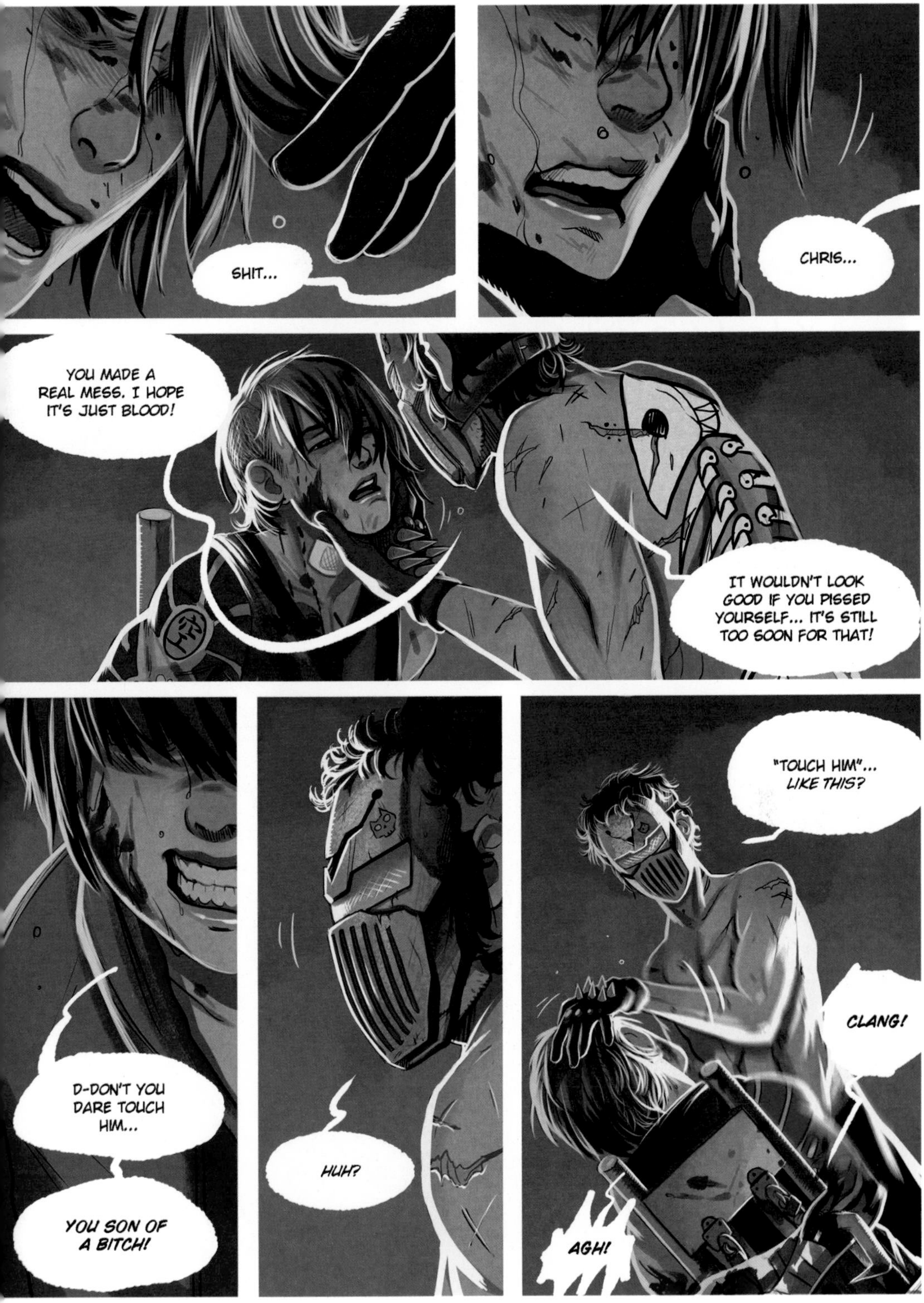
SHIT...
CHRIS...
YOU MADE A REAL MESS. I HOPE IT'S JUST BLOOD!
IT WOULDN'T LOOK GOOD IF YOU PISSED YOURSELF... IT'S STILL TOO SOON FOR THAT!
D-DON'T YOU DARE TOUCH HIM...
YOU SON OF A BITCH!
HUH?
"TOUCH HIM"... LIKE THIS?
CLANG!
AGH!

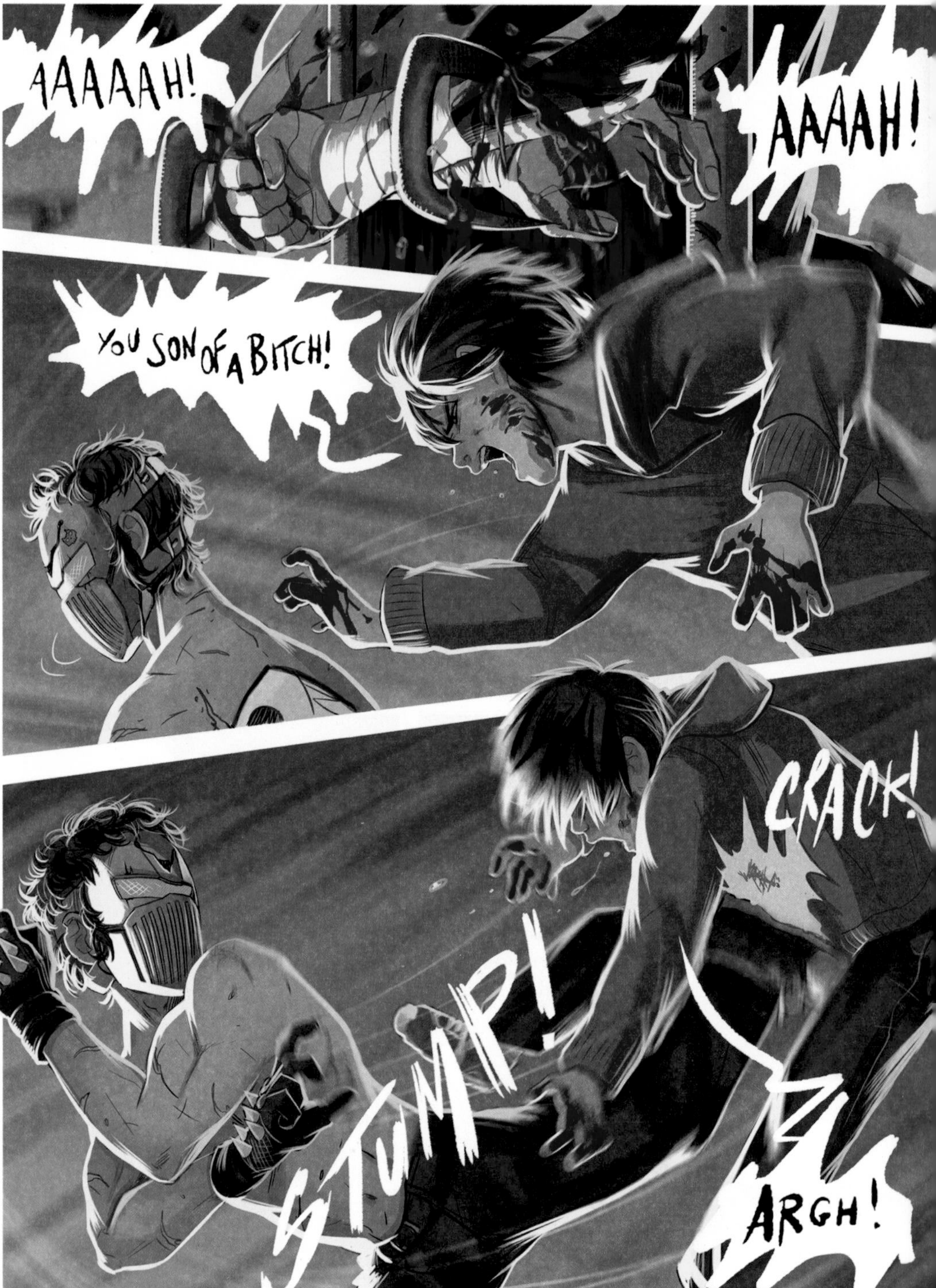
AAAAAH!
AAAAH!
YOU SON OF A BITCH!
CRACK!
STUMP!
ARGH!

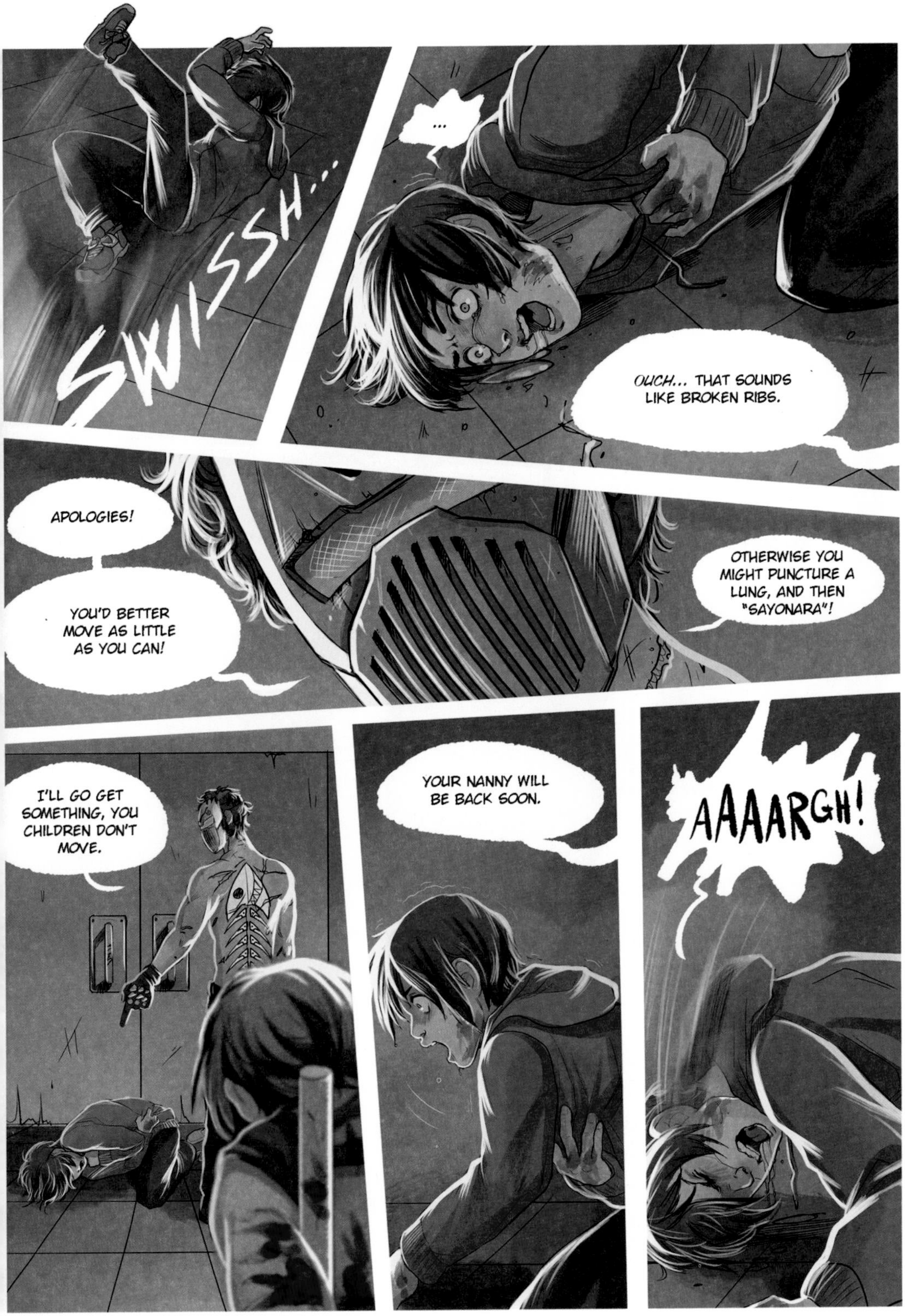
SWISSH...
...
OUCH... THAT SOUNDS LIKE BROKEN RIBS.
APOLOGIES!
YOU'D BETTER MOVE AS LITTLE AS YOU CAN!
OTHERWISE YOU MIGHT PUNCTURE A LUNG, AND THEN "SAYONARA"!
I'LL GO GET SOMETHING, YOU CHILDREN DON'T MOVE.
YOUR NANNY WILL BE BACK SOON.
AAAARGH!

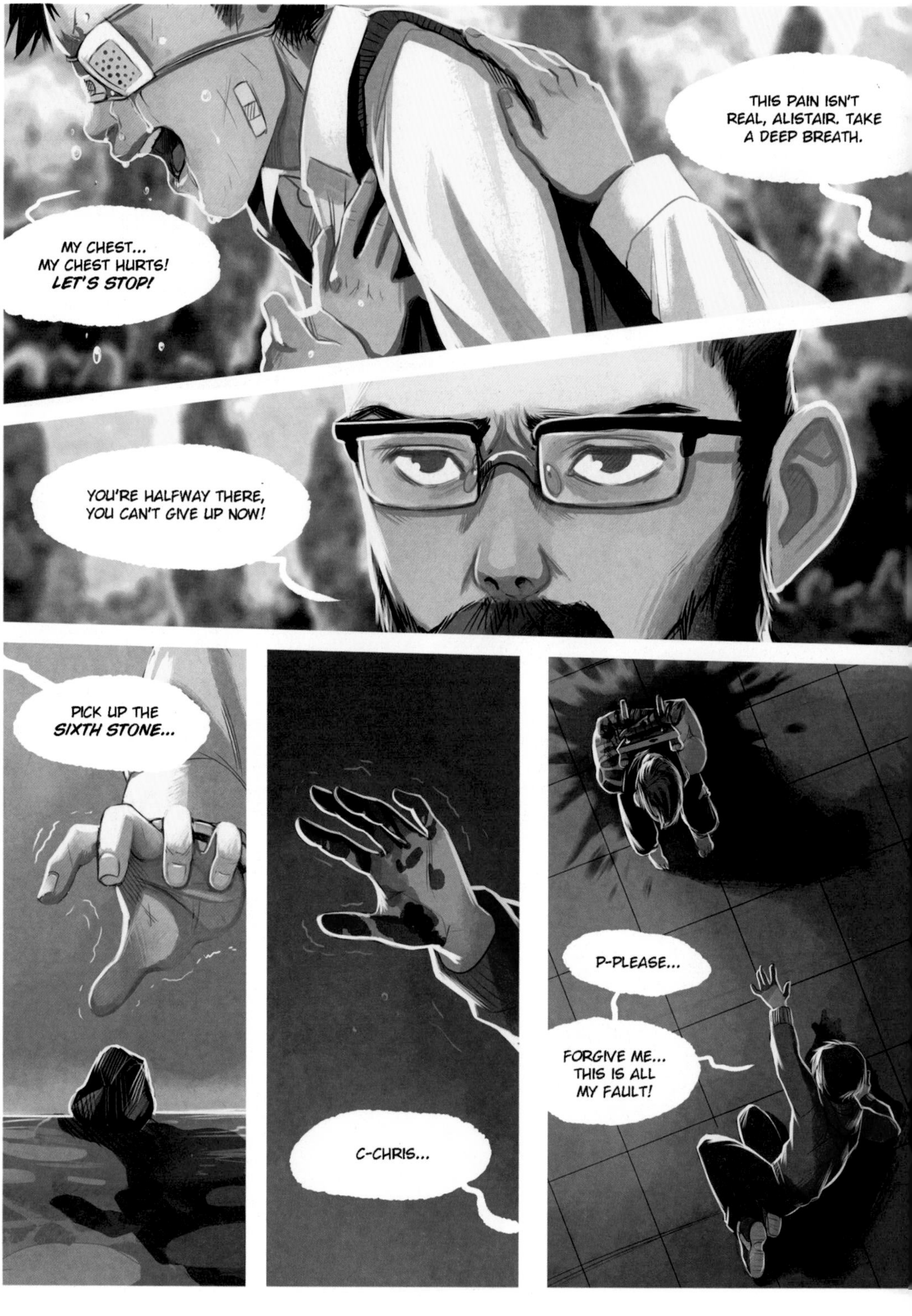
THIS PAIN ISN'T REAL, ALISTAIR. TAKE A DEEP BREATH.
MY CHEST... MY CHEST HURTS! LET'S STOP!
YOU'RE HALFWAY THERE, YOU CAN'T GIVE UP NOW!
PICK UP THE SIXTH STONE...
C-CHRIS...
P-PLEASE...
FORGIVE ME... THIS IS ALL MY FAULT!

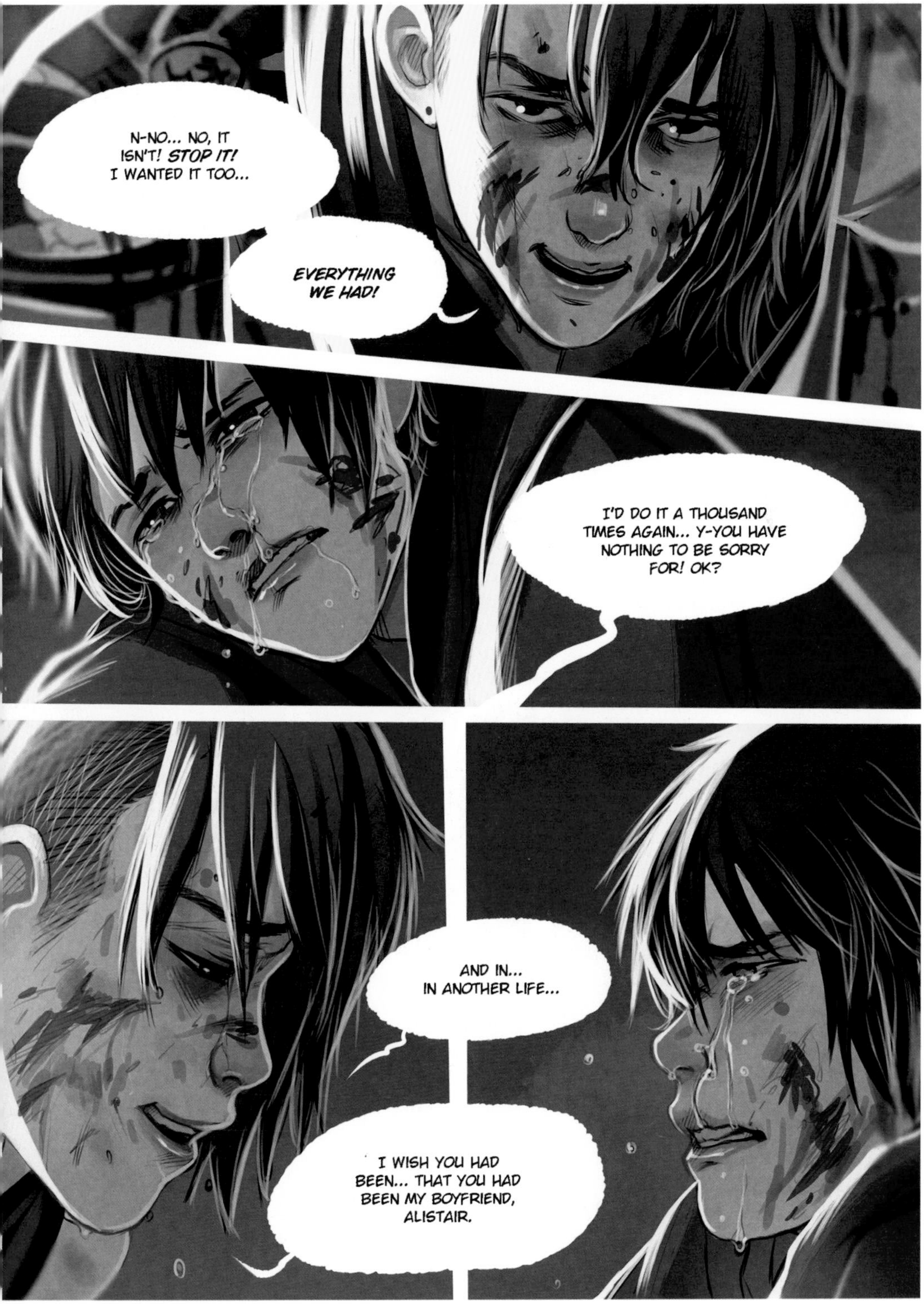
N-NO... NO, IT ISN'T! *STOP IT!* I WANTED IT TOO...
EVERYTHING WE HAD!
I'D DO IT A THOUSAND TIMES AGAIN... Y-YOU HAVE NOTHING TO BE SORRY FOR! OK?
AND IN... IN ANOTHER LIFE...
I WISH YOU HAD BEEN... THAT YOU HAD BEEN MY BOYFRIEND, ALISTAIR.

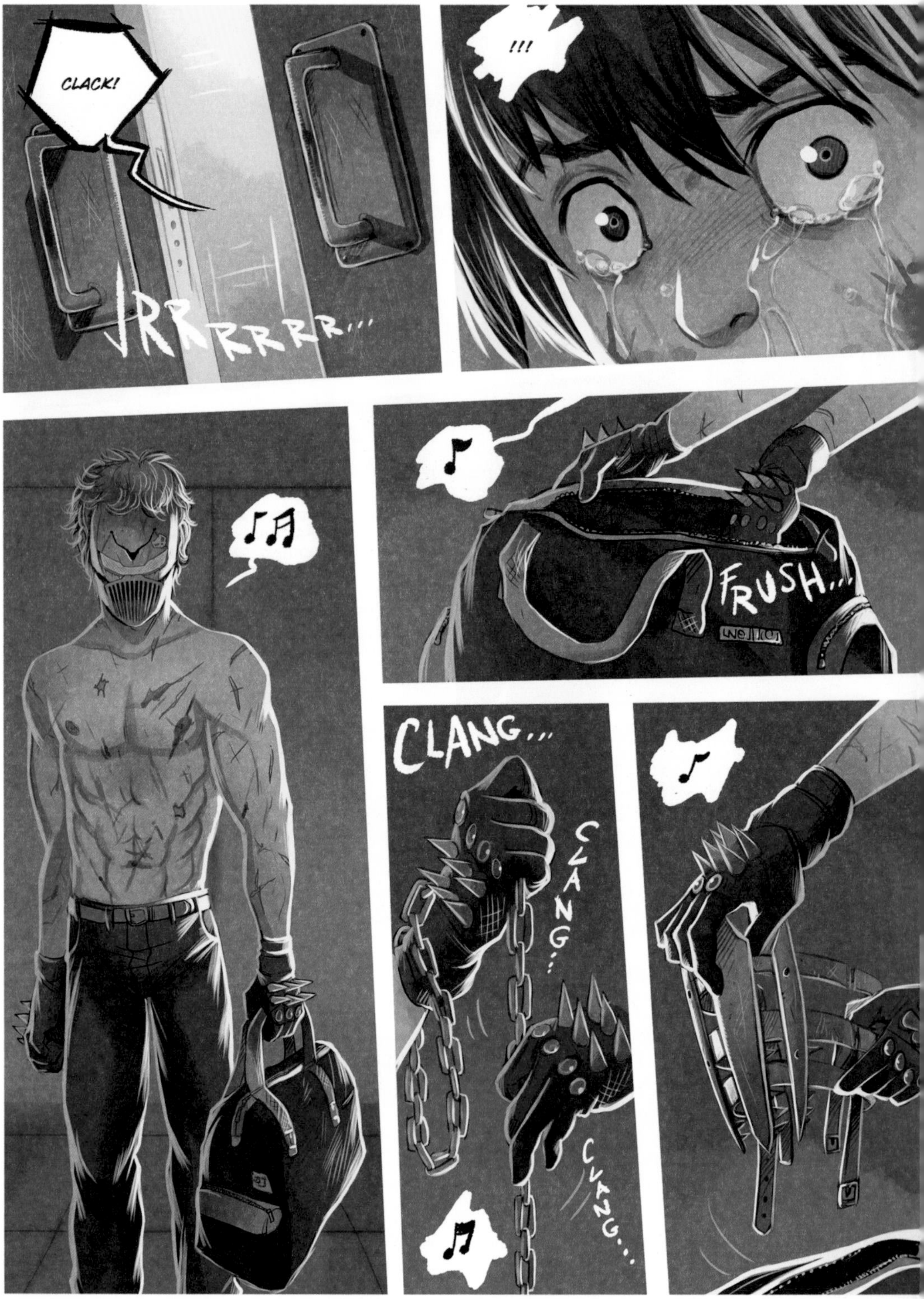
CLACK!
VRRRRRRR...
!!!
♪
FRUSH...
CLANG...
CLANG...
CLANG...
♪

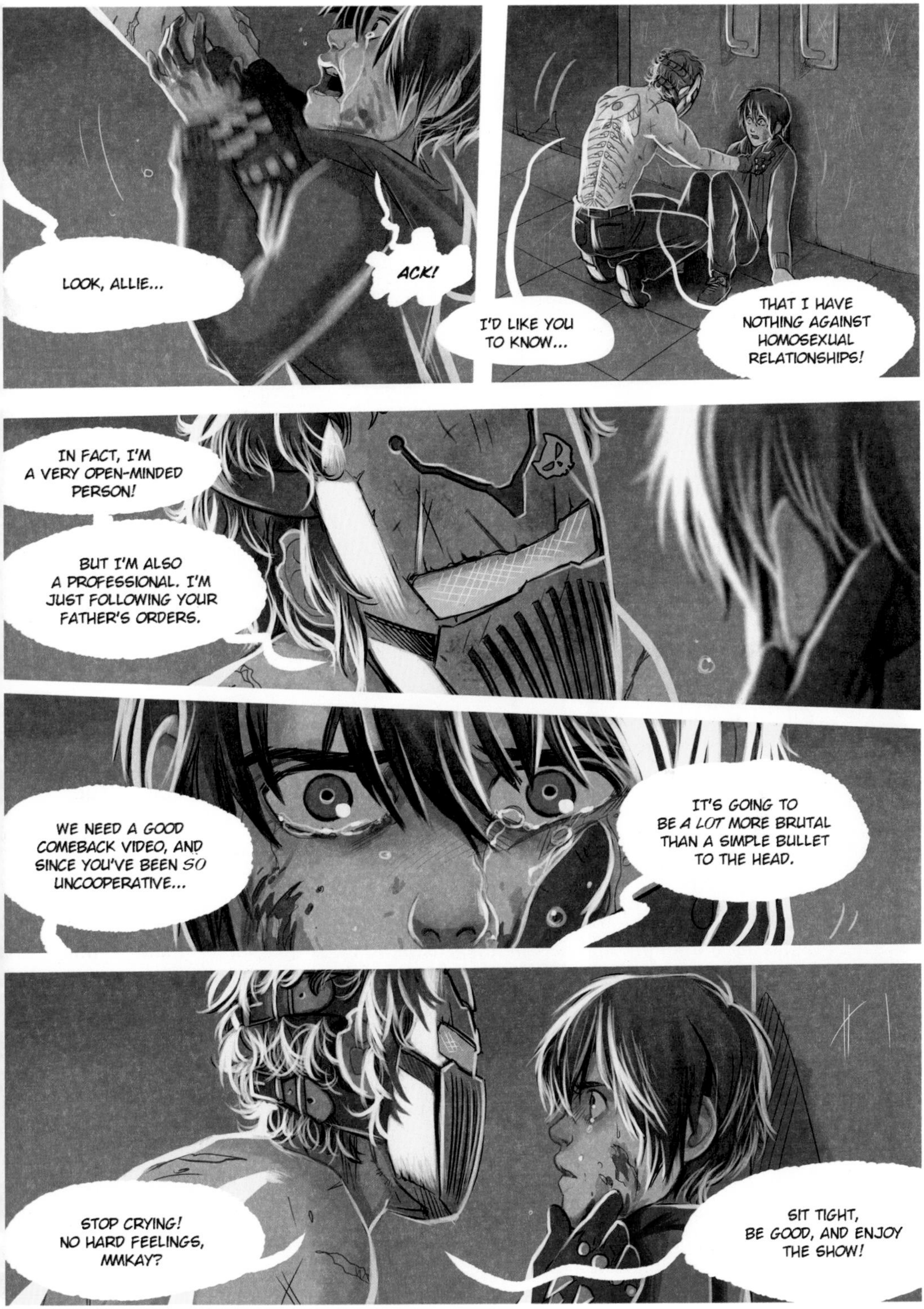
LOOK, ALLIE...
ACK!
I'D LIKE YOU TO KNOW...
THAT I HAVE NOTHING AGAINST HOMOSEXUAL RELATIONSHIPS!
IN FACT, I'M A VERY OPEN-MINDED PERSON!
BUT I'M ALSO A PROFESSIONAL. I'M JUST FOLLOWING YOUR FATHER'S ORDERS.
WE NEED A GOOD COMEBACK VIDEO, AND SINCE YOU'VE BEEN *SO* UNCOOPERATIVE...
IT'S GOING TO BE *A LOT* MORE BRUTAL THAN A SIMPLE BULLET TO THE HEAD.
STOP CRYING! NO HARD FEELINGS, MMKAY?
SIT TIGHT, BE GOOD, AND ENJOY THE SHOW!

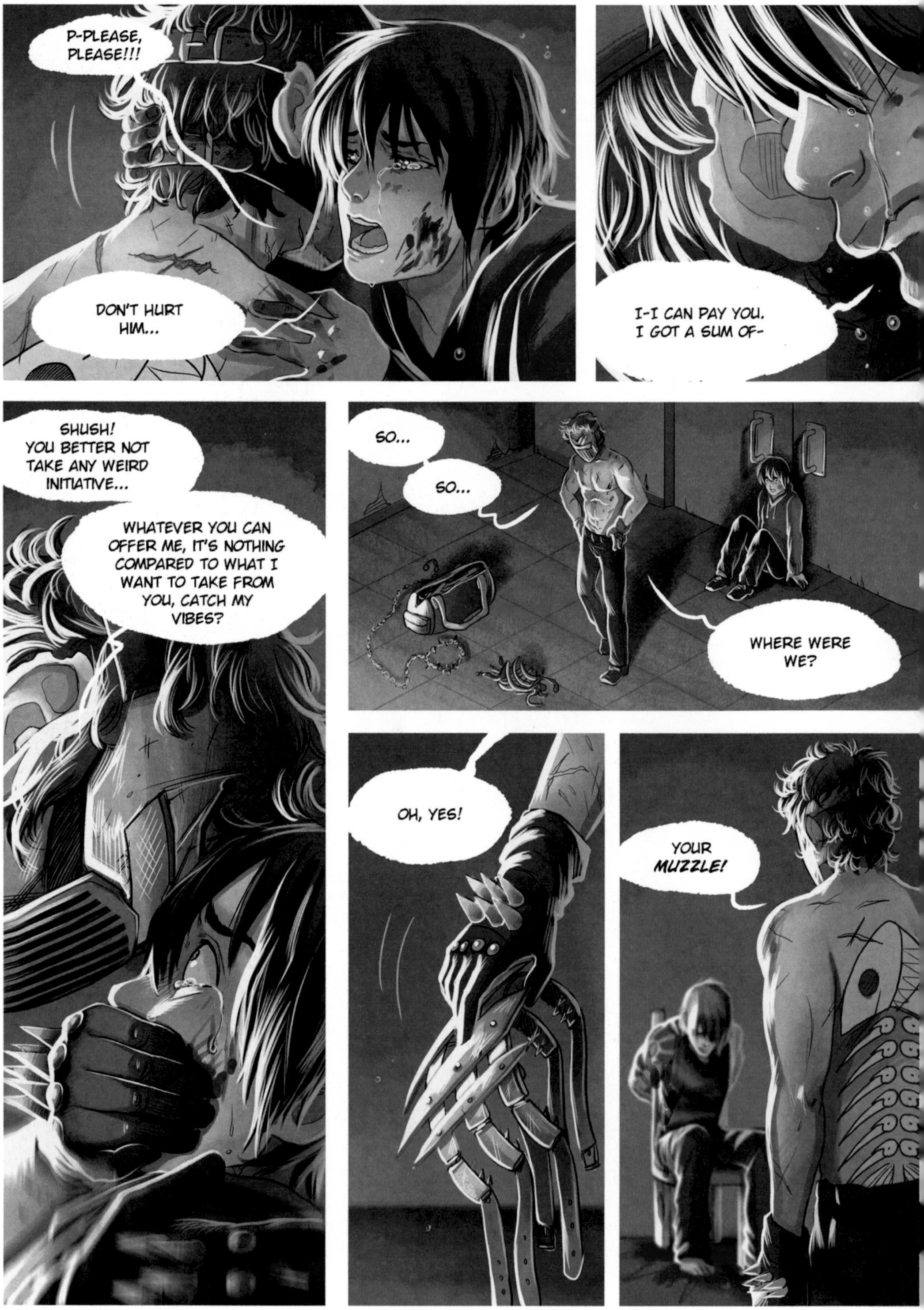
P-PLEASE, PLEASE!!!
DON'T HURT HIM...
I-I CAN PAY YOU. I GOT A SUM OF-
SHUSH! YOU BETTER NOT TAKE ANY WEIRD INITIATIVE...
WHATEVER YOU CAN OFFER ME, IT'S NOTHING COMPARED TO WHAT I WANT TO TAKE FROM YOU, CATCH MY VIBES?
SO...
SO...
WHERE WERE WE?
OH, YES!
YOUR *MUZZLE!*

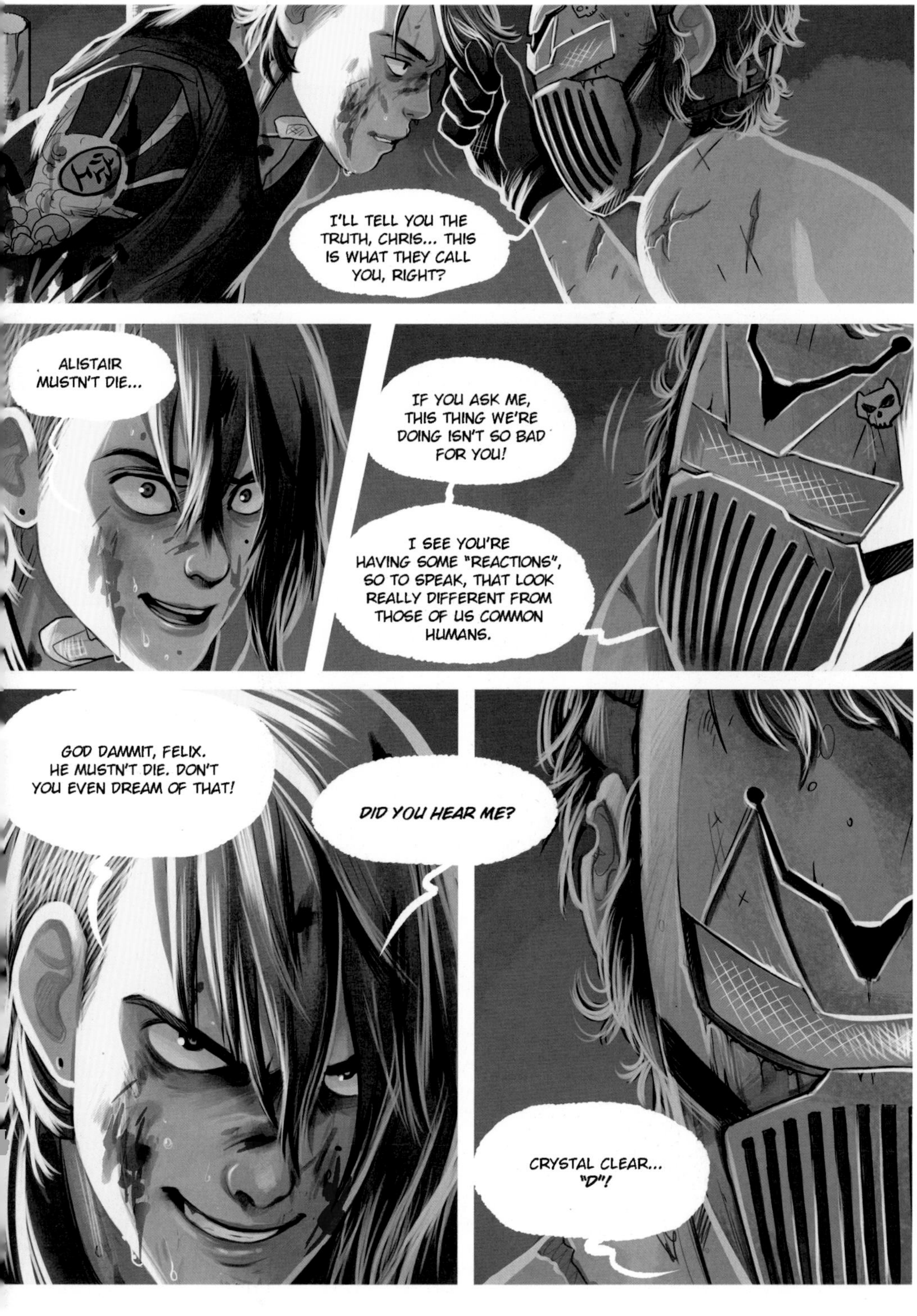
I'LL TELL YOU THE TRUTH, CHRIS... THIS IS WHAT THEY CALL YOU, RIGHT?
ALISTAIR MUSTN'T DIE...
IF YOU ASK ME, THIS THING WE'RE DOING ISN'T SO BAD FOR YOU!
I SEE YOU'RE HAVING SOME "REACTIONS", SO TO SPEAK, THAT LOOK REALLY DIFFERENT FROM THOSE OF US COMMON HUMANS.
GOD DAMMIT, FELIX. HE MUSTN'T DIE. DON'T YOU EVEN DREAM OF THAT!
DID YOU HEAR ME?
CRYSTAL CLEAR... "D"!

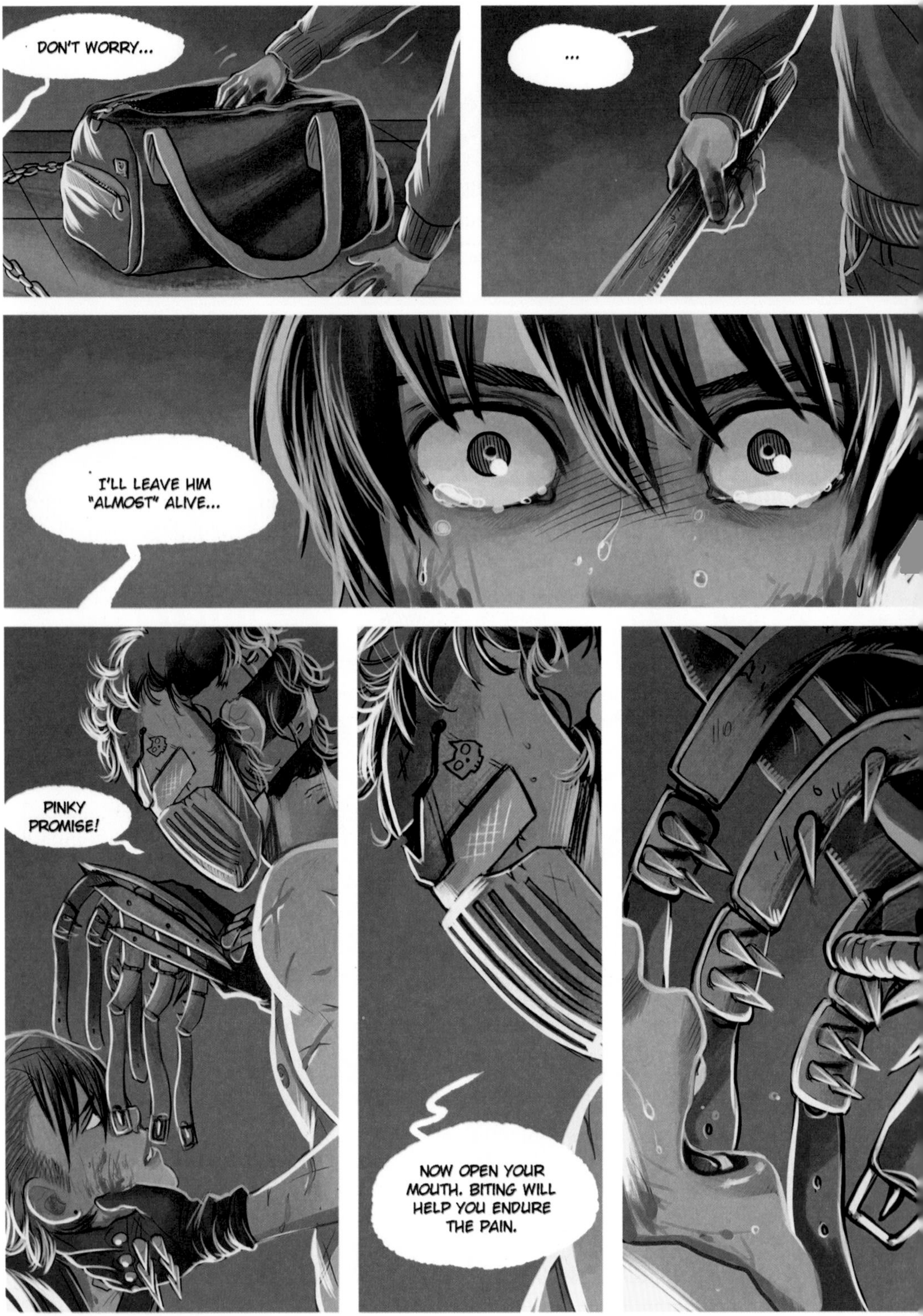
DON'T WORRY...
...
I'LL LEAVE HIM "ALMOST" ALIVE...
PINKY PROMISE!
NOW OPEN YOUR MOUTH. BITING WILL HELP YOU ENDURE THE PAIN.

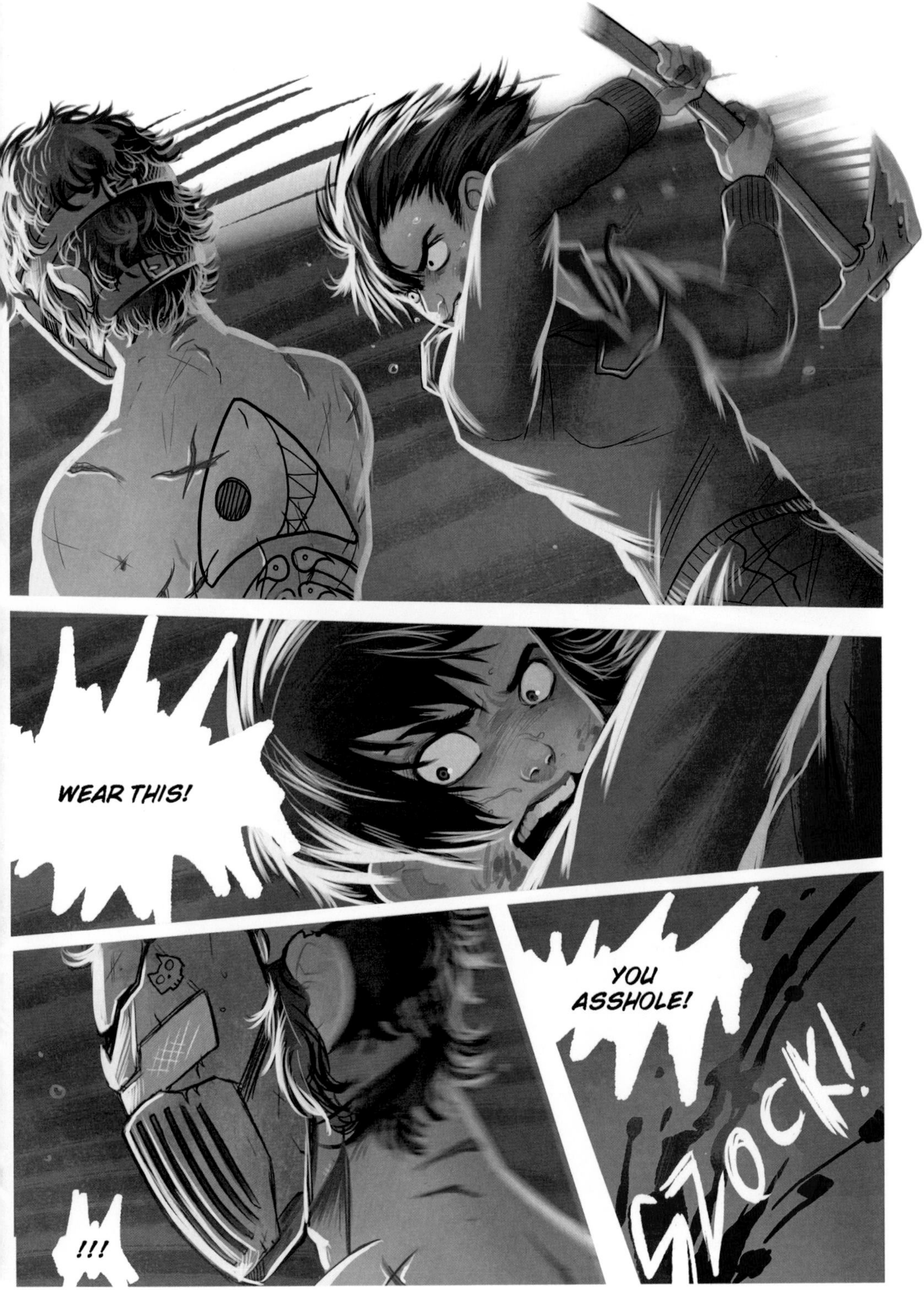
WEAR THIS!
!!!
YOU ASSHOLE!
ZOCK!

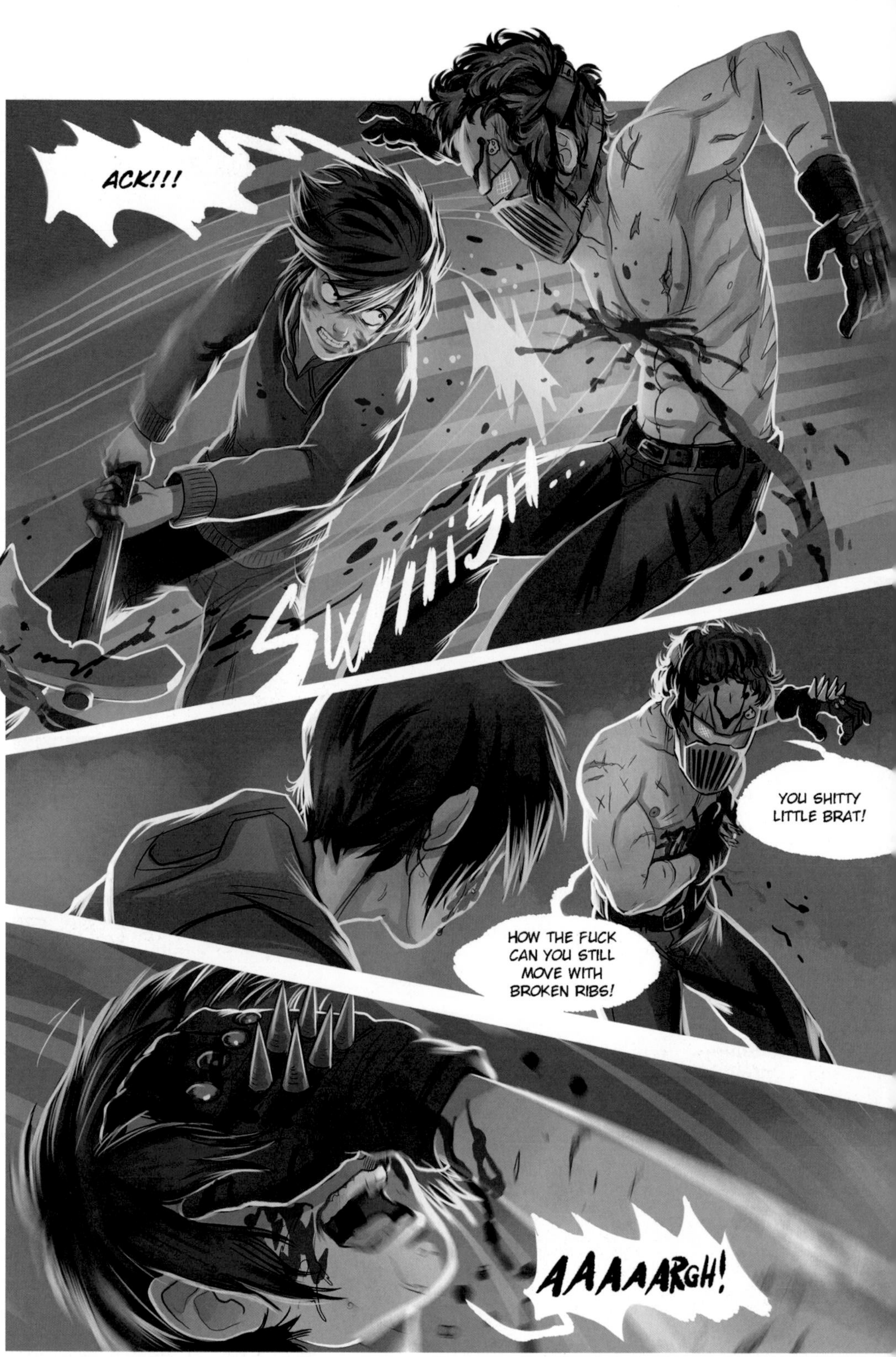
ACK!!!
SWIIIISH...
YOU SHITTY LITTLE BRAT!
HOW THE FUCK CAN YOU STILL MOVE WITH BROKEN RIBS!
AAAAARGH!

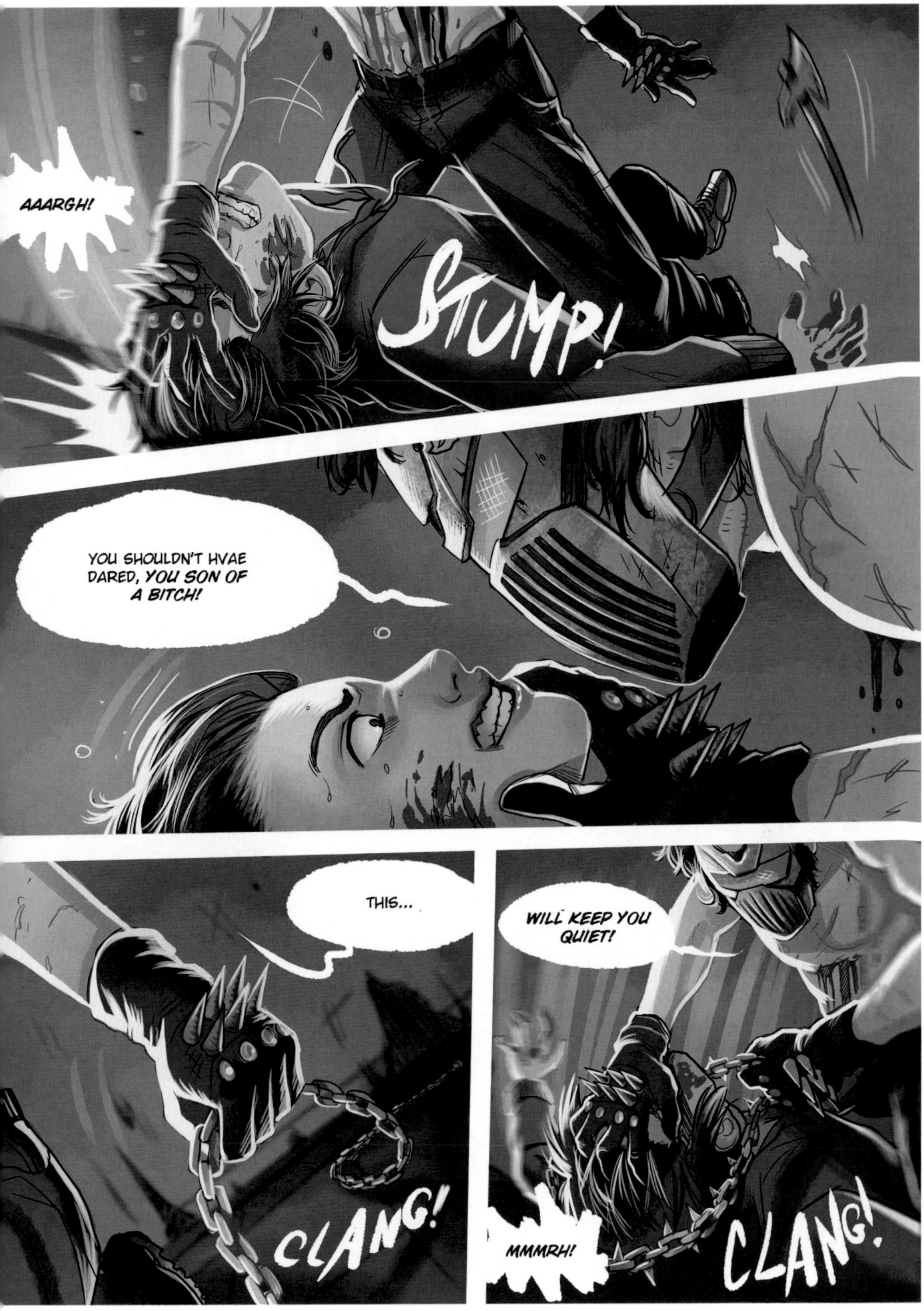
AAARGH!
STUMP!
YOU SHOULDN'T HVAE DARED, YOU SON OF A BITCH!
THIS...
CLANG!
WILL KEEP YOU QUIET!
MMMRH!
CLANG!

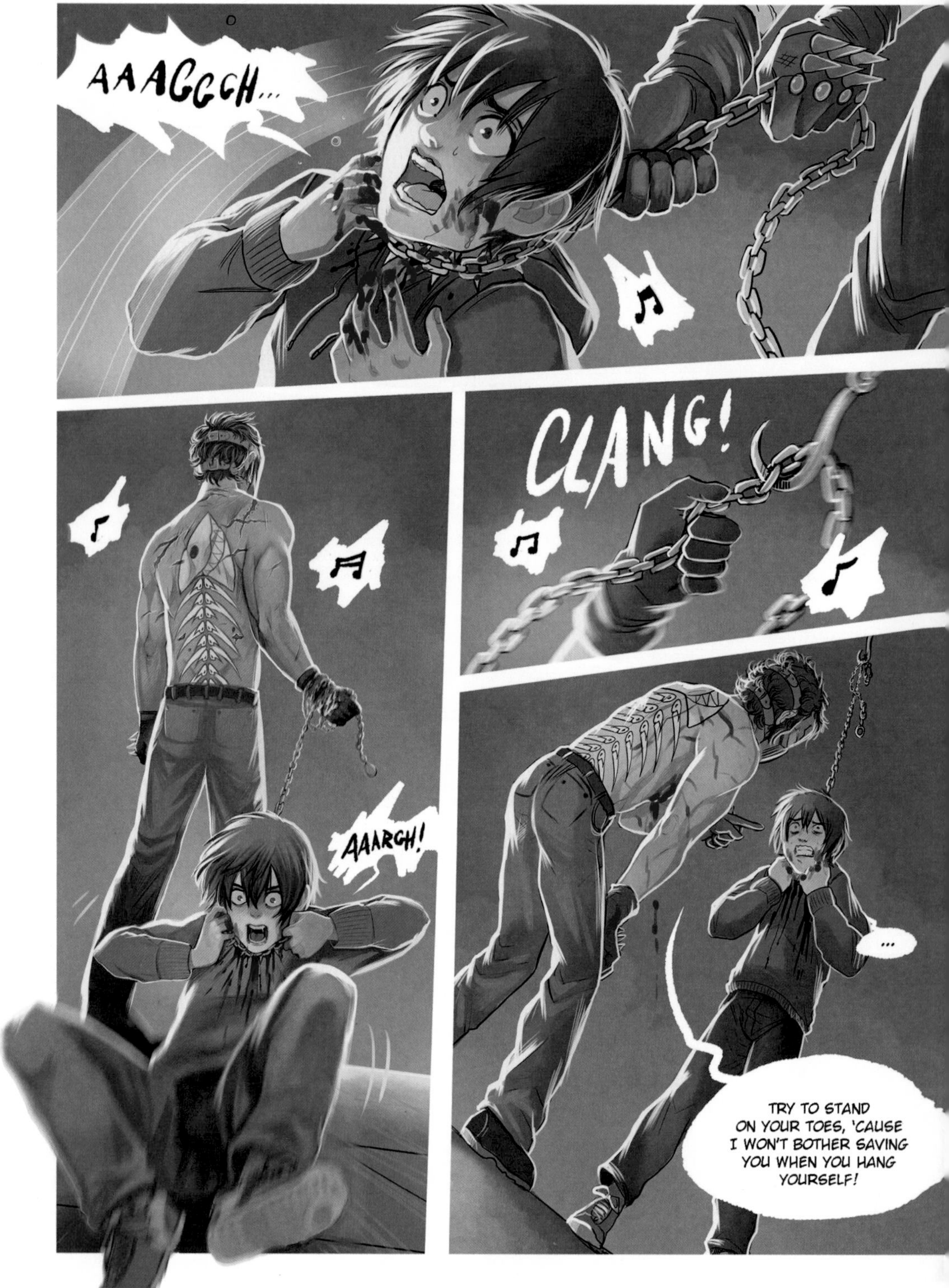
AAAGGGH...
♫
CLANG!
♪
♫
♫
♪
AAARGH!
...
TRY TO STAND
ON YOUR TOES, 'CAUSE
I WON'T BOTHER SAVING
YOU WHEN YOU HANG
YOURSELF!

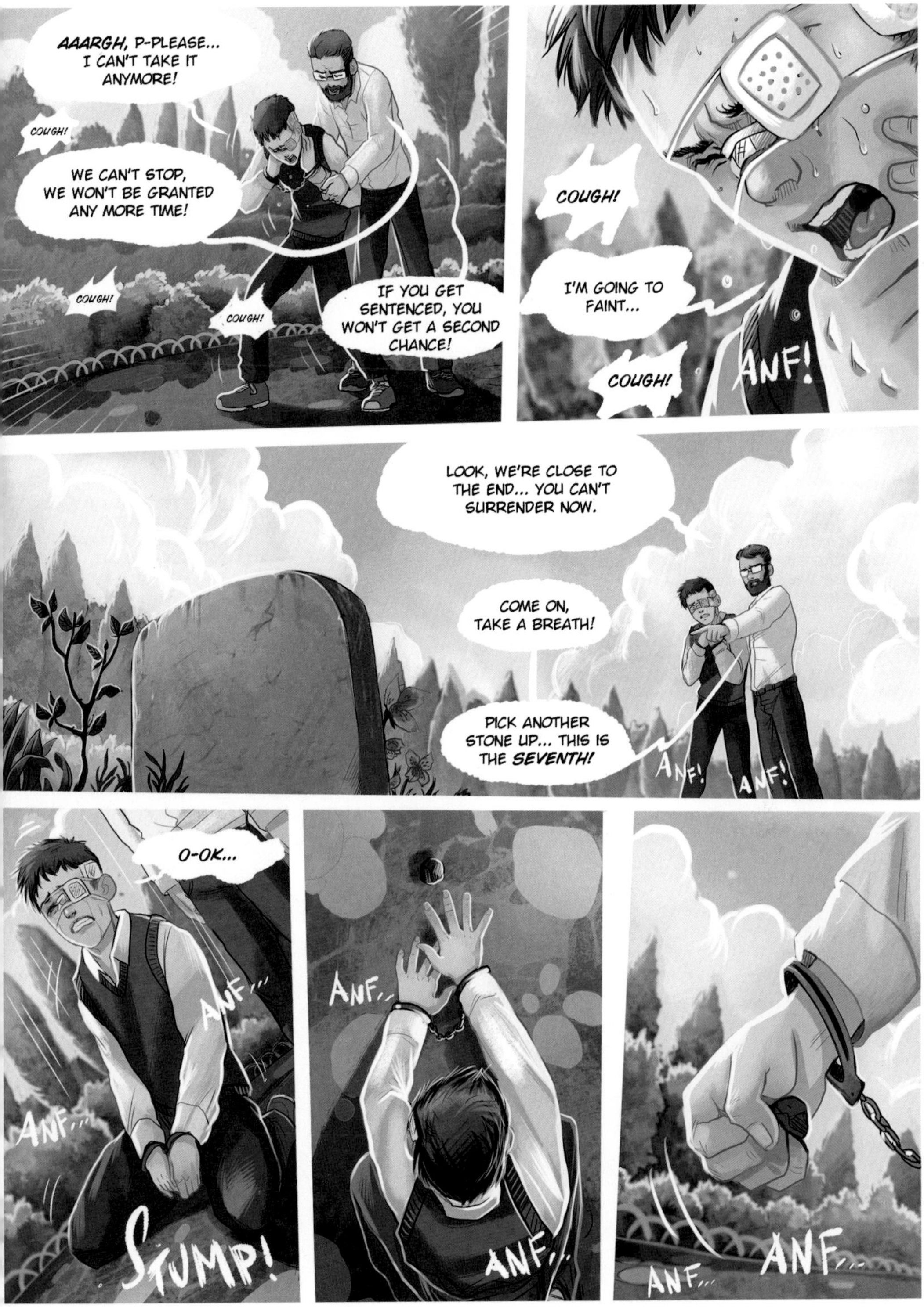

AAARGH, P-PLEASE... I CAN'T TAKE IT ANYMORE!
COUGH!
WE CAN'T STOP, WE WON'T BE GRANTED ANY MORE TIME!
COUGH!
COUGH!
IF YOU GET SENTENCED, YOU WON'T GET A SECOND CHANCE!
COUGH!
I'M GOING TO FAINT...
COUGH!
ANF!
LOOK, WE'RE CLOSE TO THE END... YOU CAN'T SURRENDER NOW.
COME ON, TAKE A BREATH!
PICK ANOTHER STONE UP... THIS IS THE SEVENTH!
ANF!
ANF!
O-OK...
ANF...
ANF...
STUMP!
ANF...
ANF...
ANF...
ANF...

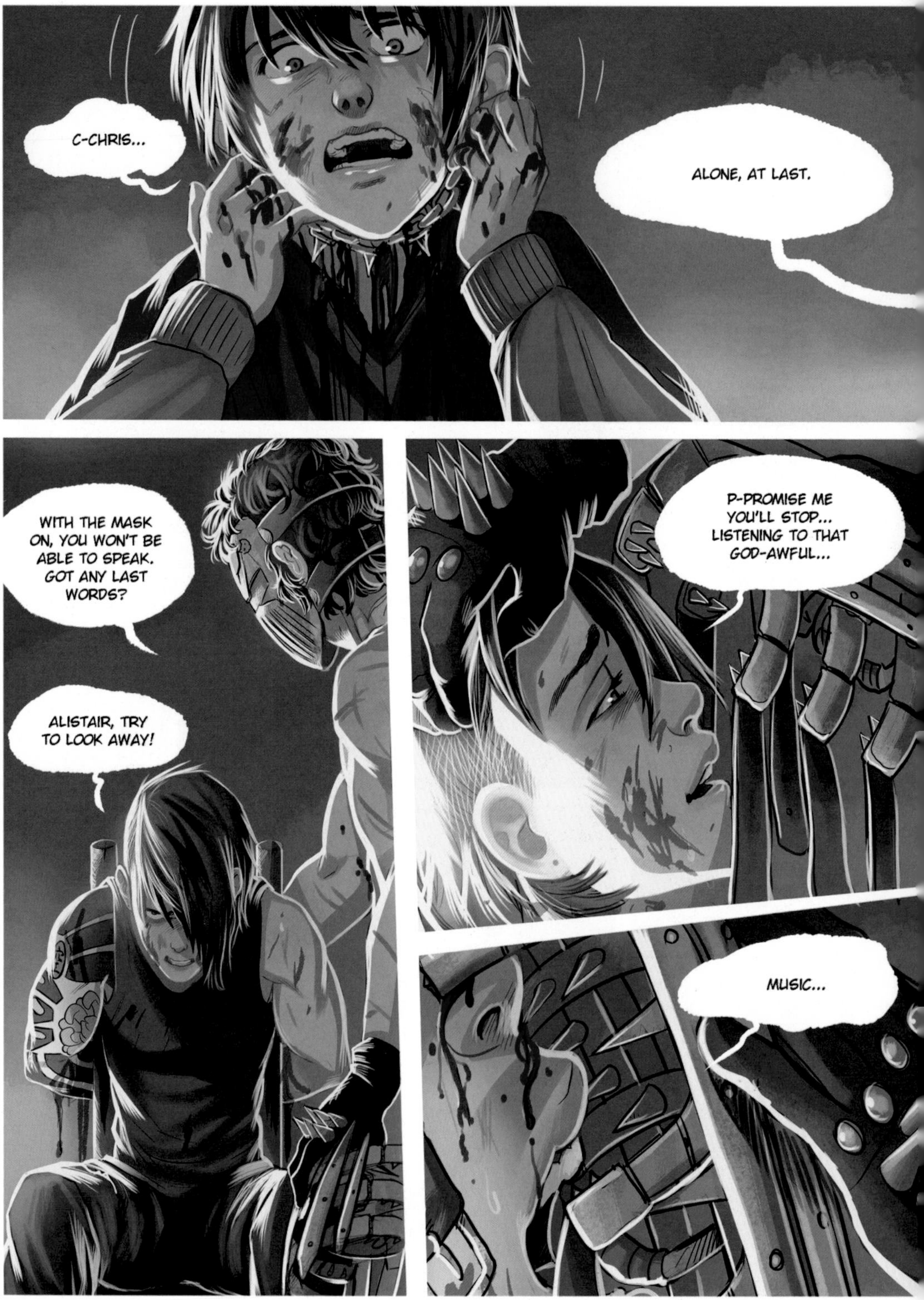
C-CHRIS...
ALONE, AT LAST.
WITH THE MASK ON, YOU WON'T BE ABLE TO SPEAK. GOT ANY LAST WORDS?
ALISTAIR, TRY TO LOOK AWAY!
P-PROMISE ME YOU'LL STOP... LISTENING TO THAT GOD-AWFUL...
MUSIC...

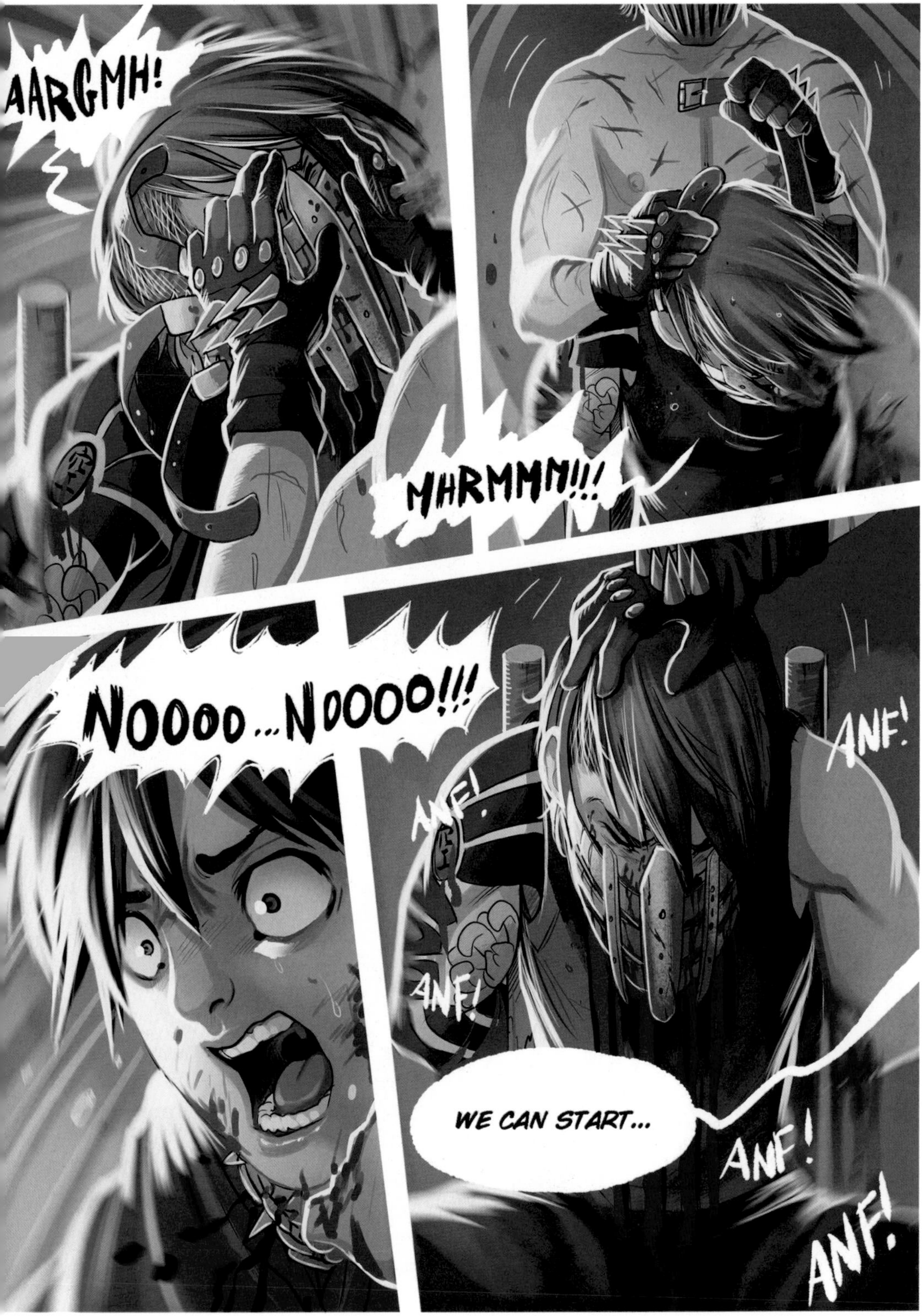
AARGMH!
MHRMMM!!!
NOOOO...NOOOO!!!
ANF!
ANF!
ANF!
WE CAN START...
ANF!
ANF!

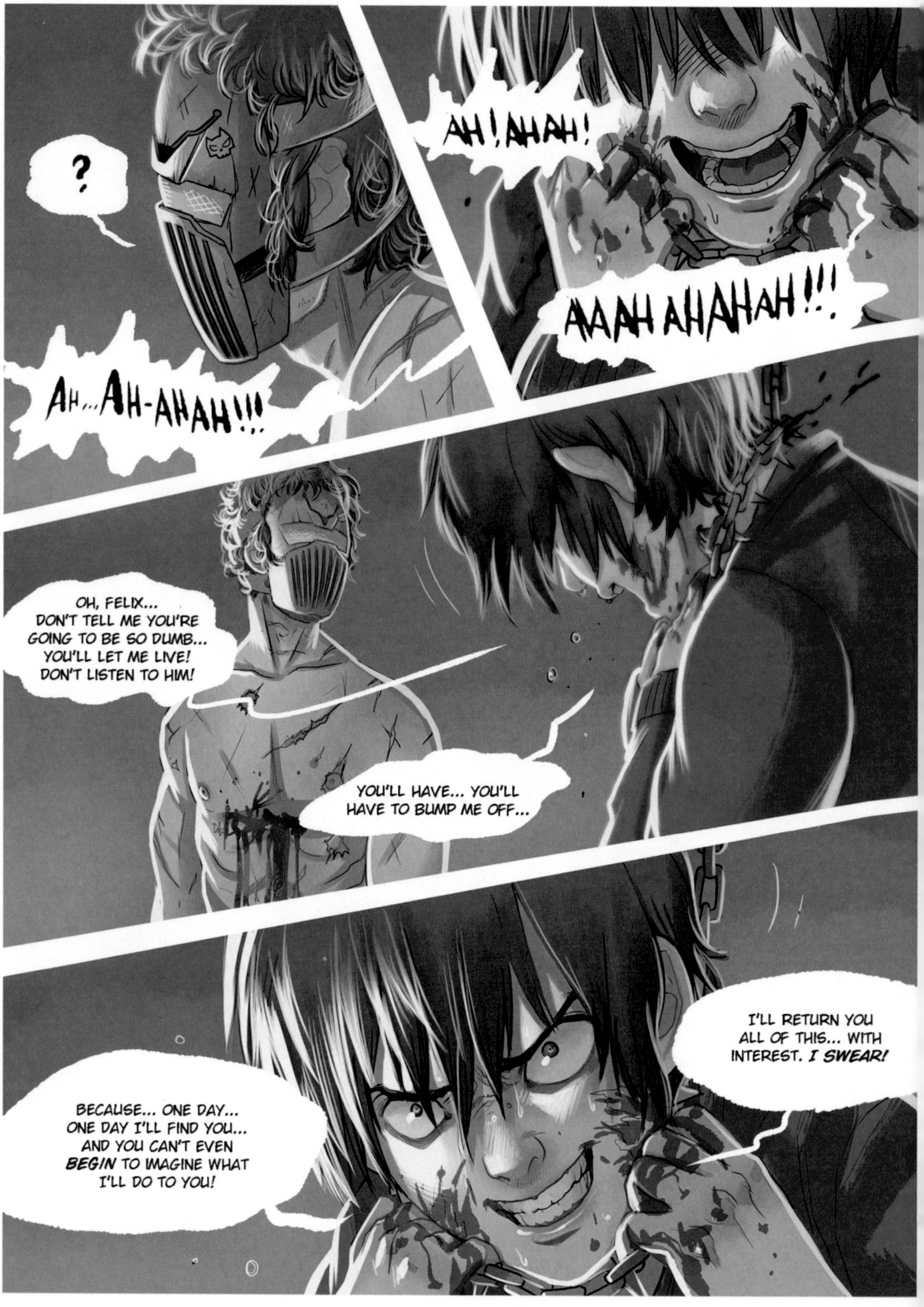
?
AH...AH-AHAH!!!
AH! AHAH!
AAAH AHAHAH!!!
OH, FELIX... DON'T TELL ME YOU'RE GOING TO BE SO DUMB... YOU'LL LET ME LIVE! DON'T LISTEN TO HIM!
YOU'LL HAVE... YOU'LL HAVE TO BUMP ME OFF...
BECAUSE... ONE DAY... ONE DAY I'LL FIND YOU... AND YOU CAN'T EVEN *BEGIN* TO IMAGINE WHAT I'LL DO TO YOU!
I'LL RETURN YOU ALL OF THIS... WITH INTEREST. ***I SWEAR!***

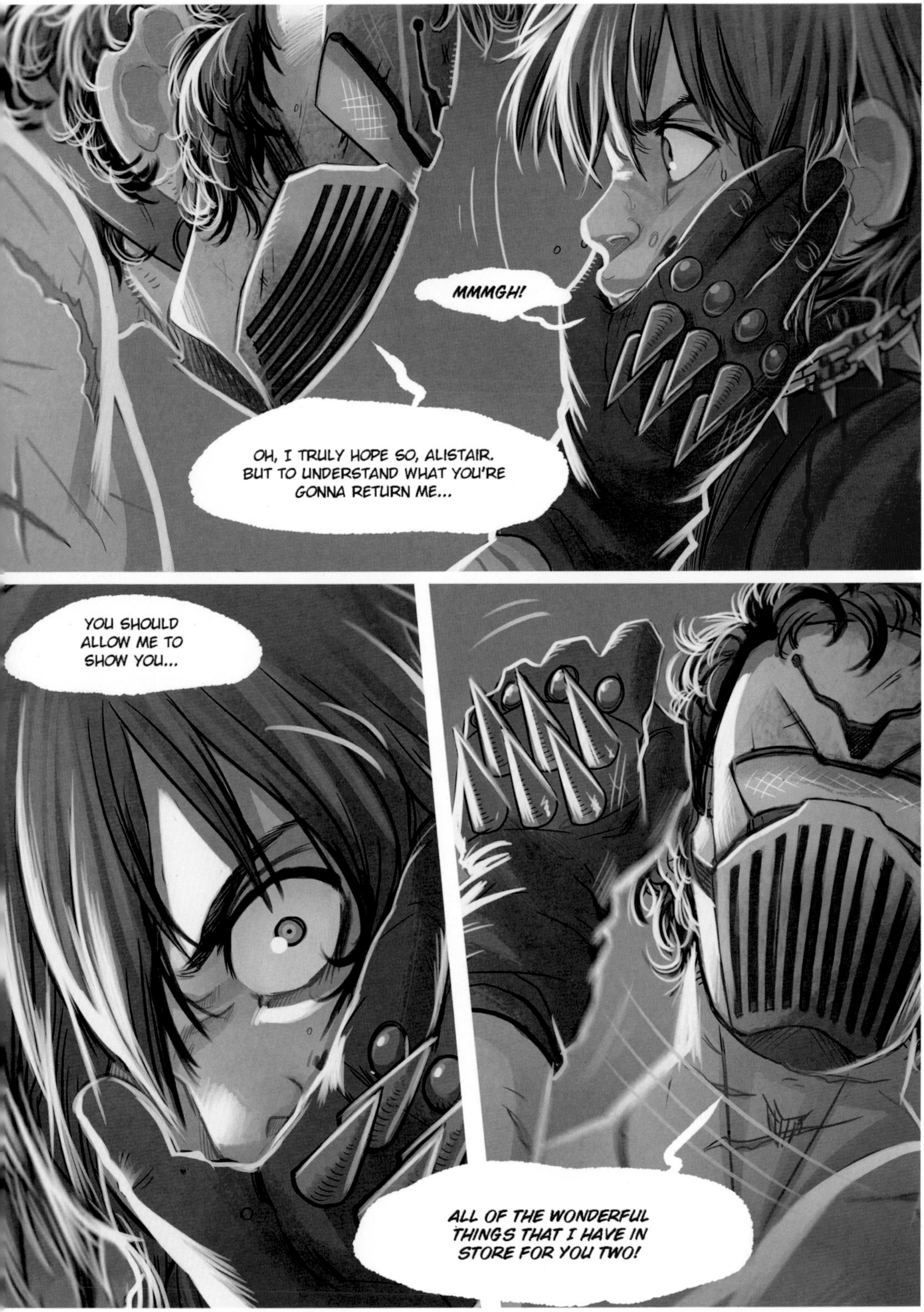
MMMGH!
OH, I TRULY HOPE SO, ALISTAIR. BUT TO UNDERSTAND WHAT YOU'RE GONNA RETURN ME...
YOU SHOULD ALLOW ME TO SHOW YOU...
ALL OF THE WONDERFUL THINGS THAT I HAVE IN STORE FOR YOU TWO!

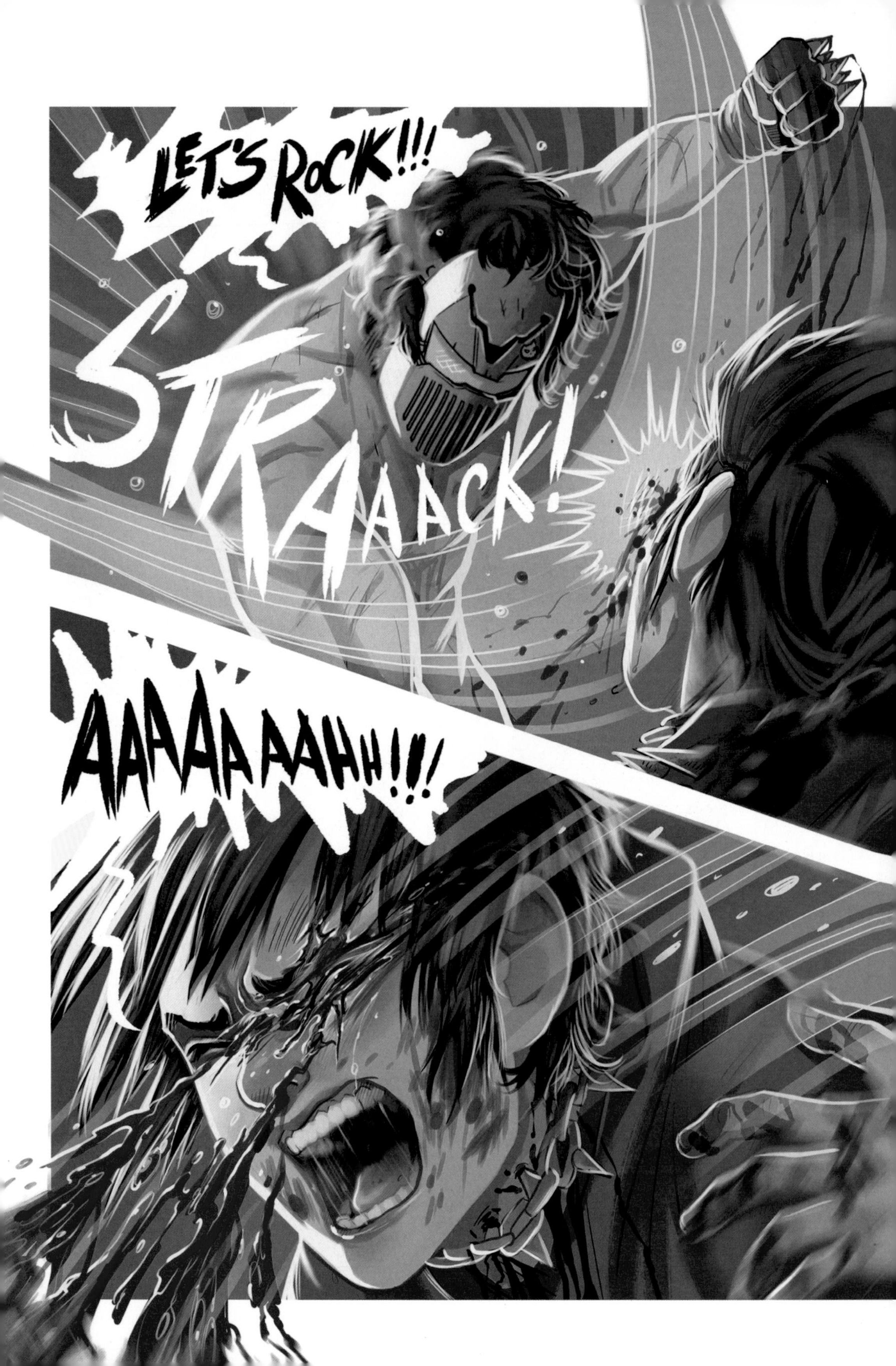
LET'S ROCK!!!
STRAAACK!
AAAAAAAHH!!!

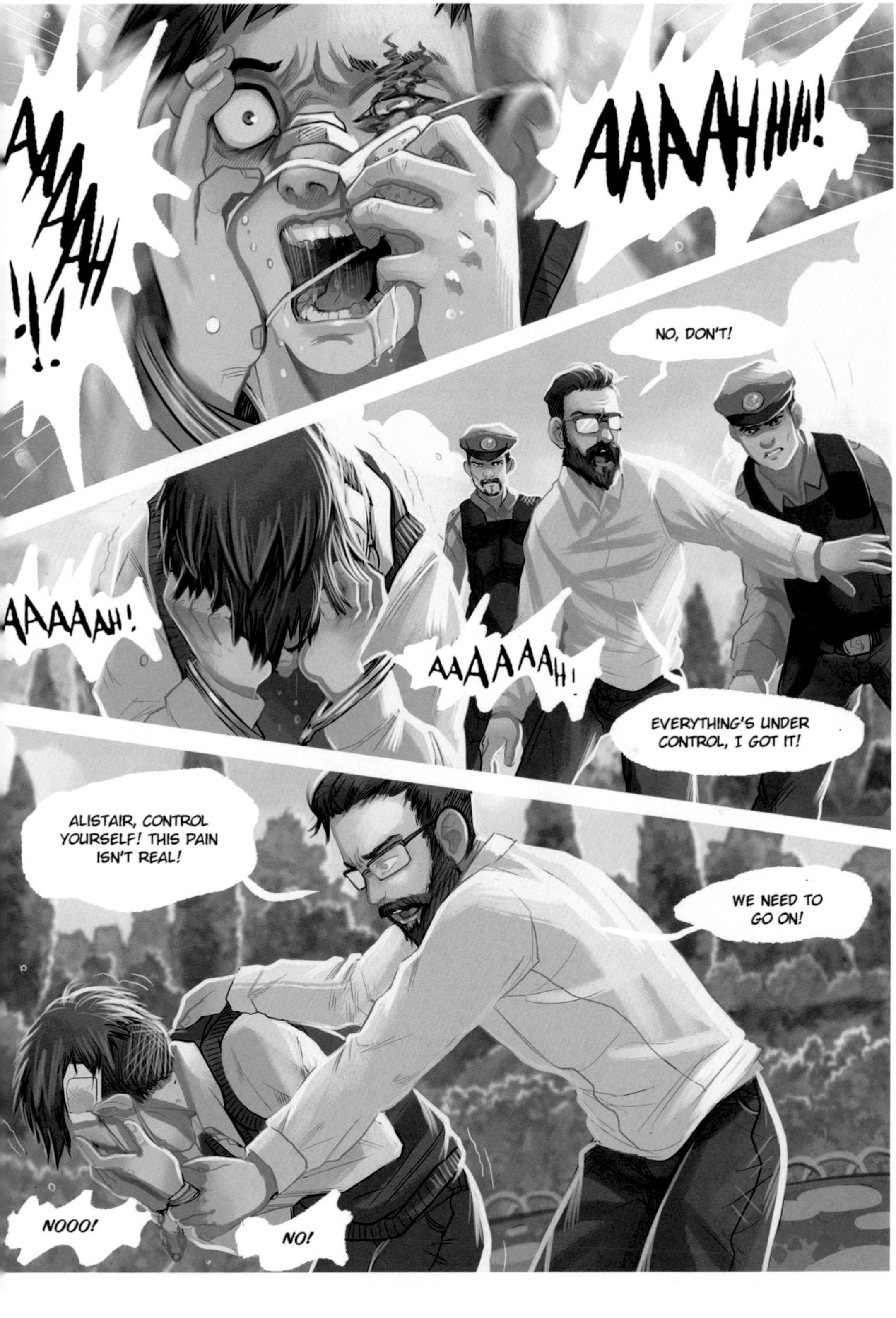
AAAAAH!!!
AAAAHHH!
NO, DON'T!
AAAAAH!
AAAAAAH!
EVERYTHING'S UNDER CONTROL, I GOT IT!
ALISTAIR, CONTROL YOURSELF! THIS PAIN ISN'T REAL!
WE NEED TO GO ON!
NOOO!
NO!

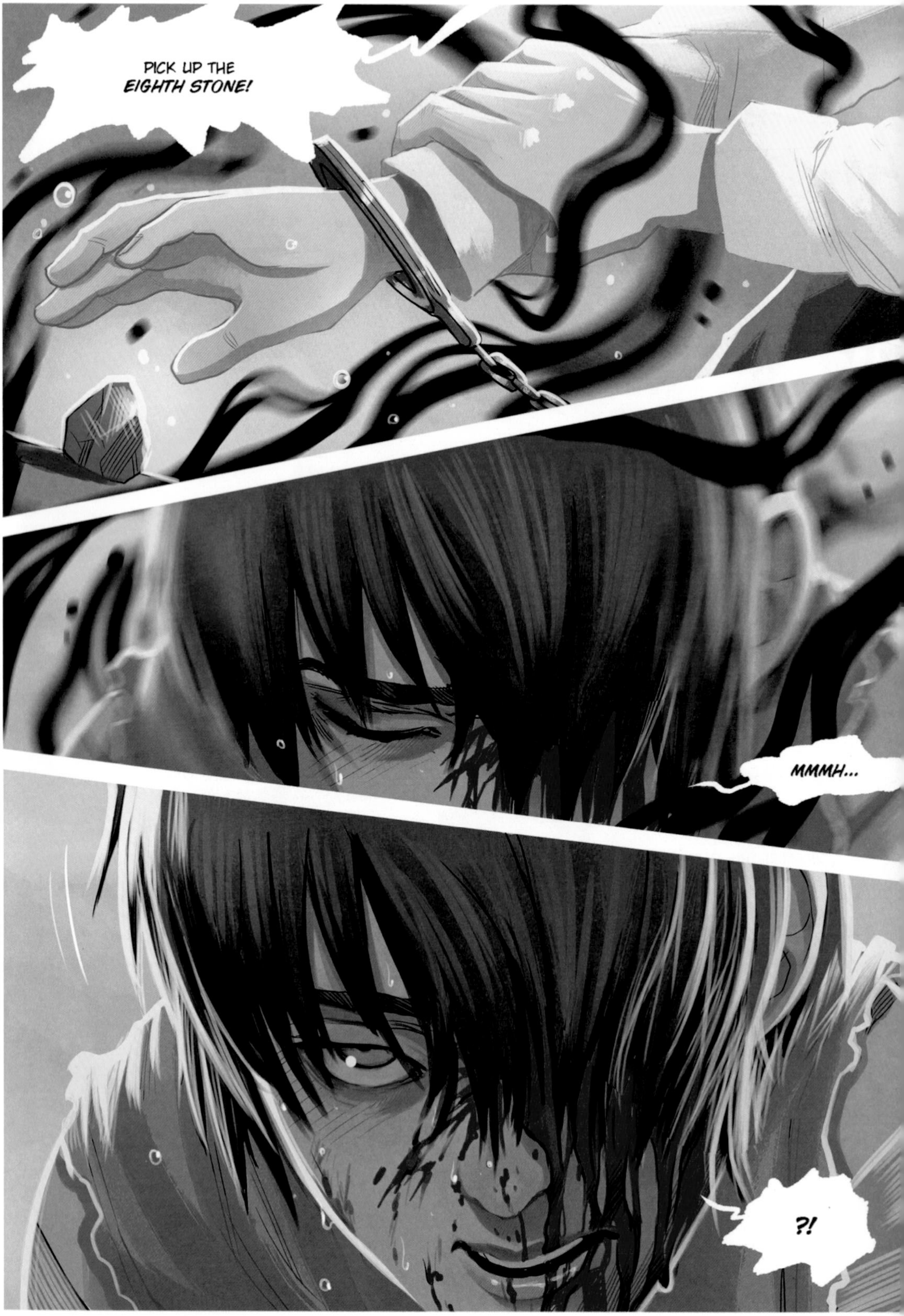
PICK UP THE EIGHTH STONE!
MMMH...
?!

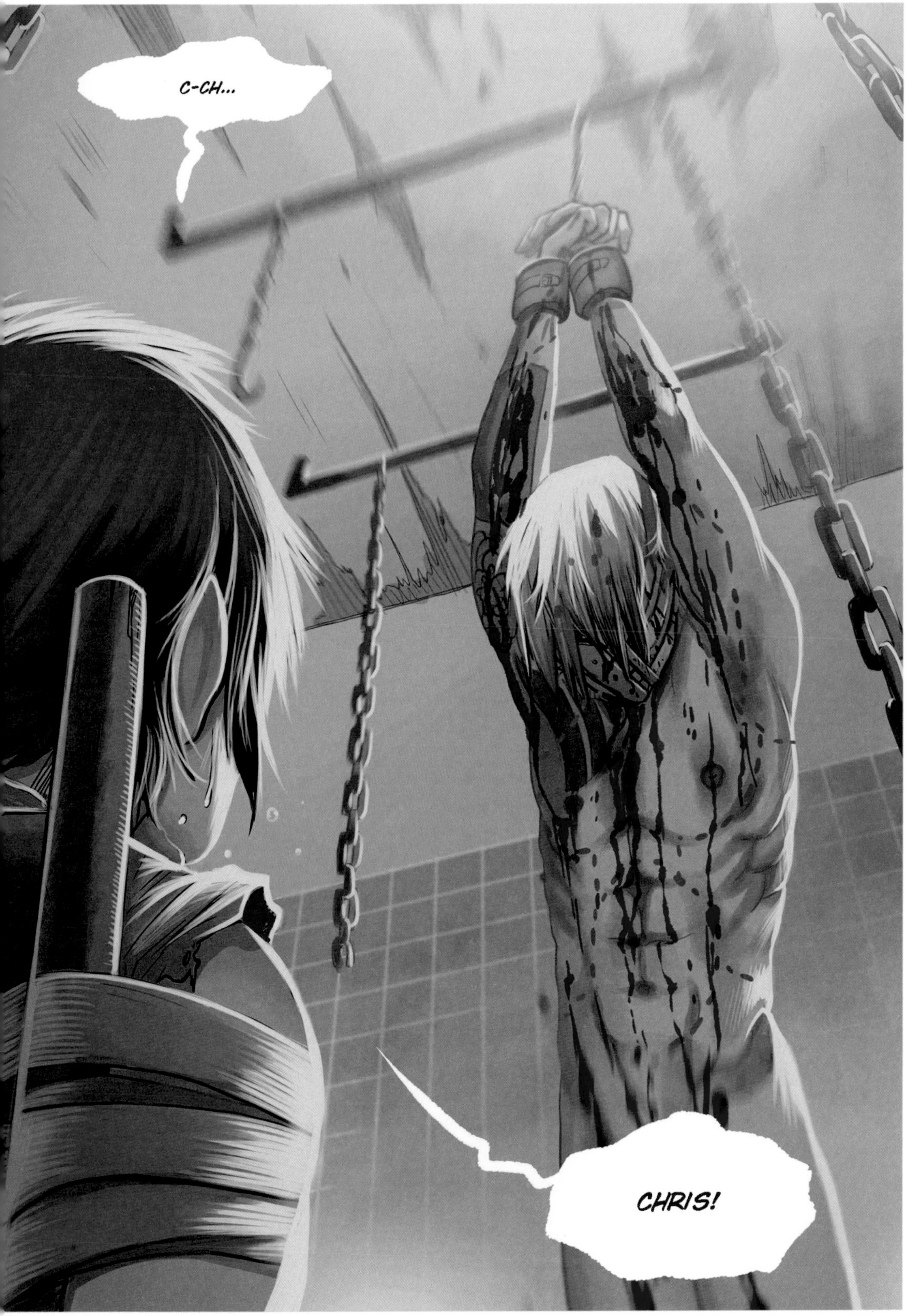
C-CH...
CHRIS!

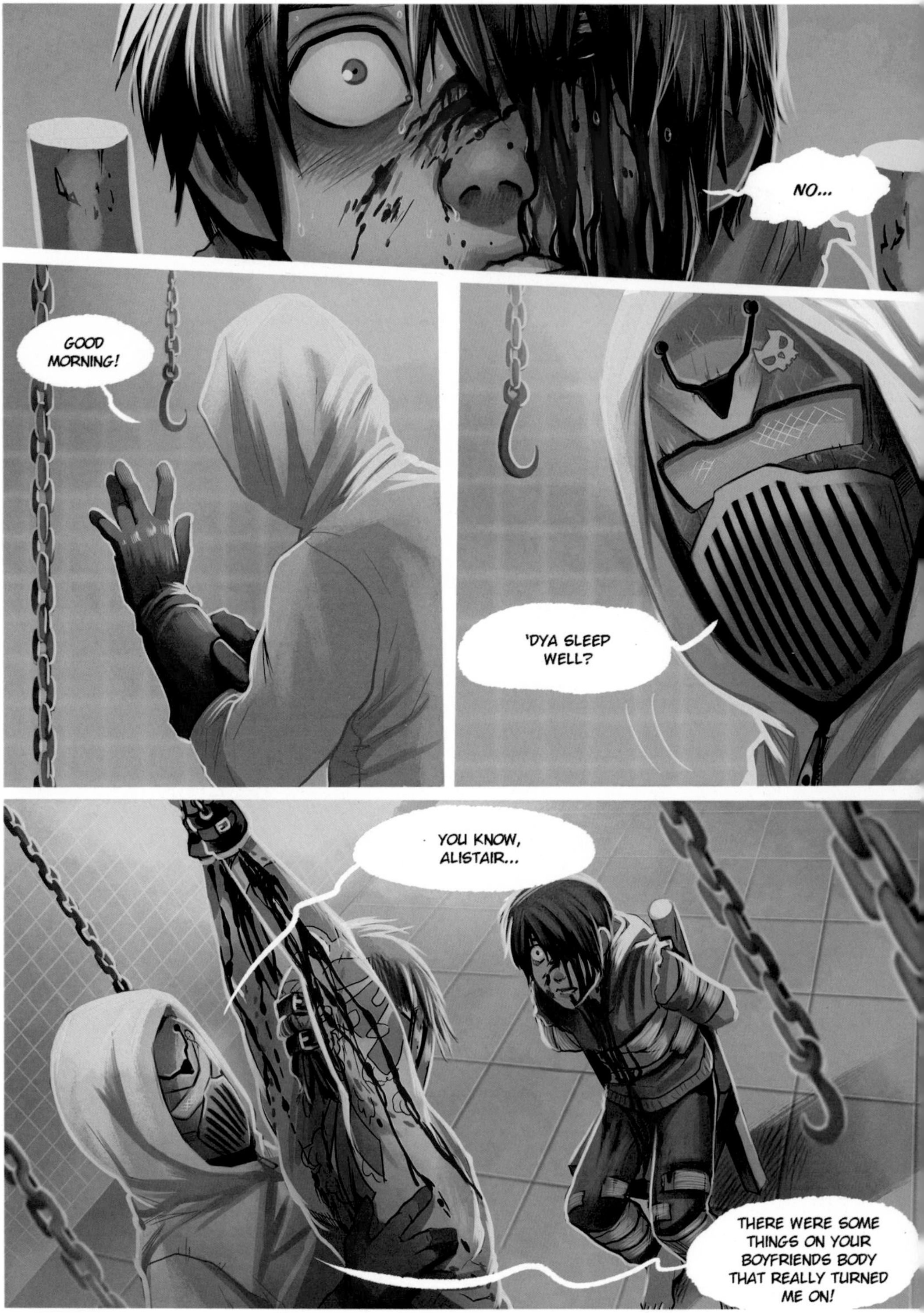
NO...
GOOD MORNING!
'DYA SLEEP WELL?
YOU KNOW, ALISTAIR...
THERE WERE SOME THINGS ON YOUR BOYFRIENDS BODY THAT REALLY TURNED ME ON!

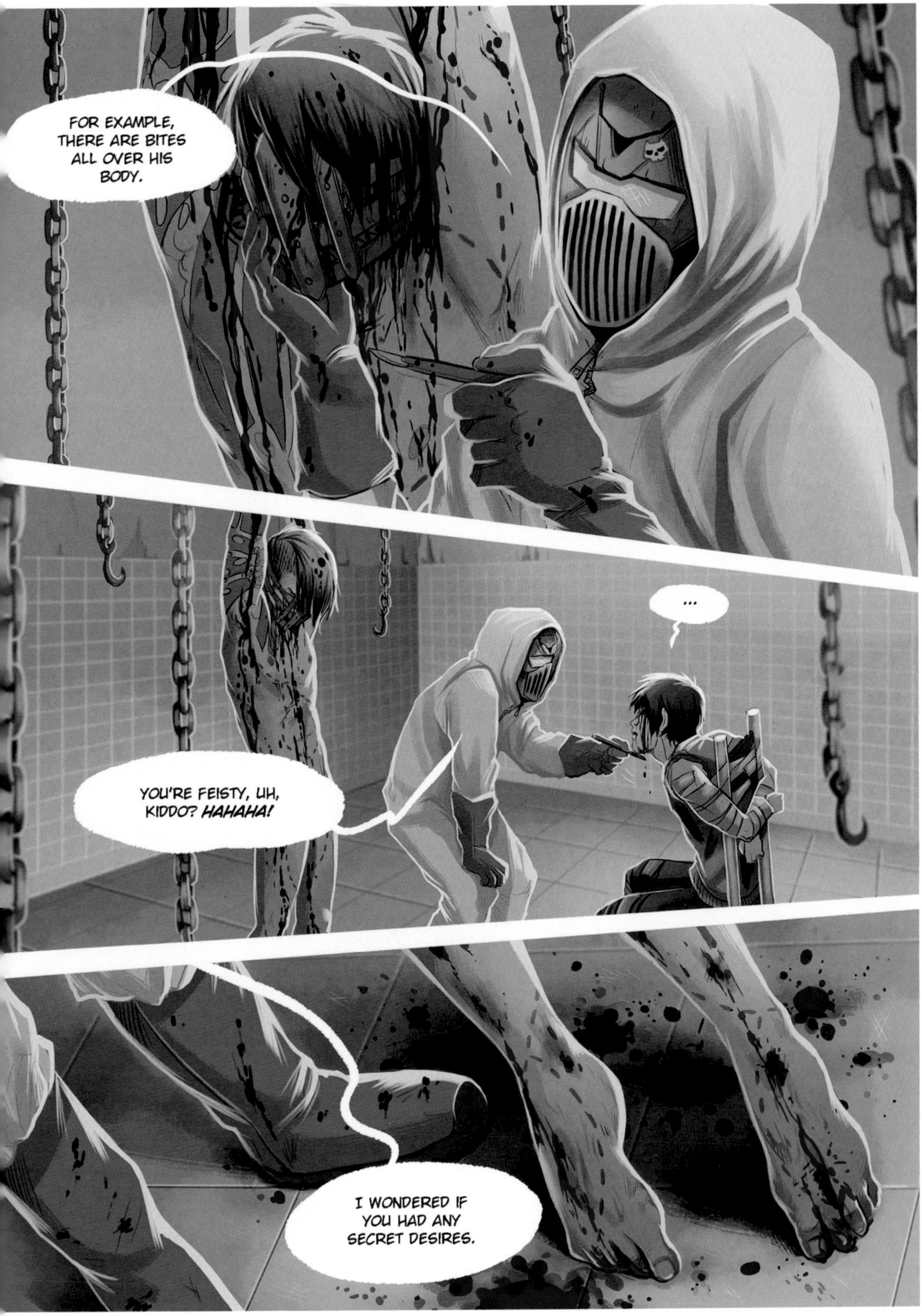
FOR EXAMPLE, THERE ARE BITES ALL OVER HIS BODY.
...
YOU'RE FEISTY, UH, KIDDO? HAHAHA!
I WONDERED IF YOU HAD ANY SECRET DESIRES.

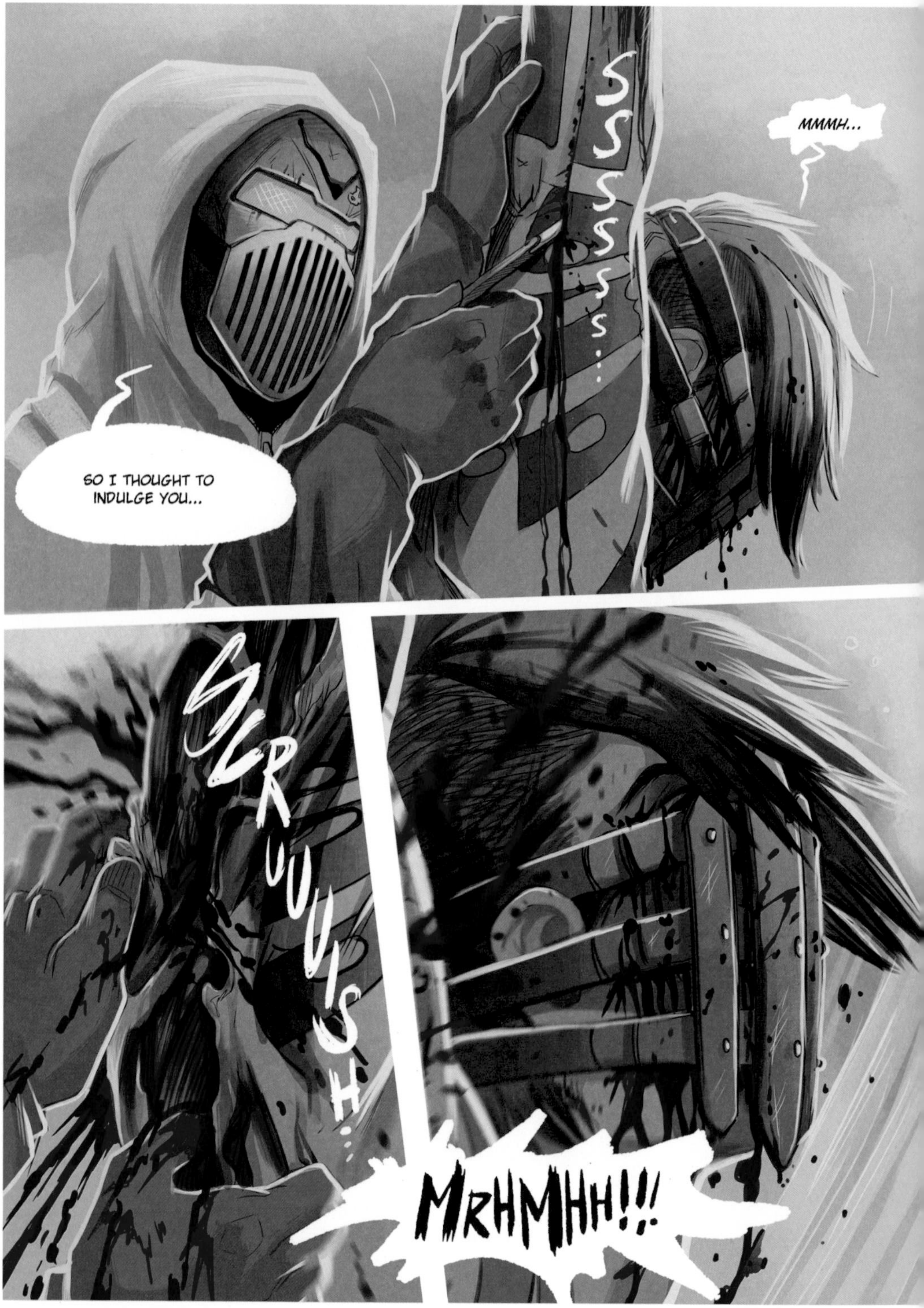
SSSSSS...
MMMH...
SO I THOUGHT TO INDULGE YOU...
SCHRUUUUISH...
MRHMHH!!!

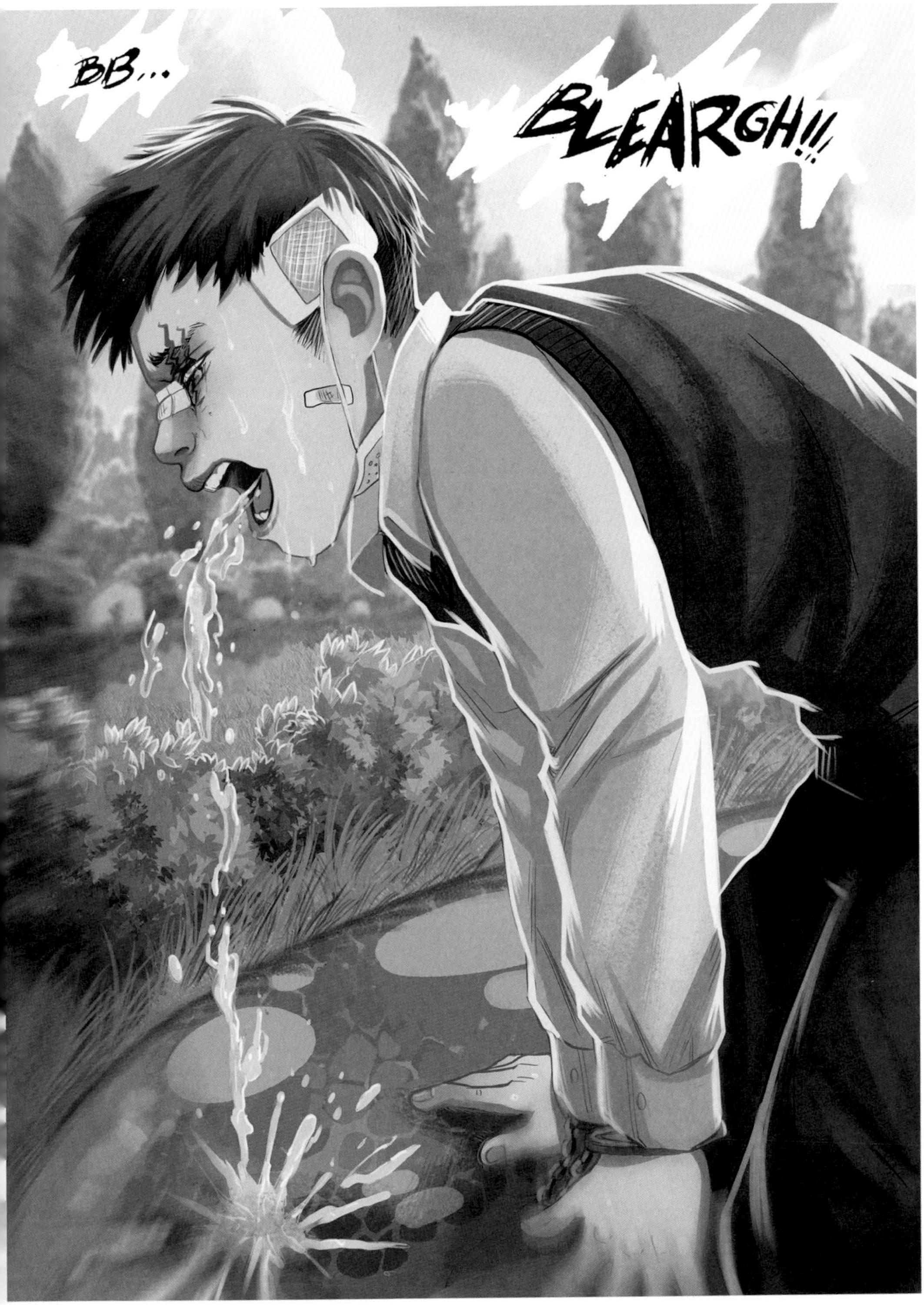
BB...
BLEARGH!!

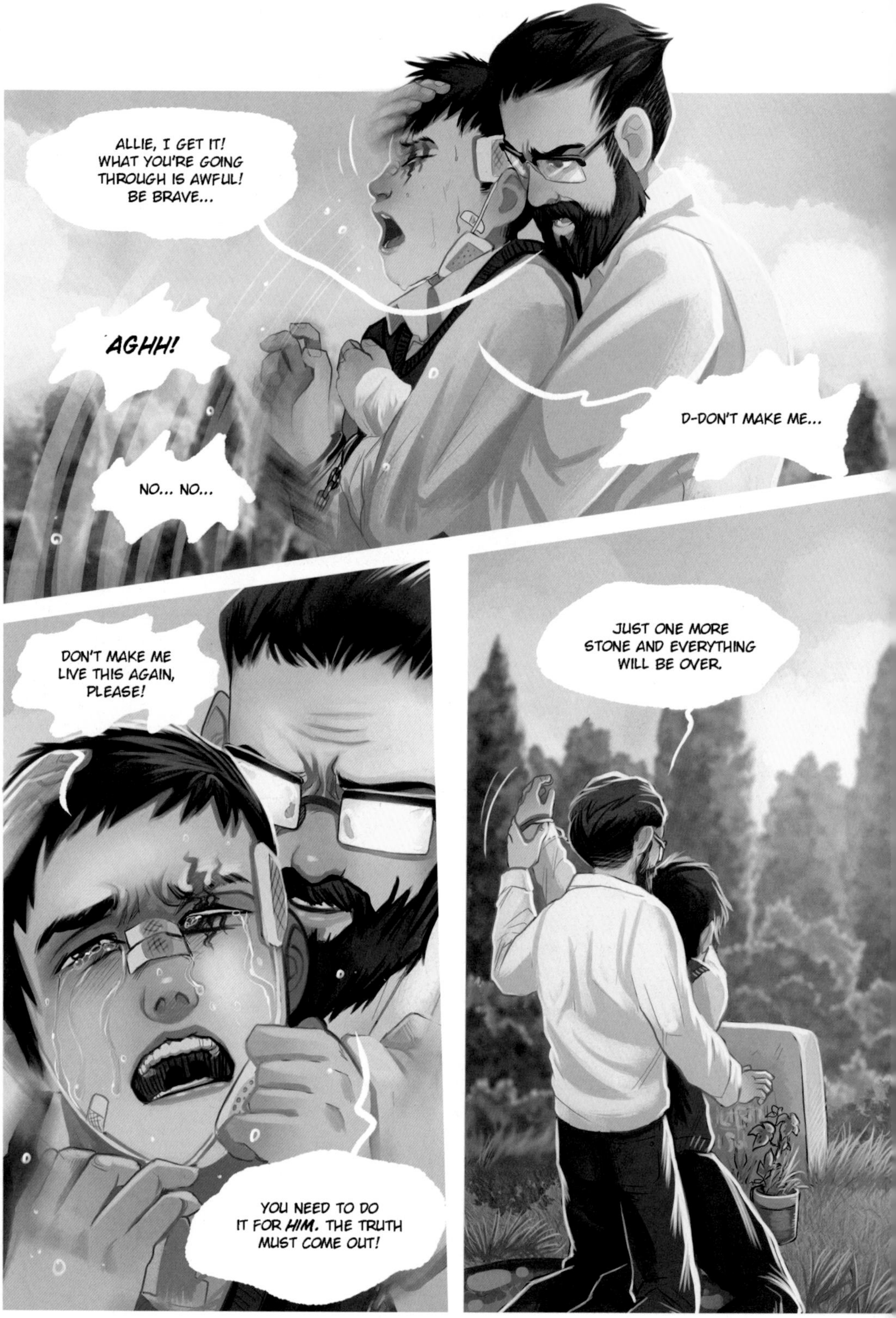
ALLIE, I GET IT! WHAT YOU'RE GOING THROUGH IS AWFUL! BE BRAVE...
AGHH!
NO... NO...
D-DON'T MAKE ME...
DON'T MAKE ME LIVE THIS AGAIN, PLEASE!
YOU NEED TO DO IT FOR ***HIM.*** THE TRUTH MUST COME OUT!
JUST ONE MORE STONE AND EVERYTHING WILL BE OVER.

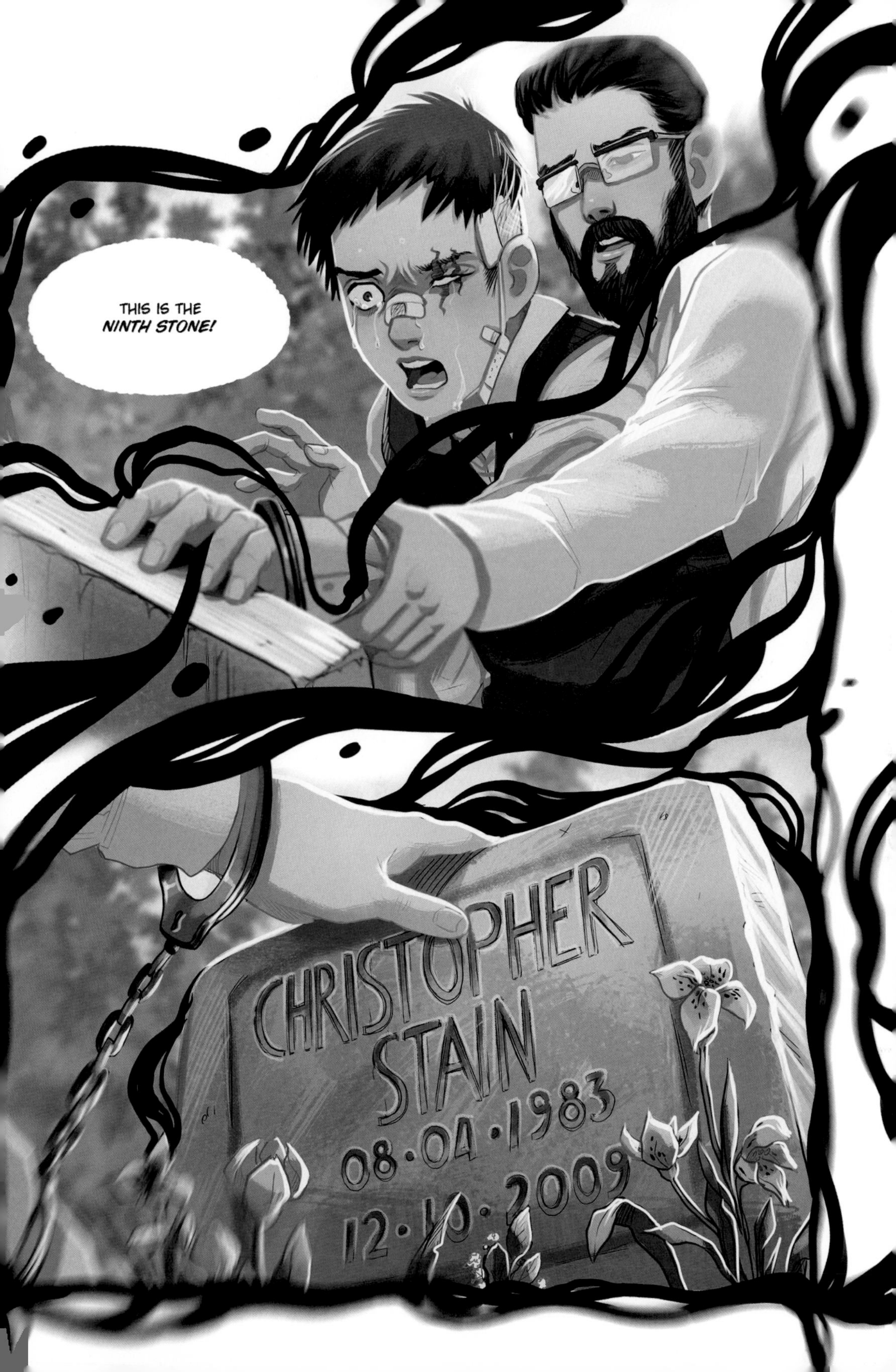

THIS IS THE *NINTH STONE!*
CHRISTOPHER STAIN
08·04·1983
12·10·2009

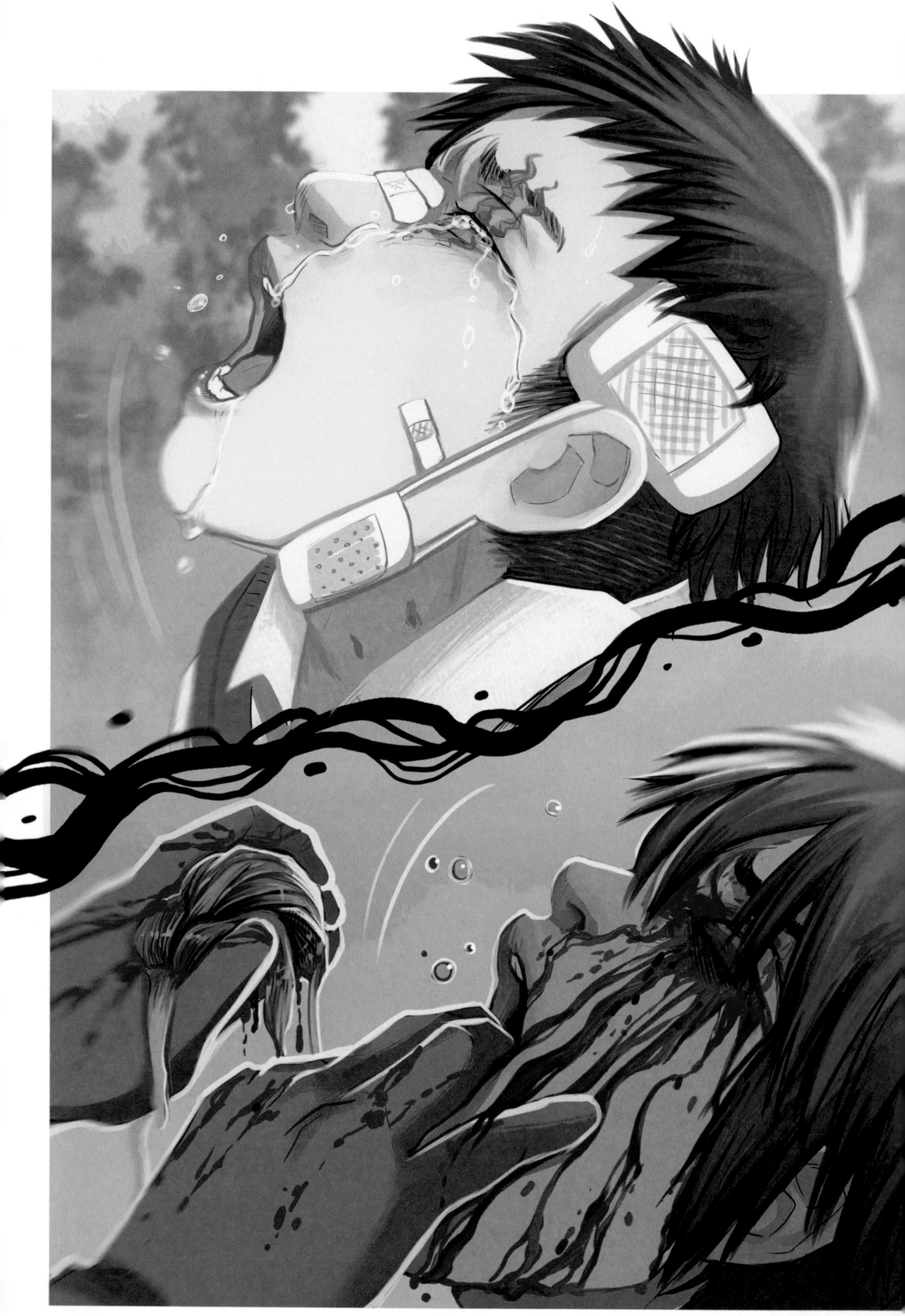

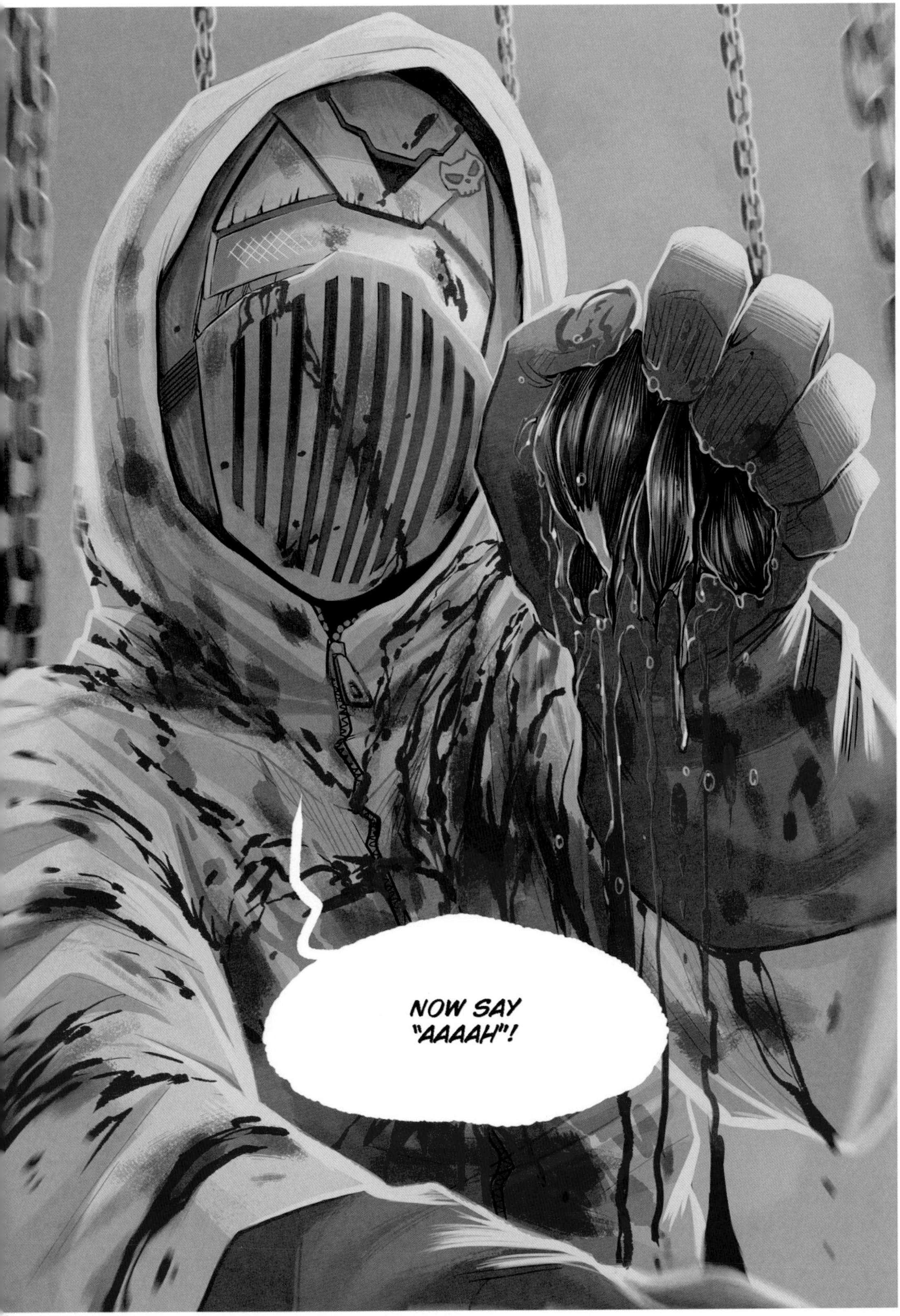
NOW SAY "AAAAH"!

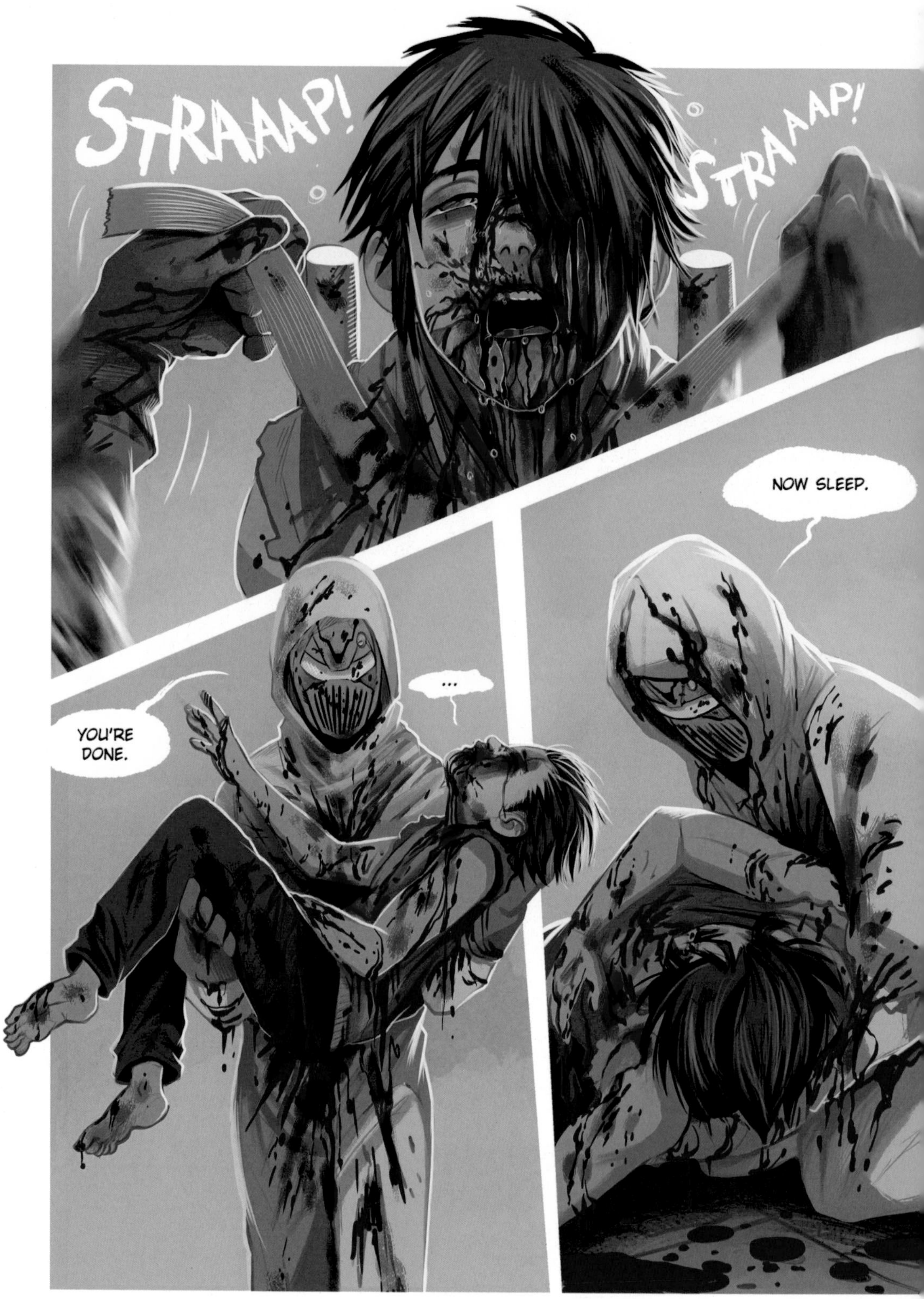
STRAAAP!
STRAAAP!
NOW SLEEP.
YOU'RE DONE.
...

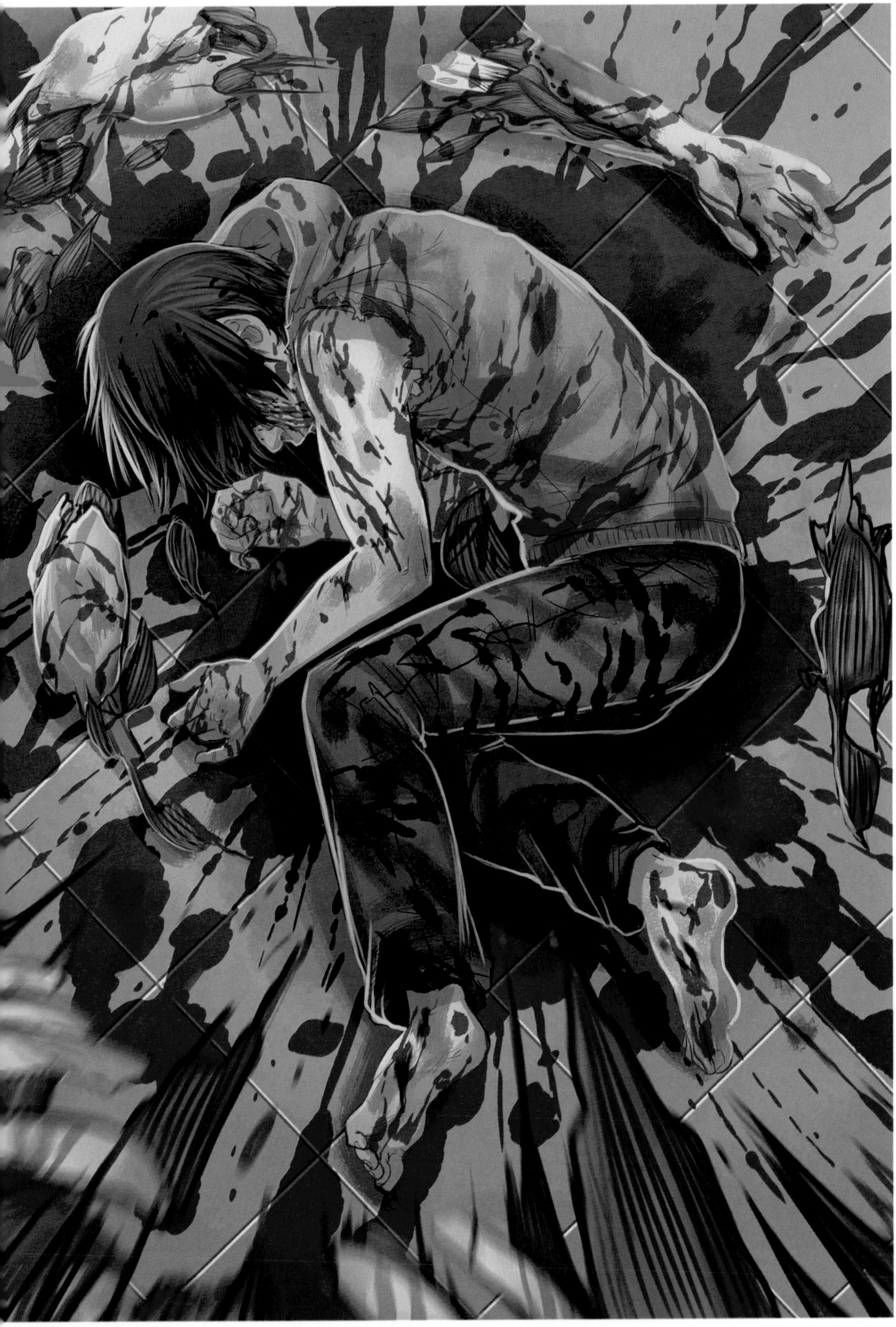

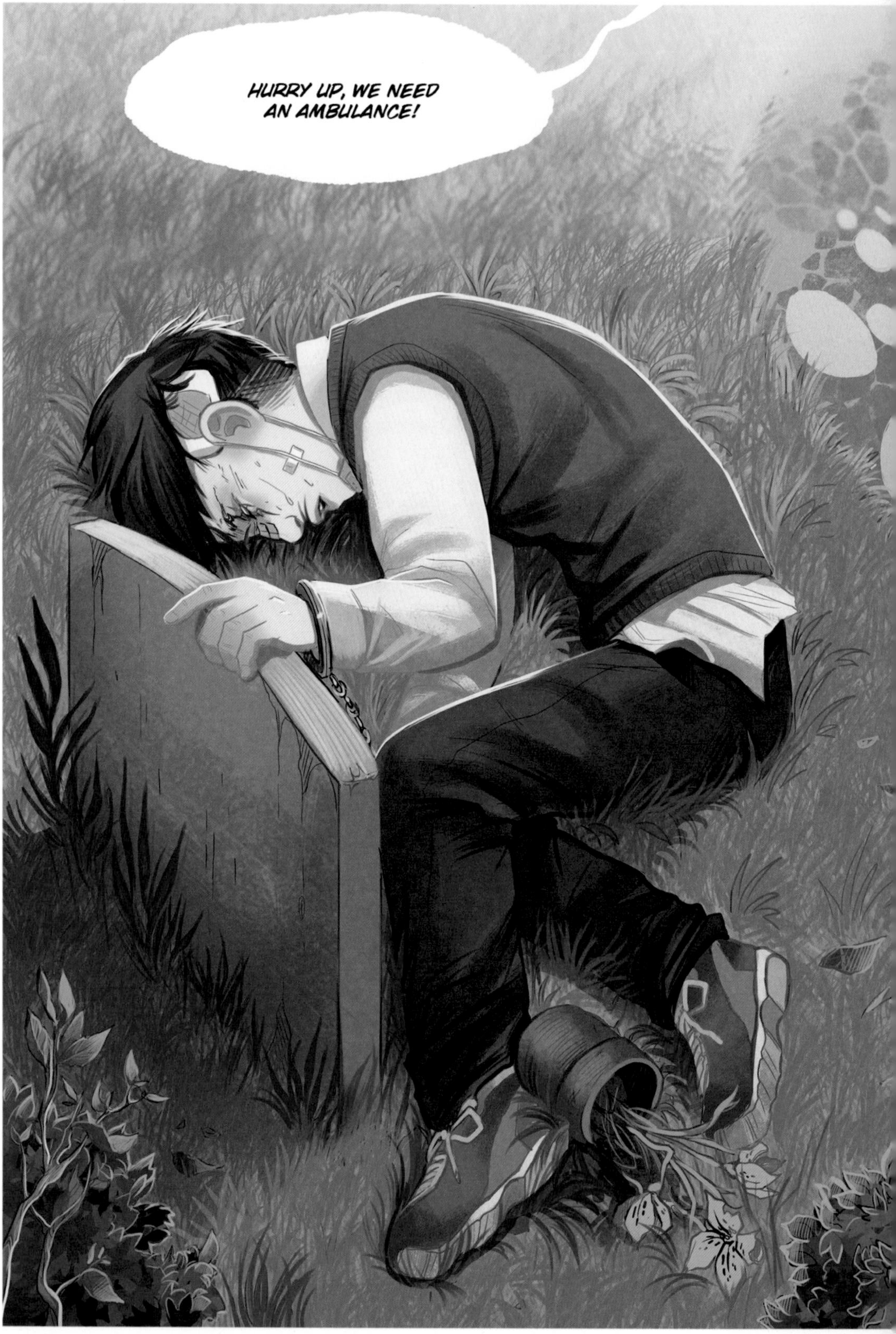
HURRY UP, WE NEED AN AMBULANCE!

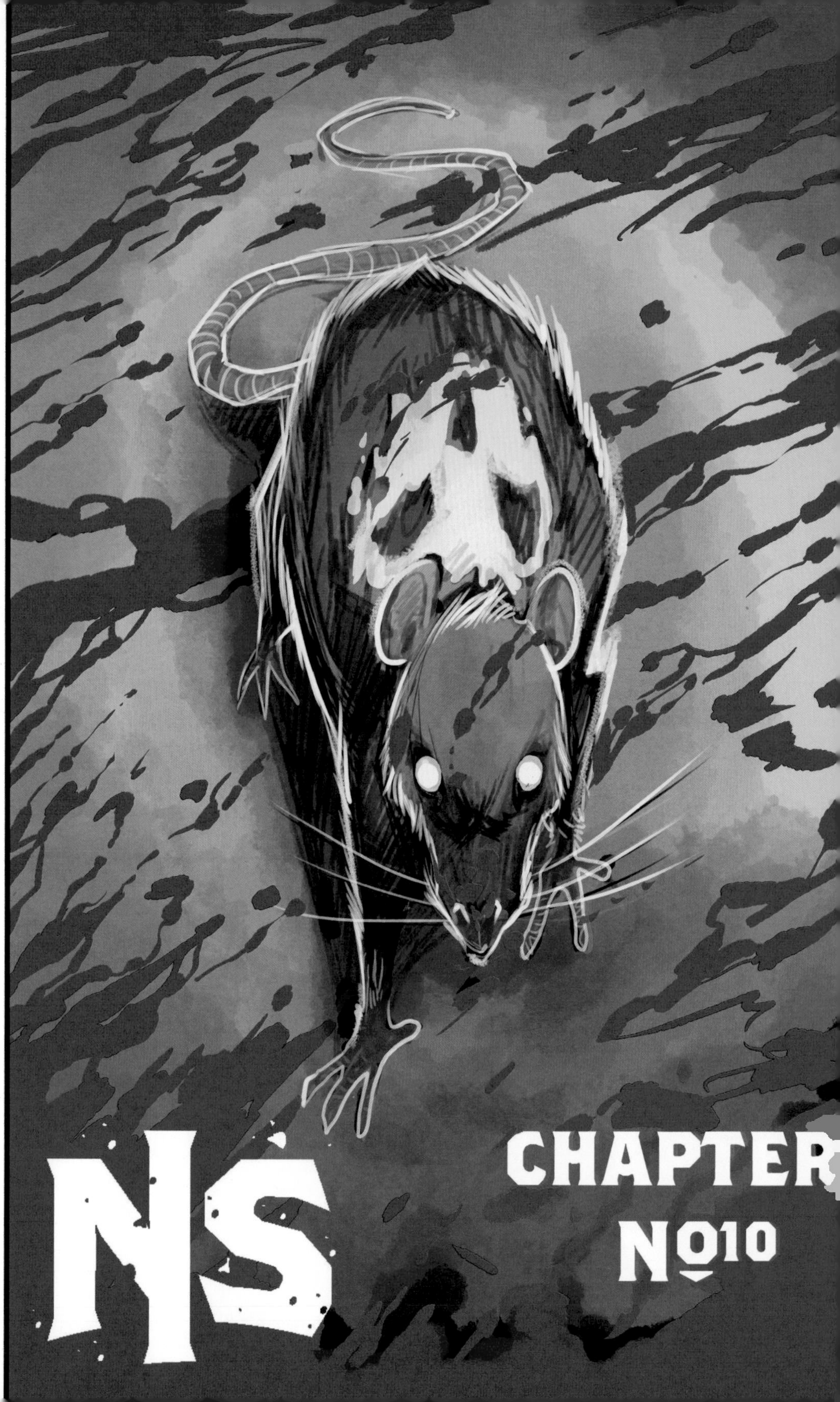
NS
CHAPTER
№10

ABOMINATION.

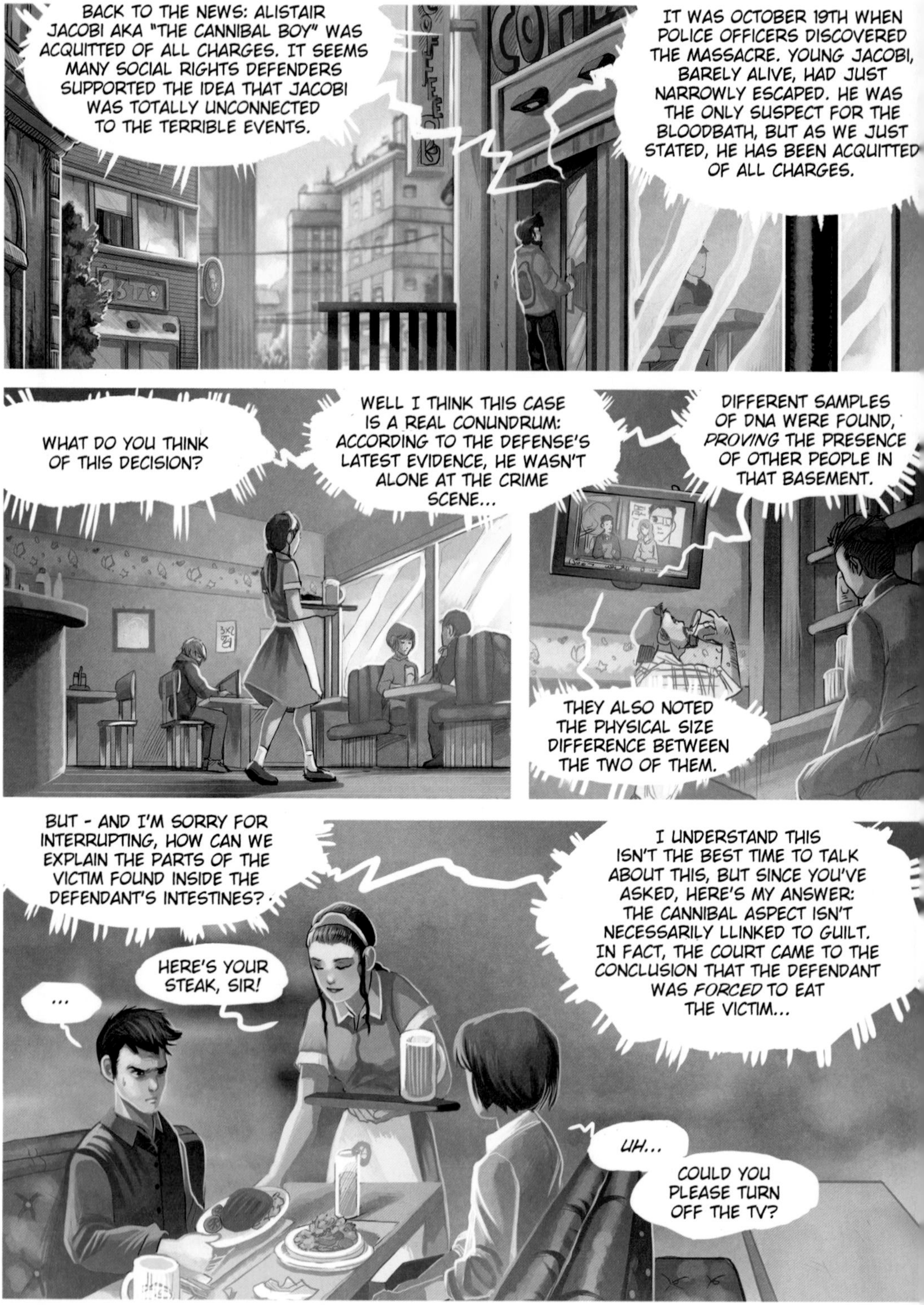
BACK TO THE NEWS: ALISTAIR JACOBI AKA "THE CANNIBAL BOY" WAS ACQUITTED OF ALL CHARGES. IT SEEMS MANY SOCIAL RIGHTS DEFENDERS SUPPORTED THE IDEA THAT JACOBI WAS TOTALLY UNCONNECTED TO THE TERRIBLE EVENTS.
IT WAS OCTOBER 19TH WHEN POLICE OFFICERS DISCOVERED THE MASSACRE. YOUNG JACOBI, BARELY ALIVE, HAD JUST NARROWLY ESCAPED. HE WAS THE ONLY SUSPECT FOR THE BLOODBATH, BUT AS WE JUST STATED, HE HAS BEEN ACQUITTED OF ALL CHARGES.
WHAT DO YOU THINK OF THIS DECISION?
WELL I THINK THIS CASE IS A REAL CONUNDRUM: ACCORDING TO THE DEFENSE'S LATEST EVIDENCE, HE WASN'T ALONE AT THE CRIME SCENE...
DIFFERENT SAMPLES OF DNA WERE FOUND, *PROVING* THE PRESENCE OF OTHER PEOPLE IN THAT BASEMENT.
THEY ALSO NOTED THE PHYSICAL SIZE DIFFERENCE BETWEEN THE TWO OF THEM.
BUT - AND I'M SORRY FOR INTERRUPTING, HOW CAN WE EXPLAIN THE PARTS OF THE VICTIM FOUND INSIDE THE DEFENDANT'S INTESTINES?
I UNDERSTAND THIS ISN'T THE BEST TIME TO TALK ABOUT THIS, BUT SINCE YOU'VE ASKED, HERE'S MY ANSWER: THE CANNIBAL ASPECT ISN'T NECESSARILY LLINKED TO GUILT. IN FACT, THE COURT CAME TO THE CONCLUSION THAT THE DEFENDANT WAS *FORCED* TO EAT THE VICTIM...
...
HERE'S YOUR STEAK, SIR!
UH...
COULD YOU PLEASE TURN OFF THE TV?

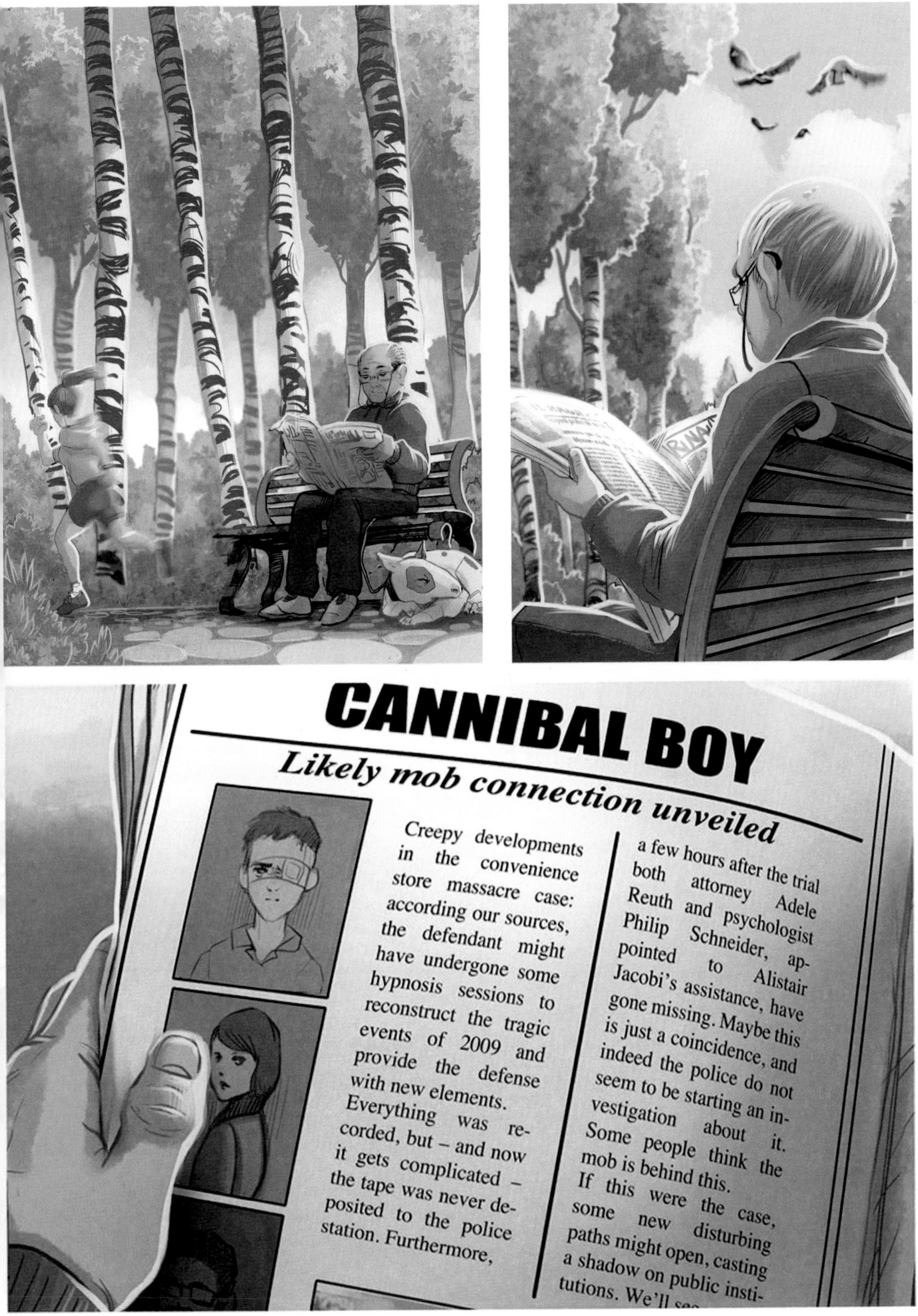
CANNIBAL BOY
Likely mob connection unveiled
Creepy developments in the convenience store massacre case: according our sources, the defendant might have undergone some hypnosis sessions to reconstruct the tragic events of 2009 and provide the defense with new elements. Everything was recorded, but – and now it gets complicated – the tape was never deposited to the police station. Furthermore,
a few hours after the trial both attorney Adele Reuth and psychologist Philip Schneider, appointed to Alistair Jacobi's assistance, have gone missing. Maybe this is just a coincidence, and indeed the police do not seem to be starting an investigation about it. Some people think the mob is behind this. If this were the case, some new disturbing paths might open, casting a shadow on public institutions. We'll

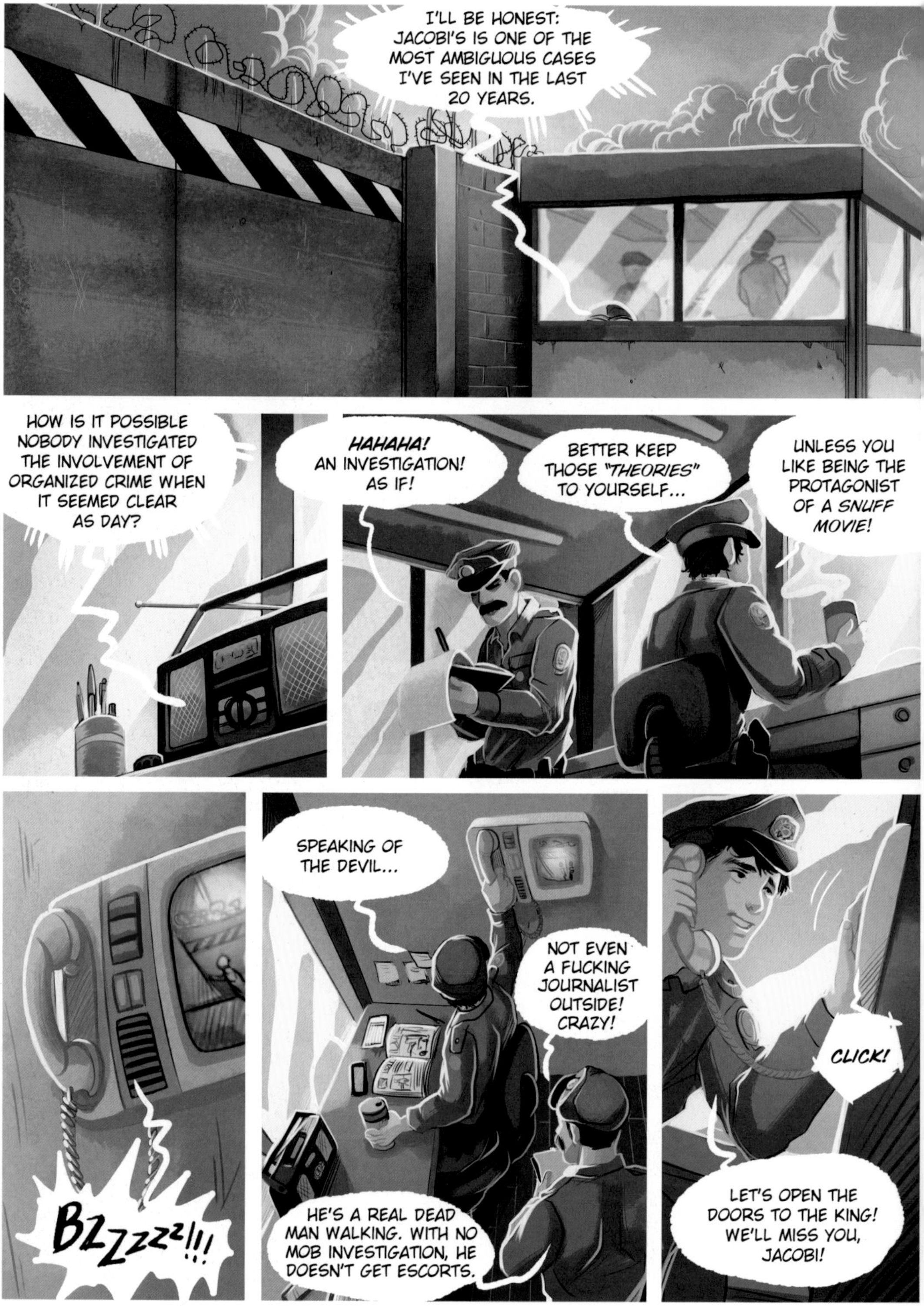
I'LL BE HONEST: JACOBI'S IS ONE OF THE MOST AMBIGUOUS CASES I'VE SEEN IN THE LAST 20 YEARS.
HOW IS IT POSSIBLE NOBODY INVESTIGATED THE INVOLVEMENT OF ORGANIZED CRIME WHEN IT SEEMED CLEAR AS DAY?
HAHAHA! AN INVESTIGATION! AS IF!
BETTER KEEP THOSE "*THEORIES*" TO YOURSELF...
UNLESS YOU LIKE BEING THE PROTAGONIST OF A *SNUFF MOVIE!*
BZZzzz!!!
SPEAKING OF THE DEVIL...
NOT EVEN A FUCKING JOURNALIST OUTSIDE! CRAZY!
HE'S A REAL DEAD MAN WALKING. WITH NO MOB INVESTIGATION, HE DOESN'T GET ESCORTS.
CLICK!
LET'S OPEN THE DOORS TO THE KING! WE'LL MISS YOU, JACOBI!

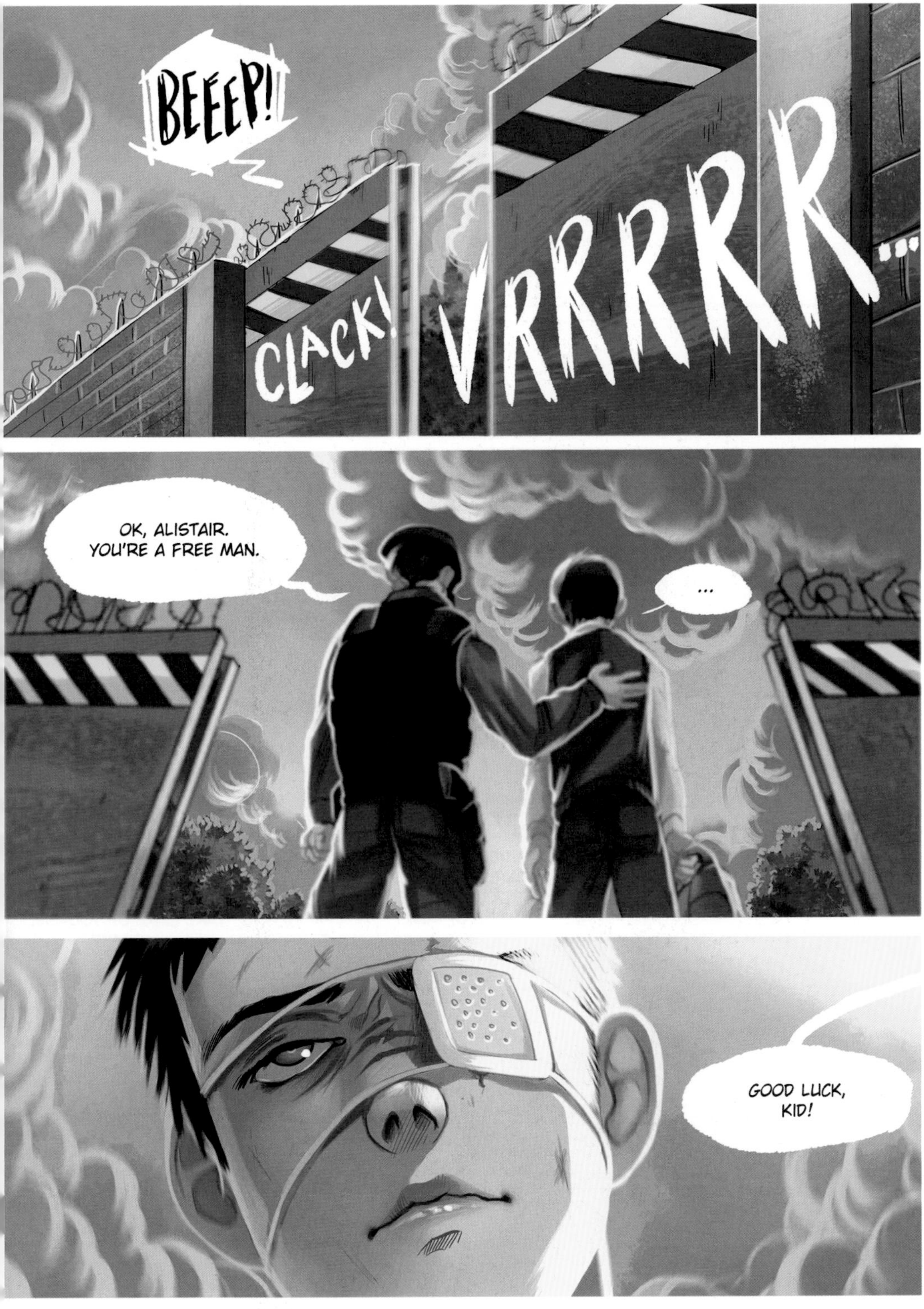
BEEEP!
CLACK!
VRRRRRR...
OK, ALISTAIR. YOU'RE A FREE MAN.
...
GOOD LUCK, KID!

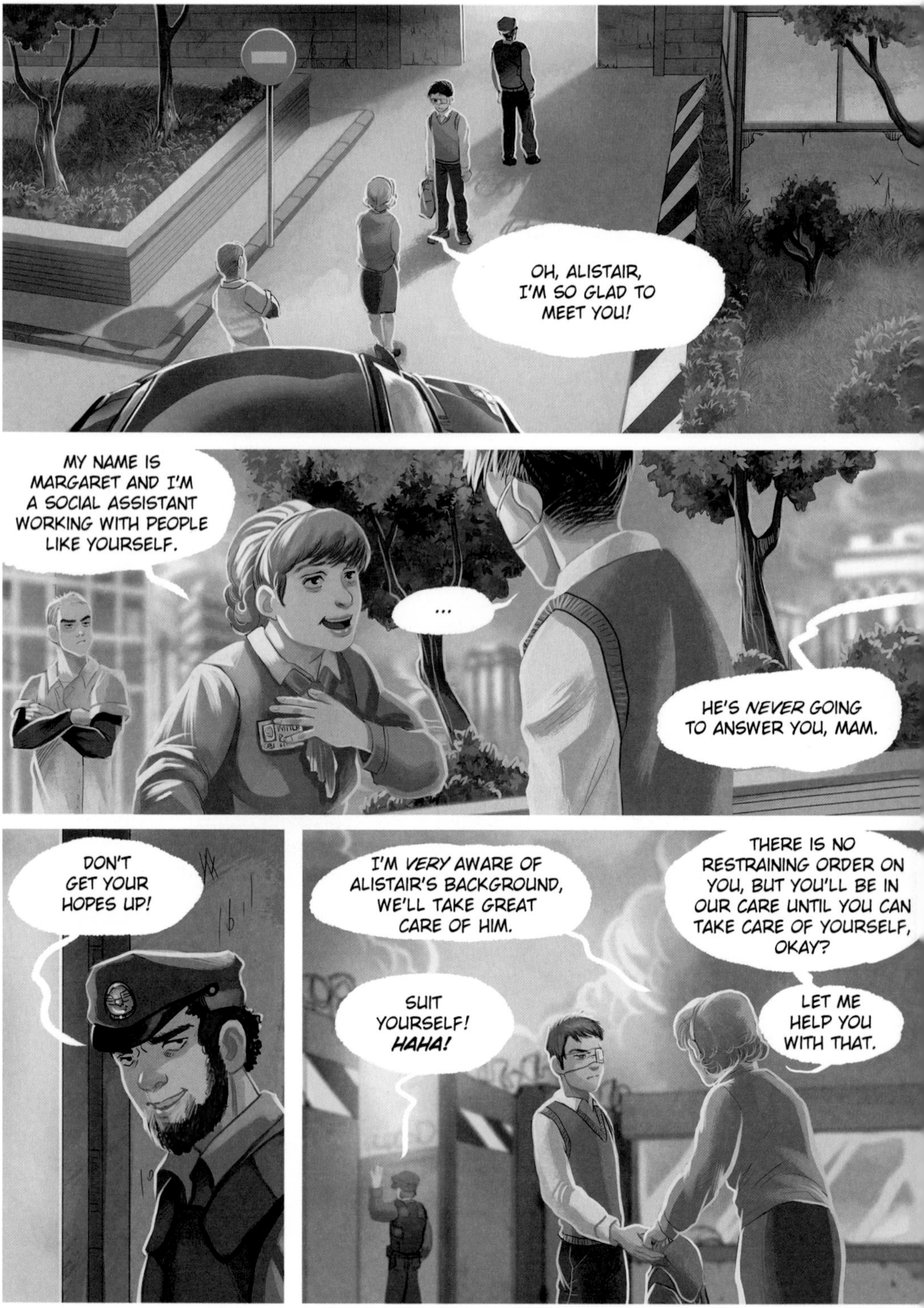
OH, ALISTAIR, I'M SO GLAD TO MEET YOU!
MY NAME IS MARGARET AND I'M A SOCIAL ASSISTANT WORKING WITH PEOPLE LIKE YOURSELF.
...
HE'S *NEVER* GOING TO ANSWER YOU, MAM.
DON'T GET YOUR HOPES UP!
I'M *VERY* AWARE OF ALISTAIR'S BACKGROUND, WE'LL TAKE GREAT CARE OF HIM.
THERE IS NO RESTRAINING ORDER ON YOU, BUT YOU'LL BE IN OUR CARE UNTIL YOU CAN TAKE CARE OF YOURSELF, OKAY?
SUIT YOURSELF! ***HAHA!***
LET ME HELP YOU WITH THAT.

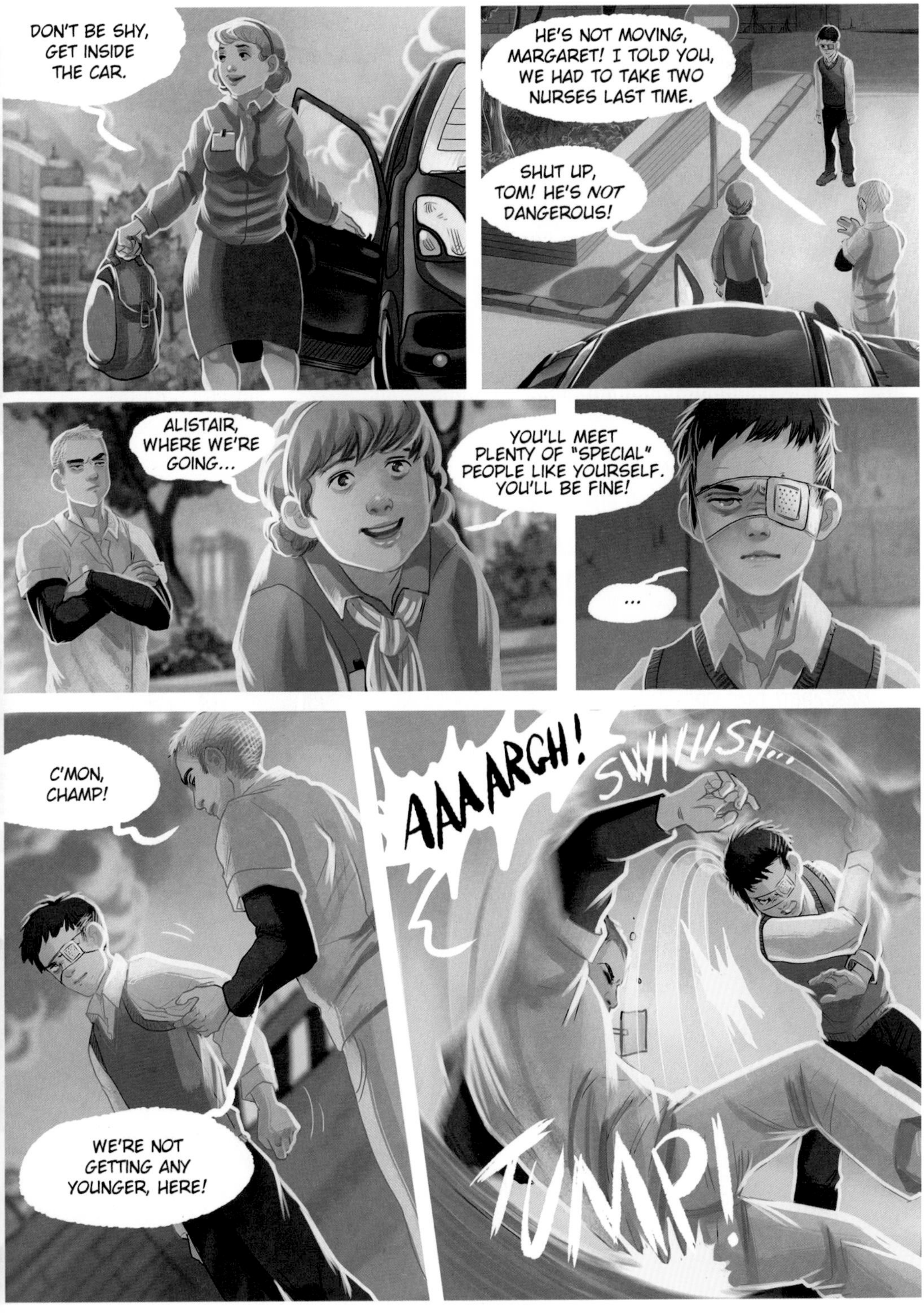
DON'T BE SHY, GET INSIDE THE CAR.
HE'S NOT MOVING, MARGARET! I TOLD YOU, WE HAD TO TAKE TWO NURSES LAST TIME.
SHUT UP, TOM! HE'S NOT DANGEROUS!
ALISTAIR, WHERE WE'RE GOING...
YOU'LL MEET PLENTY OF "SPECIAL" PEOPLE LIKE YOURSELF. YOU'LL BE FINE!
...
C'MON, CHAMP!
WE'RE NOT GETTING ANY YOUNGER, HERE!
AAAARGH!
SWIIISH...
TUMP!

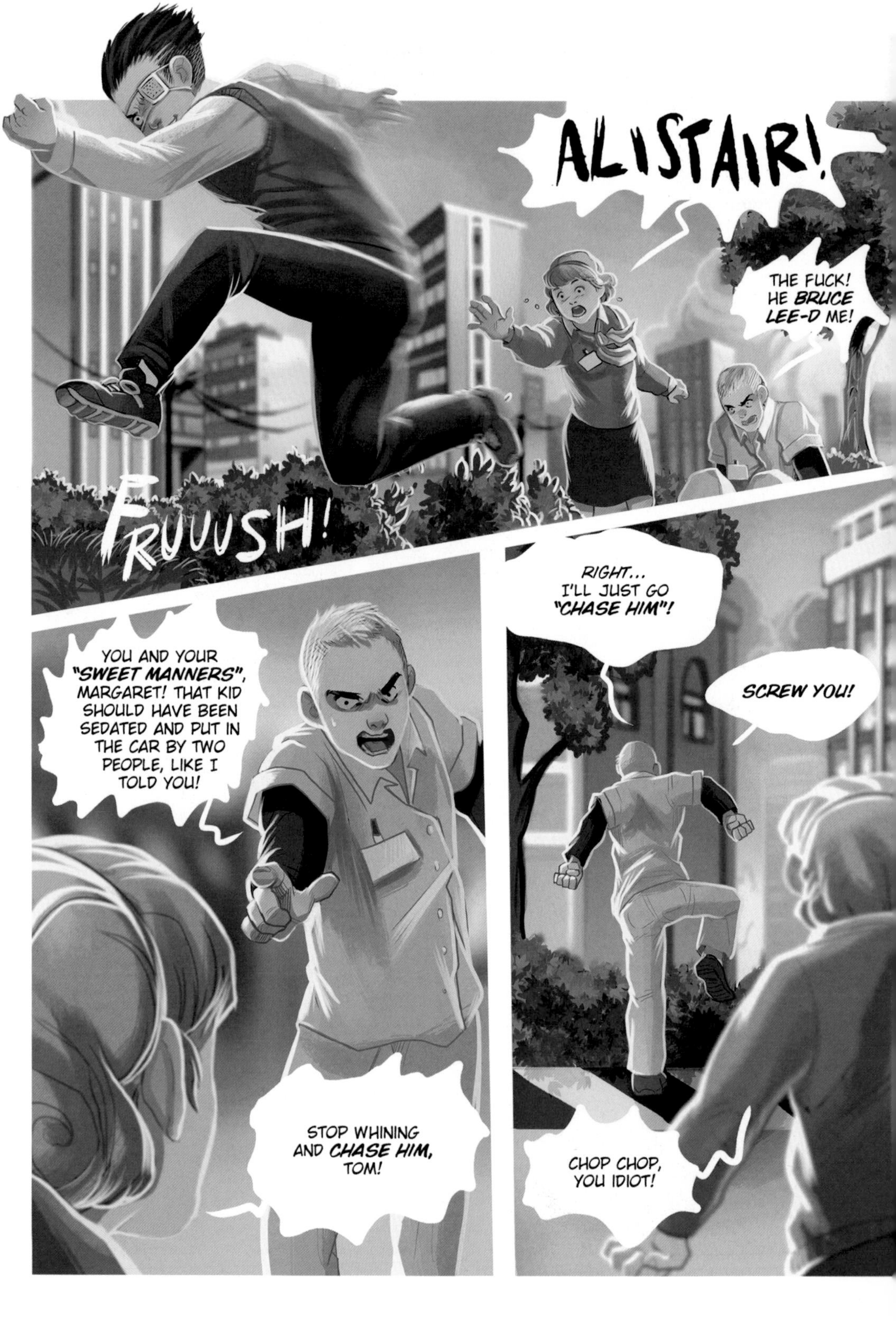
ALISTAIR!
THE FUCK! HE BRUCE LEE-D ME!
FRUUUSH!
YOU AND YOUR "SWEET MANNERS", MARGARET! THAT KID SHOULD HAVE BEEN SEDATED AND PUT IN THE CAR BY TWO PEOPLE, LIKE I TOLD YOU!
STOP WHINING AND CHASE HIM, TOM!
RIGHT... I'LL JUST GO "CHASE HIM"!
SCREW YOU!
CHOP CHOP, YOU IDIOT!

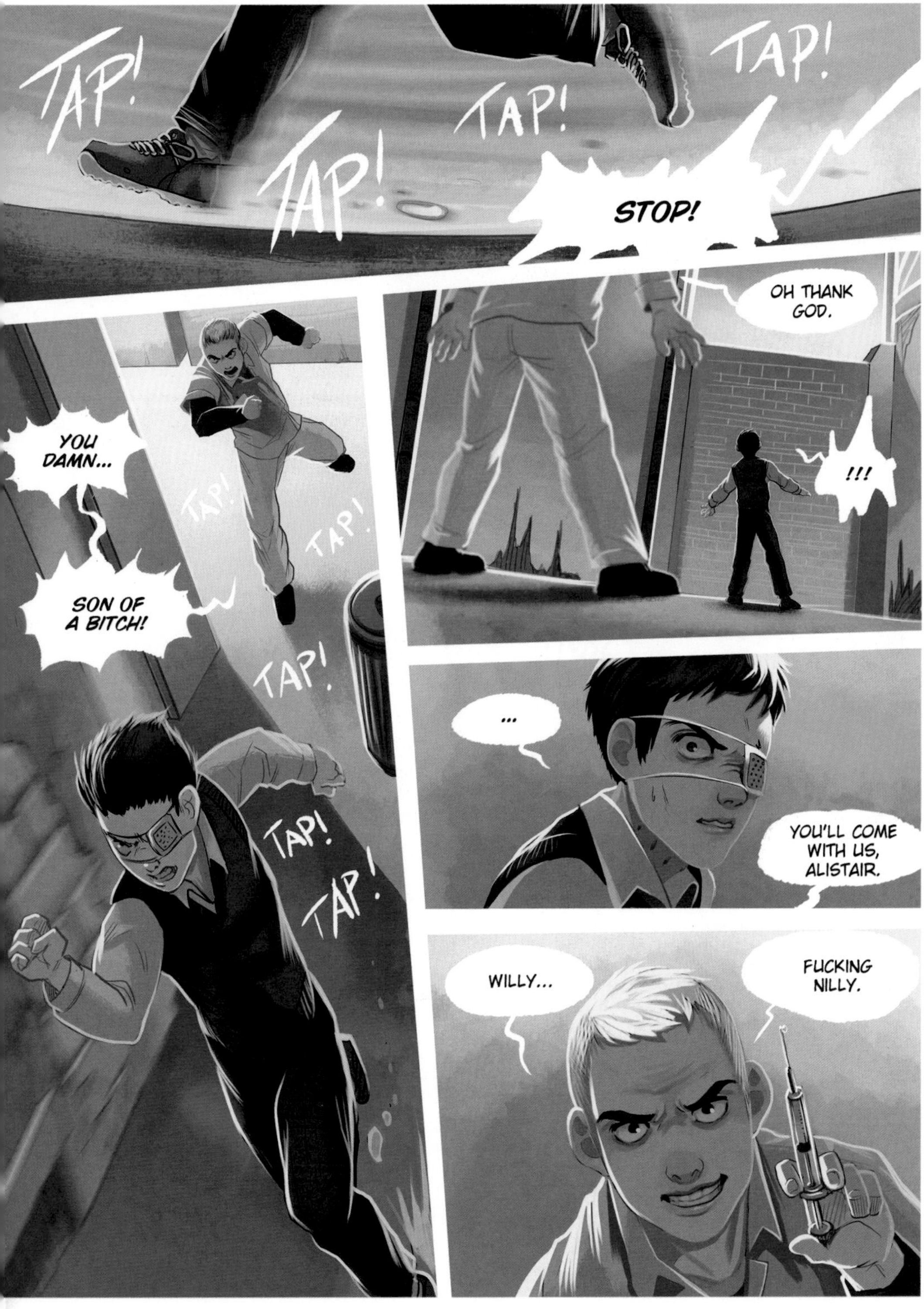
TAP!
TAP!
TAP!
TAP!
STOP!
YOU DAMN...
SON OF A BITCH!
TAP!
TAP!
TAP!
TAP!
TAP!
OH THANK GOD.
!!!
...
YOU'LL COME WITH US, ALISTAIR.
WILLY...
FUCKING NILLY.

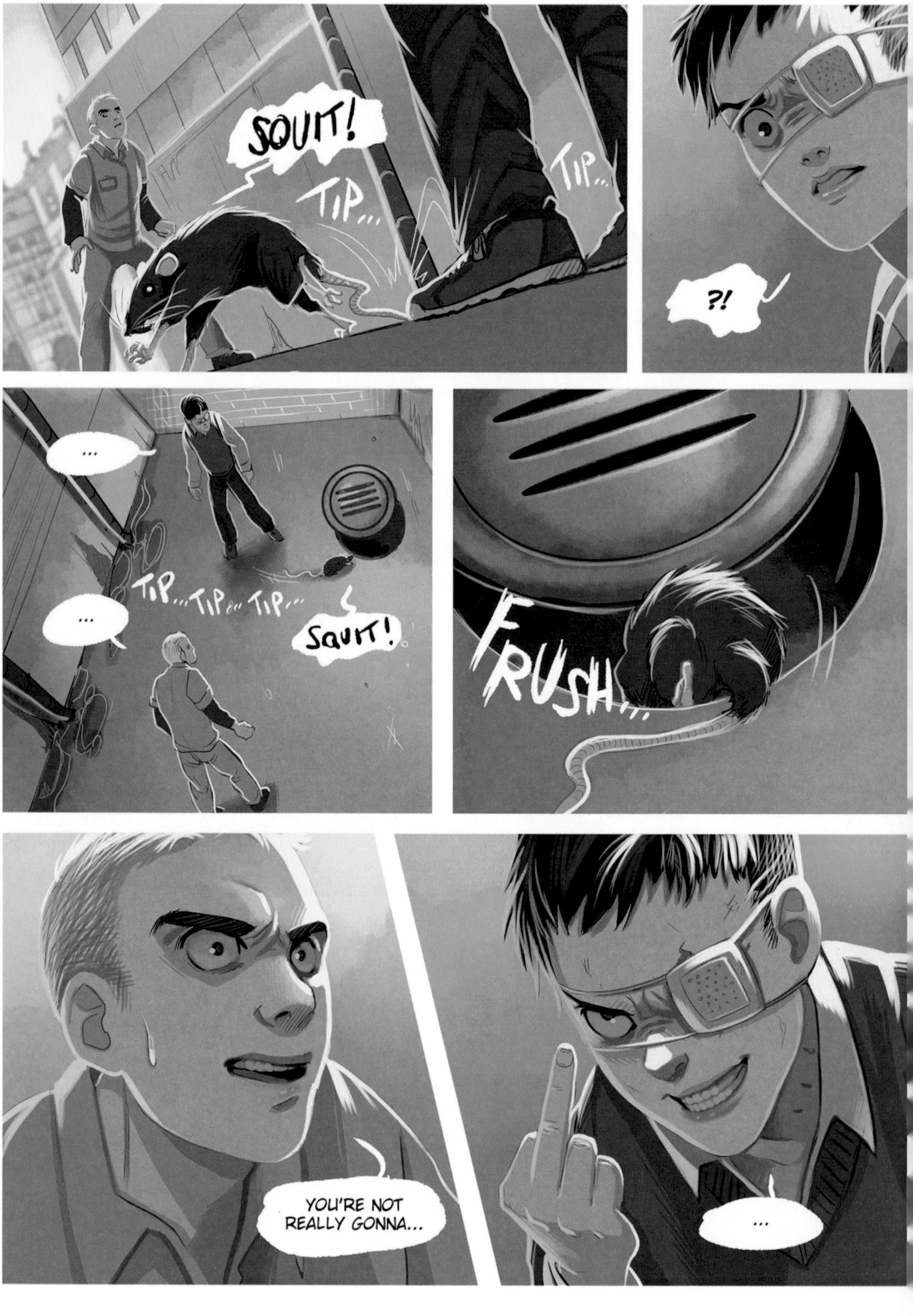
SQUIT!
TIP...
TIP...
?!
...
TIP... TIP... TIP...
...
SQUIT!
FRUSH...
YOU'RE NOT REALLY GONNA...
...

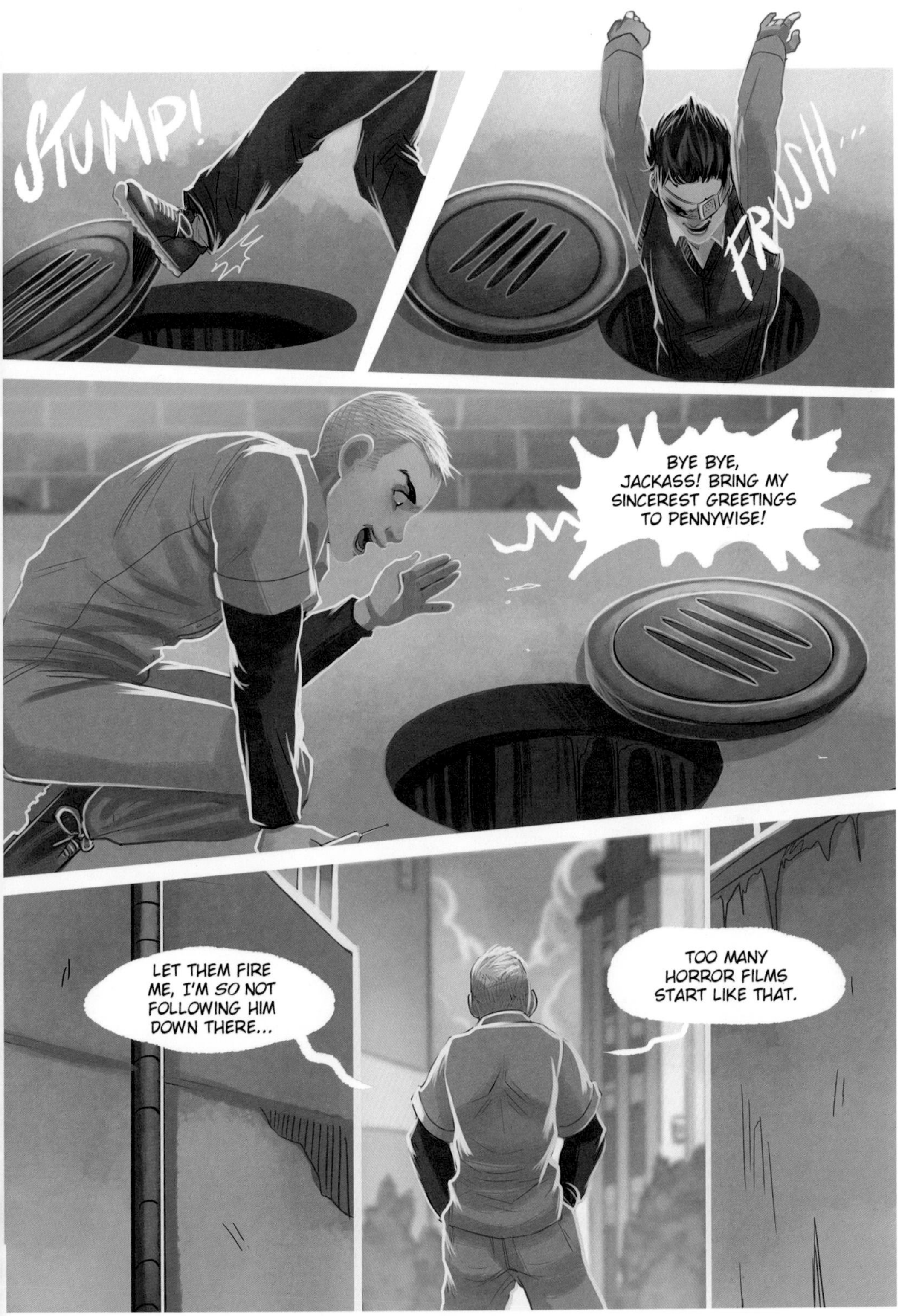
STUMP!
FRUSH...
BYE BYE, JACKASS! BRING MY SINCEREST GREETINGS TO PENNYWISE!
LET THEM FIRE ME, I'M *SO* NOT FOLLOWING HIM DOWN THERE...
TOO MANY HORROR FILMS START LIKE THAT.

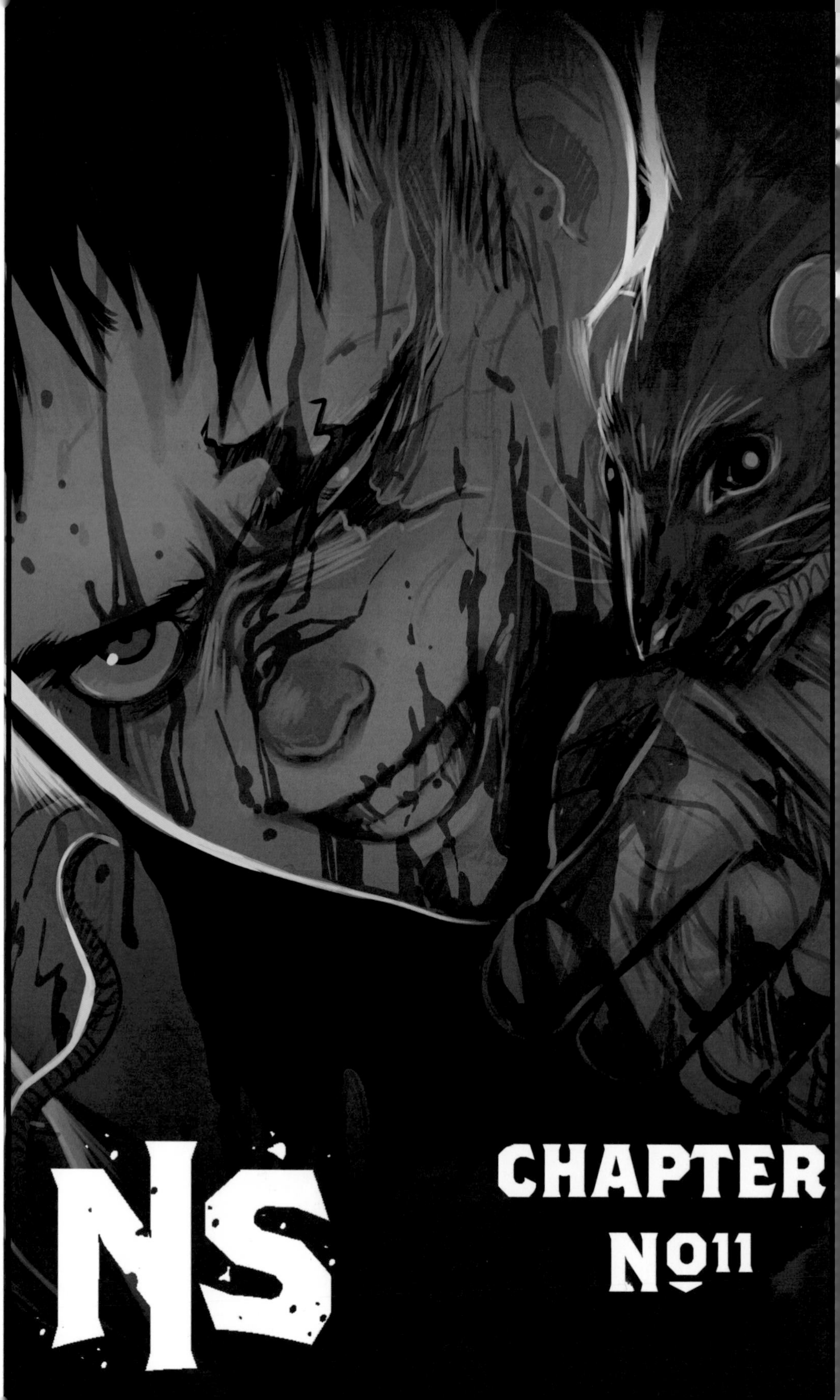
NS
CHAPTER
Nº11

SIX YEARS LATER.

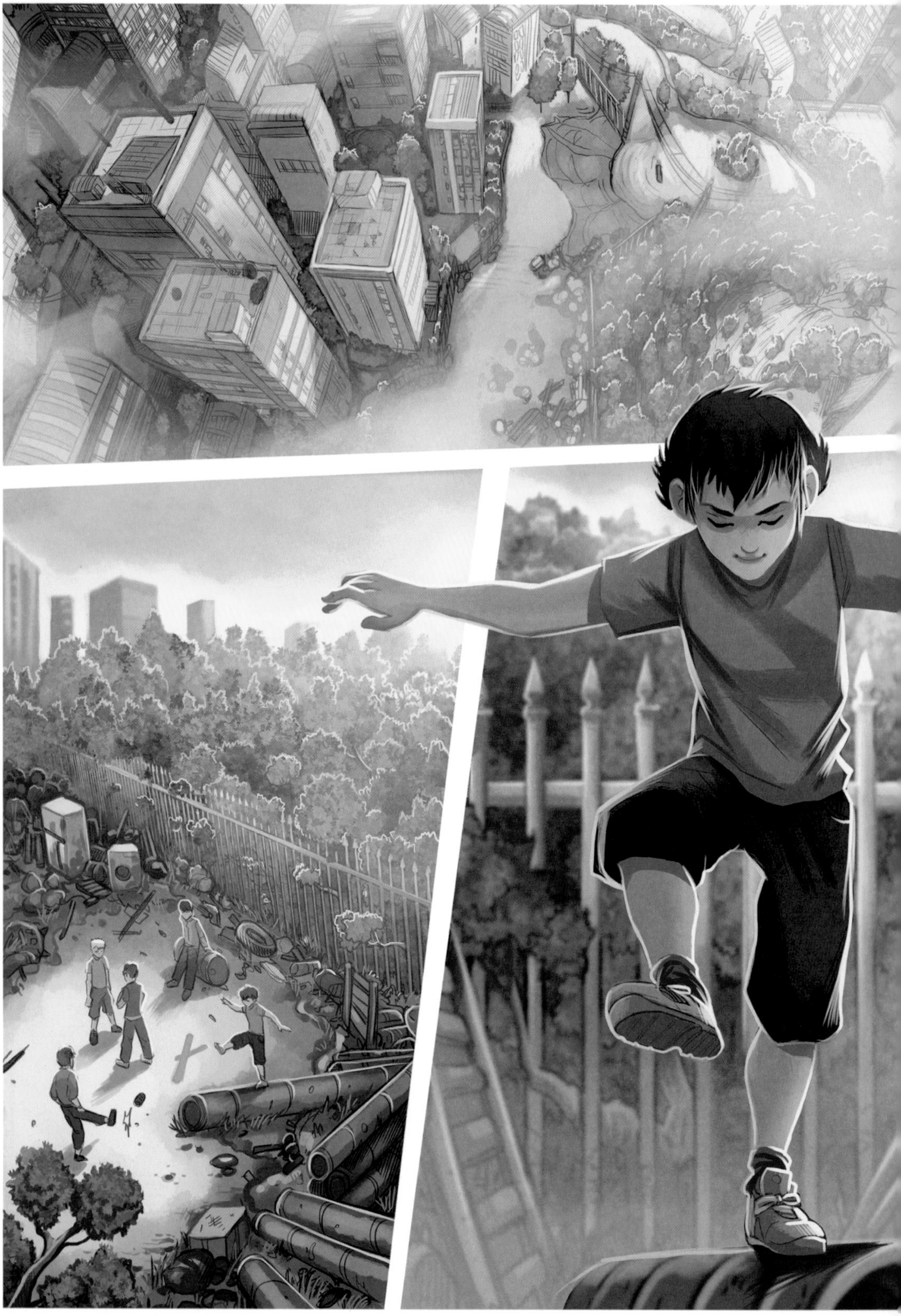

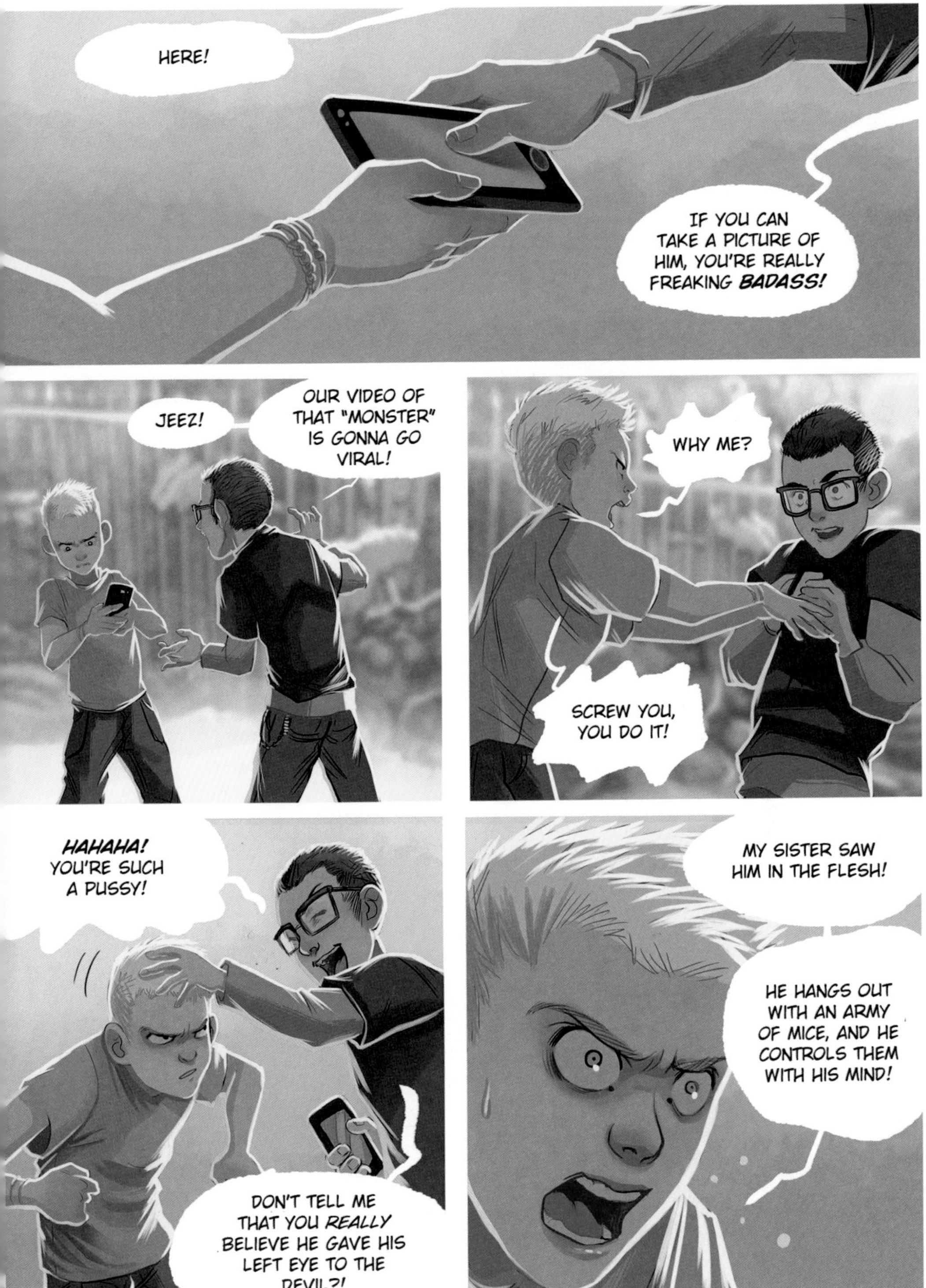
HERE!
IF YOU CAN TAKE A PICTURE OF HIM, YOU'RE REALLY FREAKING **BADASS!**
JEEZ!
OUR VIDEO OF THAT "MONSTER" IS GONNA GO VIRAL!
WHY ME?
SCREW YOU, YOU DO IT!
HAHAHA! YOU'RE SUCH A PUSSY!
DON'T TELL ME THAT YOU *REALLY* BELIEVE HE GAVE HIS LEFT EYE TO THE DEVIL?!
MY SISTER SAW HIM IN THE FLESH!
HE HANGS OUT WITH AN ARMY OF MICE, AND HE CONTROLS THEM WITH HIS MIND!

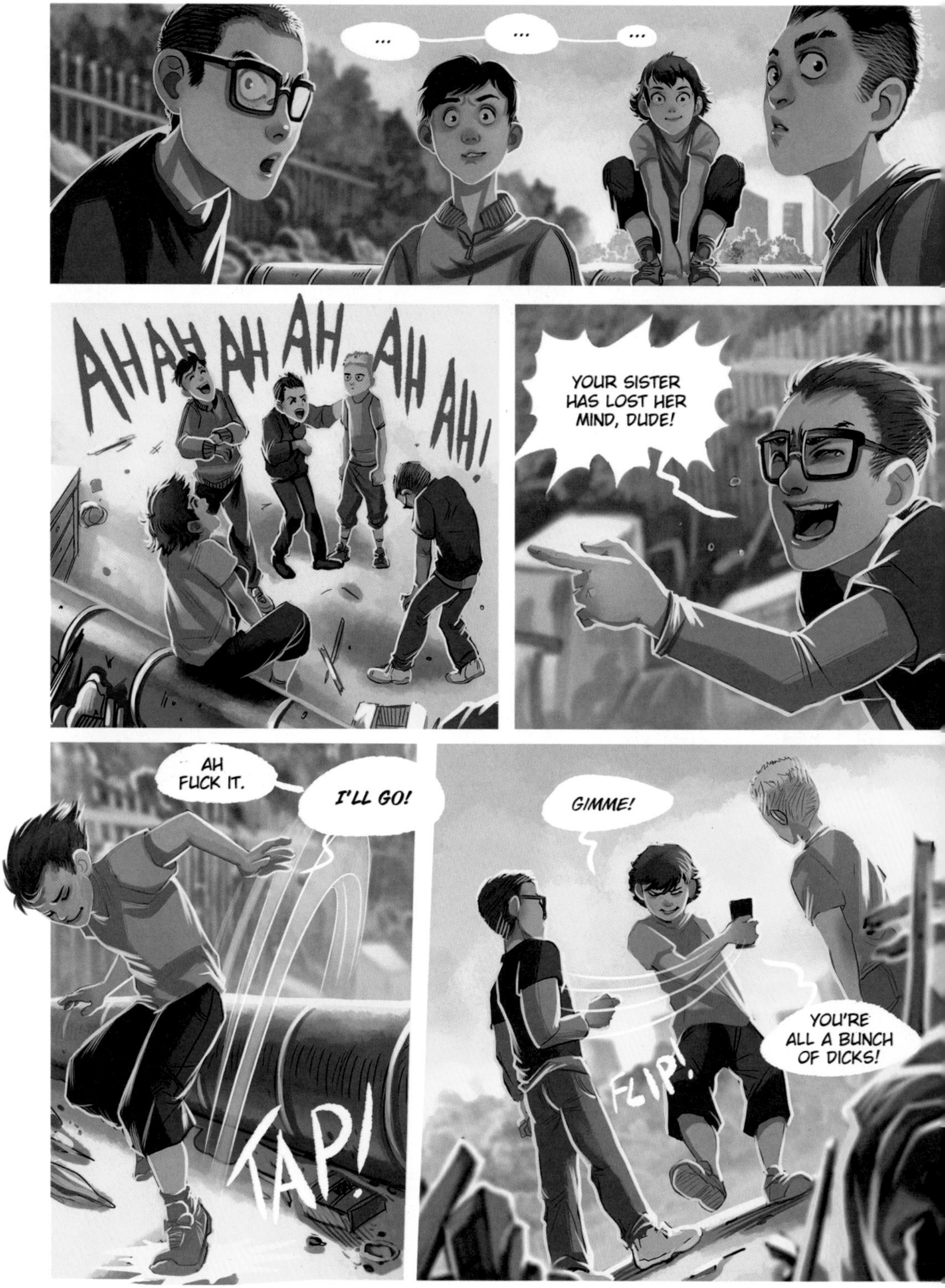
...
...
...
AHAHAH AH AH AH AH!
YOUR SISTER HAS LOST HER MIND, DUDE!
AH FUCK IT.
I'LL GO!
TAP!
GIMME!
FLIP!
YOU'RE ALL A BUNCH OF DICKS!

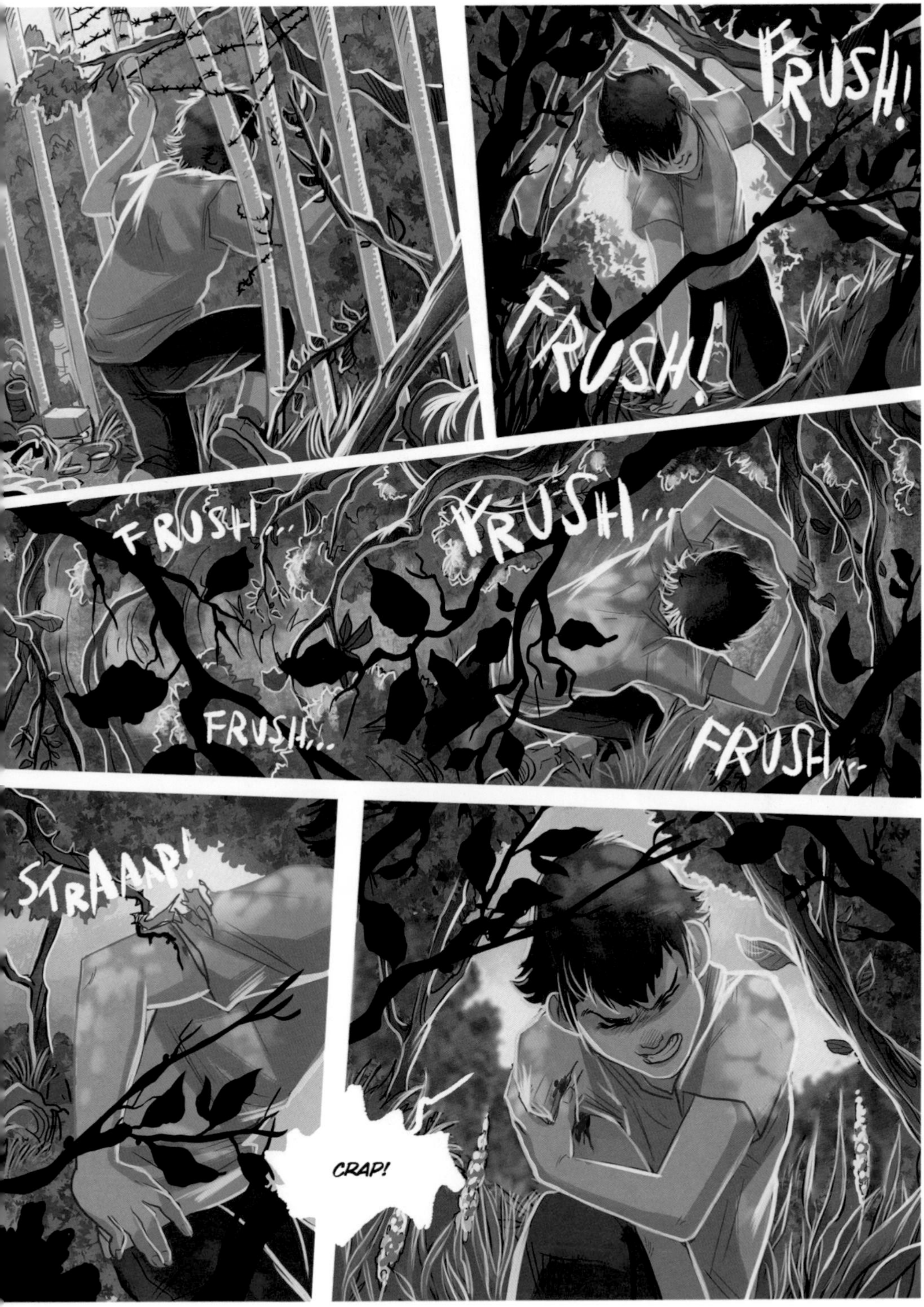
FRUSH!
FRUSH!
FRUSH...
FRUSH...
FRUSH...
FRUSH...
STRAAAP!
CRAP!

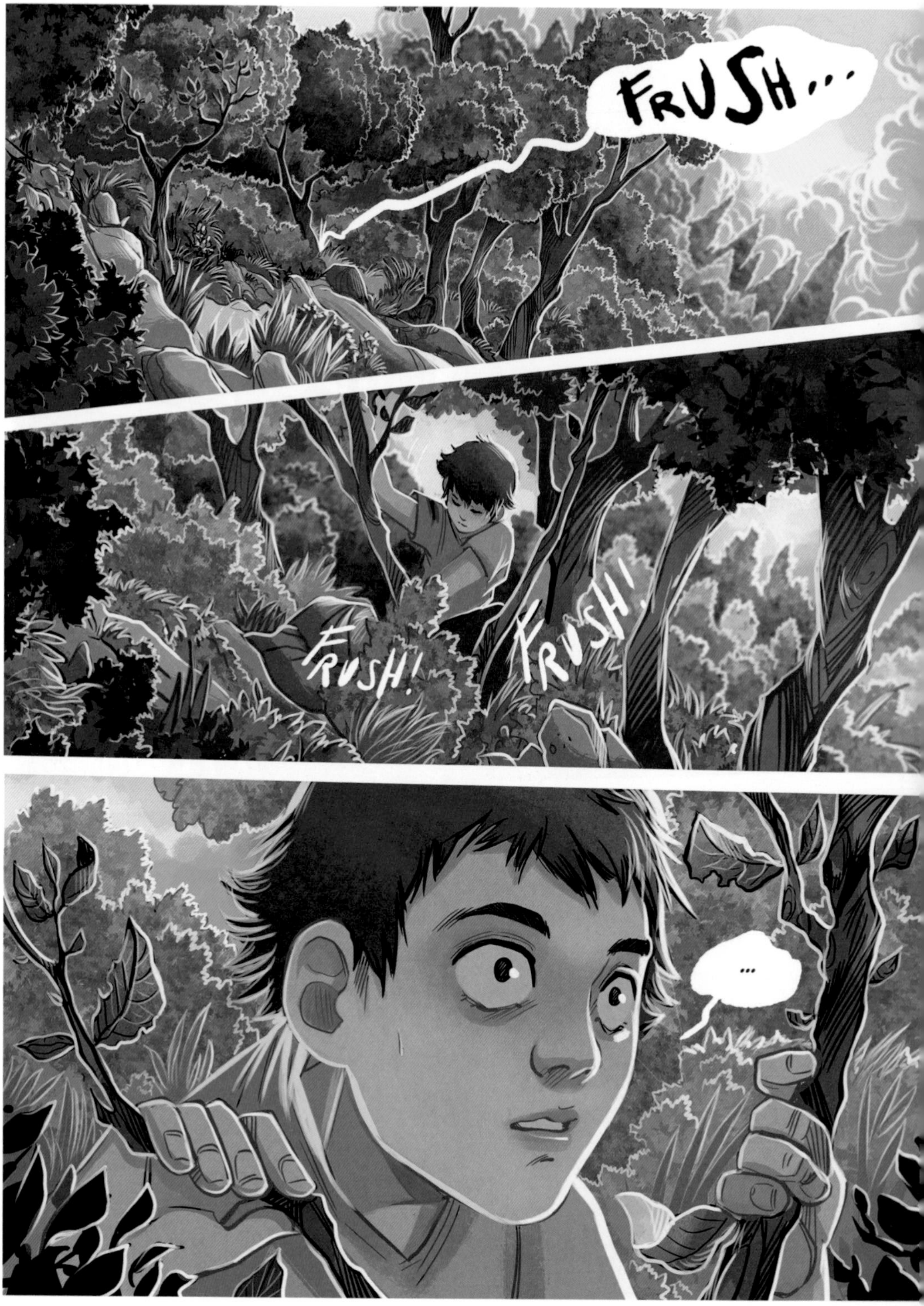
FRUSH...
FRUSH!
FRUSH!
...

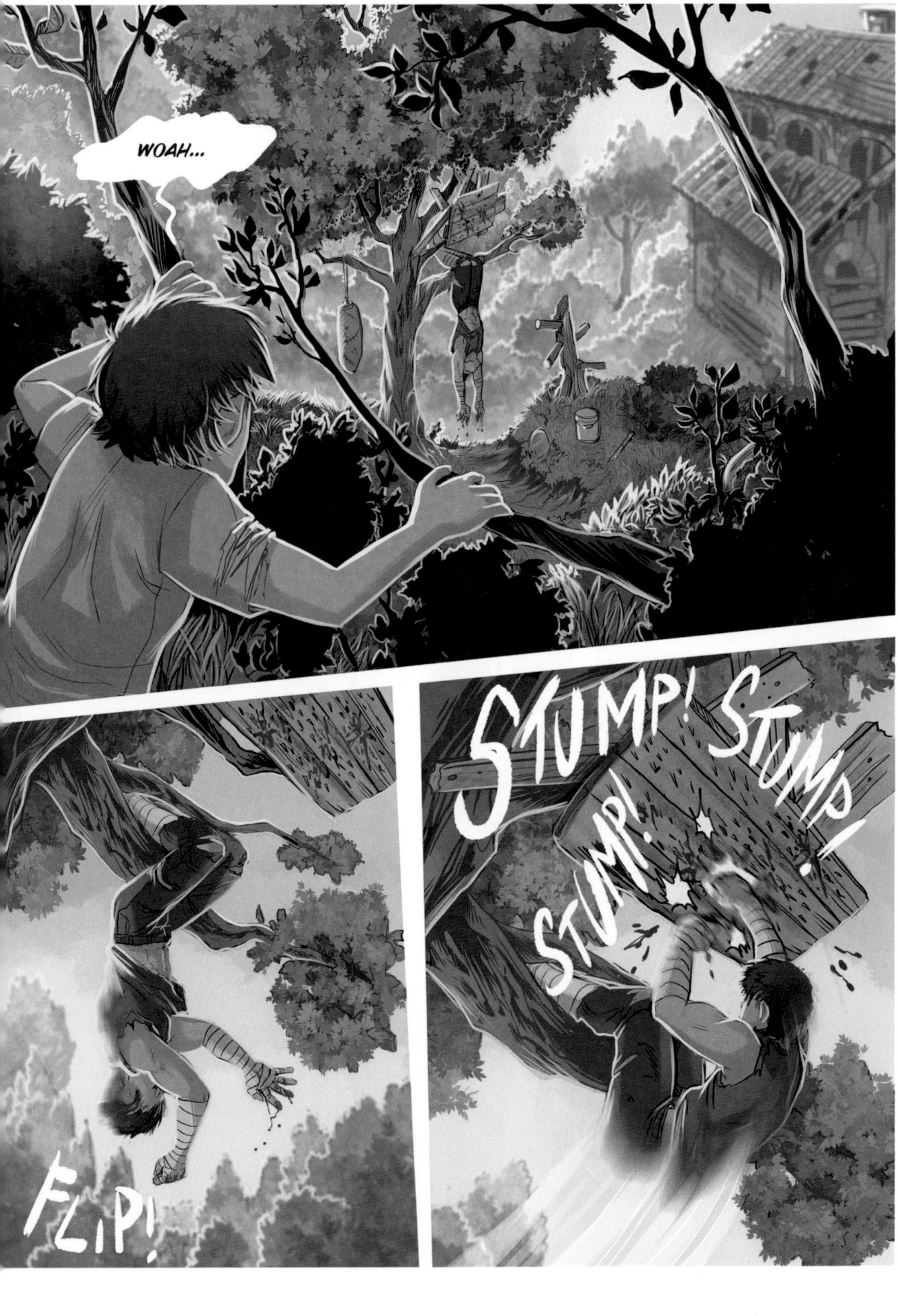
WOAH...
FLIP!
STUMP! STUMP!
STUMP! STUMP!

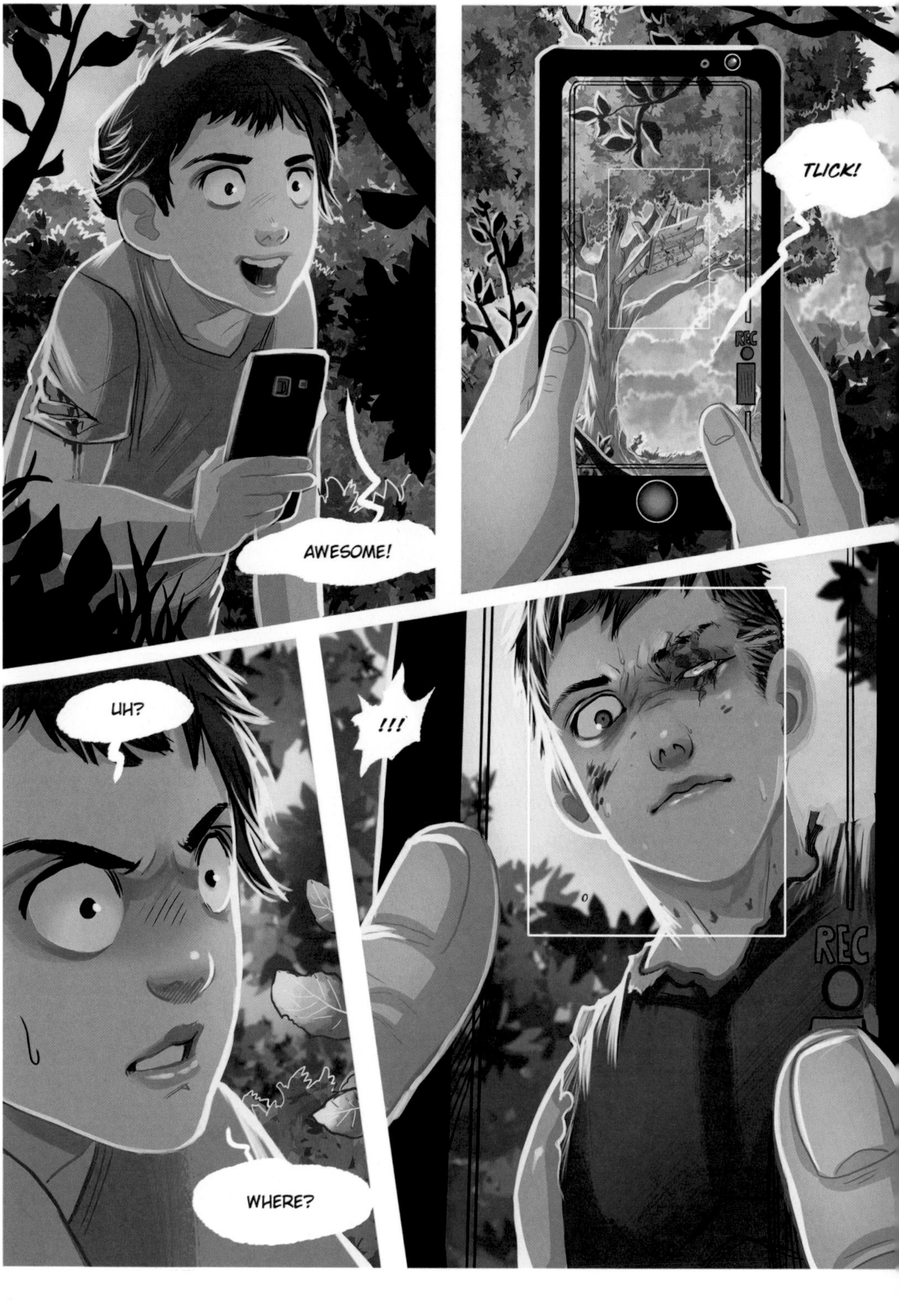
AWESOME!
TLICK!
REC
UH?
WHERE?
!!!
REC

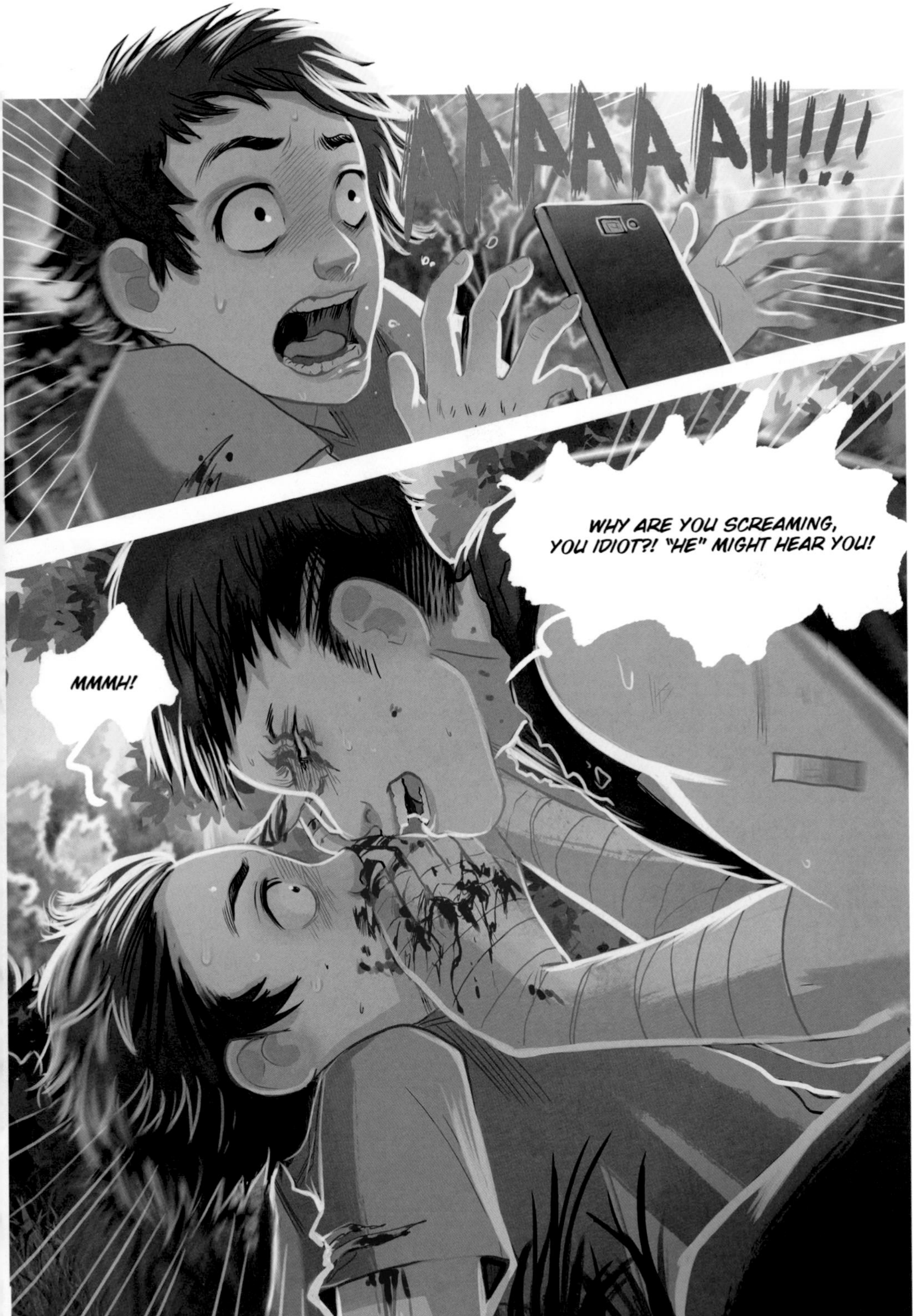
AAAAAAH!!!
WHY ARE YOU SCREAMING, YOU IDIOT?! "HE" MIGHT HEAR YOU!
MMMH!

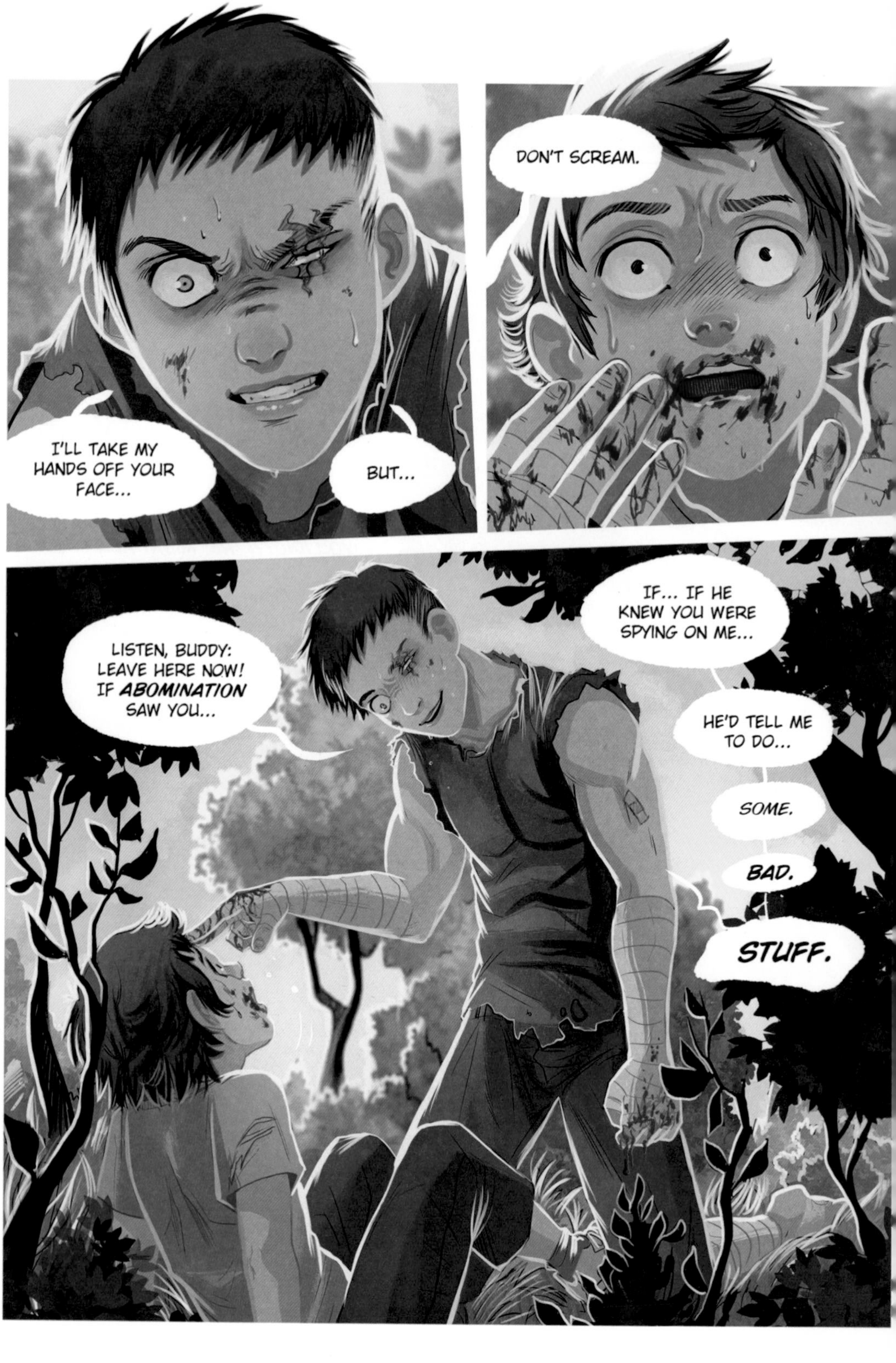
I'LL TAKE MY HANDS OFF YOUR FACE...
BUT...
DON'T SCREAM.
LISTEN, BUDDY: LEAVE HERE NOW! IF ABOMINATION SAW YOU...
IF... IF HE KNEW YOU WERE SPYING ON ME...
HE'D TELL ME TO DO...
SOME.
BAD.
STUFF.

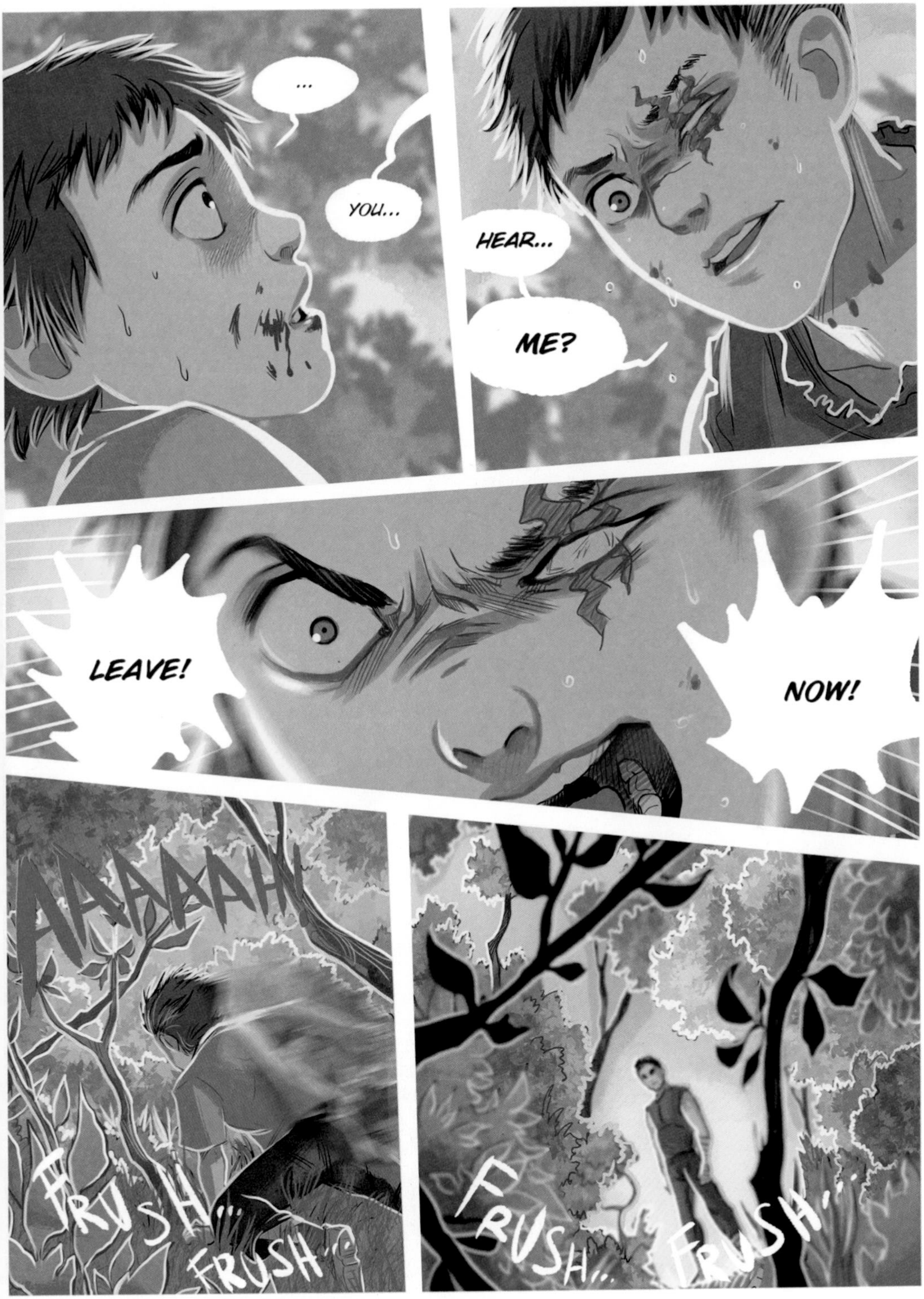
...
YOU...
HEAR...
ME?
LEAVE!
NOW!
AAAAAH
FRUSH...
FRUSH...
FRUSH...
FRUSH...

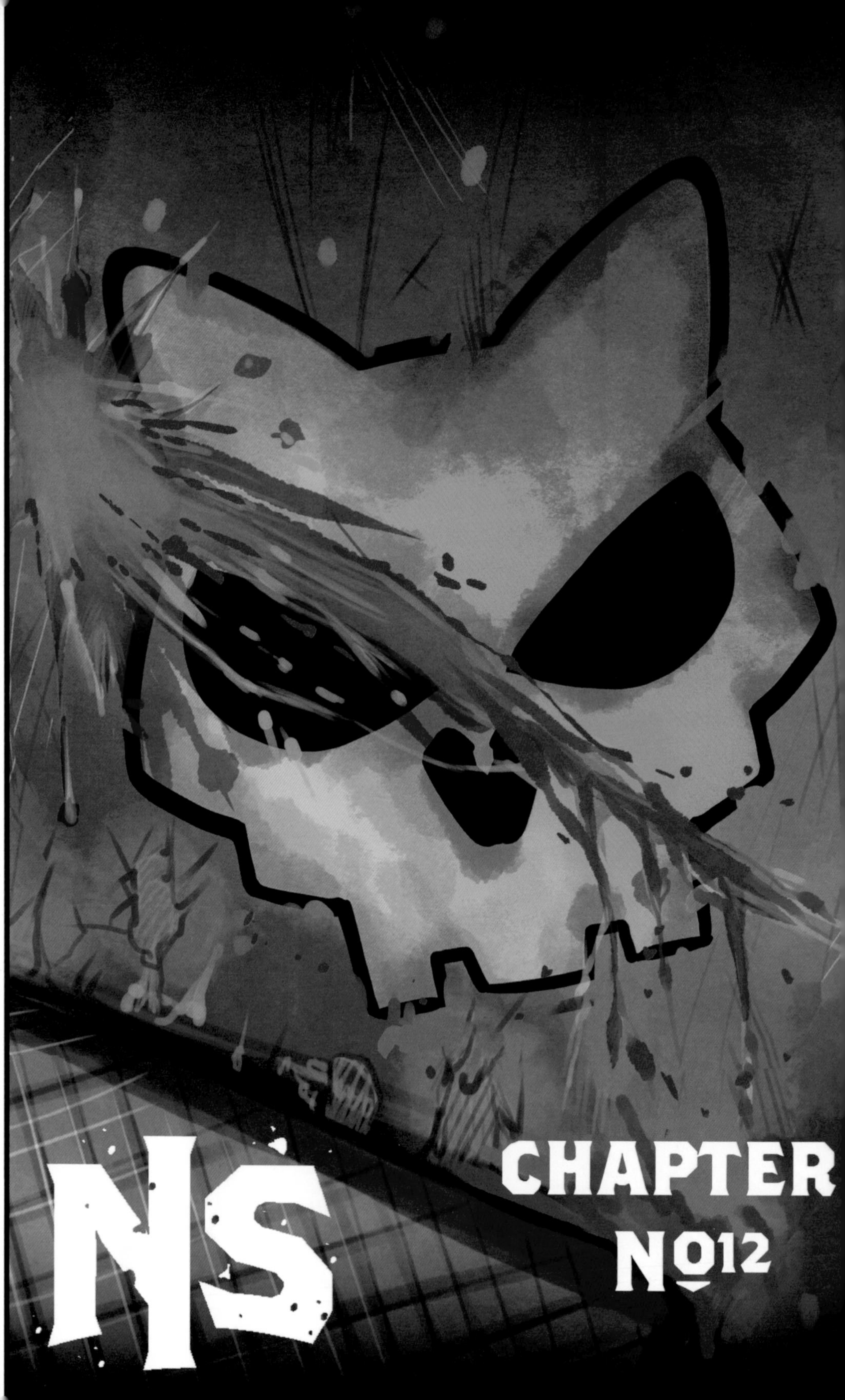
NS
CHAPTER
Nº12

FELIX.

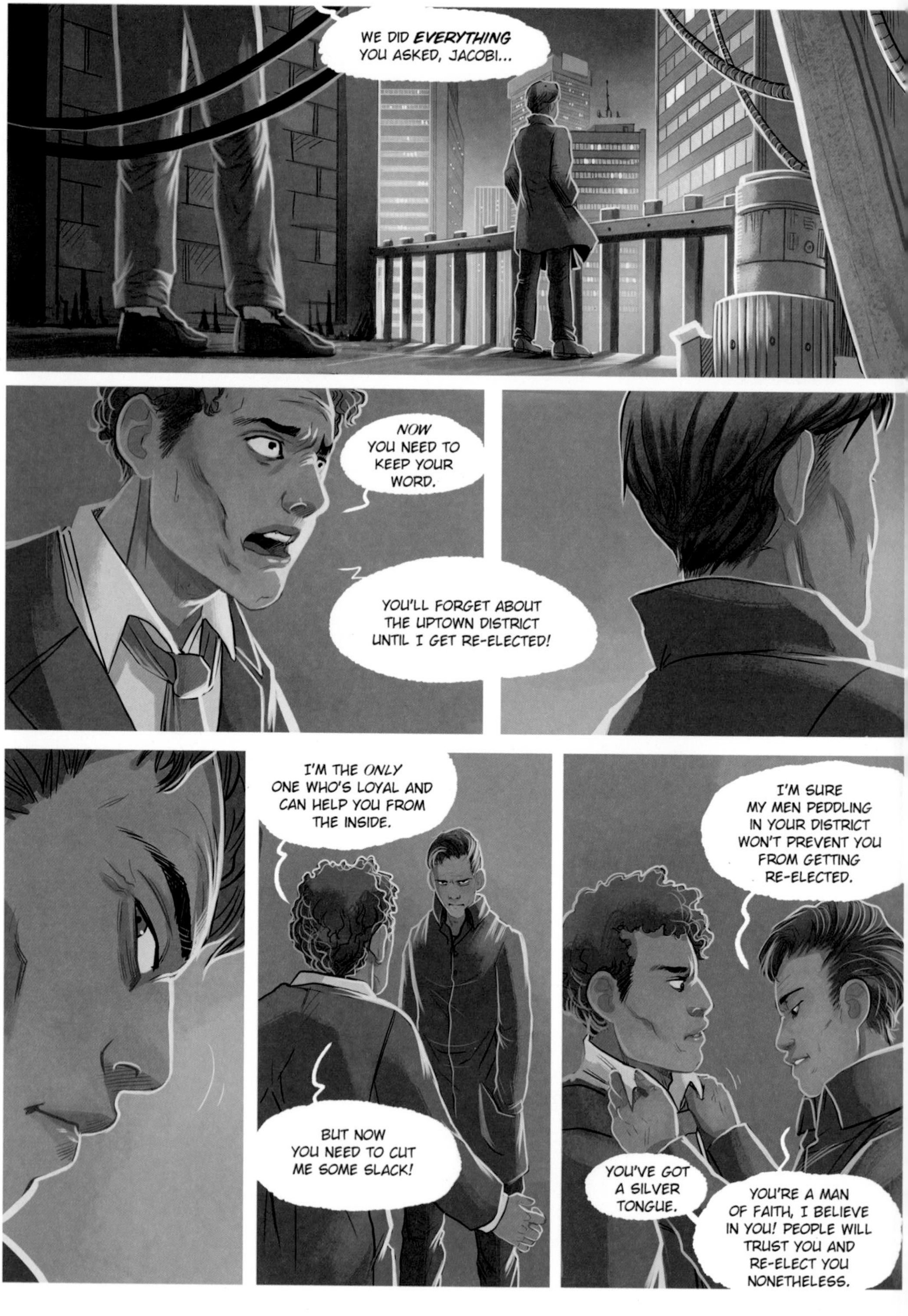
WE DID EVERYTHING YOU ASKED, JACOBI...
NOW YOU NEED TO KEEP YOUR WORD.
YOU'LL FORGET ABOUT THE UPTOWN DISTRICT UNTIL I GET RE-ELECTED!
I'M THE ONLY ONE WHO'S LOYAL AND CAN HELP YOU FROM THE INSIDE.
BUT NOW YOU NEED TO CUT ME SOME SLACK!
I'M SURE MY MEN PEDDLING IN YOUR DISTRICT WON'T PREVENT YOU FROM GETTING RE-ELECTED.
YOU'VE GOT A SILVER TONGUE.
YOU'RE A MAN OF FAITH, I BELIEVE IN YOU! PEOPLE WILL TRUST YOU AND RE-ELECT YOU NONETHELESS.

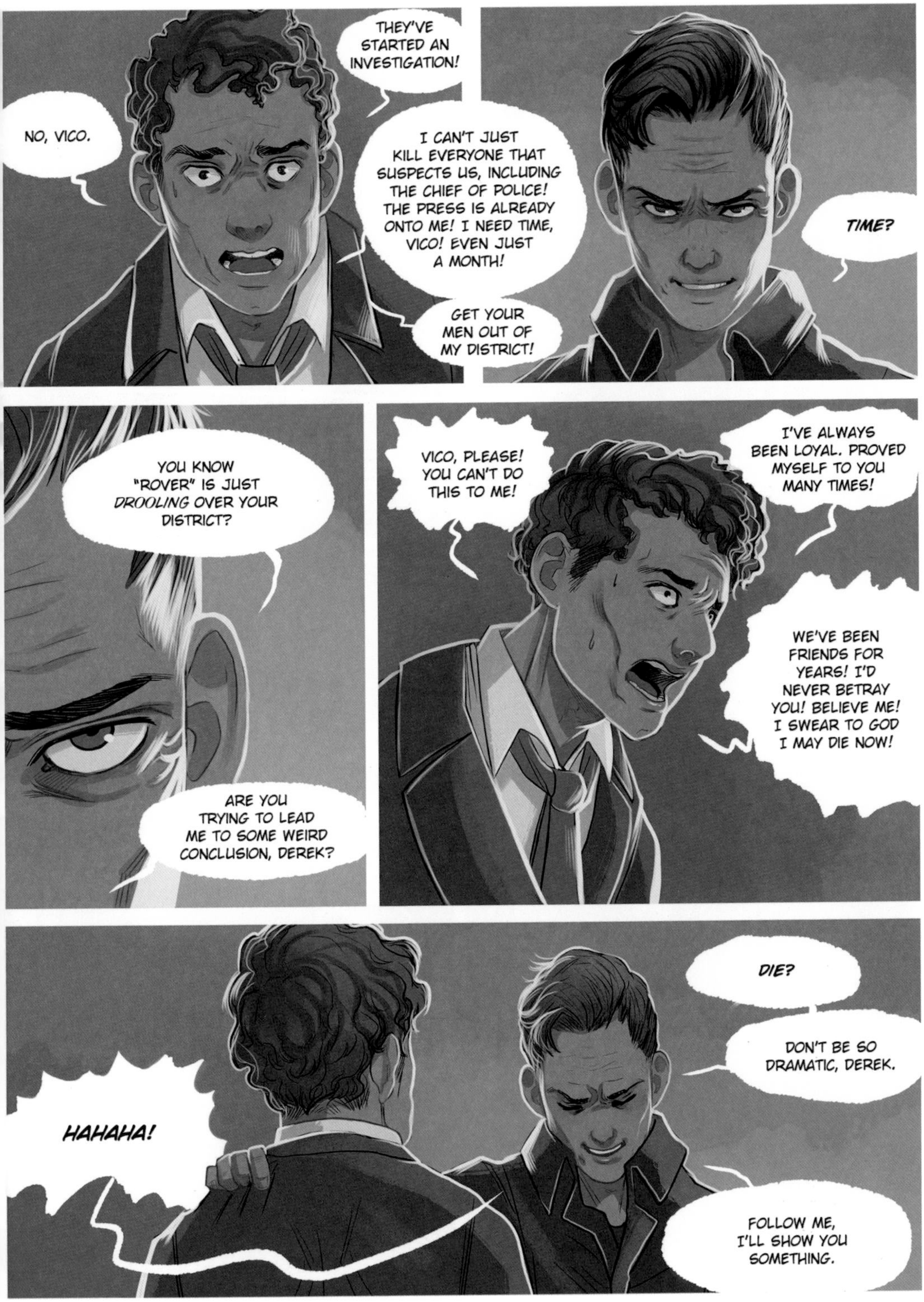
NO, VICO.
THEY'VE STARTED AN INVESTIGATION!
I CAN'T JUST KILL EVERYONE THAT SUSPECTS US, INCLUDING THE CHIEF OF POLICE! THE PRESS IS ALREADY ONTO ME! I NEED TIME, VICO! EVEN JUST A MONTH!
GET YOUR MEN OUT OF MY DISTRICT!
TIME?
YOU KNOW "ROVER" IS JUST DROOLING OVER YOUR DISTRICT?
ARE YOU TRYING TO LEAD ME TO SOME WEIRD CONCLUSION, DEREK?
VICO, PLEASE! YOU CAN'T DO THIS TO ME!
I'VE ALWAYS BEEN LOYAL. PROVED MYSELF TO YOU MANY TIMES!
WE'VE BEEN FRIENDS FOR YEARS! I'D NEVER BETRAY YOU! BELIEVE ME! I SWEAR TO GOD I MAY DIE NOW!
HAHAHA!
DIE?
DON'T BE SO DRAMATIC, DEREK.
FOLLOW ME, I'LL SHOW YOU SOMETHING.

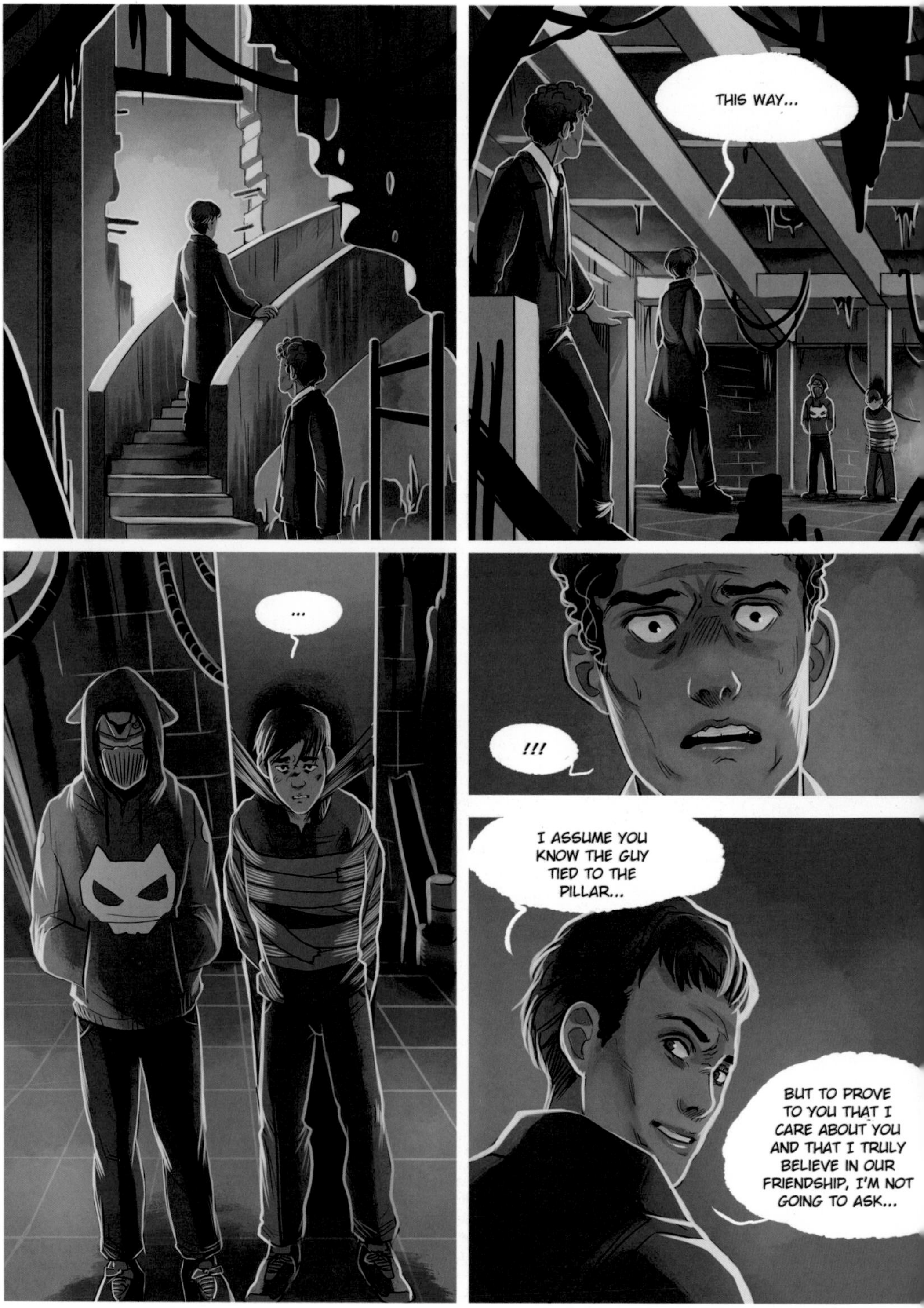
THIS WAY...
...
!!!
I ASSUME YOU KNOW THE GUY TIED TO THE PILLAR...
BUT TO PROVE TO YOU THAT I CARE ABOUT YOU AND THAT I TRULY BELIEVE IN OUR FRIENDSHIP, I'M NOT GOING TO ASK...

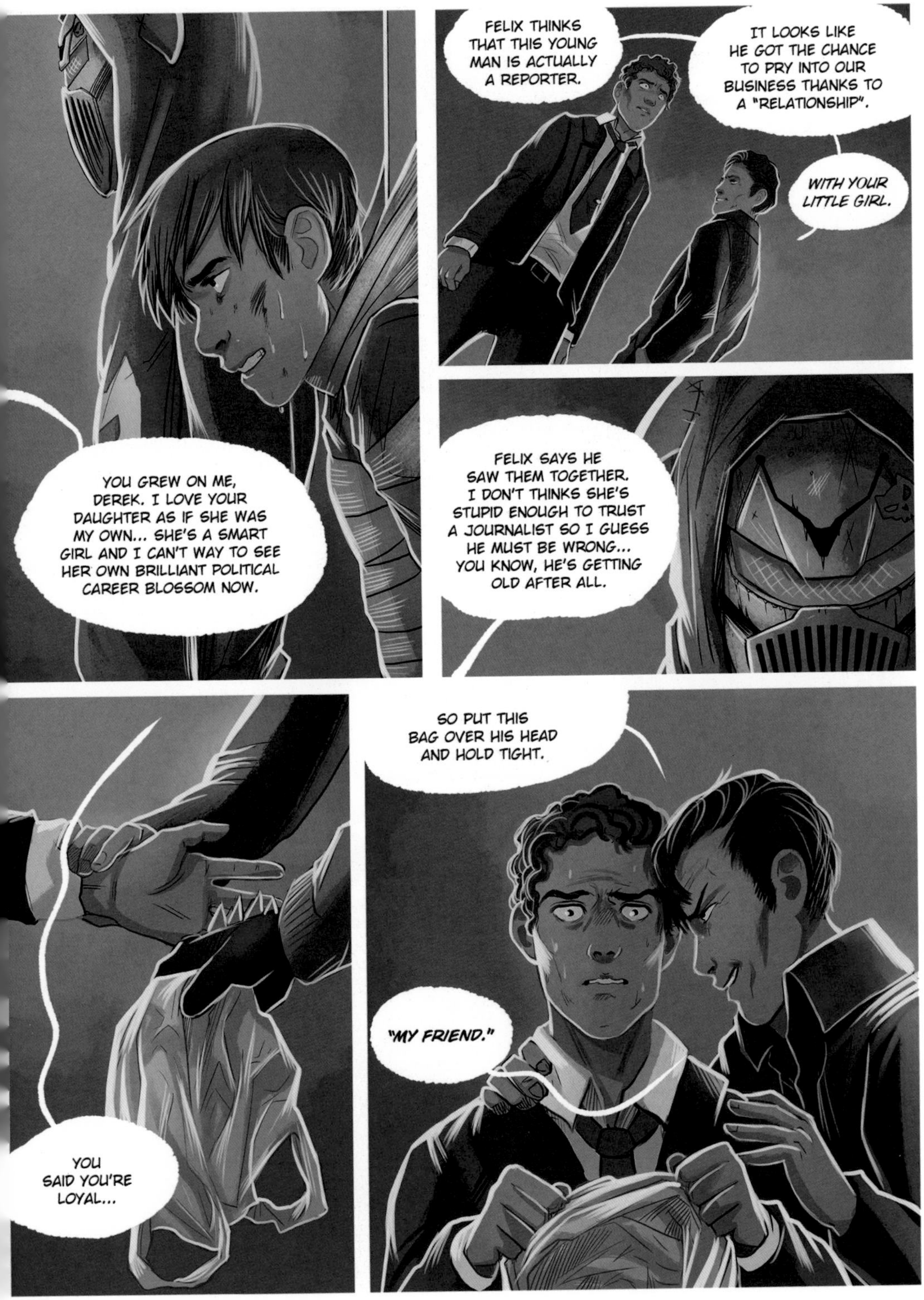
YOU GREW ON ME, DEREK. I LOVE YOUR DAUGHTER AS IF SHE WAS MY OWN... SHE'S A SMART GIRL AND I CAN'T WAY TO SEE HER OWN BRILLIANT POLITICAL CAREER BLOSSOM NOW.
FELIX THINKS THAT THIS YOUNG MAN IS ACTUALLY A REPORTER.
IT LOOKS LIKE HE GOT THE CHANCE TO PRY INTO OUR BUSINESS THANKS TO A "RELATIONSHIP".
WITH YOUR LITTLE GIRL.
FELIX SAYS HE SAW THEM TOGETHER. I DON'T THINKS SHE'S STUPID ENOUGH TO TRUST A JOURNALIST SO I GUESS HE MUST BE WRONG... YOU KNOW, HE'S GETTING OLD AFTER ALL.
YOU SAID YOU'RE LOYAL...
SO PUT THIS BAG OVER HIS HEAD AND HOLD TIGHT.
"MY FRIEND."

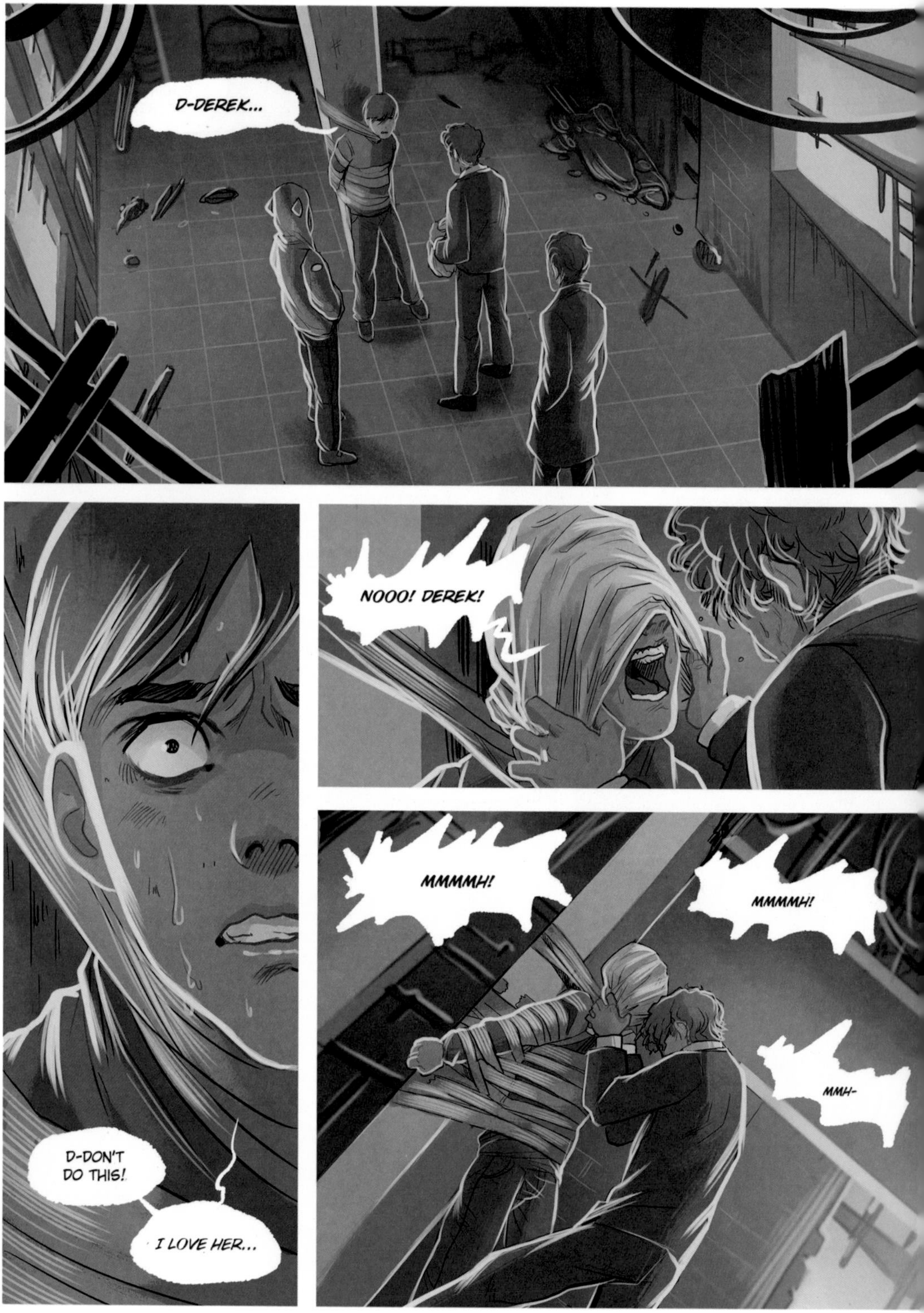
D-DEREK...
D-DON'T DO THIS!
I LOVE HER...
NOOO! DEREK!
MMMMH!
MMMMH!
MMH-

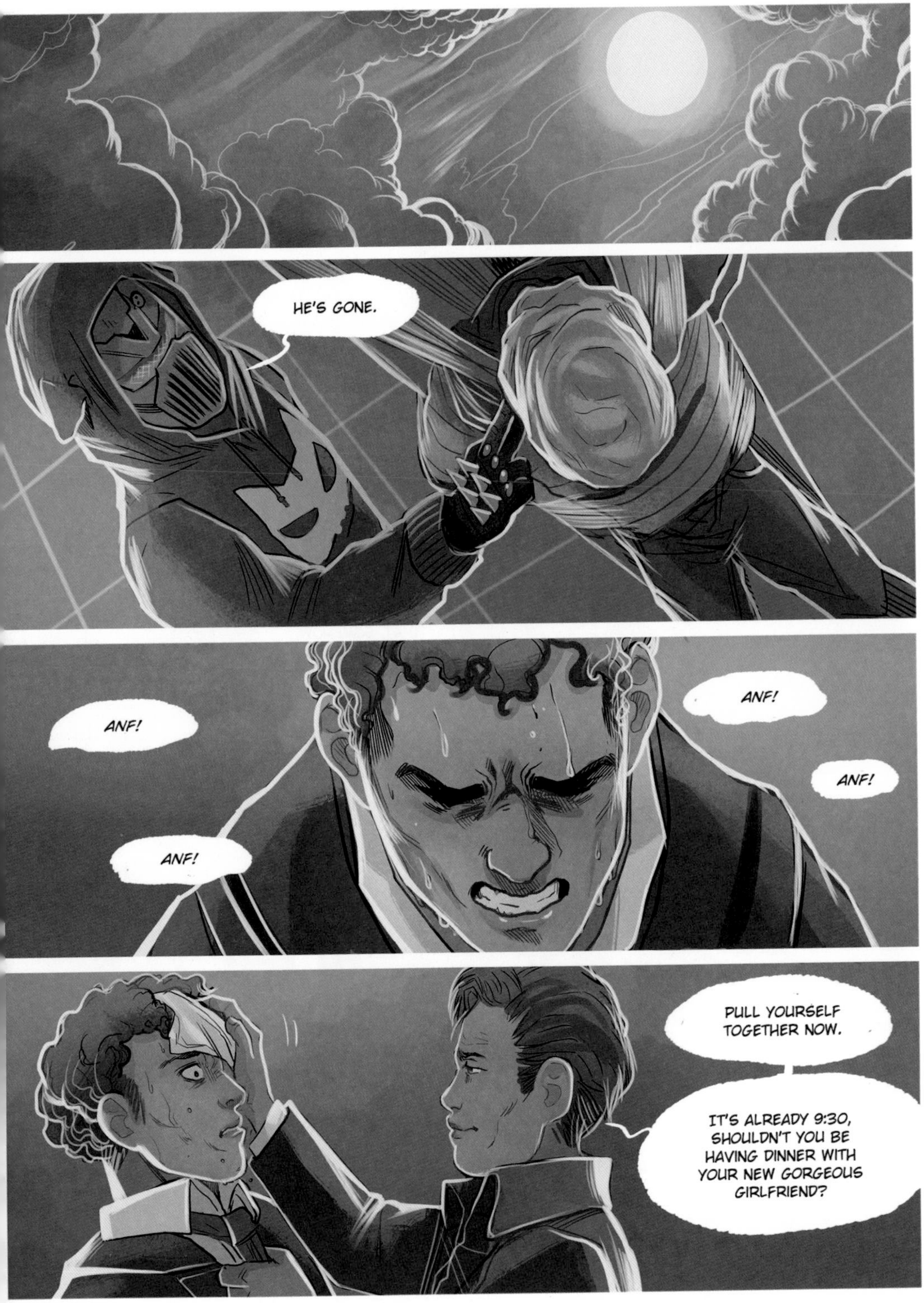
HE'S GONE.
ANF!
ANF!
ANF!
ANF!
PULL YOURSELF TOGETHER NOW.
IT'S ALREADY 9:30, SHOULDN'T YOU BE HAVING DINNER WITH YOUR NEW GORGEOUS GIRLFRIEND?

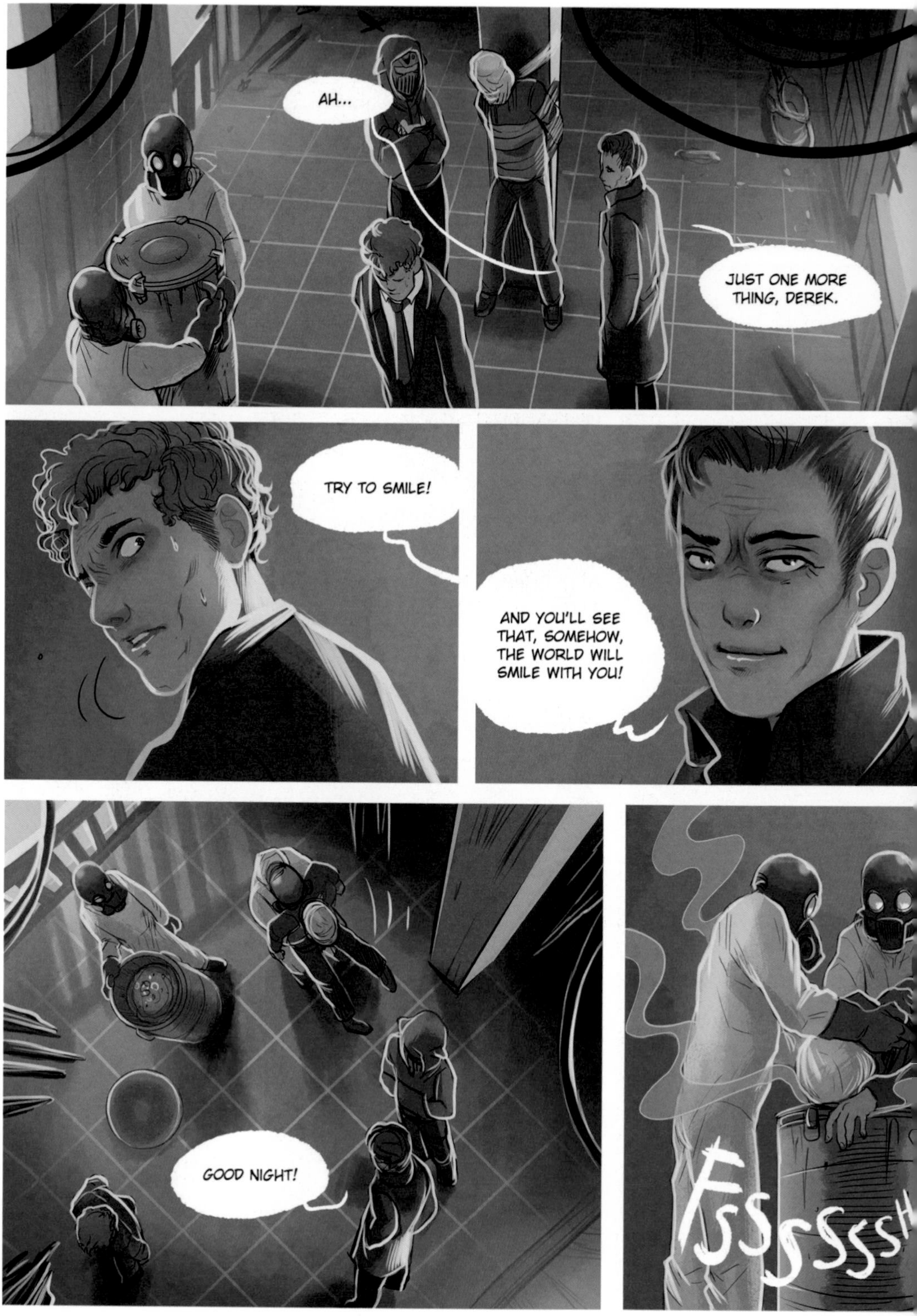
AH...
JUST ONE MORE THING, DEREK.
TRY TO SMILE!
AND YOU'LL SEE THAT, SOMEHOW, THE WORLD WILL SMILE WITH YOU!
GOOD NIGHT!
FSSSSSSH

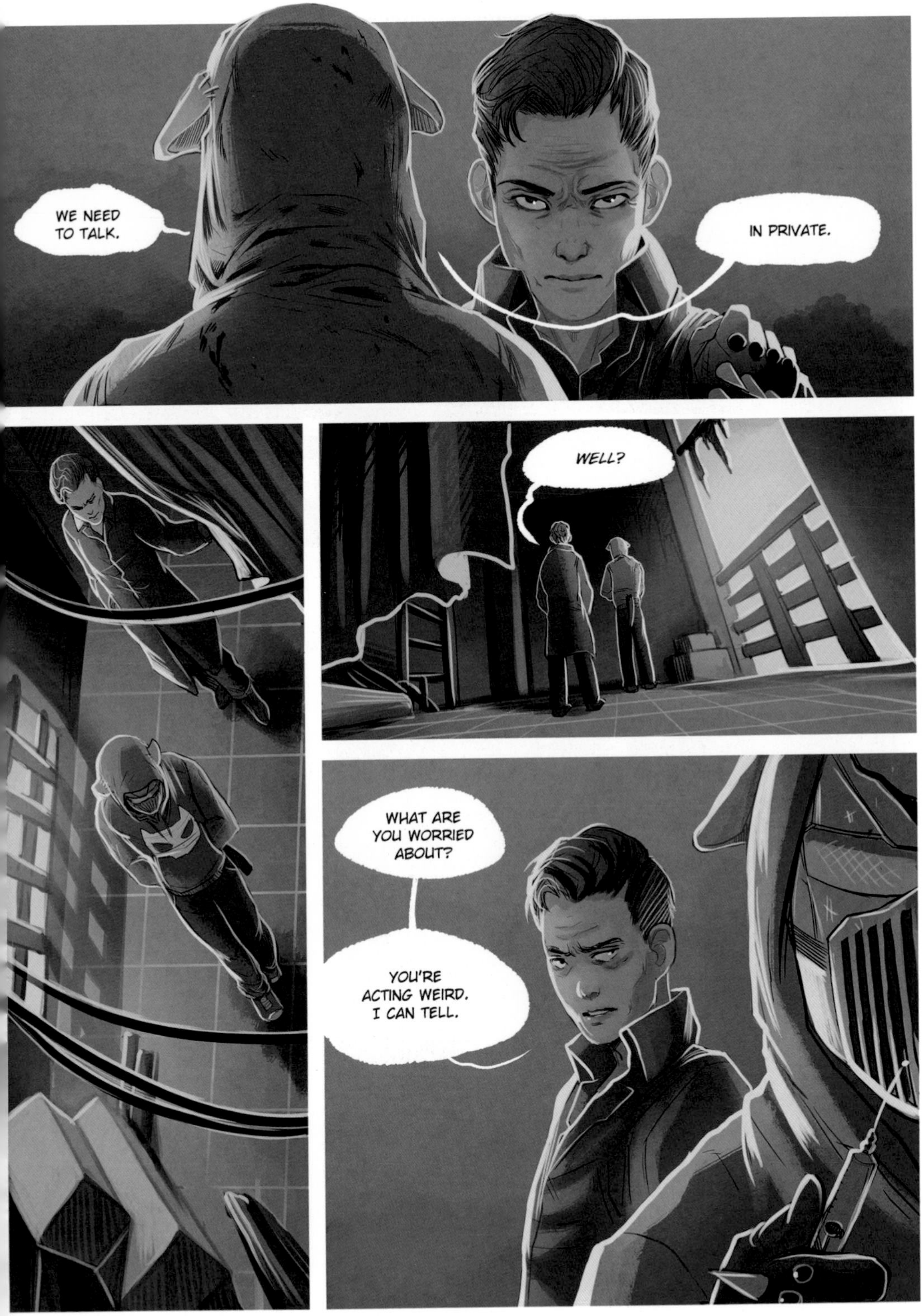
WE NEED TO TALK.
IN PRIVATE.
WELL?
WHAT ARE YOU WORRIED ABOUT?
YOU'RE ACTING WEIRD. I CAN TELL.

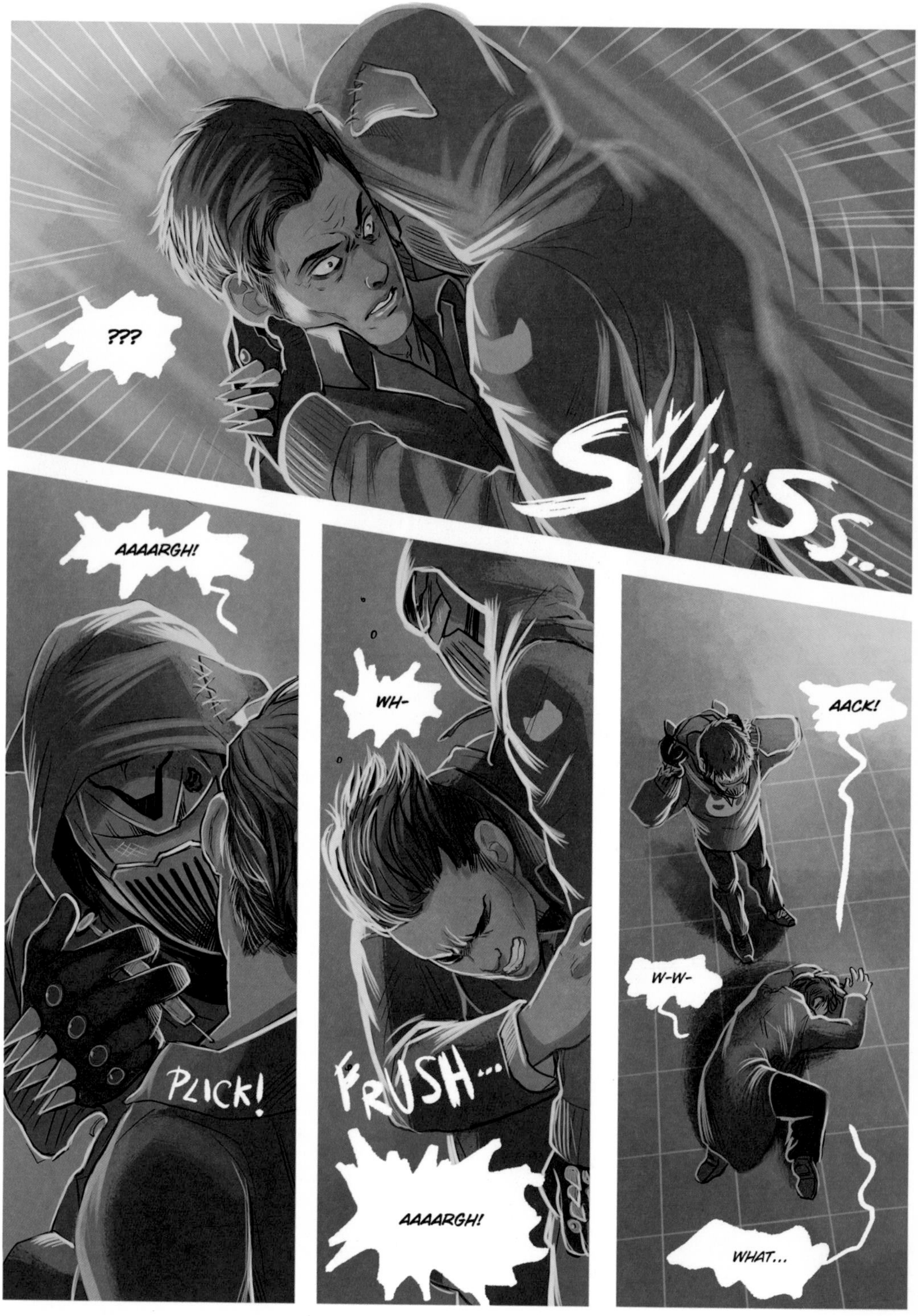
???
SWIISS...
AAAARGH!
PLICK!
WH-
FRUSH...
AAAARGH!
AACK!
W-W-
WHAT...

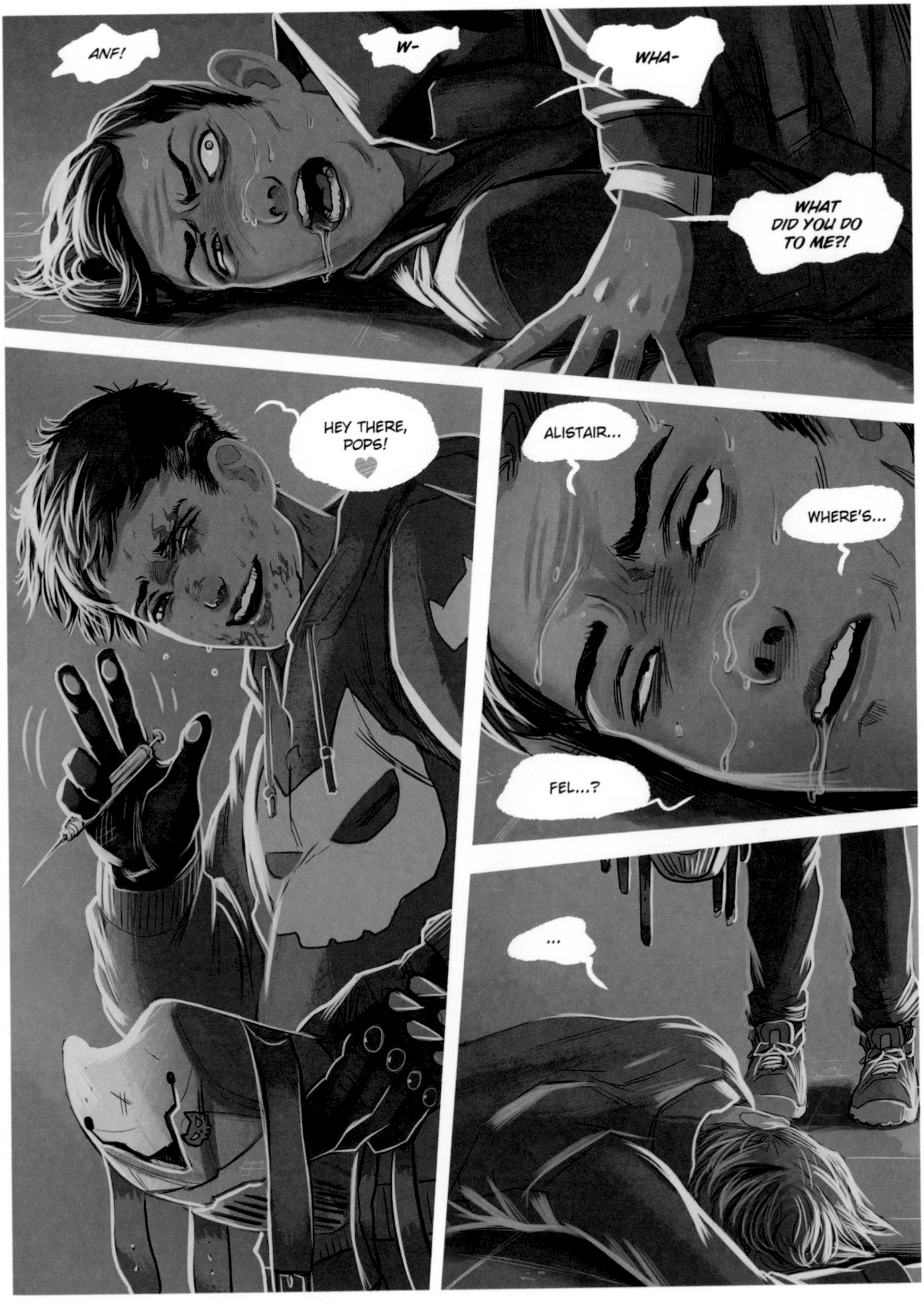
ANF!
W-
WHA-
WHAT DID YOU DO TO ME?!
HEY THERE, POPS!
ALISTAIR...
WHERE'S...
FEL...?
...

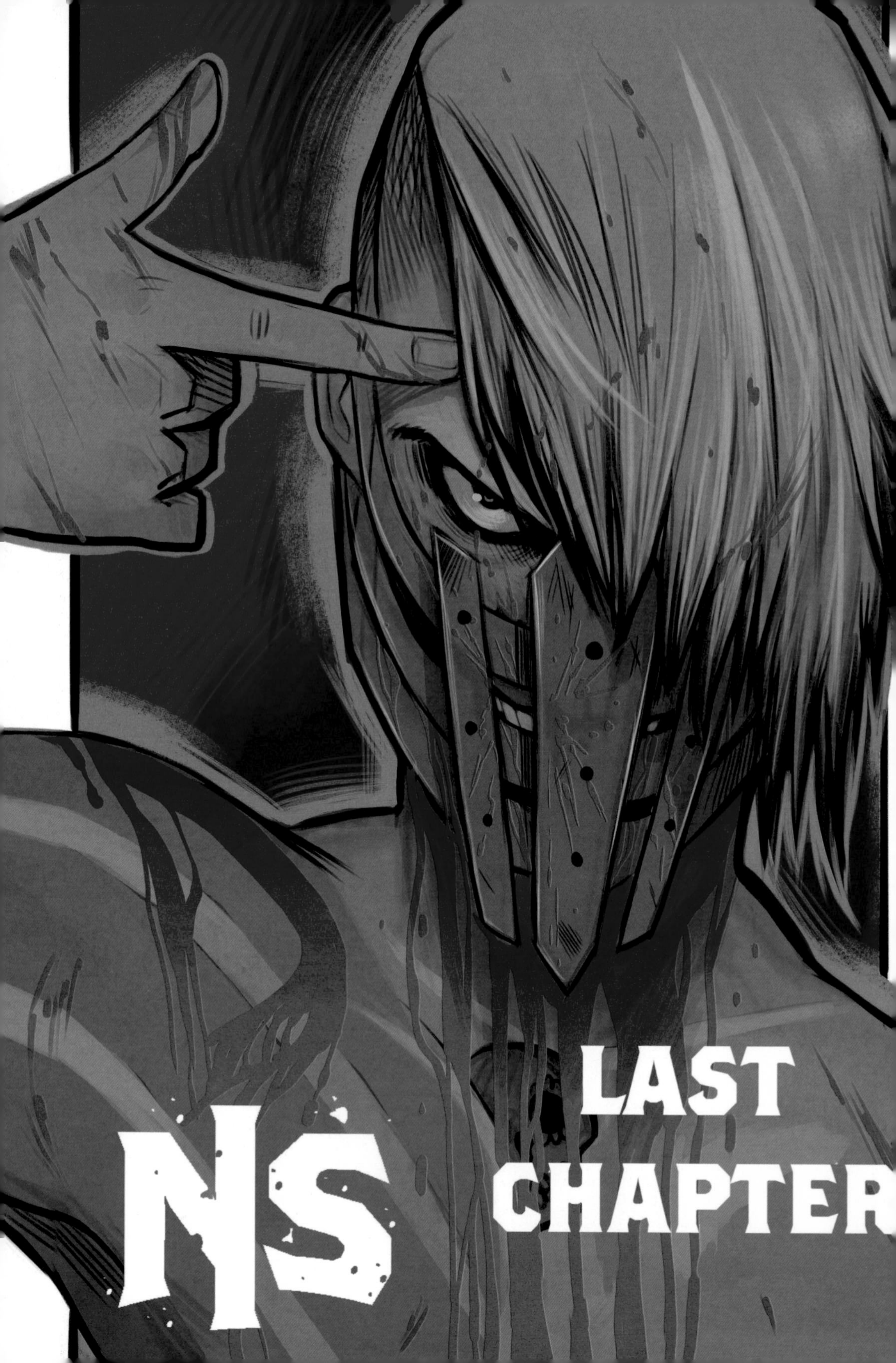
NS
LAST CHAPTER

DAMN, DAMAGE, DAMIAN.

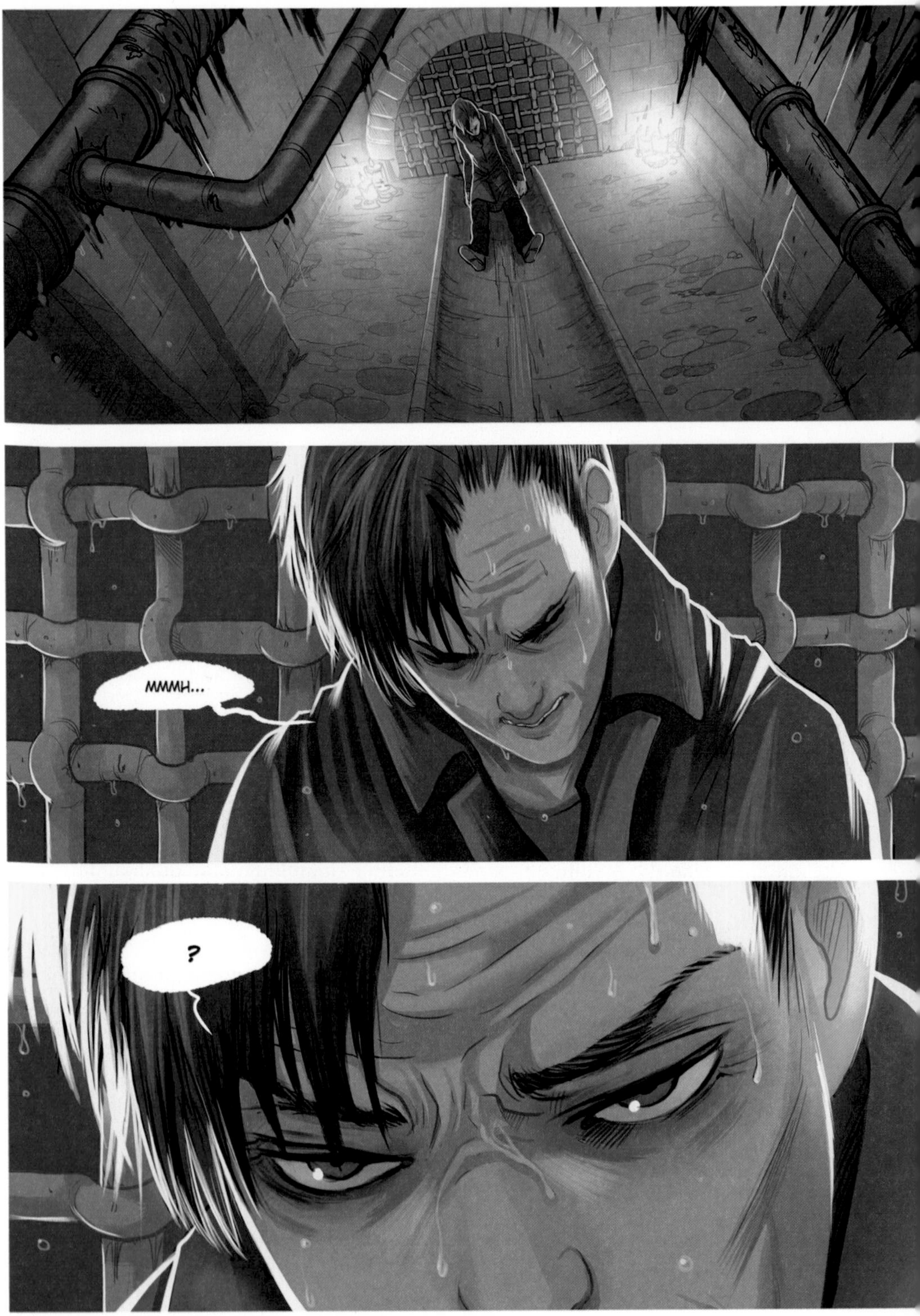
MMMH...
?

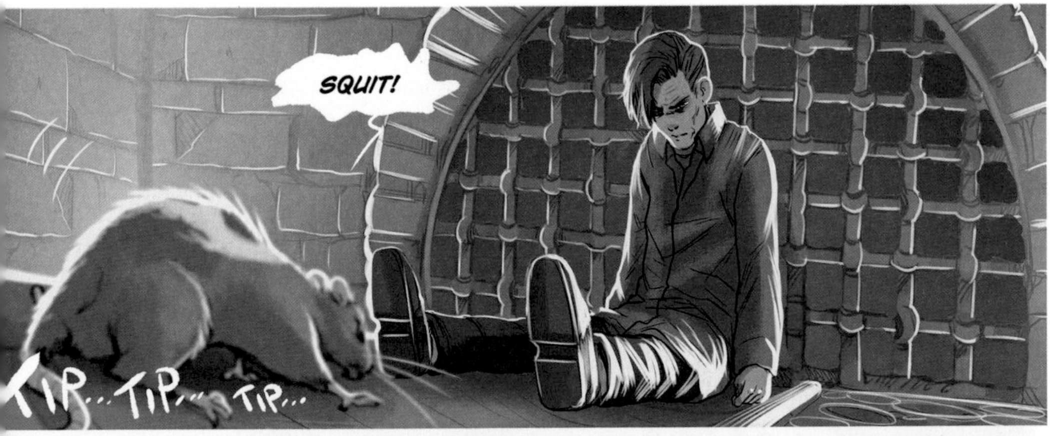
SQUIT!
TIP... TIP... TIP...

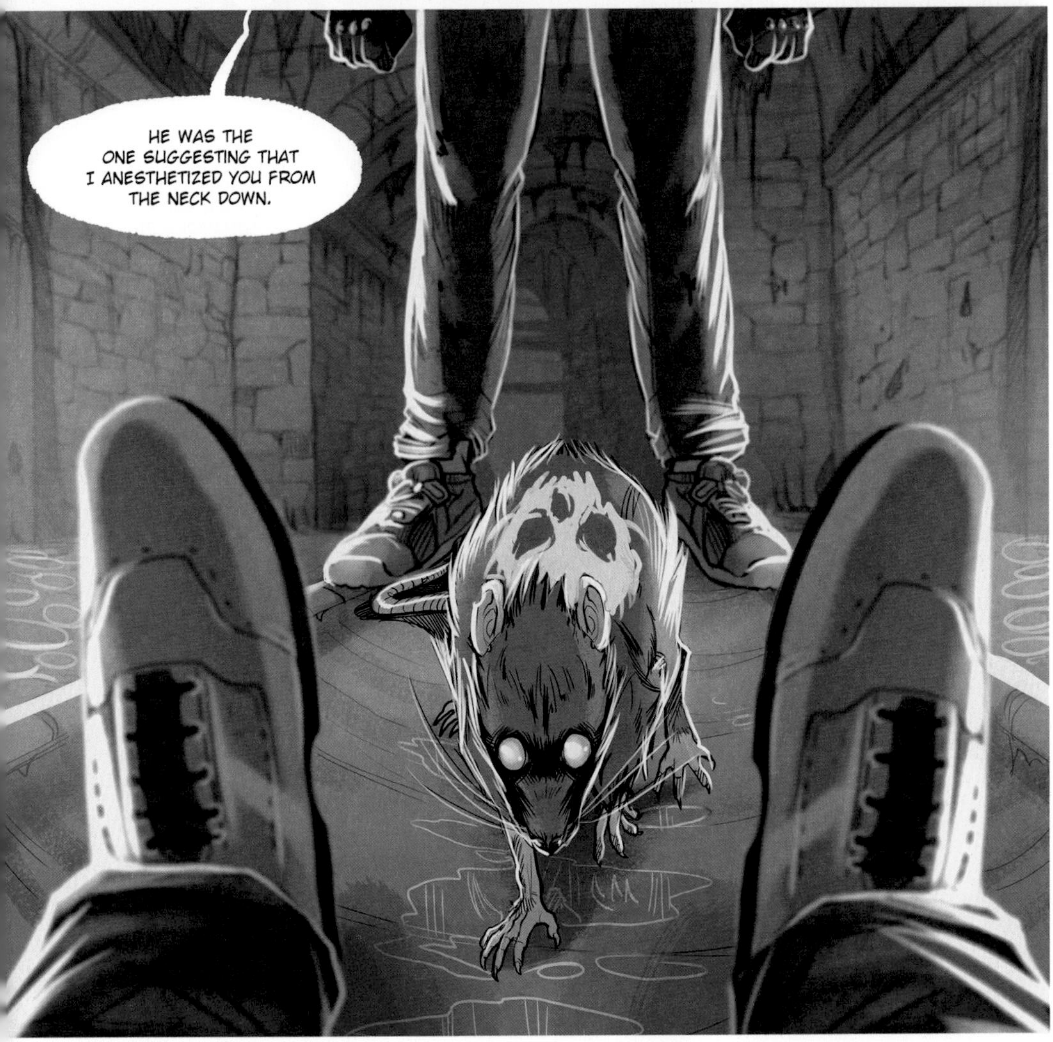
HE WAS THE ONE SUGGESTING THAT I ANESTHETIZED YOU FROM THE NECK DOWN.

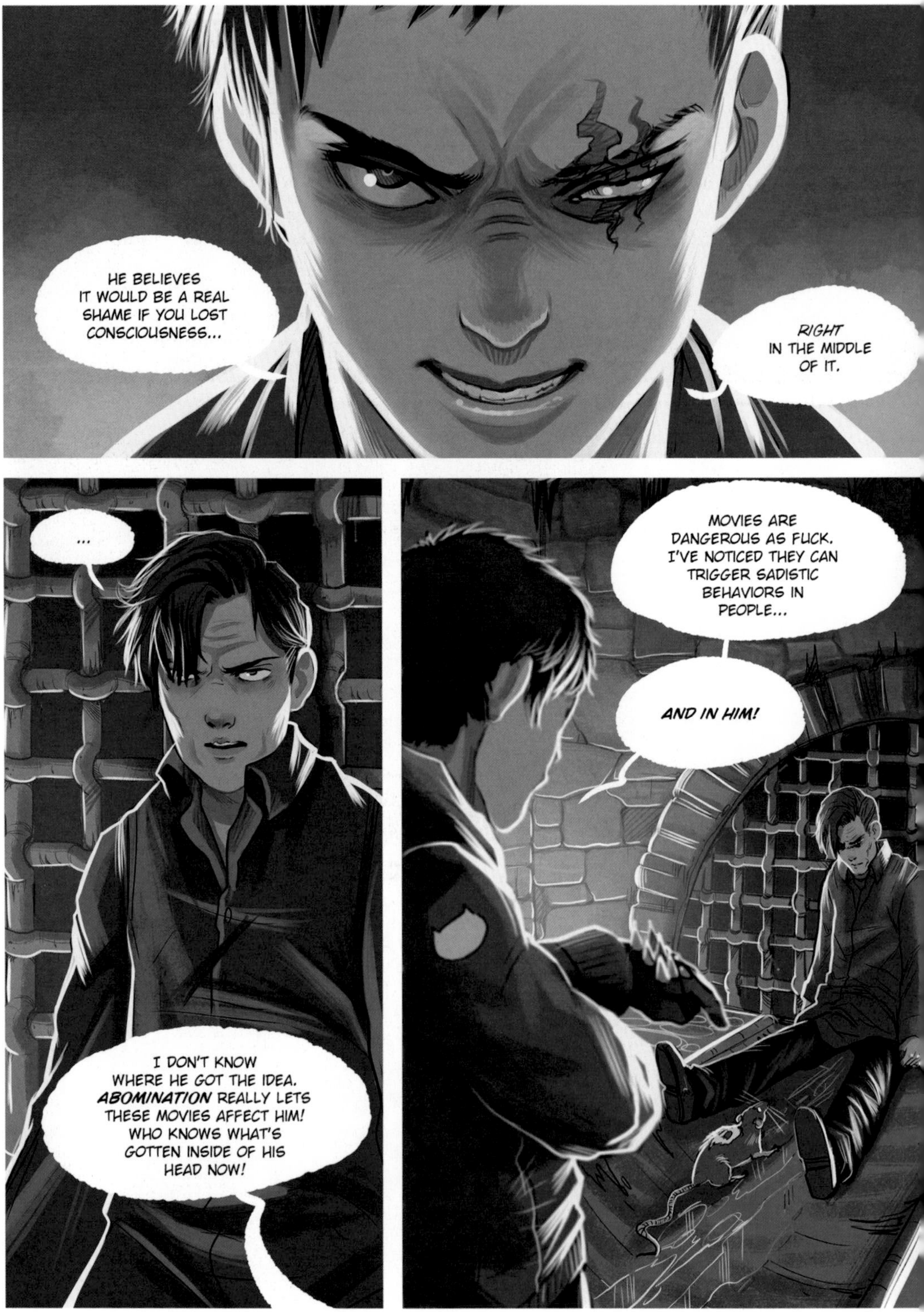
HE BELIEVES IT WOULD BE A REAL SHAME IF YOU LOST CONSCIOUSNESS...
RIGHT IN THE MIDDLE OF IT.
...
I DON'T KNOW WHERE HE GOT THE IDEA. ***ABOMINATION*** REALLY LETS THESE MOVIES AFFECT HIM! WHO KNOWS WHAT'S GOTTEN INSIDE OF HIS HEAD NOW!
MOVIES ARE DANGEROUS AS FUCK. I'VE NOTICED THEY CAN TRIGGER SADISTIC BEHAVIORS IN PEOPLE...
AND IN HIM!

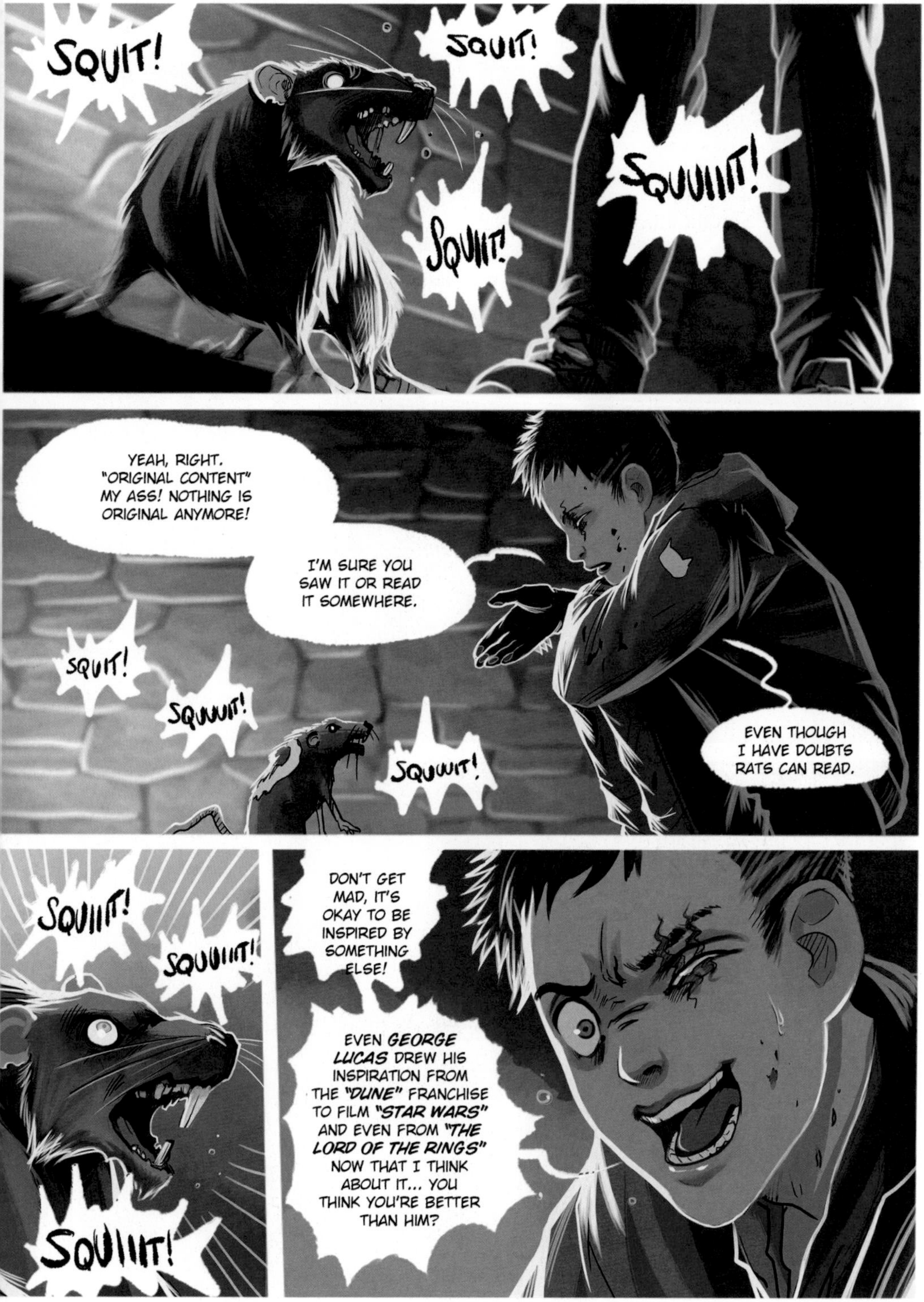
SQUIT!
SQUIT!
SQUIIIT!
SQUIIIT!
YEAH, RIGHT. "ORIGINAL CONTENT" MY ASS! NOTHING IS ORIGINAL ANYMORE!
I'M SURE YOU SAW IT OR READ IT SOMEWHERE.
SQUIT!
SQUUUIT!
SQUWIT!
EVEN THOUGH I HAVE DOUBTS RATS CAN READ.
SQUIIIT!
SQUUIIIT!
SQUIIIT!
DON'T GET MAD, IT'S OKAY TO BE INSPIRED BY SOMETHING ELSE!
EVEN GEORGE LUCAS DREW HIS INSPIRATION FROM THE "DUNE" FRANCHISE TO FILM "STAR WARS" AND EVEN FROM "THE LORD OF THE RINGS" NOW THAT I THINK ABOUT IT... YOU THINK YOU'RE BETTER THAN HIM?

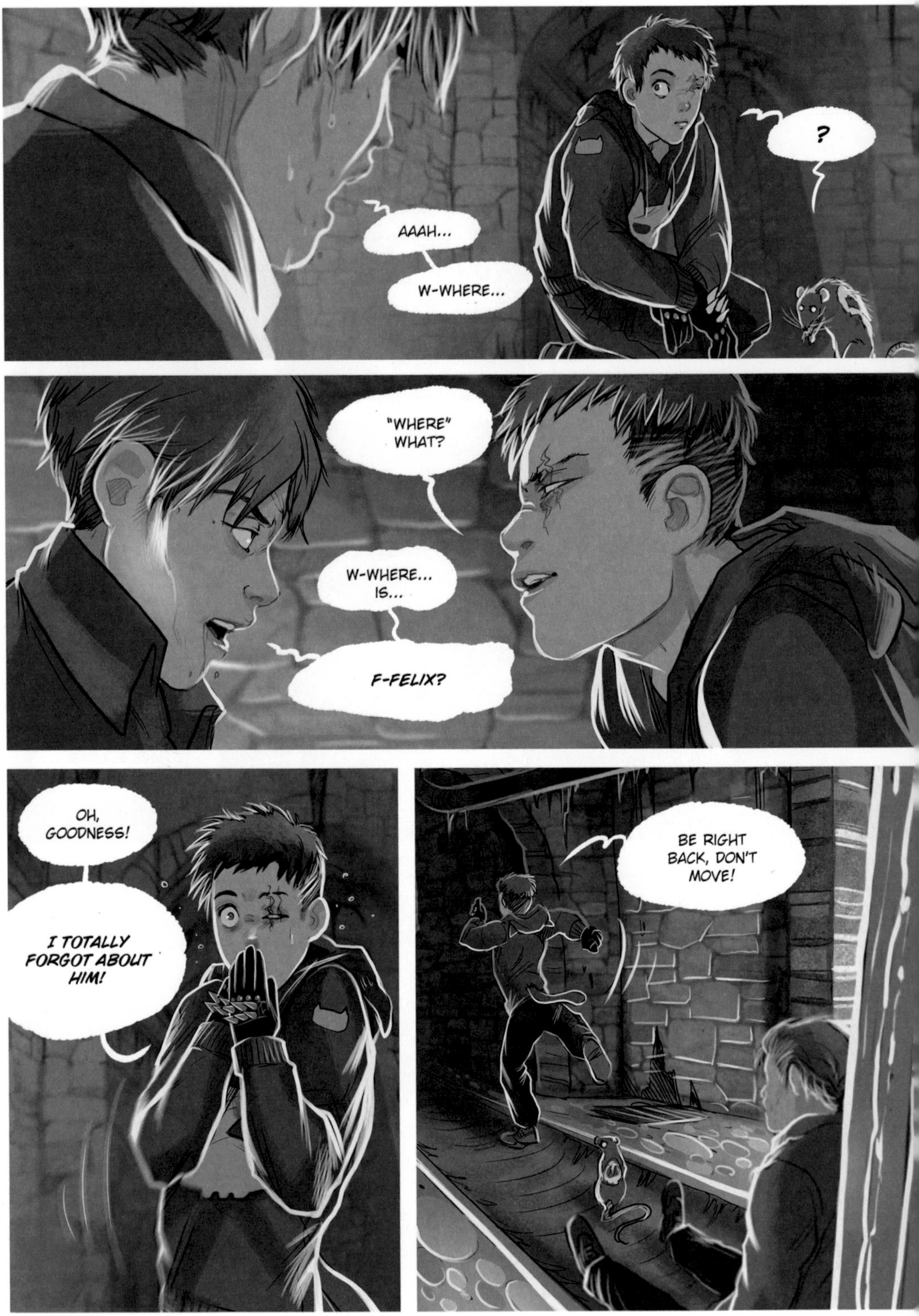
?
AAAH...
W-WHERE...
"WHERE" WHAT?
W-WHERE... IS...
F-FELIX?
OH, GOODNESS!
I TOTALLY FORGOT ABOUT HIM!
BE RIGHT BACK, DON'T MOVE!

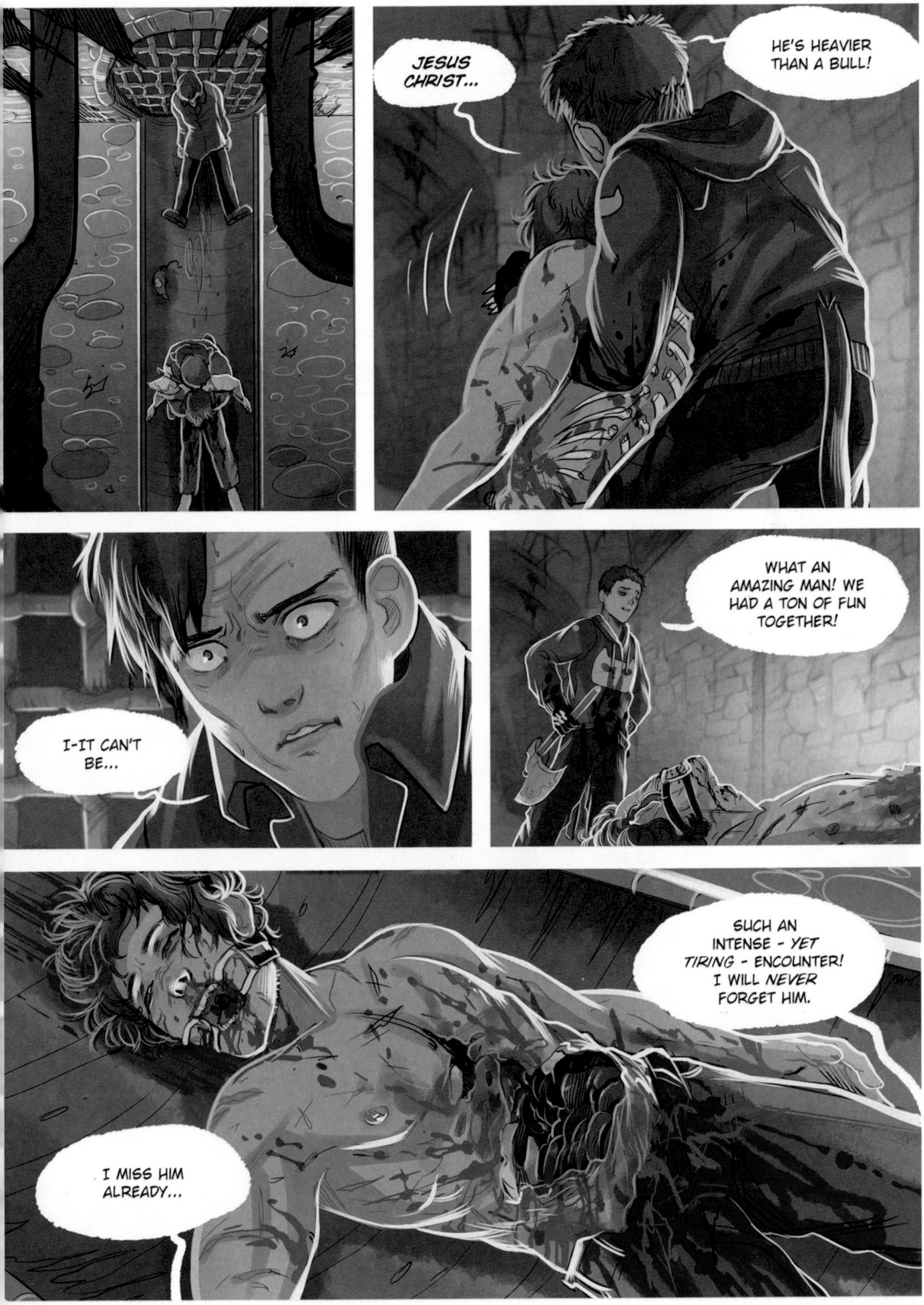
JESUS CHRIST...
HE'S HEAVIER THAN A BULL!
I-IT CAN'T BE...
WHAT AN AMAZING MAN! WE HAD A TON OF FUN TOGETHER!
SUCH AN INTENSE - *YET TIRING* - ENCOUNTER! I WILL *NEVER* FORGET HIM.
I MISS HIM ALREADY...

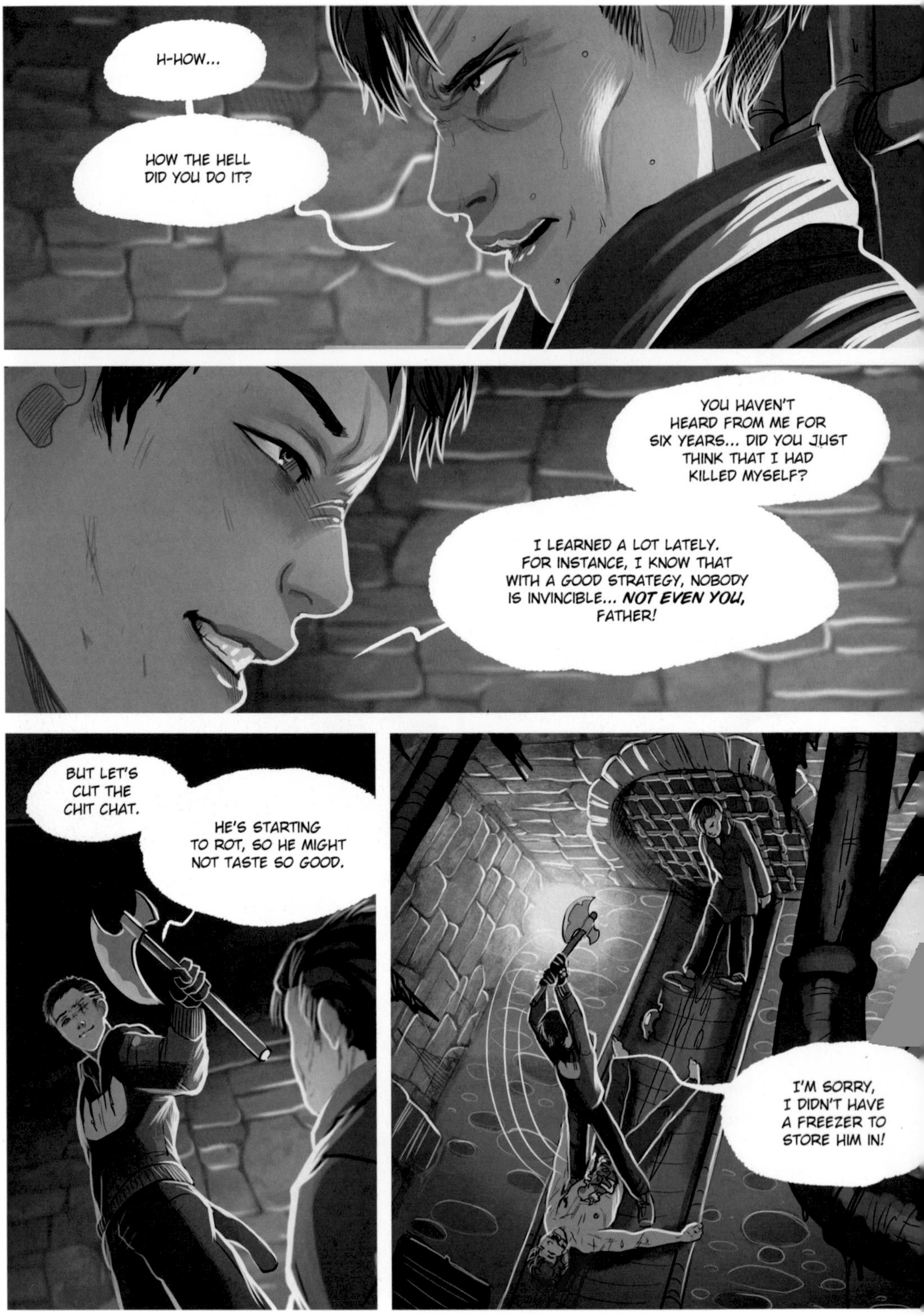
H-HOW...
HOW THE HELL DID YOU DO IT?
YOU HAVEN'T HEARD FROM ME FOR SIX YEARS... DID YOU JUST THINK THAT I HAD KILLED MYSELF?
I LEARNED A LOT LATELY. FOR INSTANCE, I KNOW THAT WITH A GOOD STRATEGY, NOBODY IS INVINCIBLE... ***NOT EVEN YOU,*** FATHER!
BUT LET'S CUT THE CHIT CHAT.
HE'S STARTING TO ROT, SO HE MIGHT NOT TASTE SO GOOD.
I'M SORRY, I DIDN'T HAVE A FREEZER TO STORE HIM IN!

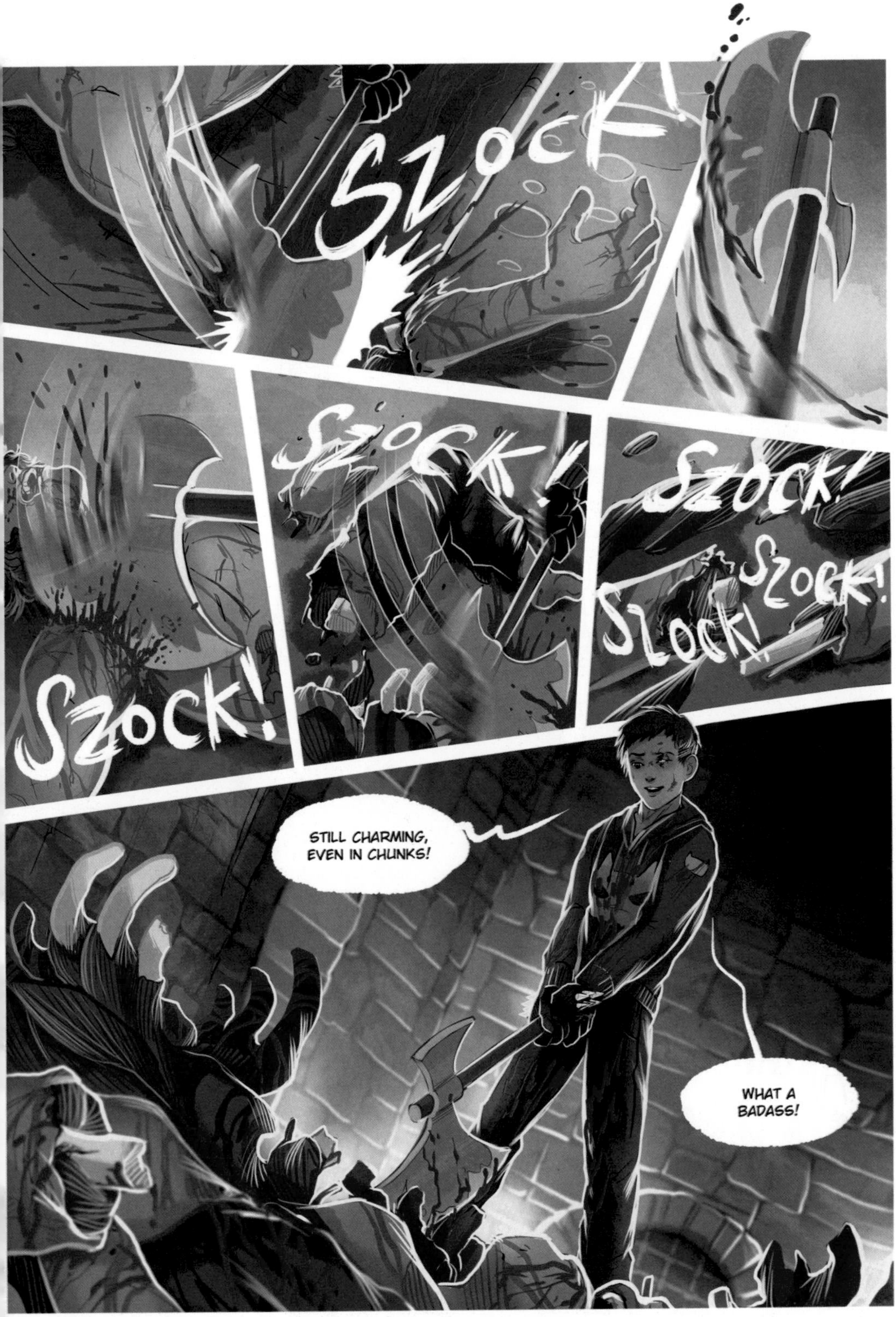
SZOCK!
SZOCK!
SZOCK!
SZOCK!
SZOCK!
SZOCK!
STILL CHARMING, EVEN IN CHUNKS!
WHAT A BADASS!

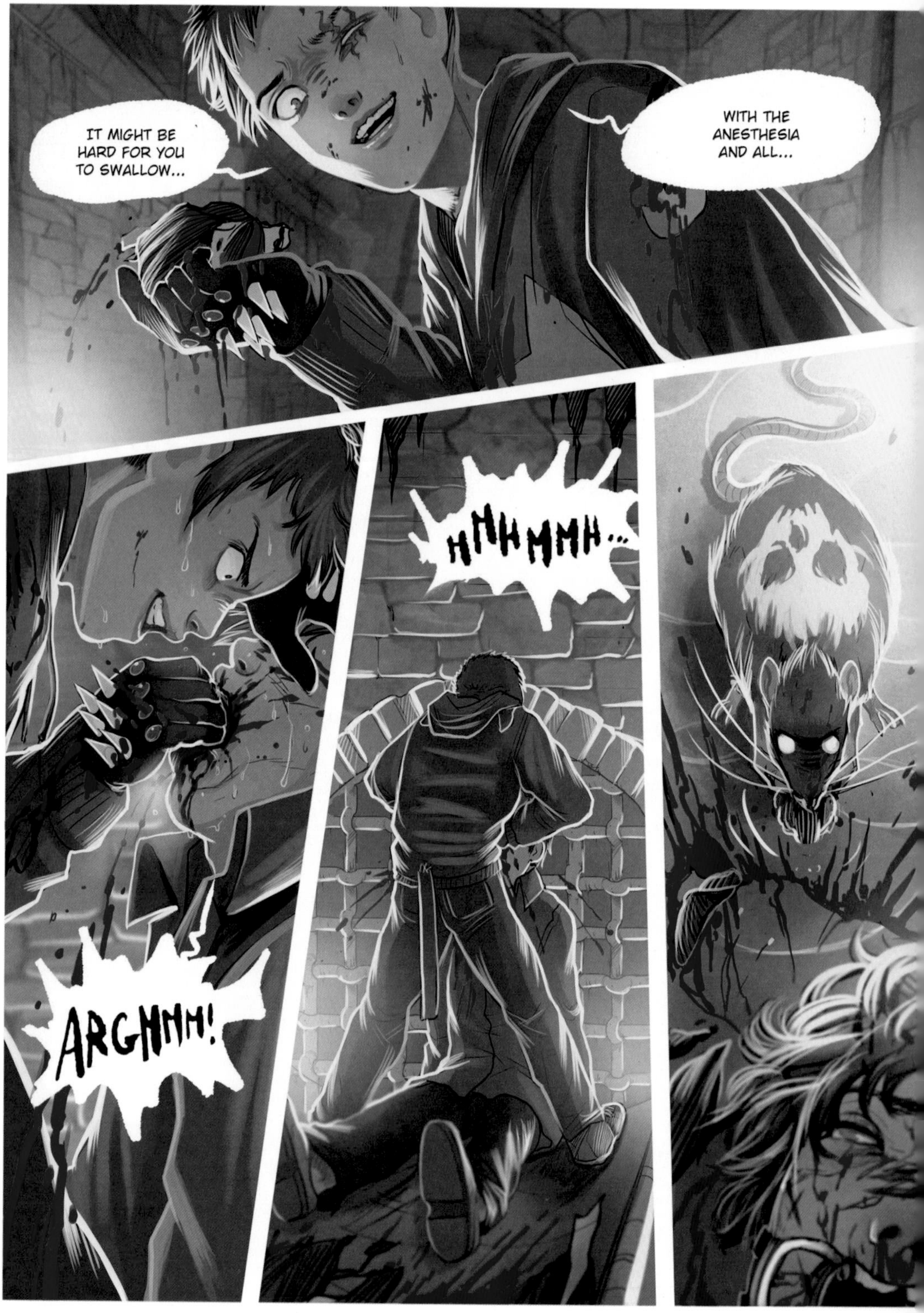
IT MIGHT BE HARD FOR YOU TO SWALLOW...
WITH THE ANESTHESIA AND ALL...
ARGHMM!
HMHMMH...

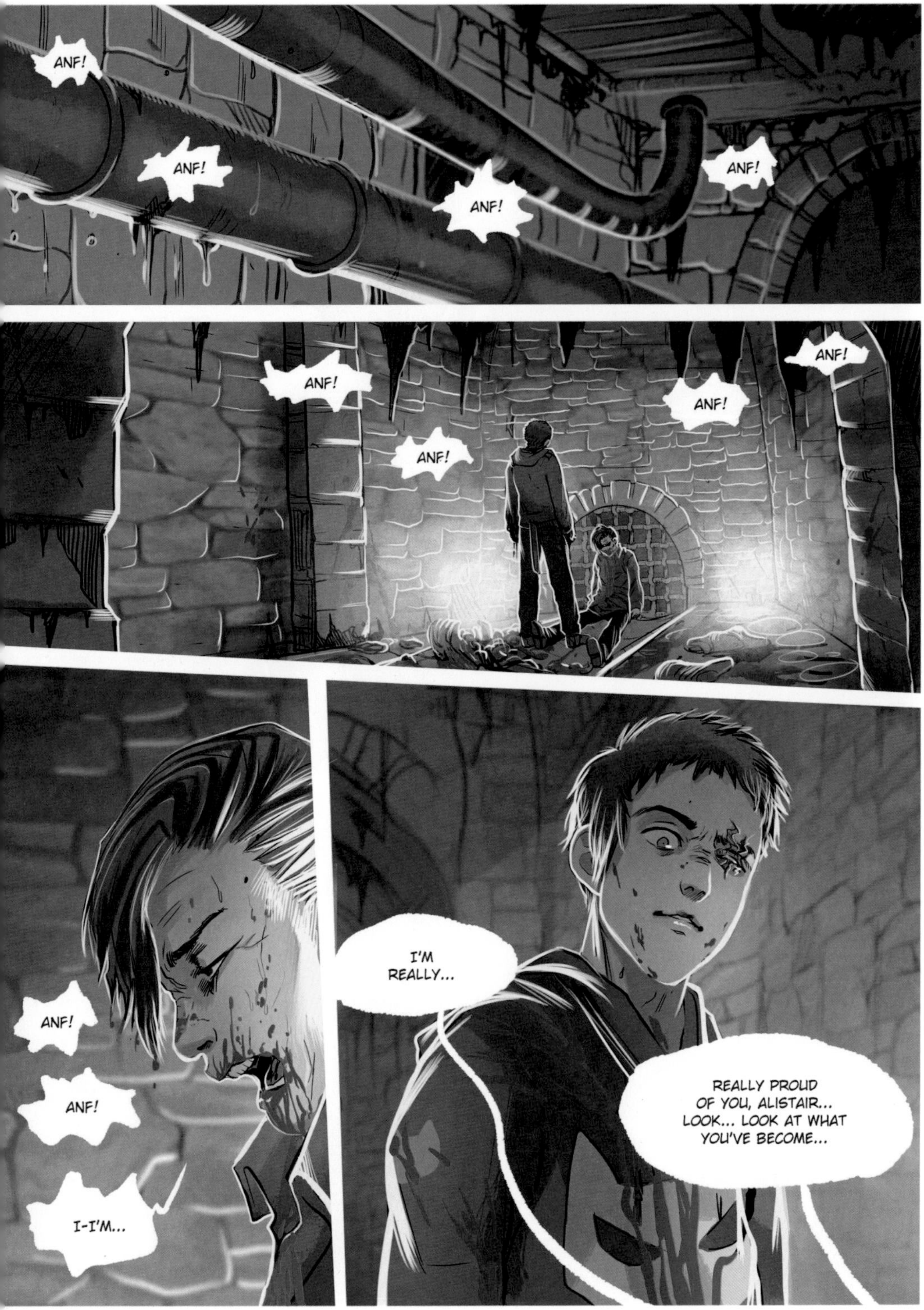
ANF!
ANF!
ANF!
ANF!
ANF!
ANF!
ANF!
ANF!
ANF!
ANF!
I-I'M...
I'M REALLY...
REALLY PROUD OF YOU, ALISTAIR... LOOK... LOOK AT WHAT YOU'VE BECOME...

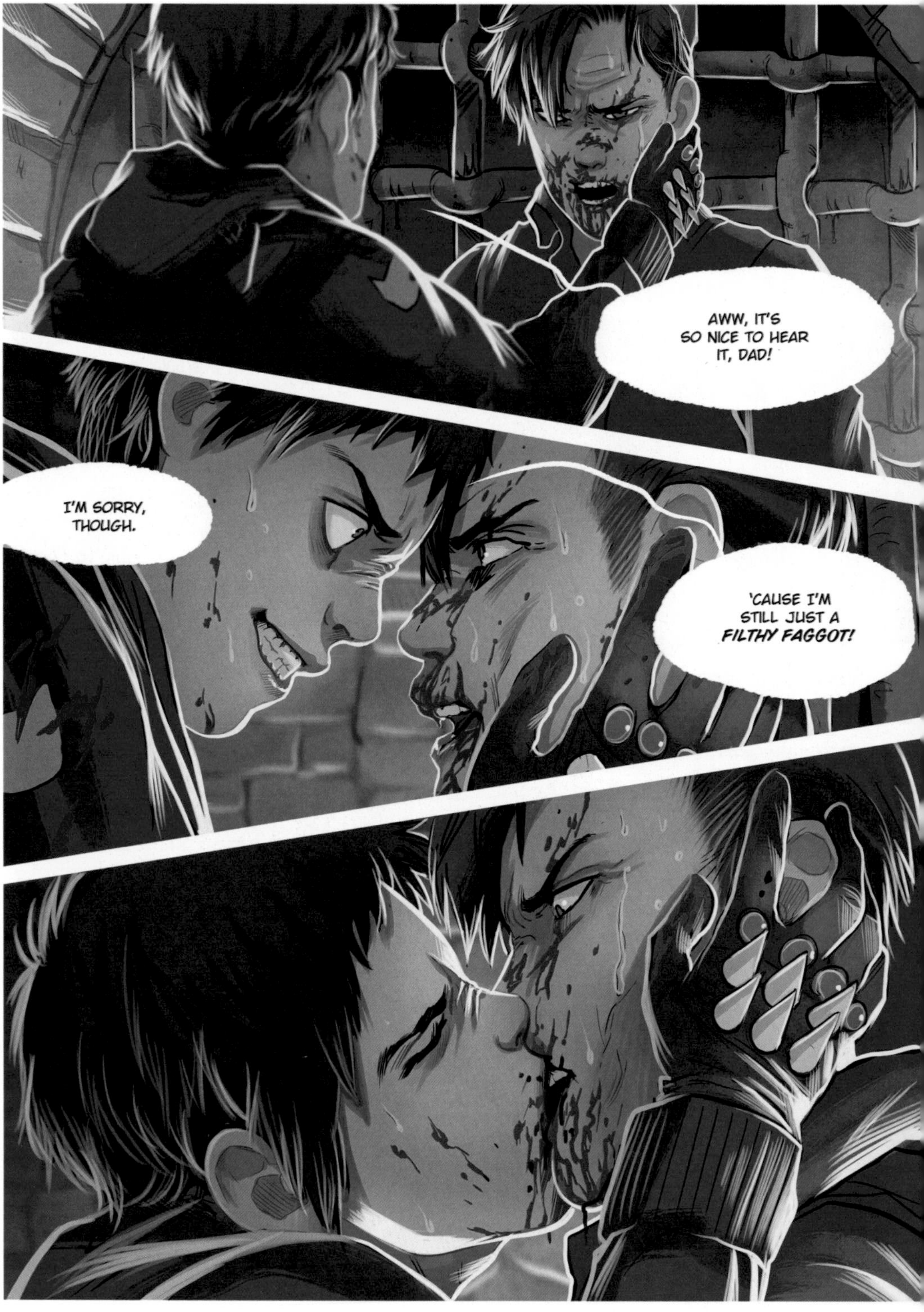
AWW, IT'S SO NICE TO HEAR IT, DAD!
I'M SORRY, THOUGH.
'CAUSE I'M STILL JUST A *FILTHY FAGGOT!*

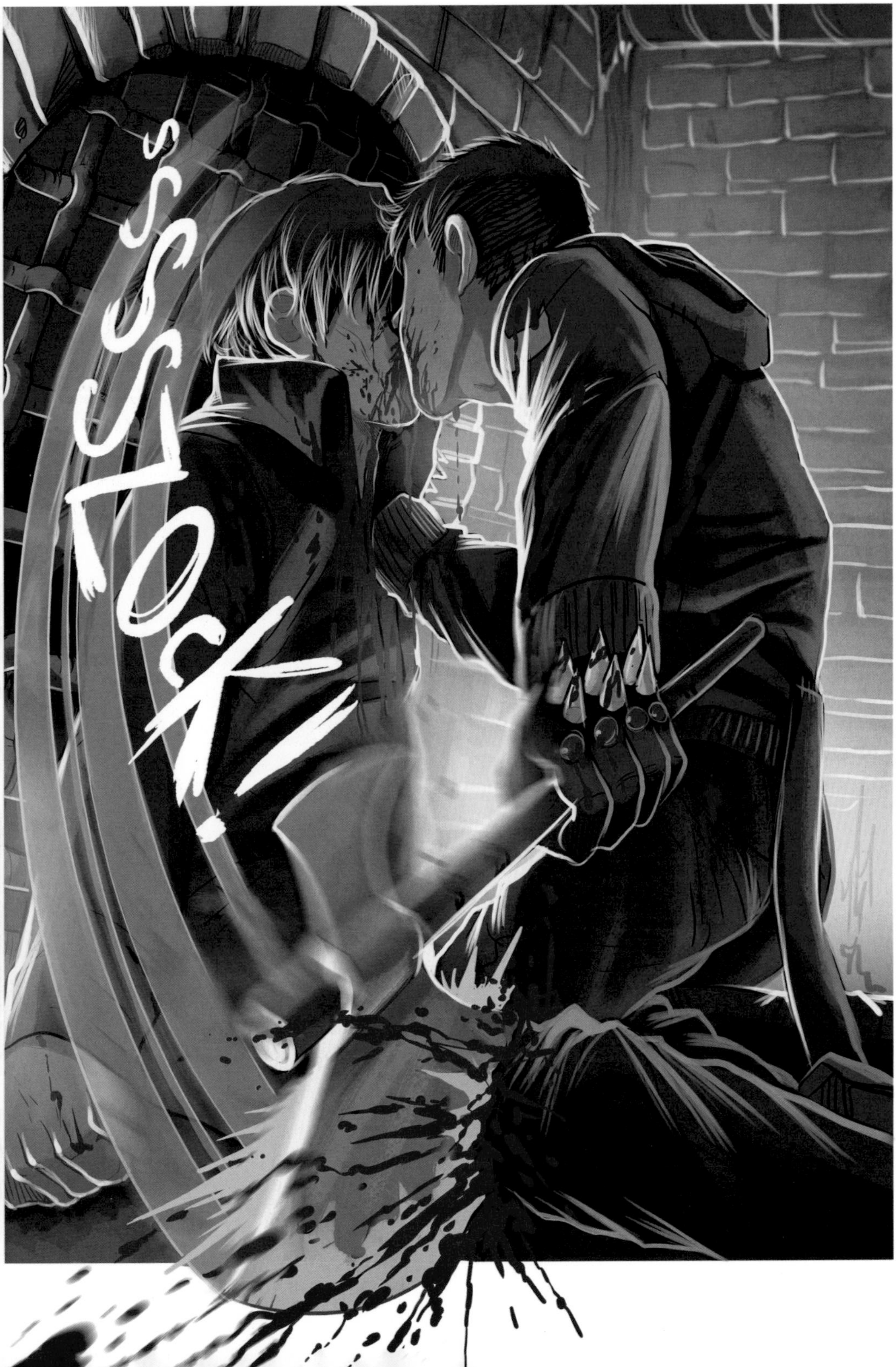
SSSTOCK!

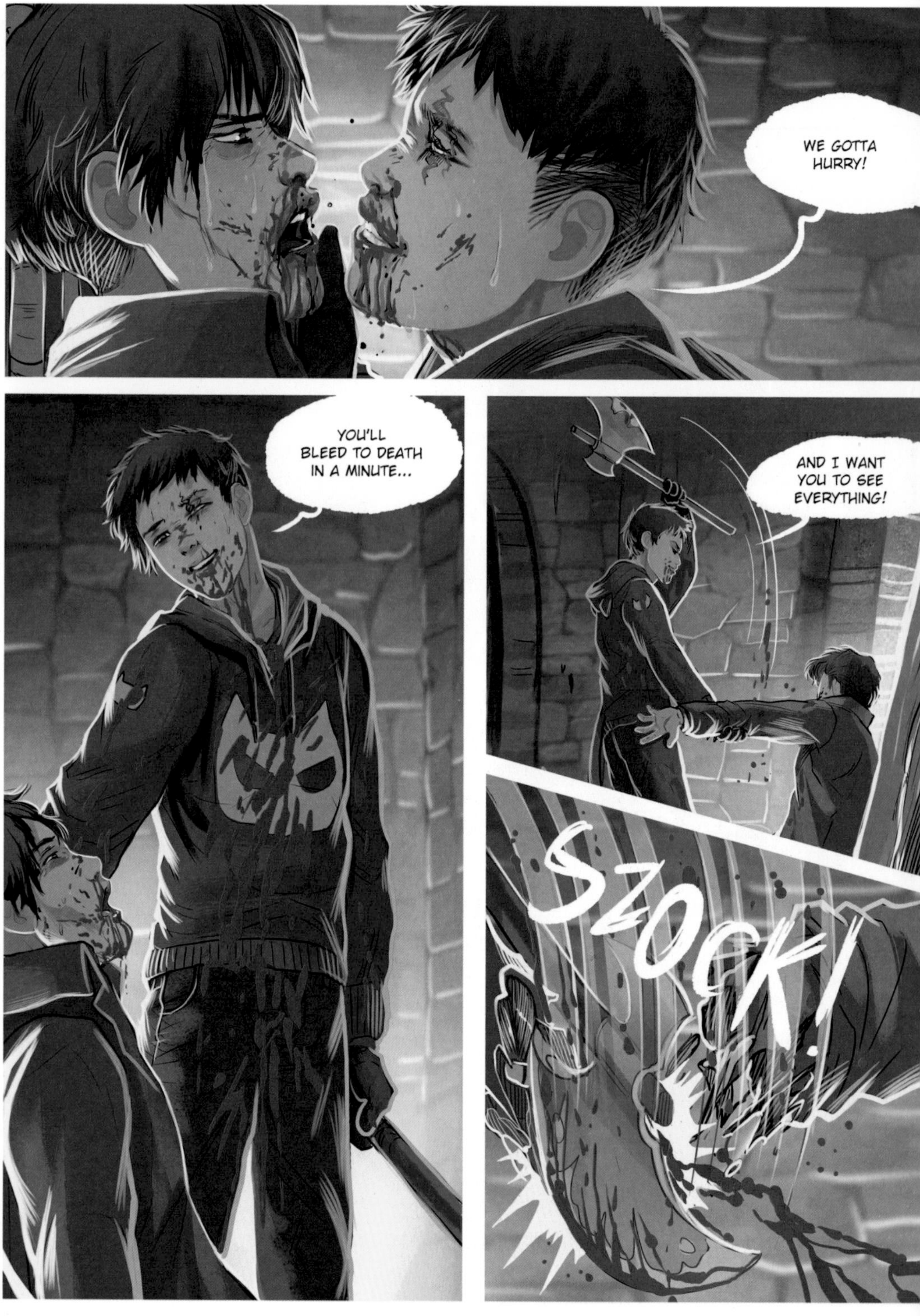
WE GOTTA HURRY!
YOU'LL BLEED TO DEATH IN A MINUTE...
AND I WANT YOU TO SEE EVERYTHING!
SZOCK!

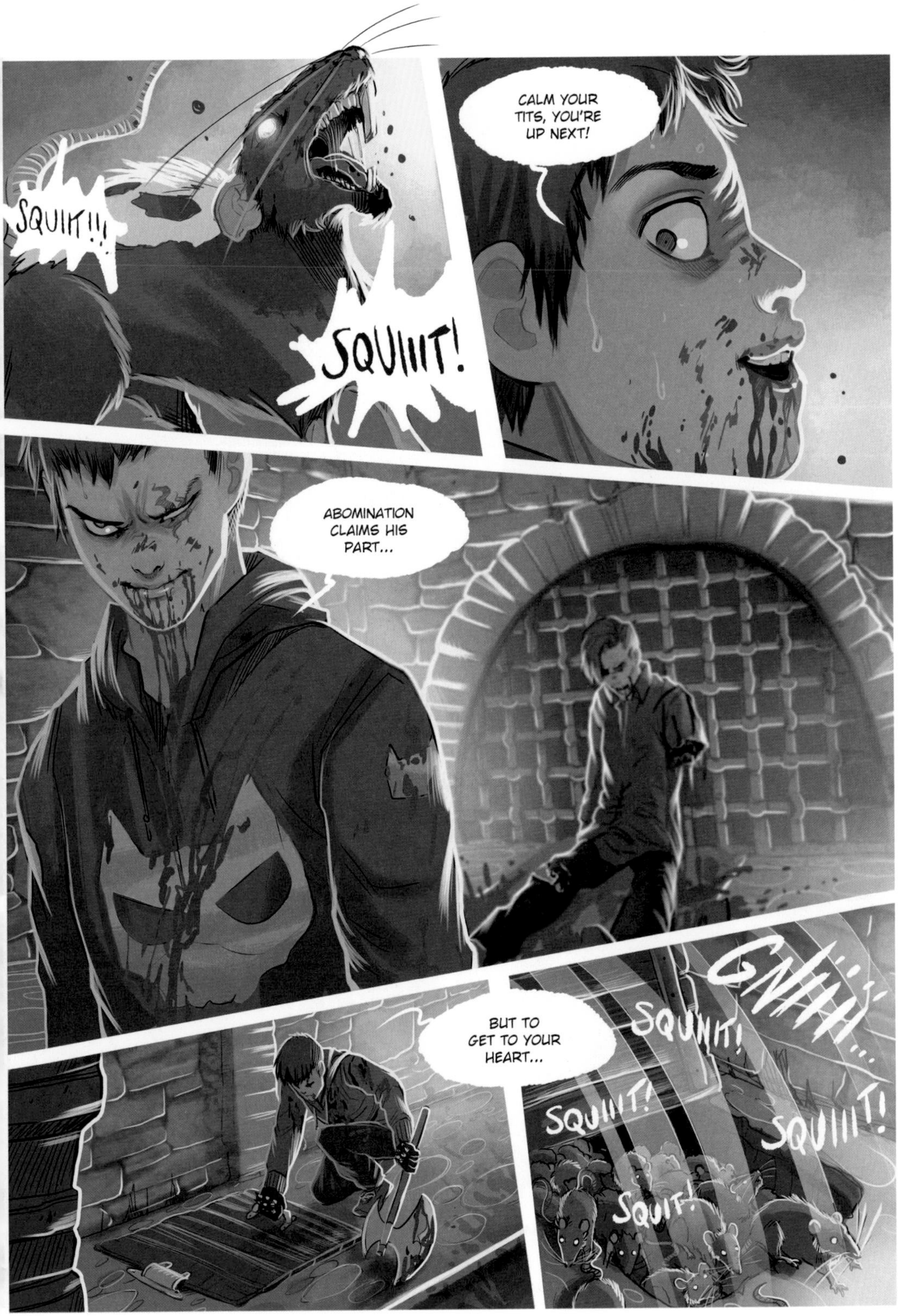
SQUIK!!!
SQUIIIT!
CALM YOUR TITS, YOU'RE UP NEXT!
ABOMINATION CLAIMS HIS PART...
BUT TO GET TO YOUR HEART...
GNIIII...
SQUNIT!
SQUIIT!
SQUIIIT!
SQUIT!

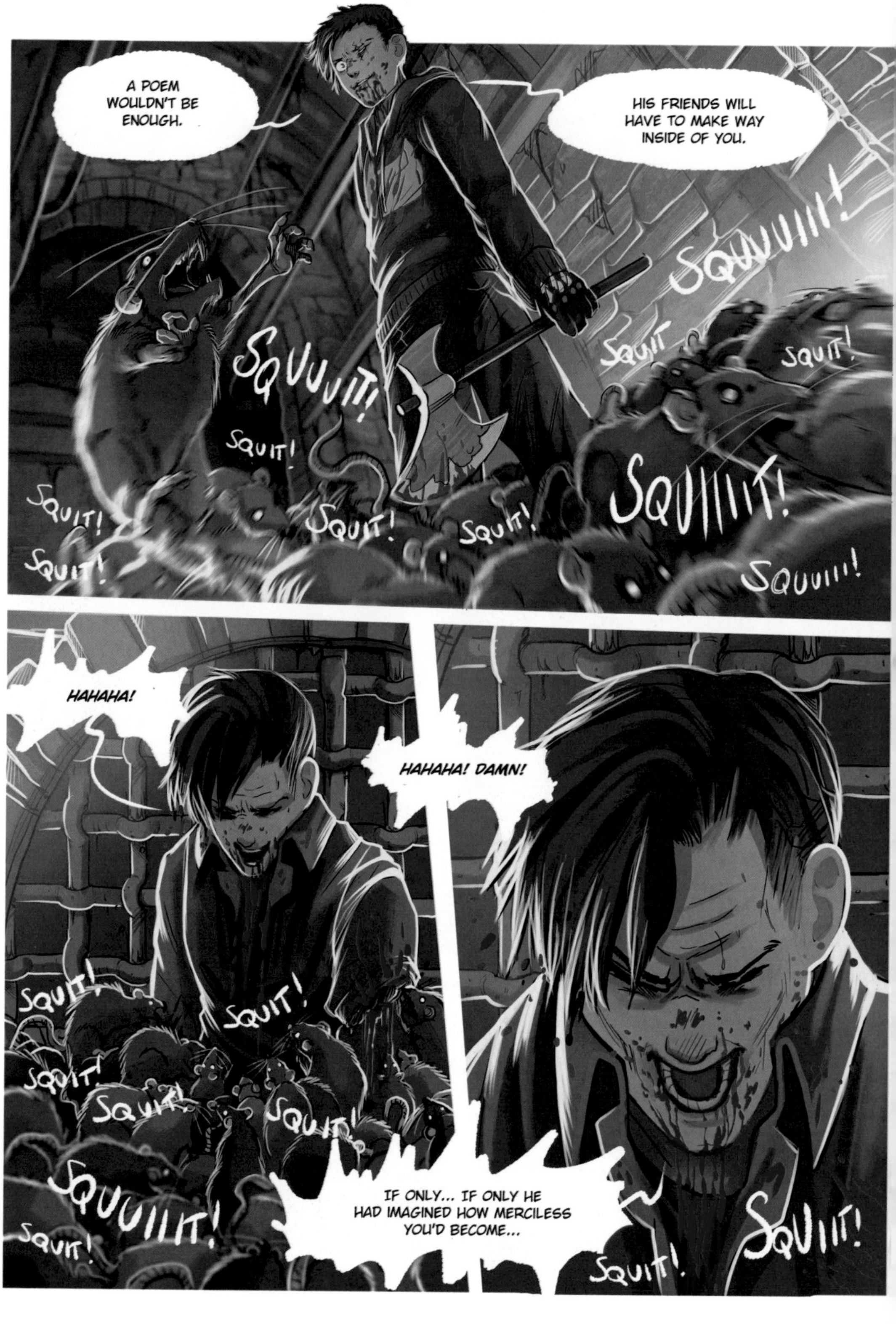
A POEM WOULDN'T BE ENOUGH.
HIS FRIENDS WILL HAVE TO MAKE WAY INSIDE OF YOU.
SQUUUIII!
SQUUUIT!
SQUIT!
SQUIT!
SQUIT!
SQUIT!
SQUIT!
SQUIT!
SQUIT!
SQUIIIIT!
SQUUIII!
HAHAHA!
HAHAHA! DAMN!
SQUIT!
SQUIT!
SQUIT!
SQUIT!
SQUIT!
SQUUIIIIT!
SQUIT!
IF ONLY... IF ONLY HE HAD IMAGINED HOW MERCILESS YOU'D BECOME...
SQUIIT!
SQUIT!

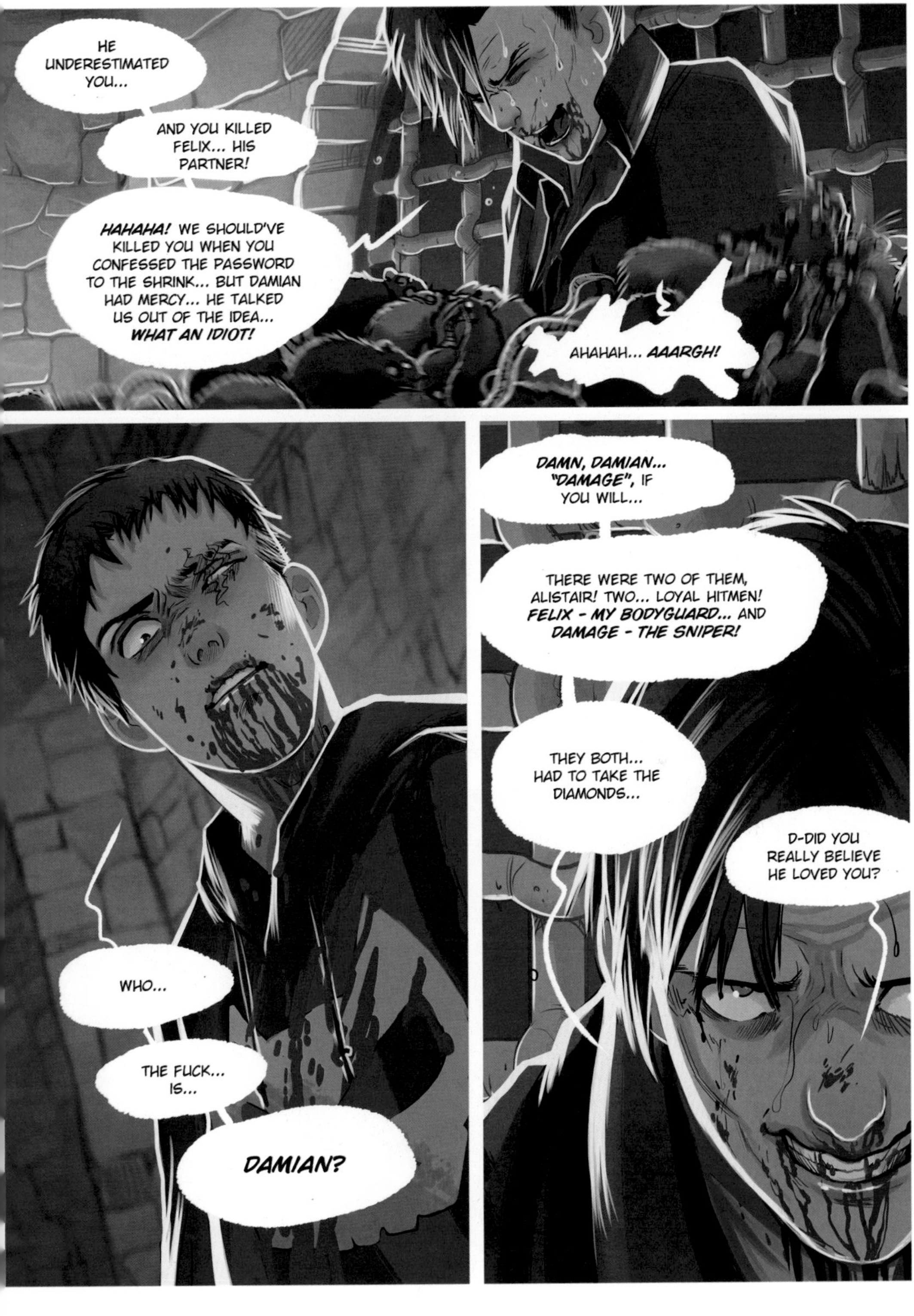

HE UNDERESTIMATED YOU...
AND YOU KILLED FELIX... HIS PARTNER!
HAHAHA! WE SHOULD'VE KILLED YOU WHEN YOU CONFESSED THE PASSWORD TO THE SHRINK... BUT DAMIAN HAD MERCY... HE TALKED US OUT OF THE IDEA... WHAT AN IDIOT!
AHAHAH... AAARGH!
WHO...
THE FUCK... IS...
DAMIAN?
DAMN, DAMIAN... "DAMAGE", IF YOU WILL...
THERE WERE TWO OF THEM, ALISTAIR! TWO... LOYAL HITMEN! FELIX - MY BODYGUARD... AND DAMAGE - THE SNIPER!
THEY BOTH... HAD TO TAKE THE DIAMONDS...
D-DID YOU REALLY BELIEVE HE LOVED YOU?

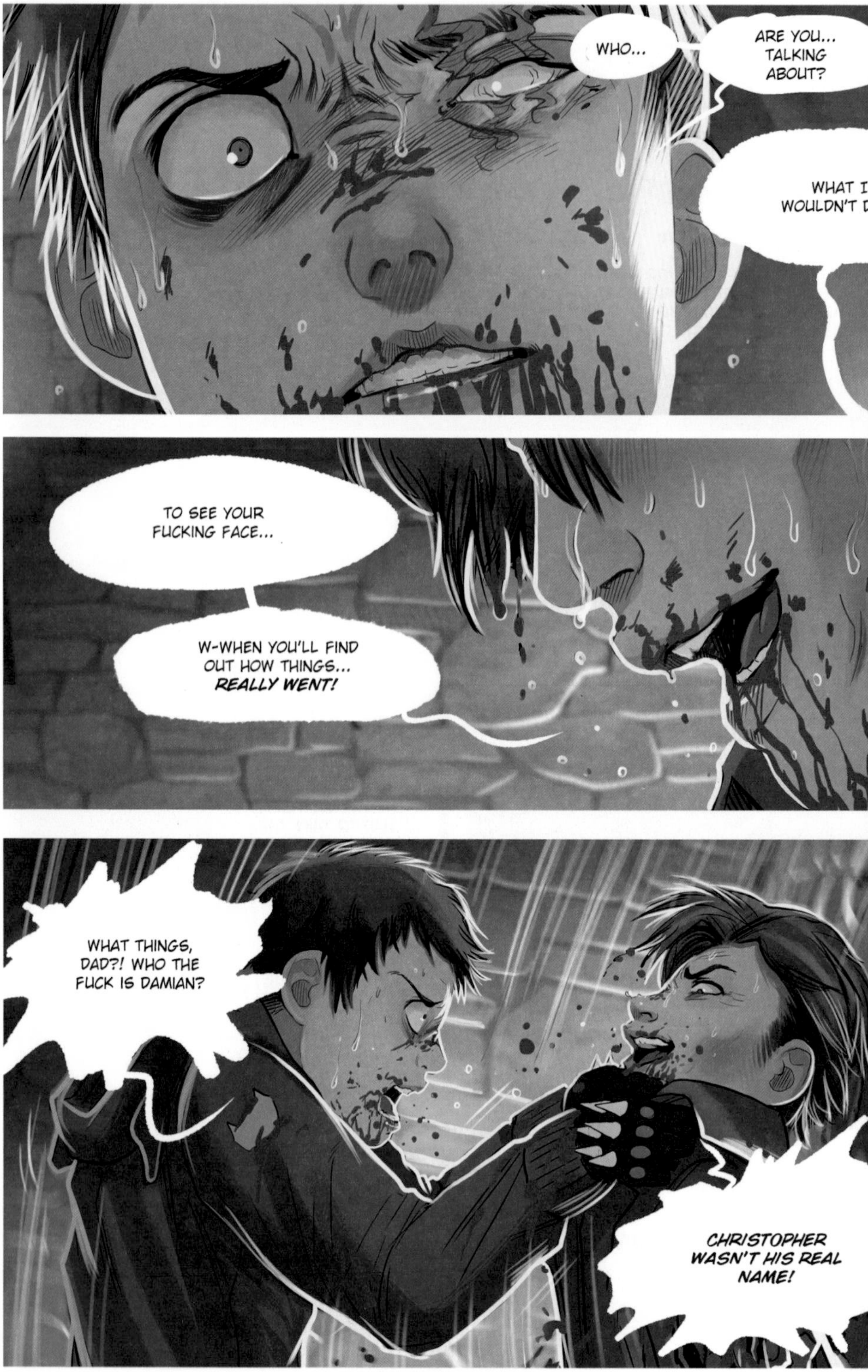
WHO...
ARE YOU... TALKING ABOUT?
WHAT I WOULDN'T DO...
TO SEE YOUR FUCKING FACE...
W-WHEN YOU'LL FIND OUT HOW THINGS... ***REALLY WENT!***
WHAT THINGS, DAD?! WHO THE FUCK IS DAMIAN?
CHRISTOPHER WASN'T HIS REAL NAME!

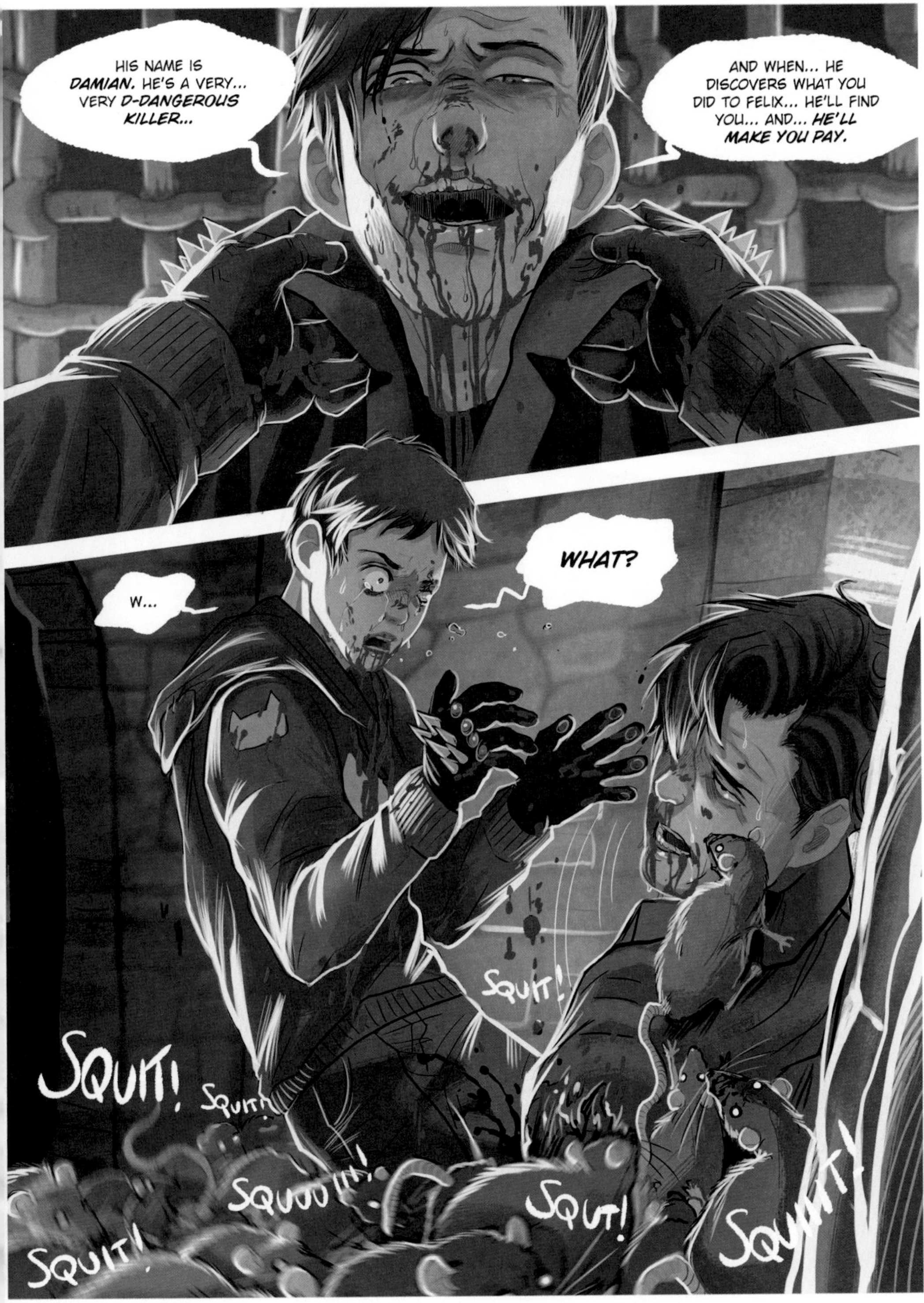
HIS NAME IS DAMIAN. HE'S A VERY... VERY D-DANGEROUS KILLER...
AND WHEN... HE DISCOVERS WHAT YOU DID TO FELIX... HE'LL FIND YOU... AND... HE'LL MAKE YOU PAY.
W...
WHAT?
SQUIT!
SQUIT!
SQUIT!
SQUT!

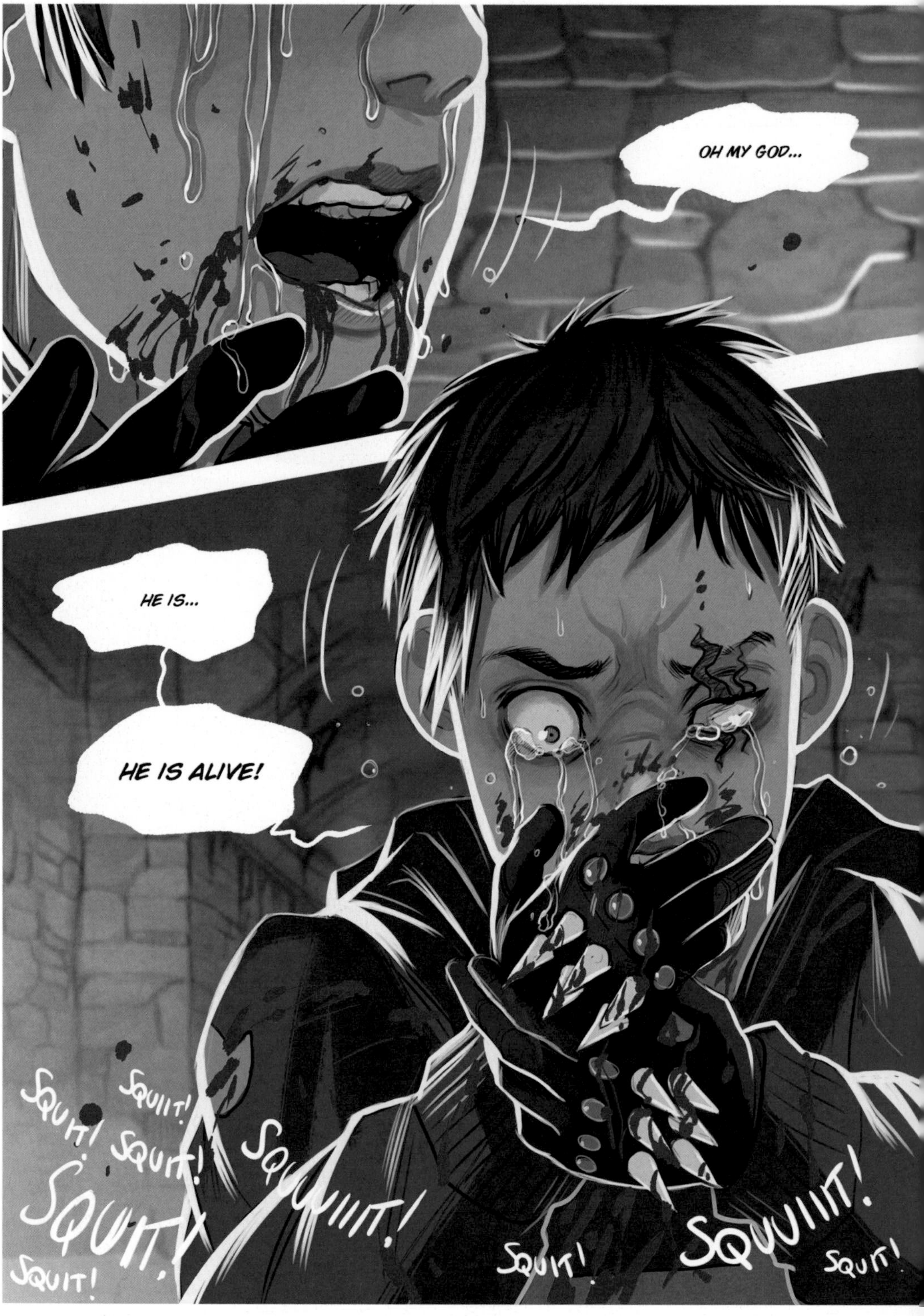
OH MY GOD...
HE IS...
HE IS ALIVE!
SQUIIT!
SQUIT! SQUIT!
SQUIT!
SQUIT!
SQUUIIIT!
SQUIT!
SQUUIIIT!
SQUIT!

END OF THE FIRST PART
OF THE TRILOGY

EXTRAS

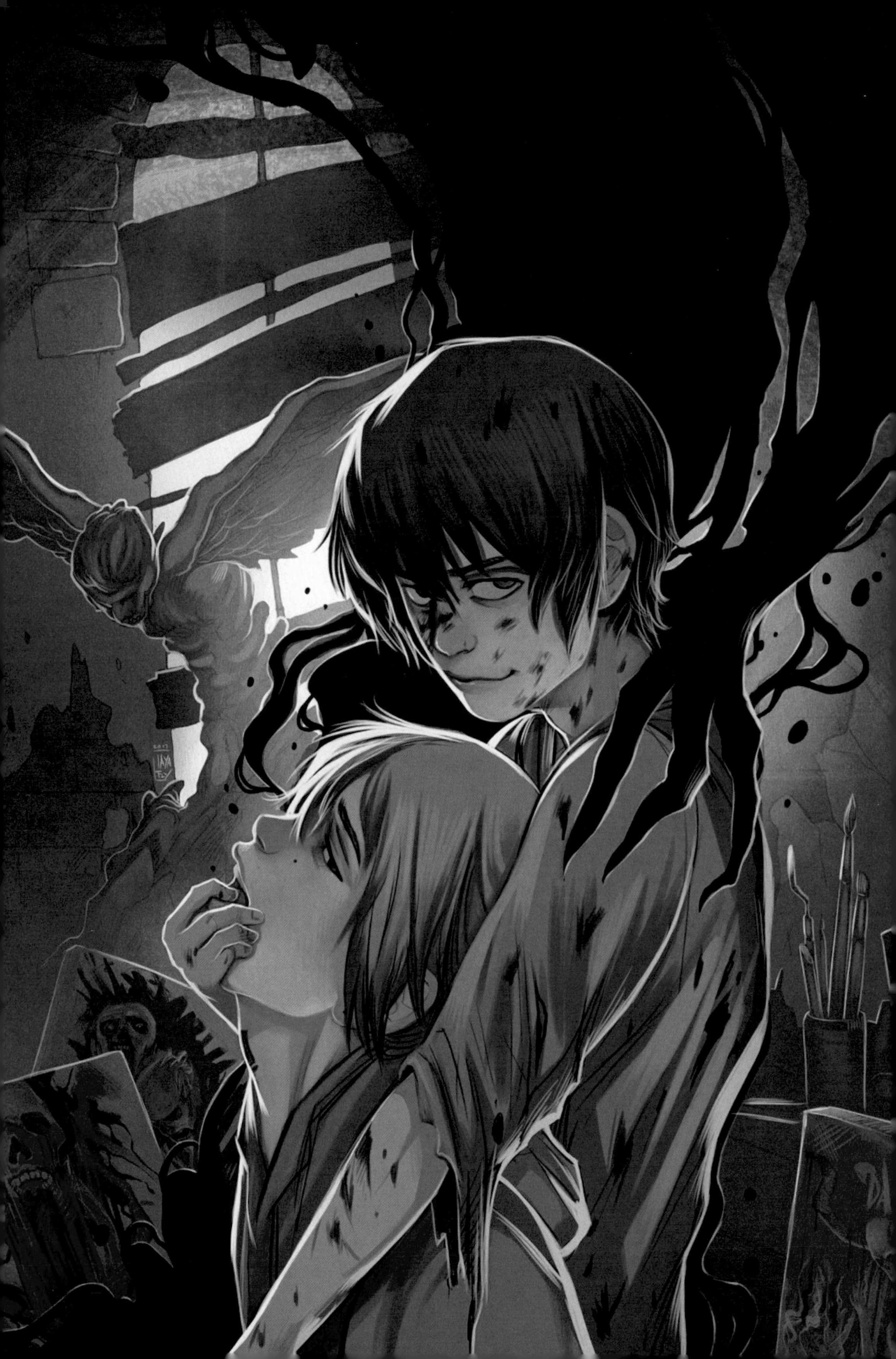

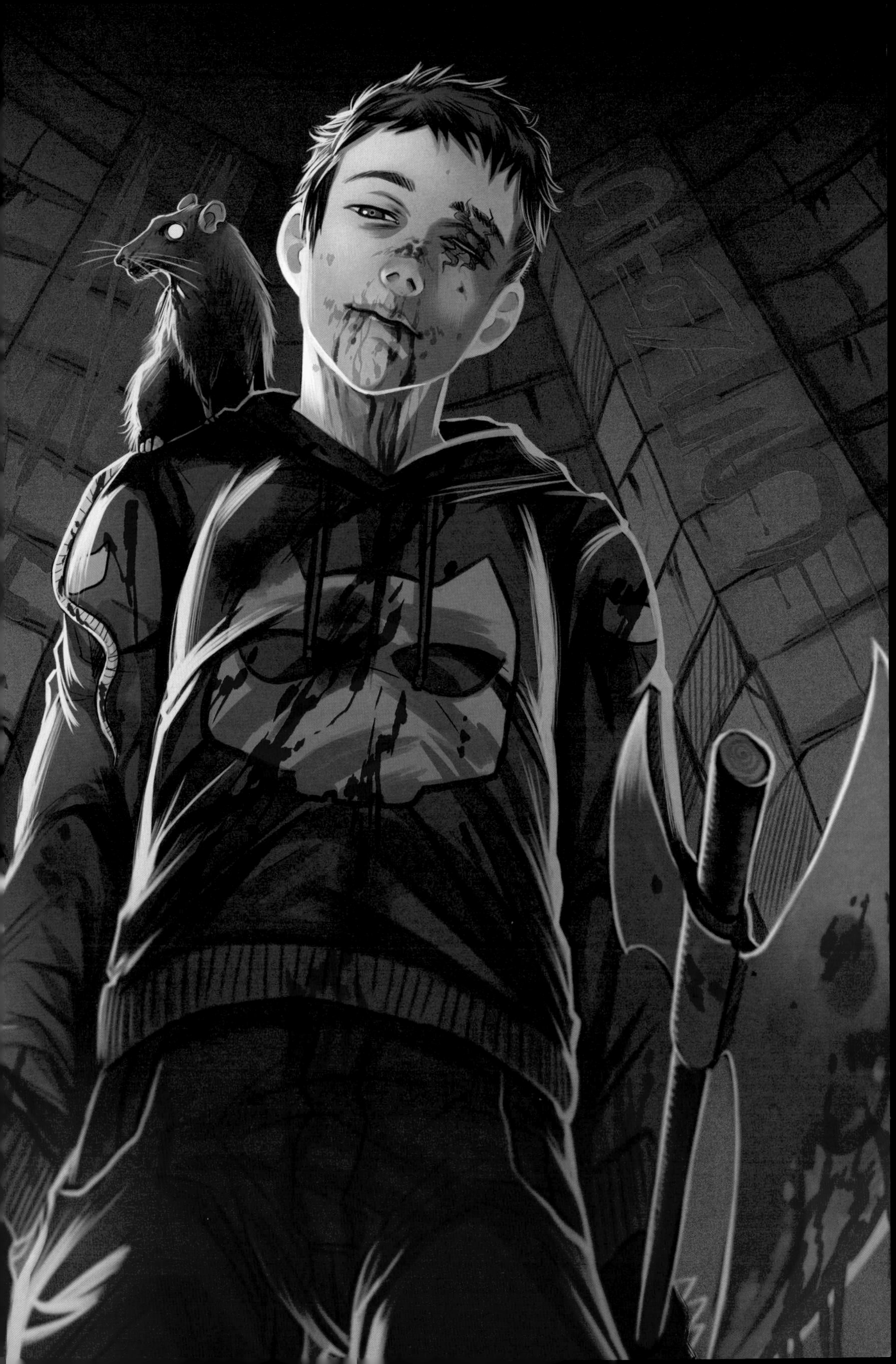

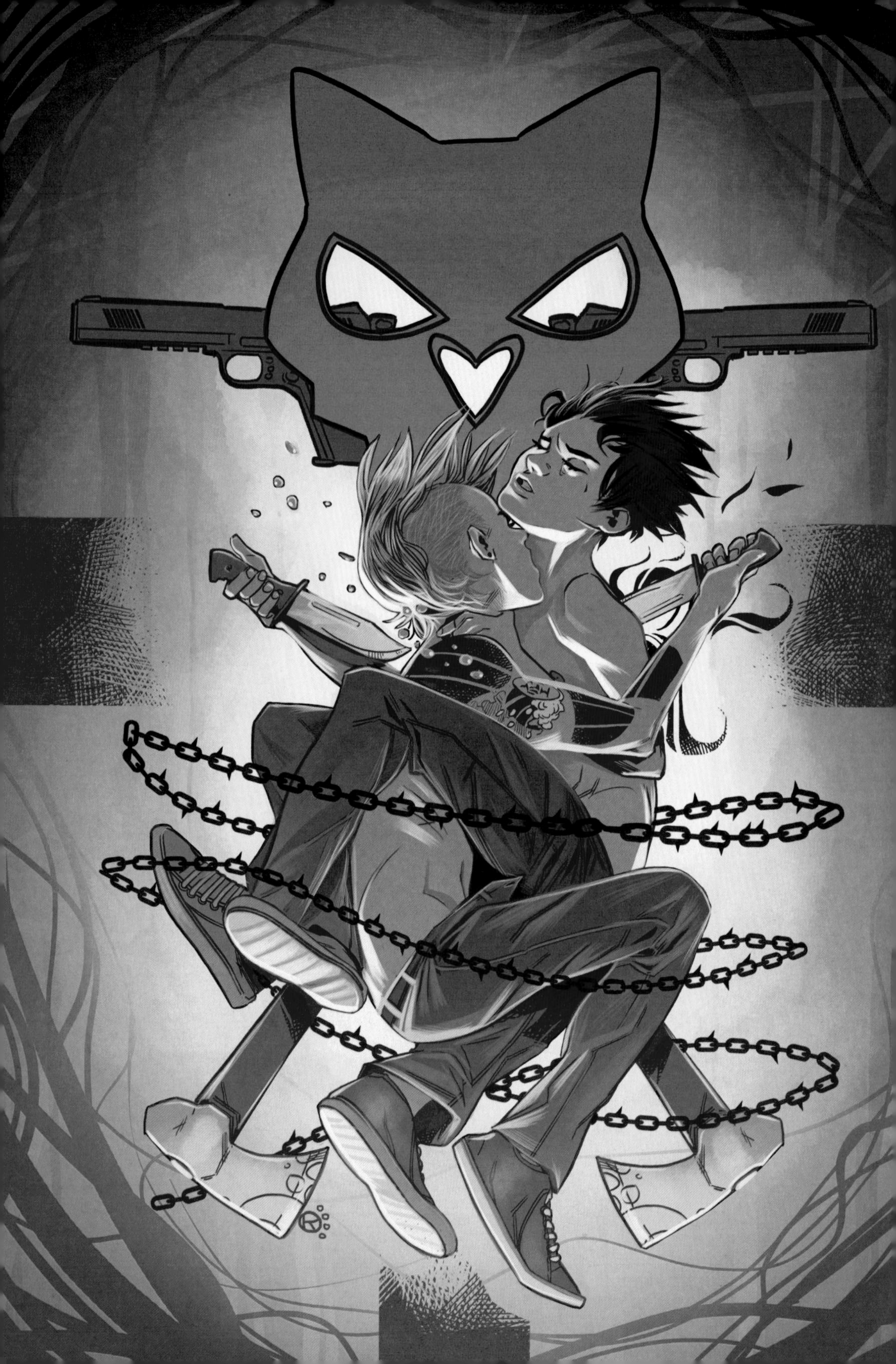

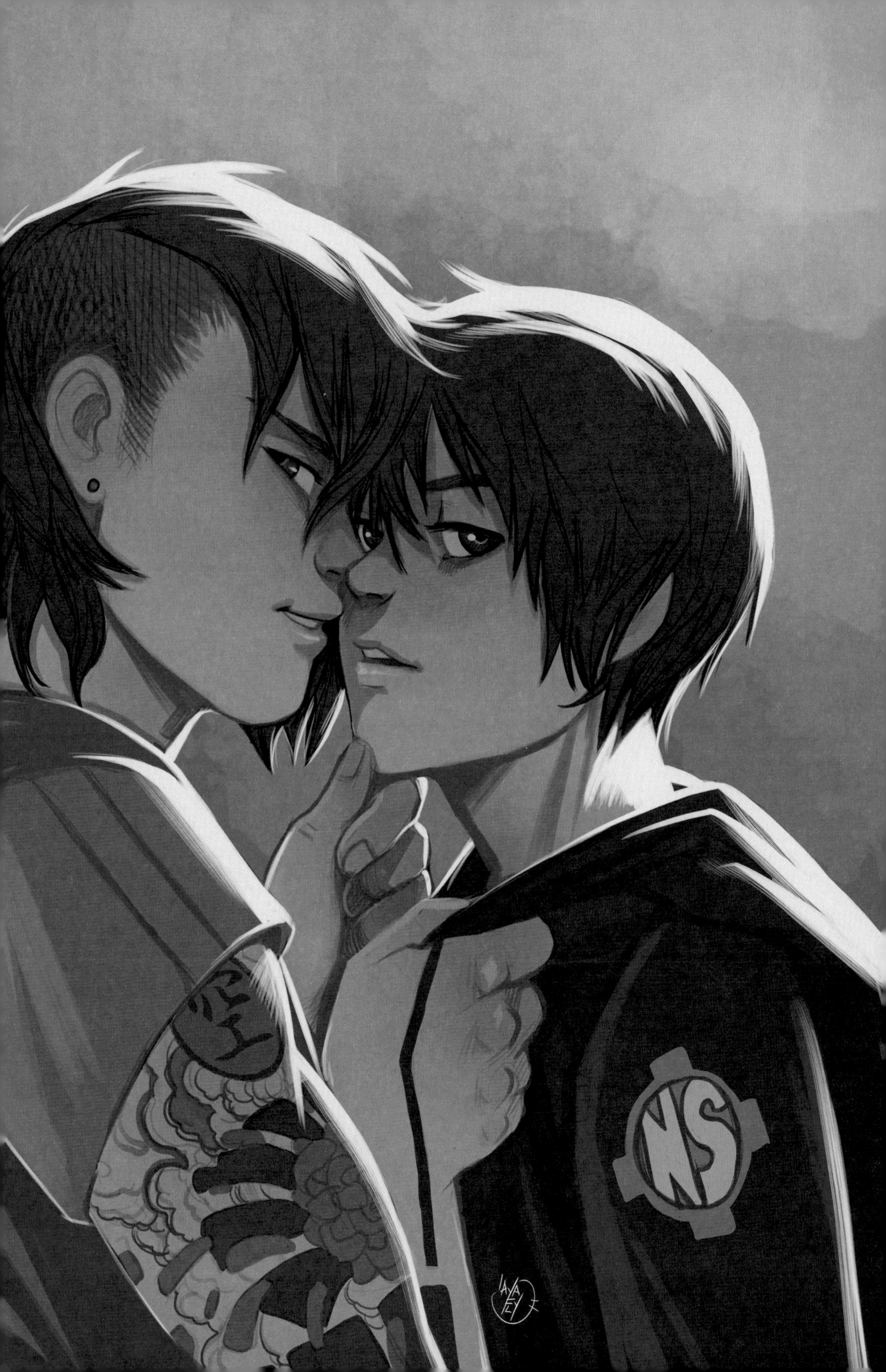

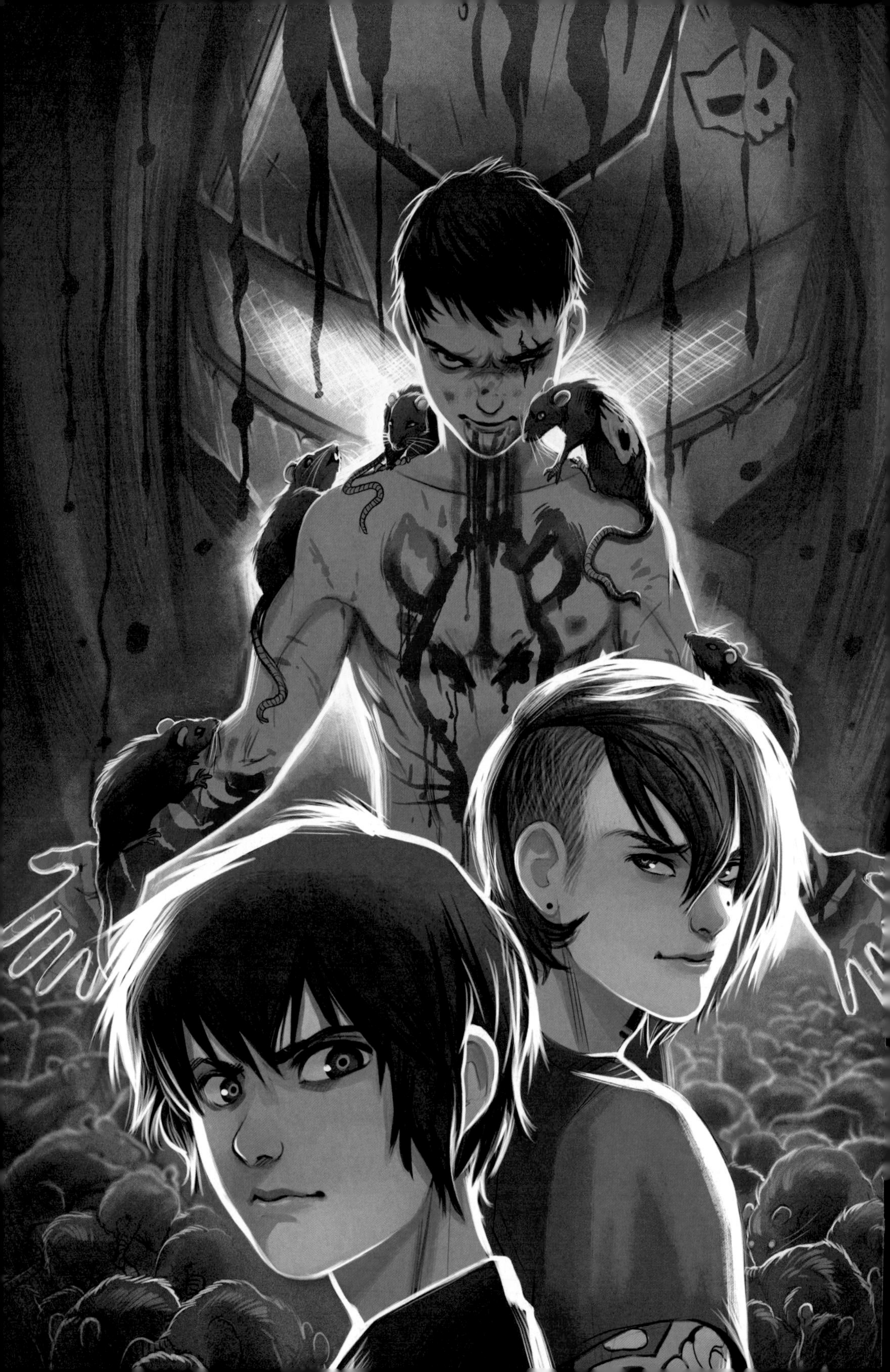

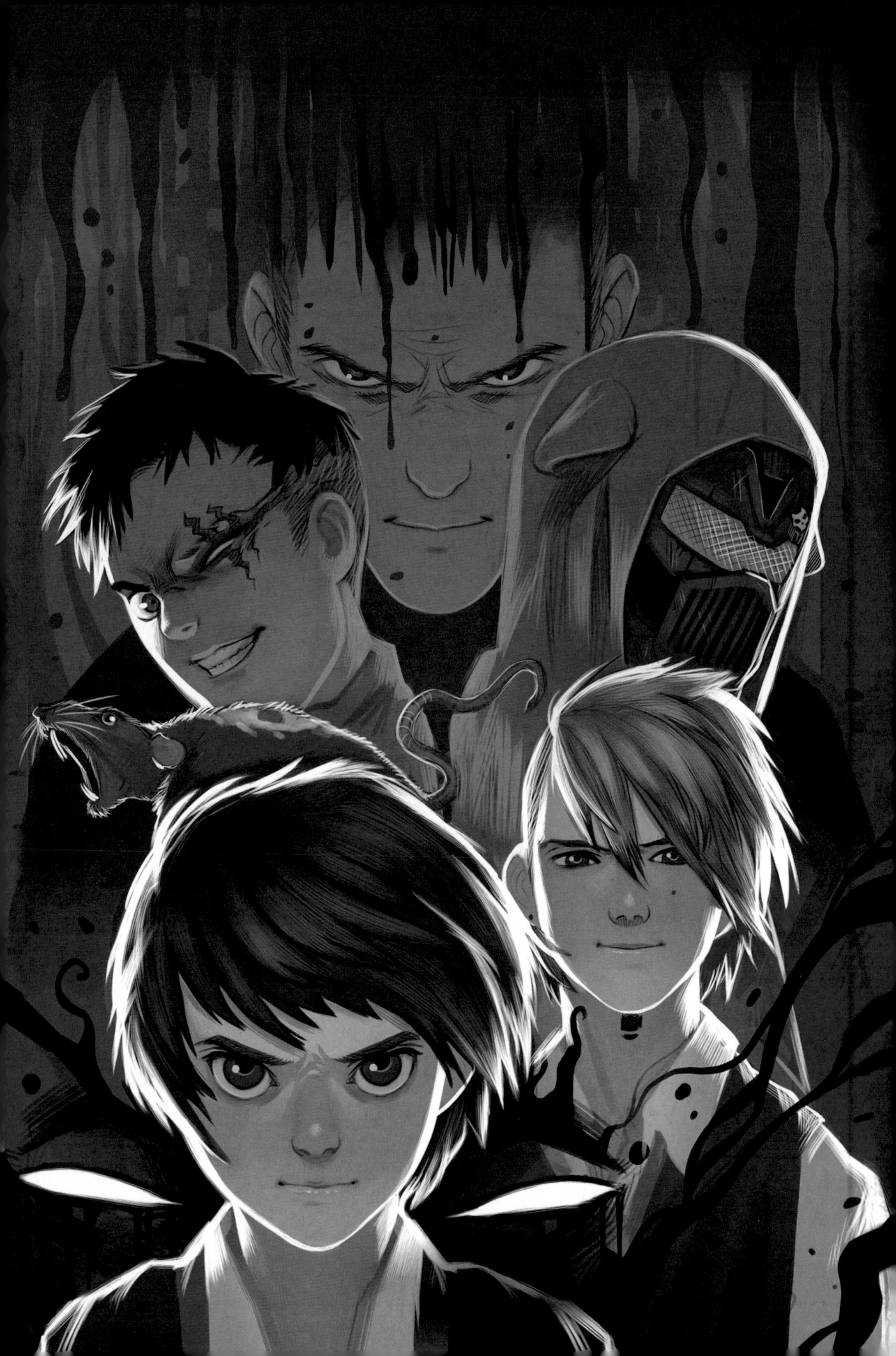

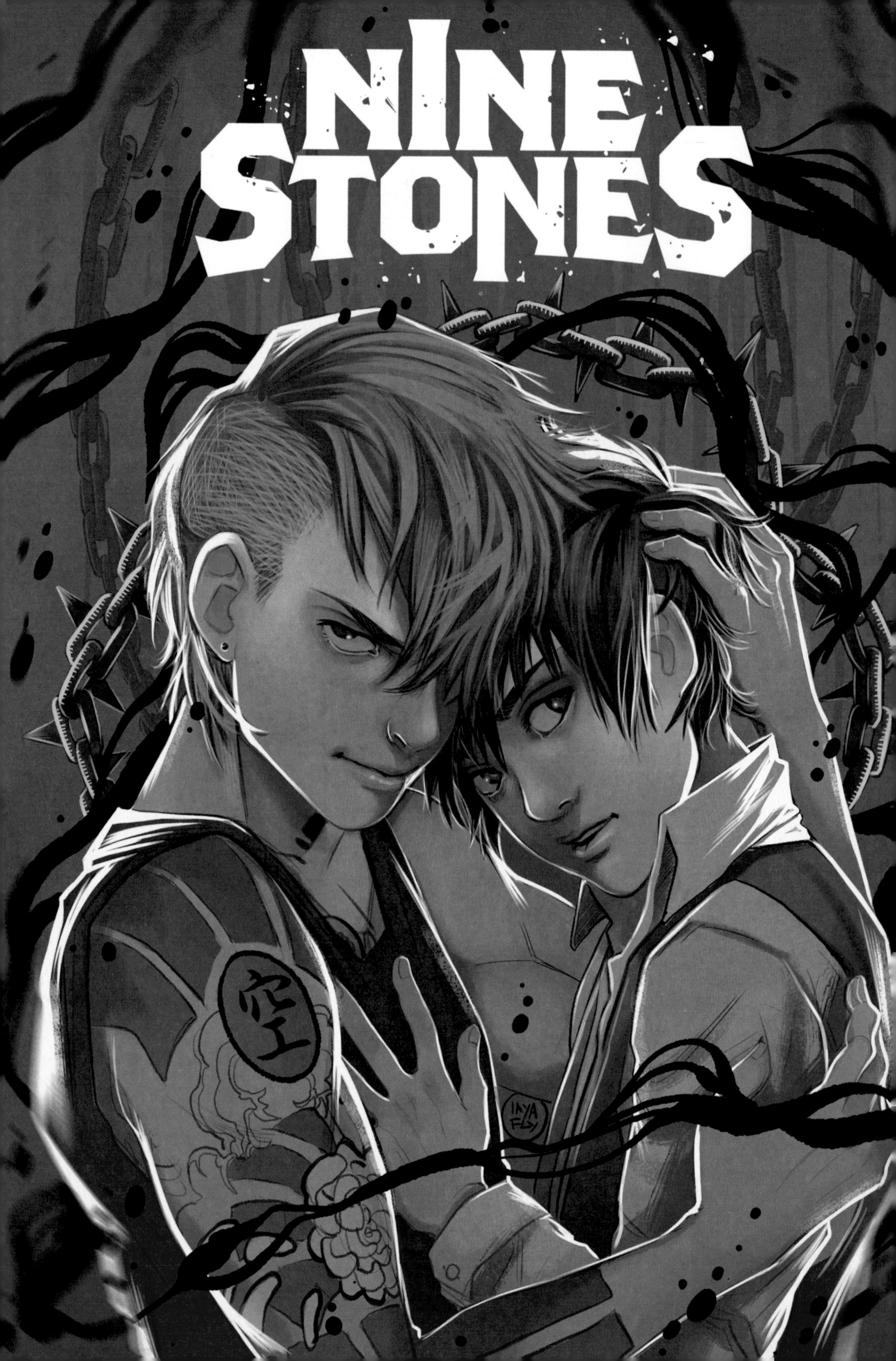
NINE
STONES
空

ALL HAIL BEHEMOTH